Lights and Shadows
of a
Macao Life

*The Journal of Harriett Low,
Travelling Spinster*

Lights and Shadows
of a
Macao Life

*The Journal of Harriett Low,
Travelling Spinster*

PART TWO: 1832–1834

Edited by
Nan P. Hodges and Arthur W. Hummel

© 2002 by Nan P. Hodges

Published in the United States of America for Nan P. Hodges by The History Bank, Woodinville, WA, design and production by Sandra J. Harner

Publisher's Cataloging-in-Publication Data
(Provided by Quality Books, Inc.)

Hillard, Harriet Low, 1809–1877.
    Lights and shadows of a Macao life : the journal of
Harriett Low, travelling spinster / edited by Nan P.
Hodges and Arthur W. Hummel. -- 1st ed.
    p. cm.
    Includes index.
    "[T]hird version of Harriett Low's journal but the
first to include the complete journal as she wrote it.
In 1900 ... an abridged and greatly altered version--'My
mother's journal.' In 1953 ... in 'The China trade
post-bag of the Seth Low family of Salem and New York,
1829–1873.'"--Introd.
    LCCN 2001039134
    ISBN 0-938106-29-5

    1. Hillard, Harriet Low, 1809–1877--Diaries.
2. Women--United States--Biography. 3. Macau (China :
Special Administrative Region)--Social life and customs
--19th century.   I. Hodges, Nan Powell. II. Hummel,
Arthur William, 1884– III. Hillard, Harriet Low,
1809–1877. My mother's journal. IV. Hillard, Harriet
Low, 1809–1877. Journal. V. Title.

CT275.H59869A3 2002   951.26'033'092
              QBI01-201472

To order:

Please send $37.50 plus $5.00 shipping and handling to: Bear Creek Books, PO Box 366, Winthrop, WA 98862.

For multiple book orders, please inquire about discount pricing and shipping for two or more copies. For library discounts, resale terms and course adoption, please contact Nan P. Hodges, (509) 996-3162 or by e-mail: bearcreekbooks@methow.com.

Frontispiece. The Praya Grande, Macao, *Thomas Allom, ca. 1840*

Map art created by Corinna Campbell-Sack

Printed in Canada by Quality Color Press, Edmonton, Alberta

Contents

Volume V
August 1, 1832–March 22, 1833

Macao August 1st 1832 No. 5

Aug 1st What an authoress I am, my 5th book. Fancy them given to the <u>public</u>. <u>Oh *tempora*</u>. <u>O *Mores*</u>. What an <u>amalgamation</u>. How many more shall I write in China? I hope not many, for it will be the same thing over and over again. I must change the scene or my readers will withdraw their attention I fear. For the writer grows lazy and inactive for want of stimulus and something interesting to relate. It is now a week since I finished my other and I hardly know what has happened, except that the elements have been in a great <u>rage</u> and every thing in the form of mats has had a <u>violent</u> <u>ague</u>.

But to begin the 1st which was last Wednesday—

Caroline & I after dinner went to the Peña Church. A most lovely evening. We were above every body except a few old padres who live in the Convent. We could have a view of every part of the town. The sea, and the atmosphere was so clear that we could see the Islands at a great distance. We spent an hour in <u>meditation</u>. My thoughts were of many <u>colours</u>. All nature seemed in perfect harmony, but to look upon the busy town and to fancy, the discords, the misery, the wretchedness that might be found in that little space, made one almost wish to be void of reflection; and then to reverse the picture and think how delightful it might be. We stopped till the vesper Bell had given its accustomed warning and came down. We came home. Mr. Wood came in and said "good bye." We dressed and spent the evening with Mrs. Thornhill, a small party. Had some fine music. I listened and people were kind enough not to disturb me much. I was not disposed to talk much.

2^d Mr. Sullivan came this morning *pour dire adieu*. The *Union* goes today. Carried Uncle, Wood, Sullivan, Gillespie to Canton. They started at 1/2 past 12. A northerly wind, which feels like <u>fire</u> upon your face, and every symptom of a Typhoon—barometer falling— but they will go and think they shall get up there before it comes. Before night the clouds portend a storm—black and threatening. Hot enough—a heavy surf rolling in. Went to the Company's dinner, had a tolerable pleasant time. Had some fine music after dinner. 5 un- married ladies there. Three Miss Pereiras there, "came out" tonight.

3 Wind began to blow this morning early, and increased till night. Blew a Typhoon. You may judge how anxious we were about Uncle— a dismal day enough, and then to think how many poor creatures will suffer. I do dread these gales, not that there is any danger for ourselves, but the Ships. Fortunately we heard about dark that Uncle was seen above Lintin yesterday so we made ourselves easy for the night as no doubt he will find shelter.

Went to bed early, for it blew dreadfully, and I felt half <u>seasick</u>, the house <u>rocked</u> so. You will laugh, but the house really had an un- pleasant motion and being shut up on every side was quite dreadful.

4 Moderated this morning. Lost some of our mats and some tile, but no material damage.

Mr. Whiteman & Inglis called this morning. Say it was a very severe gale; every one dreadfully anxious about the *Union*. Mr. Vachell in this morning. Says the damage in the inner harbour is very great. Dead bodies floating about in every direction; ships driven on shore, some dismasted; houses unroofed, and some utterly de- stroyed and every thing horrid. Mrs. Thornhill called to see if Aunt was comfortable. She had to take to the "go down" [warehouse] during the gale as her rooms were unroofed. The ceiling of one room came down <u>slap</u>. We are very fortunate. Rainy afternoon. Read all the afternoon and spent the evening very pleasantly with Mrs. Macondray. She suffered but little in the gale.

5th I intended to have gone to Church to day but read till it was too late. So read two sermons to each other. After dinner walked to the Campo with Mr. Blight; he spent the evening with us. About 10 Aunt had a letter from Uncle at which you may judge we were very thankful. He dispatched a boat as soon as he got on shore to relieve our anxiety. They fortunately got inside the river but were excessively uncomfortable and arrived only yesterday morning. Had three anchors down and lost one. Boat behaved finely. The gale was felt very much in Canton.

6th Ibar & Gordon came down yesterday and called this morning. "His Grace" [Gordon] is looking as <u>well</u> as <u>ever</u> and quite as irresistible. Did not see Ibar.

Had a book and note from Wood this evening saying Blight has heard the news of his mother's and brother's death. Poor fellow! He will feel it deeply. He has always spoken of his mother very affectionately and seemed to think it impossible <u>she could die</u>, and she seemed to be the only person he cared about going home for. To feel "the last link is broken" that bound him to home, how cheerless is the thought of returning. He has been gone 11 years, has had many afflictions. And how unavailing is our grief on such occasions for the loss of a mother is indeed irreparable.

We spent the evening alone. Caroline and I had a serious "<u>consu</u>" before we went to bed on sundry <u>important</u> <u>topics</u>.

7 Wrote a note to Canton this morning. Spent an hour or so with Mrs. Macondray. Met Dr. College and Van Basil there. Had a long talk with <u>both</u> and some <u>fun</u>.

Went out to the Campo after dinner. A lovely evening. His grace of Gordon took tea with us. Set on the terrace, tried very hard to keep awake, but found it difficult.

8 Capt. [Philip] Dumaresq[1] called this morning, Capt. of the *Martha*. Lost a mast in the gale. The *Don Quixote* returned dismasted. The *Spartan* went out to sea the morning of the gale and picked up the crew of the *Fair Armenian*, at least 44 of 60, mostly Malays. She sunk off the great Ladrones. Just from Java, went down without their saving a shirt to their backs. A narrow escape enough. Oh the losses and accidents are beyond account, every day something new. There is hardly a green shrub or tree to be seen about this place. Every green thing looks as though a fire had passed over it—dismal enough. Gordon, Dumaresq and Blight spent the evening with us. Poor Blight exerts himself manfully, but seems dull. Capt. D. says he saw Father in New York and he looked about <u>35</u>. Could it be him?

9 Looked over the Lord Chancellor's Speech this morning. It is long enough if that will recommend it. Drew a little, Caroline read aloud. Henry Robinson called, a queer muster. His brother has lately received the title of a Baronet without <u>estate</u> or <u>fortune</u>—now we have a <u>Sir</u> George & <u>Lady</u> Robinson. Had a long talk with Aunty about going home & etc. Think there is a possibility of our going home in 1834. Oh I hope so. After dinner read *Granby, a novel*[2]—pretty good. No walk & no company.

10 Mr. Blight & Dumaresq called. Mrs. Macondray spent the day with us—Mr. & Mrs. Davis the evening—which has been so pleasant. We had a walk this afternoon. The moon fulled tonight, and so still and clear, we have been sitting on the terrace all the eve'g, and now my dear sister I have retired to my room. I had a walk this afternoon, with his Grace [Gordon] and Dumaresq. Too heavenly a night not to have one near that could feel and express your feelings for you—worse, than nothing to have to spend it with those you have not one feeling in common with. Well so it is. I have to walk, smile, and talk with every one that comes along—and now it is midnight. I left the terrace with every thing calm and quiet. "Not a breath the blue wave to curl," not a sound disturbed the solemn silence, the <u>light</u> of the heathen worshipper had just expired, the last piece of <u>paper</u> had blown away. They had prostrated themselves for the last time, whether with a sincere heart only him, who knows the secrets of all hearts <u>can</u> know. And every [sound?] was hushed and seemed as though it was impossible that it could even be disturbed—but alas "all that's bright must fade," [Thomas Moore, *All That's Bright*] and now I hear the sound of distant thunder. So short, so fleeting are all earthly enjoyments—but the mosquitoes begin to warn me that it is their <u>dinner</u> hour, so I shall bid you and them good night and not allow them to indulge their <u>sanguinary</u> <u>propensities</u> upon me. (I can't see my lines.)

11 Spent part of this morning in reading history, then <u>mended</u> a dress. A terrible hot day. After dinner had just undressed and made myself comfortable on my couch and the boy brought me your <u>interesting</u> letter per *Louisa*, enclosing the very pretty card of the new firm [Seth Low & Co., New York]. I am delighted to hear you are so happy and prospering. I long more and more to be with you. I am much obliged for your exertions in my behalf my dear, and as a reward will say your letter was quite <u>satisfactory</u>. It carries me home at once and I can imagine just how you live, what you talk about, and how you look. I suspect you will begin to think of getting married now. I shall hate to hear of it before I get home. I feel positive I shall start the moment the 5 years have expired, and if my health is not perfectly good before. I am now however very well—and <u>hope</u> I shall remain so. I have been much amused with Josiah's [Josiah Orne Low][3] letter; there is so much <u>nature</u> in it. He is really quite <u>sentimental</u>.

After I had read my letters, dressed and called on Mrs. Whiteman. She has a sweet little babe. Went to the "Campo." Met his Grace [Gordon] who waited upon us home. Excessively tired, had some tea and no company, so put on a loose gown. Set on the terrace talking with Caroline and Aunty and admiring the beautiful lightning, at a distance that brilliant forked lightning. Had very little thunder here.

We were thinking what a field this would be for a novelist. There is not two people in the place whose lives and characters would not afford ample <u>stuff</u> for a novel. I will endeavour some time when I am not lazy to sketch some of their characters.

12 Sunday Hot enough! Up late, slept soundly. Came out to breakfast and saw a couple of letters directed to my Ladyship per *Italy*. Knowing they were old, I quietly eat my breakfast and then took them to the verandah, where I had quite a <u>feast</u>. Then read some of them to Caroline and we were both at home in imagination. That dear little Ellen, how I long to see her. Josiah's amused me much; he seems a funny fellow as he always was. They make me sigh and yet make me feel happy. I have just finished one of Buckminster's sermons. Could not go to Church, as Aunty was going. Vachell preaches today for the first time since his sickness. It is too hot to dress and here I set in my own room quite *en déshabillé*, with nothing but a <u>camisa</u> [chemise] and a black silk skirt on. Think I'll read again. No opportunities to answer letters at present unless via Manilla. I must enquire.

After dinner read till Mr. Blight came in, but as it was rainy we could not walk.

13 Read French this morning. Rec^d a note from Canton this morning addressed to "<u>Mesdames H. Low & Co.</u>"

Very busy this morning fitting a dress and in spite of dismal weather I felt quite happy. I find there is nothing like employment. We poor creatures have nothing we feel obliged to do and are apt to give way to the listlessness that a warm climate excites. After dinner I read History aloud to Caroline and felt better satisfied with my days work than I have for some time. Caddy has been troubled with the "indigo spirits" and I have been laughing at her. We do have dismal weather. I am sure we have not had so much unpleasant weather in all the time we have been in China as since February last.

There was a procession from the Church this afternoon. An image of an female was laid on a state bed, very richly dressed and carried around with other things, such as banners, & etc., the host. I asked Josepha what it was but was quite shocked at her literal translation from Portuguese. She said "God's Mamma had died that day."[4] They were burying her in effigy. It is horrid.

Blight, Gordon, Dumaresq, and Vachell took tea with us, all dropped in. Aunty was at Mrs. M[acondray]'s so that I had to do the honours.

14 Blowing a gale again today. Quite tremendous early this morning, and has lasted through the day, and even now at 12 o'clock tonight, it is whistling hard as ever. I pity the poor sailors. I fear we shall hear of much suffering, there must be many vessels very near.

Studied Spanish very hard this morning. Quite cool and just about gloomy enough to feel melancholy. However employment is the antidote, and I mean to be industrious. After dinner by way of amusement I read one of Shakespeare's plays. Vachell sent me a novel after dinner which I spent the evening in looking over but have read it before, and am glad for I don't want novels. I hate to see them come into the house, for they are bewitching. One must however read the novels of the day for small talk. Haven't read Scott's last [*Count Robert of Paris* (1831)] yet. Hear it's a stupid thing. Commenced Cooper's *Bravo*[5] but did not like it and would not finish it. It's a great shame he should go out of his own country for his scenes.

Have just had a consu in Caroline's room—I always go and sit down at her door to brush my hair and there we talk some times till 1 o'clock. We discussed beauty and accomplishments tonight, and concluded that sensible men looked for something more than beauty in their wives, and for our own comfort concluded that beauty gained a great deal of admiration but very little sincere love. Intellect is the thing nowadays however. How different from the days of chivalry. I am sure we should feel no interest in a hero now, let him be ever so gallant, if he knew neither how to read or write. But there the wind is whistling furiously and the clock keeps warning me of the flight of time, and I must e'en to bed, and yet I am not sleepy. But it's 1/2 past 12.

Vachell sent me this afternoon a piece of the pith such as they make what you call rice paper of.[6] I have discovered lately that rice has nothing to do with it and that it is cut with a knife from the pith of some tree. It's lighter than a feather. Shall send or <u>bring</u> you some of it. Now my dear good night.

15 Still blowing and unpleasant, though moderated a little. Capt. Dumaresq and Mr. Ward called. A company's Ship arrived this morning and spoke the *Nile* just outside. Must be in soon [I] suppose. Mat^th Daniell, alias *L'Énigme*, came in the *Duchess of Athol*. Bring news that Mr. and Mrs. Ploughden [Plowden] to come out as Chiefs [of the East India Company; they arrived two days later]—so our friends the Davis's reign has been short, but he was only chief pro tem.

Mr. Blight in this morning. Wrote a letter after dinner and then spent the evening with Mrs. Macondray. She is a very pleasant woman and we like her much. She is a general favorite.

16 The wind abated today considerably—the *Superior* arrived this morning, 96 days from Liverpool. Not much news. Cholera in Paris and <u>stopped</u> in England. Mr. Hubble [H. W. Hubbell] Supercargo, one we saw in Manilla, looks as though he knew what he was about. Gordon and Dumaresq in. Nothing of the *Nile* yet. Must have met with some accident, or got to leeward, most probable. Mr. Blight spent most of the morning with us. I felt in great spirits and did nothing but frolic. Caroline had a letter from her brother who says he leaves there in September. Oh dear, I can't believe she will ever leave me.

After dinner I dressed for a walk, but Blight came in and said it was too windy and unpleasant to walk. So I left him to take care of Caroline and Mrs. M[acondray] and Aunty settling the affairs of the nation, and I wanted to go and see somebody—and I could not think of any one I wished to see that wouldn't be more happily engaged reading letters than talking with me, for two direct Ships had just anchored and the letters were on their way to the shore. Never mind, I said I'd jump into the chair and I'd sally forth like the monkey in the fable to see the world [*Aesop's Fables*, "The Monkey Who Had Seen the World"]. So I went on to the Quay; there was *tout le monde* assembled watching the boats with anxious hearts, no doubt. I called on Mrs. Grant, but she could not see me. So I went to Mrs. Rees. I set me down at her window and such a scene of excitement I have not seen for many a day. The huge packets from one ship had just been delivered, they were just returning from the Chief's (where all packets are opened) and had not read a letter, I suppose, when an-other came—then away they went back again. Some disappointed that the first contained none for them, another pleased, and in fact the different feelings that seemed to be excited was quite wonderful. I thought if the friends could but see these poor creatures looking for a letter and the desire that was manifested, and the pleasure that was evinced by those who had rec^d a quantity, that they would de-prive themselves of many an hour's sleep to give them that pleasure. No one can ever realize it till they have seen it. I almost wished myself an English woman that I might participate in the general joy. But also joy is not the only feeling by far that is excited. No! envy, hatred, malice, and all uncharitableness. Two years ago [January 31, 1830] this Mr. P. [W.H.C. Plowden] went home a widower with scarce a friend to see him off (but it might be a long story, so I shall not begin). Now he comes back with flying colours, a married man and now he will see smiles on every face. But alas it will be but outward show! I'd not be him for all India's wealth.

Then again he has married a beautiful widow, at least a most en-chanting creature. She came here on her way to England a few years since and she broke the hearts of dozens. No one came near her with-out being slain at once, she was a most dangerous person. Her present husband is among the number. I suspect we shall have funny times here, well I shall be a quiet spectator. English people are different from what we know of Americans; they don't seem to think it any harm to have a small flirtation with married ladies. Never mind— no treason here.

Well, I saw and reflected on what I saw. I became very melan-choly and felt a sad depression of spirit, arising from different causes. Mrs. Macondray & Blight took tea with us. Oh what a trying world this is. I wish I could ever know that what I do is right. I am in a maze of perplexity—oh that I knew the consequences of certain actions and deeds that I should like to have take place, then perhaps I might insure my happiness. This has been an eventful day indeed!

17 I read French all the morning. Quite a calm warm day today. Mr. Perit, young [John Murray] Forbes, and Gordon came in this morning. No news of the *Nile* yet. Strange.

After dinner read Holms *Annals of America*,[7] then walked with Mr. Blight—Perit joined us. Dumaresq spent the evening with us. A very gentlemanly, pleasant young man. Like him much. No news today. Heard something tonight which made me angry. Do think I am tormented.

Mr. & Mrs. Ploughden landed today. She has a babe 3 weeks old, born on board Ship. At least she was to land, have not heard whether they did. Now it's 12 o'clock, so good night.

18 Calm hot day and every prospect of another gale. A north wind very like the Simoom of the desert which seems to parch everything it touches. Macao looks like Autumn now; there is not a green leaf scarcely to be seen.

Commenced Walter Scott's last novel. Find it dry and uninteresting at the <u>beginning</u>.[8] I hear they paid him a splendid compliment in Italy, by giving him a masquerade Ball and confining their dresses and characters wholly to his novels.

Mrs. Pereira called this morning. Mrs. Macondray was delivered of a fine girl this afternoon and she is quite comfortable.

We walked to the Peña this afternoon. Very hot. Blight and Reeves joined us. R. says his father [John Reeves, who had sailed for England, January 6, 1831] had a letter from Mr. [Nathan] Dunn in America who says he does not like the manner of living, that he is <u>freezing</u> to <u>death</u> and the <u>help</u> is no <u>help</u> at all. A capital story for the English.

I hear a Mrs. Trollop[e] has been ridiculing the manners and customs[9] of our good country tremendously. Blight and Forbes spent the evening with us. I got in <u>high</u> <u>spirits</u>.

19 Calm rainy morning. Hope we shall have no gale [and that] it will pass off in rain. Went out to breakfast and rec[d] letters by the *Nile* but few days later than the *Martha*. A long letter from G[eorge] B. A[rcher] which gave me great pleasure and all of which I shall answer in the course of time. I am anticipating a feast of gingerbread shortly, will I dare say be near a week before we get it. I am sure it will taste good. Believe I did not tell you I made some gingerbread, the first thing of the kind I have been guilty of for some time. In fact all I did was to mix them together, everything was weighed and ready. When it came out of the oven it proved <u>variegated</u>; that is it was covered with <u>white spots</u>—the flour was not sufficiently <u>rubbed up</u>. However people <u>said</u> it was good.

My letters prevented me from going to church as I had intended, but I read two excellent sermons at home.

Walked a short distance, but rain sent us back early. Blight spent the evening with us.

20 This morning read a little French, then Blight sent a review of Mrs. Trollope's travels in America. Some not <u>flattering truths</u> delivered, some things exaggerated but written with great spirit and <u>cleverness</u> (English).[10]

After dinner read Holmes *Annals of America*, rather dry. Blight came in and brought Vigne's *Six Months in America*.[11] Read one volume this evening—rather interesting, apparently written without prejudice, which is very rare in these works. On the whole I should think very just.

21 This morning translated some Spanish, *Las Ruinas*. Read the second vol. of Vigne. Like it very well, most of it. *Flora* arrived, commissions from Paris via Batavia. News from Uncle and lots of excitement. Caro [had] letters from her brother. Did a little work.

After dinner looked over *Count Robert of Paris* but it is too <u>stupid</u>—cannot get through with them. After dinner walked with Blight—Vachell joined us out as far as the hill, then went to the barrier. Mr. J. P. S[turgis] and J. Forbes bore down and "<u>Uncle J.</u>" walked home with me. He and J. Blight, Dumaresq and Ward took tea with us. Now my dear I am going to bed, so good night. Must go and give Caro a kiss, and will fancy it's you. Oh!

22 This morning was lying reading on my couch and the boy brought me something in the form of a note, which on examination proved an anonymous production addressed to Miss Low, which if you will not say is vanity I will copy for your perusal. I suspect who <u>may</u> be the <u>author</u>—he endeavoured to conceal the handwriting, but did <u>not</u> succeed.

> There is a winning charm of gentle nature
> On all thy being like a perfume thrown
> Making each beauty both of mind and feature

Inseparable—<u>not</u> to be <u>singly</u> known.
Something there is that as an unseen power
Subdues the wonted current of our thought
Leaving the heart all passive - But one hour
Of <u>thy</u> sweet converse, and the Soul is fraught
With feelings of a cast, oh! <u>too</u> deeply wrought.
                    - Macao -

(I hear via <u>Sandwich</u> <u>Islands</u> that this foolish affair was written by a
Mr. Ward Supercargo of the *Don Quixote.* - February 1833.)
    We guess and I think rightly. Soon after receiving this I got <u>a</u>
<u>letter</u> which put the acrostic out of my head.
    Blight, Gordon, Perit and Whiteman called. Walked after din-
ner. Dumaresq and Ward joined us and we spent a very pleasant
evening upon the terrace. <u>An</u> <u>eventful</u> <u>day</u>.

23^d Spent this day much as usual, studying and reading. Some visitors, I <u>suppose</u>, but I forget <u>who</u>.
    Rained all day. Oh no, terrible hot I <u>remember</u>. Gordon spent
the evening with us. Quite exhausted with the heat and glad to
tumble into bed as soon as he made his exit.

24 Nothing new today—rains and blows a gale, dreadful weather.
Went to see Mrs. Macondray today. got a pretty baby. <u>Uncle</u> <u>Jem</u>
[J. P. Sturgis] & Blight took tea with us.

25 This morning rec^d things per *Nile*, gingerbread, & etc., which I
shall notice per letter. It is delightful to see or taste any thing from
home. Think the dresses very pretty. Cleared up a little just at night
so that we strolled out a little way. Were met by a <u>bevy</u> <u>of</u> <u>beaux</u>. Filed
off Caroline with Blight and Gordon, I with Sturgis and Dumaresq.
All spent the evening with us and J. Forbes. Some "funny bits"—and
laughable. I wish I could venture to take off every one and put them
down in their true colours. Oh! what a book I should have—to note
all the funny things said in this house—the inconsistencies of <u>men</u>![12]
It would be as good as a play. This last summer has been the most
amusing one I have ever passed in Macao, rich—<u>big</u> with <u>events</u>! Mr.
Plowden called this morning. Blight and Dumaresq in.

26th Sunday Went to Church this morning—Dumaresq went with
me. Ame[rican] Ship *Potomac* arrived from Java—letter for
C[aroline]—Capt Condry in her. Wished to call, but the weather

was so bad had to carry his ship into the "Moon." The "Cap Sing Moon"[13] is called the Moon for shortness, but sounds very odd to hear people so quietly telling of taking up their abode in the <u>Moon</u> till the new teas come. You fancy they are about to leave this "mundane sphere."

Matt Daniell alias *L'Énigme* called this morning. Looks as <u>wishy-washy</u> as ever—on his way to England.

Dumaresq spent the evening with us. Since his departure Cary and I have been thinking what different ideas or feelings we have now from what we had when we left home. A few years makes some difference in our feelings, and we see the same things in very different lights on an acquaintance with the world. I often sigh from the bottom of my heart to think I have to become reconciled to things that once the bare mention of would make me shudder—wicked, wicked world. Why were we created? Now my dear good night. There is no use in <u>thinking</u>.

27 Up early this morning and wrote French exercises. Went to Mrs. Davis's this morning and then to Mrs. Macondray's and stayed till 3. Mr. College came in and we had a long chat on a variety of subjects.

Received a letter from my friend Mrs. Cartwright this morning via St. Helena. She was at the Cape. Give me a description of her passage and the passengers, one of which deserves to be tarred and feathered. Indeed I know of no punishment too bad for her—a Mrs. B[eaucaut], of whom I have given you a history in <u>No. 4</u>. [June 7, 1832, vol.4] I had some pity for her then, but now I've not a spark. "Oh woman, when thou art bad, Hell itself affords no fouler friend [fiend]." [a variation on Homer, *Odyssey*, XI, l.531] But there let her rest if she can.

I was delighted to hear from Mrs. C., for if she had forgotten me I should have no longer believed that there was such a thing as <u>friendship</u>.

Dumaresq and Sturgis walked with us this afternoon. S. spent the eve.

28 This morning after reading some Spanish we sallied forth to make some calls. First perpetrated a visit on Miss Morrison. She looked cross and ugly and the Dr. [Robert Morrison] "grinned a ghastly smile," on the whole gracious—Madame had gone to the Campo to take an airing. Then went to Mrs. Pereira's. The mistress of the Palace was agreeable, her <u>amiable</u> son gave us a tune upon the "Accordion," a new instrument just come out. Dare say you have seen it—rather pretty. Called on <u>Lady</u> Robinson, not at home. Then on Mrs. Thornhill, had our fortunes told. The part which most <u>depressed</u> my <u>spirits</u> was regarding my <u>future spouse</u>. He will be <u>whimsical</u> & <u>changeable</u>, but another part says he will be an <u>honour</u> to his <u>country</u>.

Then called at Mrs. Daniell's to see Mrs. Plowden, but were disappointed. We are very anxious to see her. Then called on Mrs. Grant. Had a discussion upon matrimony. C. & I for the sake of argument railed against it. Dropped into Mrs. Davis's and finished off with Mrs. Macondray's. Came home at 3 perfectly exhausted, one of the hottest days we have had. Tiresome work going out in the morning. Only do it for new comers once. Came home, found a lot of new goods just come from France. My kind Uncle and Aunt overload me, & I know not how to repay it. Went to the Peña after dinner with Blight and Forbes, and spent the evening *sans cérémonie* with Lady Robinson. Called her Mrs. all the time; could not think to say <u>Lady</u>. Caroline and I had a long <u>consu</u> in her room. I am <u>plagued</u>.

29 Had <u>a</u> <u>letter</u> this morning which I answered <u>short</u> and <u>sweet</u>. Hope I shall have no more from the <u>same source</u>. Forbes spent the morning with us. Dreadful hot day. Saw Sullivan and others land about 3. Uncle is coming down the last of the week.

Dumaresq called for us to walk. Went to the Peña. Ibar, Cox, and Perit joined us. Otadue, our old Spanish master has returned to Manilla. The *Angenora* arrived there from France. I hoped letters for me, but no! Luky ought to have written. Dumaresq, Blight, Sullivan, & Forbes took tea with us. Chief subjects of conversation, Mrs. Trollope's book on America and other travellers in that happy country, which they <u>abuse</u> delightfully.

A letter received from Canton to the pair of Mesdames H. Low and Co—a <u>letter</u> of <u>Introduction</u>.

Thundershower tonight. 12 o'clock and so good night.

30 Blowing a gale today. Read and worked as usual. Dumaresq came in to tea, said a Dutch Ship [*Sophia*] has gone on shore by the gap, close by us—lost her rudder, parted their cables, and is now <u>bumping</u> upon the rocks. All Macao there in the midst of rain and wind, to lend assistance or gratify curiosity. Any excitement is I believe agreeable in Macao, and even a Shipwreck serves for <u>amusement</u>.

Gordon took tea with us and bid us Adieu for this Season. Were engaged at the Company's to dine, but sent an excuse.

31st Uncle arrived this morning very unexpectedly. Seems to have the luck of gales in his excursions. However he came inside and they anchored during the gale. Fortunately we did not know he had started. Spent two hours very pleasantly with Mrs. Macondray. She is a very intelligent, pleasant woman and I like her much. Walked after dinner with Blight, Sullivan, Wilkinson, & Perit joined us. W. Came down with Uncle. Mrs. Fearon and Mrs. Rees spent the evening with us looking at engravings just rec^d from Paris, some very pretty. Wound up the evening with a little good natured scandal— must have a little for seasoning.

Sept 1st Only think, the first day of Autumn and we have not had hardly any warm weather, at least not blazing hot. Lots of gales and rain.

The *Sylph*[14] in 17 days from Calcutta, shortest passage ever known. Brings accounts of lots of people coming here from Calcutta. So our gay season will soon commence; fashionables too! I don't like Calcutta people though, they only abuse the place and make every one dissatisfied. Read history all the morning. Did not feel very well and stayed in my own room till near dinner, believe the gingerbread disorders my stomach. Blight and Forbes in. Had a present from Mr. Rieves, a quantity of "Drawing Room Scrap Sheets," filled with scraps of poetry, short extracts, Anecdotes, Charades, Enigmas, Conundrums, & etc., very prettily got up.

Walked after dinner with Blight, went to see the Ship. Looks melancholy, broadside on the rocks. Wilkinson and Forbes spent the evening with us.

2d Did not go to Church, read two sermons at home. Mrs. Davis came in and we had a long talk about that Mrs. Trollope's book, which the English are all crowing over. It is as much as we can do to fight for our country and our refinement. I believe the sole motive of publishing this book is to put down the spirit of emigration to the United States and to drive them to Canada. Mrs. D. thinks to suppress the spirit of *égalité* that prevails in England now. She certainly writes with great spirit, but the idea of her going over with Fanny Wright[15] is enough to tell what class of society she visited in.

She tells many truths but much that is false, or at least facts so embellished or <u>discoloured</u> that there is no such thing as weighing the facts. I will not pretend to say that there is that degree of <u>refinement</u> in America that there is in England, nor do I believe there is, but I know there is decency and civility, elegance and luxury—but not to the extent there is in England. But they will laugh, and they may, if they will believe every word that is written, by every person who chooses to wield the pen.

3 Wrote most of the morning. Began to make a fortune teller. Blight & Wilkinson called. Walked after dinner with Blight. Forbes spent the evening with us. A very pleasant youth—agreeable manners and unsophisticated. Is not much indebted to nature for beauty.

4 This morning tried to read, but rec^d a letter from S[usan] Orne, giving me an account of her engagement to Mr. Schibler. She seems to be desperately enamoured and over head and ears in love. I am sure she has my most sincere wishes for her happiness. I dare say she will be quite as happy as though she had <u>money</u>, that seems to be the *sine qua non* nowadays, but for my own part it is I think a secondary consideration.

This news quite unsettled me. Sullivan made us a call and then I went to Mrs. Macondray's and stayed till dinner time. Came home, had no walk. Blight spent the evening with us. Finished our <u>fortune teller</u>. As we composed the sentences, we made them to suit our <u>friends</u>.

5 Uncle had a new secretary from France yesterday, and he has transferred his old desk to me, so that I am now quite magnificent—and quite at the height of my ambition—with room enough for every thing and my <u>arms</u> beside. Suspect I shall be more <u>eloquent</u> than <u>ever</u>.

The *Asia* arrived yesterday and brought <u>quantities</u> of people— Mr. & Mrs. N. Alexander & family, Mr. & Mrs. Donolly and an <u>ancient spinster</u>, a Miss Barlow or Barwell. There are more coming I believe. Rainy and squally today & yesterday. Mr. Blight, Forbes, & Dumaresq came in this morning. They say the *John Gilpin* is in from Baltimore. <u>Hope</u> I shall have some letters, but <u>fear</u>—those two feelings are twins I believe, they seem inseparable.

Went to see Mrs. Macondray tonight. Lindsay and my *recherché* admirer, Gutzlaff,[16] returned today from the North. Hear their expedition is satisfactory. They met with a warm reception wherever they went. Sold all their goods and could have sold lots of opium had they have had it.

We have been playing Loo tonight. Dumaresq, Blight, & Forbes were here—and now here I am scribbling away. The winds are whistling, all are in bed but me, and it is near 12. Think I shall say good night.

6ᵗʰ Hear this morning the *Israel* [Capt. W. Crocker] has arrived, from Boston. Sailed 12 of May. So I shall have some letters. Hear J. Thorndike has departed this life and left his money for someone else to enjoy. Oh the vanity of all earthly possessions, one's life spent in hoarding money to die and leave. Well may we say "All is vanity." [Ecclesiastes 1:2] I spent the morning very industriously in reading and studying. Find my new desk quite magnificent. Mr. Calvo called this morning to say Adieu, he leaves for Mexico tomorrow. Going to seek his fortune poor fellow, he knows not how. Says Macao is <u>Mui triste</u>.

Our organ that we have long expected arrived today after much trouble & tribulation.

Walked out after dinner. Met Mrs. Ploughdon, was introduced to her. Saw a great many other strangers. The Campo was quite gay. Mrs. P. is very pretty, & pleasing manners—should have liked her better had she not have asked me if I did not wish to go home. Such a question!

Met Sullivan and Blight, stayed on the hills a long time for the night is perfect. Mr. S. is happy in his <u>self complacency</u> and is I suspect perfectly satisfied. We had a long chat about a variety of matters. "His Excellencies grandson" [grandson of Governor James Sullivan (1744–1808) of Massachusetts] does not get worshipped by us. Came home soon after tea. Dumaresq came in and introduced Mr. Dana, <u>parson Dana's</u> son,[17] of Marblehead to us, good stout looking Yankee. Brought me a letter from Nat. [N.P. Knapp] The others are all under lock and key yet. But this disturbed my peace, it mentions Caroline's Mother[18] is dead. I have not yet told her, nor do I intend. She will probably have letters from her brother tomorrow or the next day which will mention it. Poor dear girl, how she will feel it, and yet she has great <u>firmness</u>, and will bear it well perhaps, but it is an <u>awful</u> thing to lose a mother. And so far away too, heaven forbid it should be my lot. I feel sad and sick at heart.

7th C. got letters this morning from her brother. As he says nothing of the event, I of course shall not mention it till I hear further.

Forbes and C[harles S.] Bradford,[19] Supercargo of the *Gilpin* called this morning and perpetrated a long call. Mr. B. is very lively and agreeable. It seems quite delightful to see one that has any life, for the residents here appear more than half dead. Seem to take no interest in any thing, are lifeless and spiritless, energies and faculties all lying dormant. Too much exertion for them to talk or move.

Set our organ going this morning—is quite delightful, the music is very fine.

Walked after dinner. Had a very pleasant consu upon the hill with Mr. Bradford, and Dumaresq joined us. A lovely evening, and we talked of love, matrimony, & etc. generally, flirtations and nunnerys, travellers and stayers at home, foreign ladies and American ladies—and in fact our subjects were very various. He is a great enthusiast, and fancies woman all that is good and lovely; anticipations for happiness are great, and opinions of the pleasures of this world exalted. Ah poor fellow, I did not undeceive him or forewarn him that disappointments await him at every turn. No, they will come soon enough. He was engaged just before he left home. We quizzed him this evening. Those two with Forbes took tea with us. Dumaresq is a most gentlemanly quiet youth, small, good looking however, smart, spirited, and honourable feelings. A most lovely night. No letters per *John Gilpin*, no not one. Crocker of the *Israel* has locked his up in his desk and gone to Canton to learn the state of the markets before he delivers them. Very delightful. In about 10 days or a fortnight we may get them.

8th Read till 12 this morning, then dressed and spent the rest of the morning with Mrs. Mac[ondray]. Met Bradford, Dumaresq and Forbes there. After dinner went to Mrs. Fearon's, or rather "the Casa garden." You cannot fancy anything more romantic. It is a most lovely place. It is now quite in a dilapidated state, the walls were thrown down in the Typhoon, trees torn up by the roots, temples and summer houses demolished. The moon was shining beautifully through the trees and reflecting itself upon the waters *à la distance*. Oh if I could transport you out here for two days, and then set you down again in your own happy home I would. For you cannot fancy how romantic it was, it only needed Mr. D. to be my adorer and it would have been quite a scene for a romance. Seated upon a rock at the edge of a precipice, a thick wood above and below, up-turned trees, and twining shrubs around us, the moon shining brightly above us, our faithful dog Dash in the foreground. Oh how lovely. Felt tired when I got near home, went into Mrs. Macondray's, Bradford and Dumaresq took tea there, went home, found Wilkinson, Blight, Forbes, and Perit there. Now love I am going to bed so good night.

9th Went to Church this morning. Great many strangers there.

After church read Paley's *Theology*.[20] Capt. Condry, Dumaresq, and Bradford dined with us. Capt C. is a very pleasant man, has been all over the world. Is a married man of about 40. Rainy no walk. Listened to the organ this eve'g; it is very fine.

10th Capt. [James Warner] Sever[21] & John Forbes called this morning and Ibar. Was studying in my room all the evening and did not see them. Dumaresq, Forbes, & Perit spent the evening with us. Condry & Bradford took tea with us.

11th [Charles] Bradford breakfasted with us, thinking to start very early for Canton with Uncle, but they did not go till about 11. Do not like B. upon longer acquaintance—no refinement, is too forward. We bid Uncle good bye again with a prospect of a short passage and no Typhoon. Read a little. Finished *The Dutchman's Fireside* by Paulding—some scenes very amusing, written with spirit and ease, the plot very simple.[22] Spent an hour with Mrs. Macondray. Mr. King called, just from Canton.

Walked after dinner with Blight and Perit. Dumaresq joined us. We set upon the hills till the moon rose to light us home, looked splendidly as she came up from the Sea. Forbes, Blight, & Seaver spent the evening with us.

12 Spent most of the morning in writing. Aunt Low went out to call on the late arrivals. Vachell called and introduced the Rev. Mr. Wimbledon [Charles Wimberley][23] from Calcutta, "rather a severe muster." Went out to the Campo. Stopped to speak to Mrs. Daniell— she was sitting in her chair with her children playing round her. The handsome papa was entering fully into their innocent gambols. Three of the prettiest children I know of, they were rolling upon the grass, careless and happy. I was half inclined to envy the happy group, for

they must be happy, and if they are not, they are ungrateful! It was prettier than any picture I ever saw.

Mr. and Mrs. Davis, Mrs. Thornhill, Blight, & Sullivan spent the evening with us.

13 Read all the morning. Dumaresq spent an hour with us. Walked after dinner. D. joined us, then Blight, and then King & Perit. I had three of them coming home. D. left for Lintin, the rest spent the evening with us.

14th Strong northerly wind this morning. Some predict a Typhoon. Braces one up finely, I long to have a good <u>canter</u>. Wish I was at home. Are you not tired of that wish?

This morning Mr. Ibar came in. He is thinking of going to Spain this year, smart fellow enough. Capt. Sever, Blight, & Sullivan in this morning. "His Excellency" [Sullivan] felt perfectly satisfied with himself; was however very agreeable. Sever also, he is a much more refined Capt. than one generally sees. He had a liberal education and studied law some years, but possessing a spirit of Independence & being I believe in some way embarrassed, he left his law and went into the <u>forecastle</u> of a ship, where he served some time and <u>rose</u> by <u>degrees</u>. He is very pleasant and gentlemanly, but bitter <u>ugly</u>.

After dinner we went to the Campo with Blight—King & Perit joined me, and I had to <u>endure</u>. K. has lived too long in this country. He has the spirit of self love most fully imbibed, people grow so independent of other people. They depend so little upon their neighbours and so much upon their own resources for their happiness, that they after a time get very selfish and find that no company is so pleasant as their own. It is the general complaint and no one is willing to trespass upon established habits.

15 Capt. Condry called and some others, spent an hour with Mrs. Mac[ondray]. Met College there. <u>Worth</u> <u>going</u> <u>for</u>.

16 Went to Church this morning. Very cool, was really cold there for they pulled the Punkah. Many strangers there.

Capt. Sever, Blight, and Forbes were in this evening, leave in the morning for Canton.

17 Did not feel very bright this morning, but I adorned my <u>mortal frame</u> and sallied forth to pay my respects to the new arrivals. I just called on Mrs. Alexander and Miss Barwell. Saw the former, a pretty, interesting woman of easy and handsome manners. Miss B. was engaged. Then called on the lovely Mrs. Ploughdon [Plowden]— met Vachell & Whiteman there. Mrs. P. is a sweet, amiable creature, <u>perfectly white</u>, with jet black hair. Talked about Mrs. Trollope's book, which they [think] is <u>scandalous</u>, but it affords them lots of fun at the expense of Poor America. Have not yet read it. Then I called on Mrs. Donolly,²⁴ a little delicate creature, as small a person as I ever saw. Looked as though she needed a Mamma to take care of her. She is quite out of health—thinks Macao a <u>queer</u> place, and longs to get out of it, back to Calcutta. Feels lonesome and homesick, poor thing. She has a <u>handsome</u> young husband, but from a five minutes call I should judge that was all he had to recommend him, but there is no accounting for tastes.

Called on Mrs. Thornhill. Met Chay Beale & Young Pereira. Then went home with a violent headache which always follows visiting in the morning. Went to walk after dinner with Blight and felt rather better. Dumaresq took tea with us. Just returned from Lintin. Brought us a box that came from France with lots of pretty things, which were liberally bestowed upon me and made me feel uncomfortably. I almost wish they would not give me so many things. I do not feel any happier for them, and it lays me under such a weight of obligations.

18 Sullivan in this morning. We had a long argument with him, in which we flattered ourselves we had the advantage. C. & I walked out alone this afternoon. College walked out by the side of us on horseback. Tells me of a curious marriage there was at the Cathedral this morning at 5 o'clock. A Miss Paiva,²⁵ one of the most respectable families here. He says he heard all the circumstances from her brother so he can vouch for the truth of it. It seems this young lady was several times in company with a gent (I forget his name), but Capt. of the *Camoens*. She fancied him very much, but he shew no signs of partiality to her. But she was not to be foiled by that. She told her brother, she liked him and if she was married it must be him, and he must do all in his power to promote the match. I believe she did not actually propose herself, but they managed it so satisfactorily that the marriage was consummated. But think you it was love that bound him? Ah no, the <u>80,000 dol[lars]</u> was the <u>rivet</u>, when, if they should be unfortunate, where will they be—she is <u>fat</u>

and ugly, and he worships the <u>dollars</u>. He was worth nothing before and I suppose considers himself <u>fortunate</u>—but I should not think he would fancy the <u>appendage</u> he must have with the money.

I hear tonight Vachell is off to England. Mr. Wimberley is here to supply his place for 2 years.

Spent the evening with Mrs. Davis, a small party and very pleasant. A tremendous thunderstorm just after we got home.

19 Mr. Blight & Mr. Wilkinson in this morning *pour dire Adieu.* Leave for Canton tonight. Mrs. Morrison called. Went to a large party at Mrs. Daniell's. *Tout le monde et sa femme* were there, about 60— lots of strangers. Dancing and music, supper and chat, promenading and lounging. Danced with Alexander, Sullivan, Chay Beale, and Capt. Dalrymple [HCS *Orwell*]. Had a delightful time, came home about 1. Just before I went had a letter from Cousin Sally Orne and Uncle [Elijah] Porter. They put me in spirits for the evening. Written on my birth day.

Neponset just arrived. G[eorge] H. Williams[26] in her. Hope I shall see him.

20 Dumaresq in this morning, says the <u>animal</u> that came on shore from the *Neponset* had no idea when he <u>left</u> home. Indeed he could recollect nothing of the manner in which he had been living or what had occurred since that time, and yet called himself <u>Sane</u>. Oh dear how can people be so stupid.

Went to the Company's tonight, a dinner party. Dalrymple and Haylett handed me to table. Only 6 ladies there. Mrs. Plowden looked lovely. Felt tired and sleepy—very stupid after dinner and very glad to find myself in my own room.

21st Hot day. Some calls. Walked after dinner. C. & I took our seats on a hill and amused ourselves with laughing at the married ladies, perched about in different spots. Spinsters versus married ladies. I suspect all our spite is from <u>envy</u>. Not that we wish to take their happiness from them at all, but it is a feeling one cannot help—and after all our spite is only for the amusement of the moment. Dumaresq & Sullivan joined us on the hill and took tea with us. Also Mrs. Thornhill.

22d Not very well today. Read *Clarence* by Miss Sedgwick. I liked it very much. Read this evening *The Confession of an Opium Eater* [De Quincey].[27]

23ᵈ Did not go to Church, having a violent headache. Read Beattie on *Truth*[28] in connection with some other works I have been reading. Dumaresq & Perit took tea with us.

24 Went to Mrs. Macondray's this morning. Met Sullivan & S. Sturgis there. They leave for Canton tonight. Had quite a merry call.

25 Had 4 more letters per *Neponset* this morning, not much news. Dismal accounts of poor E. Hodges. Should think Mrs. Gray would feel very uncomfortable. Have been reading *Sydenham* & *Alice Paulet* today—or *The Man of the World*.[29] Very well written and very entertaining, rather a Satirical thing.

Walked out after tea. Aunt Low invited a large party to night, but they are all engaged. At least Mrs. Fearon came and Mr. Vachell, Mr. Dumaresq, and Capt. [Benoni] Lockwood.[30]

26 Reading all day. Walked with Dumaresq and Perit. Took tea at home and spent the evening with Mrs. Macondray.

27 Spent the day as usual in reading. Finished *Alice Paulet*, very well written. Cuts up the present customs of Society handsomely. Walked with Perit, Dumaresq, and Lockwood, and Bursley [captain of the American ship *Nile*] joined us. P. spent the evening with us, we had quite a <u>home</u> frolic. Caroline & I accompanied the organ by blowing on a comb as in the days of our childhood. I had a violent toothache and the moment it stopped I got up and danced, which set the others but—

Morris & Capt. Underwood[31] called.

28 A cold north wind blowing very strong, the changes here are as sudden as in America, and very trying.

Went out this morning and called on Mrs. Morrison, Mrs. Macondray, Mrs. Underwood, Lady Robinson, & Mrs. Thornhill. Mrs. U. is on her way to England from Madras. Is said to be very handsome, but she was out today and we did not see her.

Mrs. Davis had a Ball tonight and some fine music. Mrs. Underwood was there, played delightfully upon the harp and piano. Sings very sweetly. She is handsome, and sitting at her harp makes quite a picture. We had a rich treat this evening. We had Paiva and Mrs. Pereira, Mr. & Mrs. Underwood, those four sung the vesper hymn most divinely. I did enjoy it. We had some duetts, and trios, had considerable dancing. I had a most intolerable headache in consequence of going out in the morning, but the more it ached, the more I flew round and laughed and talked, for the moment I was still it seemed as though my head would burst. Stayed till about 1 and broke up.

29 Mrs. Rees, Mr. Dumaresq, Seaver, Mrs. Davis, & Mrs. Ploughdon called. Mrs. Rees leaves in a few days for Calcutta—she is an excellent woman and beloved by all.

Finished Washington Irving's last book today, *The Legends of the Alhambra*[32] written in his usual good style, the same grace of expression and beautiful language which characterizes all his works. The stories are Moorish tales and not much of any thing, in fact written by any one else or a less talented would not be read.

We went this evening to Mrs. Grant's—a most delightful party. Expected to have met Mrs. Underwood, but she was unwell and sent an excuse. We however had some very good music. A brother of Mr. Huddleston has come here with his wife from Madras, and he is a great performer on <u>many</u> wind instruments. He played the "hautboy," an instrument I have never heard before. It is very sweet and makes a most delightful accompaniment. He says it is very difficult to play, that [it] is very fatiguing. It is blown through a small reed. We had some dancing, a supper, and a very merry and delightful evening. It was very cool. Danced with Dalrymple, Mr. Davis, Mr. Young, & Mr. Vachell. Broke up early.

The last party for the season I suppose, that is gentlemen's parties, as they go to Canton on Monday.

30 Wrote a letter and sent via Manilla to the United States—also wrote to my friend Mrs. Cartwright.

Walked after dinner. Saw Mrs. Underwood on horseback—looked elegantly. She excels in this too. She had two gents with her, and all Macao was out after her. It is amusing to see the actions of people here. Our grandmother Eve bestowed her gift not only upon her daughters but her sons here and they do not check its <u>growth</u> at all.

Perit joined us and came home with us. [Spent] the evening alone. Now my dear I have brought my book up and as I have been up of late very late, I must bid you good night and shall endeavour in future to be more particular in making up my accounts daily. Good night my dear.

October 1st Monday morning. I rose rather late. Fine, cool morning. Dispatched a letter per Manilla [to] Mrs. Cartwright, wrote several notes, read my french lesson to Caroline, dressed, and a <u>call</u> of two hours from Mr. Dumaresq. Was making a <u>pen wiper</u> for Uncle, a very pretty muster. D. tried very hard to get me to <u>offer</u> to make him one, but I was determined he should <u>ask</u> if he wanted it; and he did at last.

Mr. Daniell called. The Company do not start tonight on account of northerly wind. They make any excuse to prolong the time in Macao. Dumaresq & Seaver called for us to walk; we had quite a pleasant walk. Feels like Autumn weather at home. We find a bonnet quite comfortable now. We have not worn one before for some months. You would I suppose think it very bold to go walking about without bonnets, but it is exceedingly comfortable I assure you. I put my new cottage [bonnet] on to day and admire it very much. The crown is rather small, but the ribbon is splendid. A gentleman told me that he did not hear the Sermon yesterday, my bonnet attracted his attention so much. He said it reminded him of home. I always think of you when I put it on. That and the blue gown together look very well I assure you.

D[umaresq] and Seaver spent the eve'g with us & Perit. Capt. Seaver sang to us beautifully. He has a <u>magnificent</u> voice.

About 10 Vachell came in and bid us <u>good bye</u>. He leaves for England next month. 'Tis not pleasant to say farewell to anyone, particularly one whom you have been intimate with. He leaves Macao with the Factory tomorrow morning.

3d Read a little Spanish, and some history aloud to Caroline, and then worked till dinner time. Caro & I walked after dinner with Dumaresq & Seaver—Perit joined us. They spent the eve with us. Also Mr. Chinnery, a most <u>amusing</u> man, of very good information and good sense.

4 Up in good season this morning—fitted part of a dress. A most lovely morning—first such weather as we have at home this month. Cool, bracing winds. The roses begin to come into our cheeks and we feel no need of a siesta after dinner. I spent the morning with Mrs. Macondray, tending her baby a good deal. Poor woman, she has all sorts of trouble and all alone. She has taken a violent cold, and the poor babe is pining away from hunger. Wet nurses won't

come, can't speak the language—can't get a bottle, won't feed with
a spoon, and all the ills that flesh is heir to in this miserable country. [See October 8 and 17 below] I left her at 3, came home [and]
wrote a letter to her husband. Read a little. Then Dumaresq and
Seaver called for us to walk, and we went up to Camoen's Cave.
Lovely afternoon, beautiful moon, and we sit upon a stone bench
overlooking a parapet till quite late when we bent our steps homeward after having had a very pleasant <u>consu</u> there.

Mr. Perit spent the evening with us and bid us adieu, leaves tomorrow morning for Canton. Since his departure C. & I have walked
upon the terrace about an hour <u>chatting</u>, talking of the present, past
& future. Retired to our rooms. I have had another meeting in her
room, now snugly ensconced in my own and having settled my daily
accounts, I bid you good night.

5 Spent this morning in reading and sewing, both at once. Caroline
went to Mrs. M's and I was sitting alone. I wanted to sew and read
together and I managed very well.

Walked with D[umaresq]; C. with S[eaver], a lovely evening. <u>The
two</u> spent the evening with us. We had our organ playing and I was
drawing the sides to a basket. Spent the evening very pleasantly. A
walk proposed for the Lappa.

6 Read a little French, and went to sewing. Seaver & Dumaresq came
to say every thing was ready for our trip to the Lappa. I spent an
hour with Mrs. M[acondray]. Dined at 2. D. & S. called for us at 3
and we went down to the boat. Had a delightful <u>pull</u>, up the river.
The afternoon was charming. Landed, had a pleasant walk. Only one
adventure—on crossing a ridge my foot slipt and went half way up
to one knee in thick mud. With an <u>effort</u> I pulled it out, but in such
a condition! What to do I knew not. There was so sign of my silk
stocking and purple silk shoe. I thought at first, best to let it dry, but
soon after coming to a beautiful clear running stream I thought I
would dip it and accordingly made for the brook. The cooly that
was carrying our provisions appeared to be of the same mind, for
before we arrived at the brook, he put his basket and jugs upon the
ground and came down to the stream and with the greatest nonchalance possible took up my foot and washed all the mud nicely off
with a cloth. He then took the bottom of my dress and did the same.
He brought to light the stocking and shoe, but left me in a dripping

state I assure you. If I do not get cold I am tough. This was a piece of gallantry I should never have <u>suspected</u> a Chinese to be guilty of, and note it down that it may not be forgotten. We have come to the conclusion this evening that it is some <u>lover</u> in disguise, for gallantry and kindness are not understood by the Chinese in general. After my <u>ablution</u> we proceeded to the Joss house. I have often described the place as well as in my power, but never expect to do it justice. I wish always I could transport you here. It is so delightful, so unlike any thing you have ever seen. We were saying when seated at a little square table in the piazza of the temple, if any of our friends could for an instant be dropped down there or permitted to look upon us, they would be amused. The situation was so wild, so romantic that it is impossible to give you an idea. The people were excessively civil, and even the mob only show an idle curiosity.

We wandered about for sometime, and started for home. Had a delightful walk by moonlight, "had as clear a moon as you ever saw." The water was very smooth, and we pulled round to the Praya. The Peña Church was beautifully illuminated and had a fine effect upon the water. The town looks sweetly from the water. The words of the poet may well be applied to this place "Distance lends enchantment to the view." [Thomas Campbell, *Pleasures of Hope*, Part I, l. 7]

Came home about 9, had some tea. Capt. Seaver sang to us a little, and now here I am—another day has gone. I must begin to write some letters or I shall never get them done.

7 Busy at work all the morning. Caroline read aloud to me the "*Commonplace Book of Poetry*,"[33] quotations from different American Authors. Dumaresq called, but we were not dressed and he went away. We rec^d a note to the <u>firm</u> [a note from W. W. Wood to the firm of H. Low & Co.] shortly after saying the *Walter* had arrived from England, bringing late English news, also that the *Suffolk* was on her way from Boston and the *Clematis* had been spoken with and is expected hourly. Northerly winds have been very strong of late and this ship had been 49 days making 8 degrees.

We walked after dinner. Our two beaux joined us, and we had a delightful walk. They are both so respectful and gentlemanly, indeed all the gents here are. They never by look or word show any disrespect. They spent the evening with us. It is now about 12. Caro and I have been comparing notes and discussing the merits of <u>the two</u>, and <u>wondering</u> and wishing. Oh my dear sister that I could tell you all the "<u>funny bits</u>" and the strange manoeuvres of this place or rather the people. You do not know <u>what it is</u>, to be one of two spinsters in a place. It is a distinction I would willingly give up and resign my post at any hour, but alas we cannot do as we would, here or there! Good night, my dear.

7 [8] Went to Church this morning, walked with Dumaresq. Heard Mr. Wimberley preach for the first time—liked him very well. Seemed to feel what he read, which is more than the other did. Went home, finished Beattie on *Truth*, wrote a letter. Walked after dinner with Dumaresq and Seaver. Spent the eve'g alone. Lovely night. Walked the terrace a long time <u>talking</u>.

8th [9] This morning just as [I] was out of the bathing tub, Caroline sung out and said she heard Uncle's voice in the "go down." I passed the word to Aunty and then my first impulse was to rush into the drawing room. Judging it <u>decorous</u>, I stopped and put on a dressing gown and *en papillote* sallied forth, whereupon on opening the door I discovered a stranger, a youth. I sang out Oh! and retreated <u>speedily</u>.

We were soon handed a packet of letters per *Red Rover* brought by Mr. <u>Higginson</u> from Calcutta. I had a delightful long letter of 4 sheets from Mrs. Cleveland. Made myself <u>decent</u> and met Mr. H. at breakfast. A very pleasant young man. His voice and manner of speaking is just like Edward Orne's, I cannot help thinking of him. I was busy till 2 o'clock, then spent an hour with Mrs. M[acondray]. She is obliged to give her babe to a China woman to nurse. It is very unpleasant, and grieves her much, but she cannot help it. After dinner Seaver, Dumaresq and Higginson called for us to walk. We went to the Peña. A perfect evening. They all took tea with us, and left us about 11. Capt. S. sung to us. He does sing <u>divinely</u>. He is a very superior man; had a <u>liberal education</u>, studied law three years with Gov. Lincoln and for some <u>good</u> reasons left and went into the forecastle of a Ship. Rose by degrees, is now Captain—a situation he ought not to fill for he does not like it, and his mind is too active for such a life. And [he] is a most entertaining companion, not handsome, but that is forgotten—a man of great observation, and has seen a great deal of the world and I should say a keen observer of men and manners. Dumaresq is an excellent man, very gentlemanly, very stiff in his manners, though very agreeable upon acquaintance, a little diffident, particular, obliging and very <u>smart</u>. Has been at sea since a boy. To sum him up a very fine young man though not one I should ever take a fancy to for an <u>intimate</u> <u>friend</u>.

9 [10] Read a little Spanish this morning, and then Caroline & I set together and worked till dinner time, she making a bonnet and I a gown. After dinner <u>the</u> <u>three</u> came. We went to <u>Camoen's</u> Cave; had quite a romantic walk. Mr. H[igginson] made himself very agreeable—he's a funny creature. <u>They</u> spent the evening with us, looking at pictures—"Scrap Sheets," fortune tellers, annuals, and etc., with which traps our center table abounds. Our beautiful organ at the same time delighting our ears. A few songs from Capt. S[eaver] and some pleasant <u>chat</u>, we contrive to find 11 o'clock in short time. And now it is <u>1/2</u> <u>past</u> 12 and time for me to "<u>turn</u> <u>in</u>." You will think we keep very late hours, and so we do.

10 [11] Aunt Low & I went out this morning, called on Mrs. Clifton, Mrs. Wimberley, Mrs. Alexander, & Miss Barwell, Mrs. Rees, Whiteman, and Crocket—had sundry dissertations upon children, <u>their</u> <u>rise</u> <u>&</u> <u>progress</u>. All very entertaining to me as you may suppose. Aunt L. seems to enter into the particulars with great pleasure and you would think she had 1/2 a dozen herself.

Had a note and "*Byron's Gallery*"[34] from Dumaresq. He has gone to Lintin today. Walked out with Higginson & Seaver. They spent the evening with us as usual. Aunt L. took tea with Mrs. Thornhill, but we had a most rational evening at home.

11 [12] Very busy all the morning at work. After dinner Mr. H. and Seaver called for us to walk. I undertook to pilot them through the village, but I found I had entered crowds of huts with legions of squalling children who greeted us with a shrill shout at the tops of their voices, dogs barking, and altogether a perfect Babel. Our imaginations stretched to the utmost could not convert the scenes into any thing like romance or even neatness and simplicity. And although we were let into the secrets of family arrangements as we passed their open doors and saw mothers performing the most maternal offices on every side, yet we could not compare them with the meanest villagers at home. Dirty, filthy creatures I saw no escape from it either, but after some time we made our exit and got on to the open hills, rejoiced to breathe the fresh air. Mr. H. was very agreeable. We spent a very pleasant evening, the two with us.

13 Very busy at work again. Set with Aunt Low all the morning and had a very interesting conversation with her—she is a sterling woman, and the better she is known, the more she must be respected. I never saw a person who would bear inspecting so well, so conscientious and strict in the performance of duty. Walked and spent the evening *comme à l'ordinaire*. No variety, the same people day after day, but these two* are worth something. There is something to be obtained from their conversation.

*Higginson & Sever, the two now.

14 Went to Church this morning. Mr. W[imberley] gave us an excellent sermon, the text "Choose ye this day whom ye will serve," [Joshua 24:15] indecision of character the subject. Caroline had letters from her brother per *Mary* [from Batavia], and he has not come. Poor girl is disappointed again. Hear the *Clematis* is at Manilla. Spent the evening with Mrs. Macondray. The dear Mr. College went in with me and spent part of the evening.

15 Reading most of the morning. Finished Mrs. Trollope. Like some parts of the book and others I do not. I walked with Higginson, C. with Seaver, that is the order of the day. Had a very delightful walk and chat. He is worth talking to, has sense enough, thinks for himself. They, with Mr. & Mrs. Wimberley & Mrs. Thornhill, spent the evening with us. Now it is awfully late and I must say good night.

16 I read part of the morning, got very much interested in the Life of Josephine. Was called to see Mr. Millet, who detained me an hour. Then Aunt Low had a letter from Canton of which you will undoubtedly hear more anon. It took up my attention till two, when I finished the rest of the morning in writing to Uncle.

Walked after dinner with Higginson. Spent the evening at home at the table. We all got letters. Aunt L. and I from Brother Nat, and C. from her bub. per *Fremont*—nothing new, but the disgraceful times in Congress.

17 This morning finished a dress, read some, spent an hour with Mrs. Macondray. Says there is an order issued to take from foreigners all China women, they are generally wet nurses, which will be very dreadful. Her poor babe was very near starving till she procured one, and just as it begins to recover it would be too cruel to have them taken away. Oh these mandarins are <u>too</u> barbarous. The moment they see a fellow creature making money they begin to <u>squeeze</u> them as it is termed. No doubt this is to extort money from them. Stayed at home all the evening and read the Life of Josephine. Finished it, very interesting. She was a sweet amiable creature, beloved by all, and was well tried in the schools both of prosperity and adversity. The prediction of the old sybil in the west Indias proved wonderfully true; she certainly saw into futurity.[35]

18 At home all day, reading History. I do <u>love</u> history better than any kind of reading, and I should much sooner go to sleep over a novel than in reading history. In the evening we were escorted by Higginson and Sever to the "<u>Opera</u>" where we heard <u>very</u> well performed the Opera of Cinderella [*La Cenerentola* by Rossini] in Spanish. The music was very good, the scenery pretty, and the acting very amusing. Cinderella was not <u>very</u> <u>beautiful</u>, being a <u>boy</u> of very somber hue. In her <u>home</u> dress <u>she</u> reminded me of Henriette Gelliveau. The company was chiefly Portuguese and no beauty among them. The Opera was wholly under the direction of Mr. Paiva, who deserves great credit. He wished to let his townswomen know what an Opera was, and having travelled all over Europe and possessing great musical talents himself, he undertook it and succeeded very well. We really were very much amused. Got home about 1/2 past 12. There was a farce afterwards, which was rather tedious.

19 Reading aloud to Caroline all the morning. Miss Morrison and Capt. Clifton called. I did not go out this afternoon. Higginson called and spent the evening with us. I commenced the *Fair Maid of Perth* [Sir Walter Scott] upon his recommendation. I drew all the evening. Now good night.

20 Chay Beale and Ibar called this morning. Ibar just from Canton, is going to Europe this year. Has been out here 10 years. Clifton & his wife called and the two Miss Ullmans. Read some and cut out a crape dress. Went to walk, met Dumaresq and Higginson, who joined us. D. just from Lintin. It is currently reported in Lintin & Capsing moon, that I am engaged to D. and Caroline to Sever. And all for why, because they have been seen walking with us a few evenings.

Poor creatures, I wonder any gentleman dares to walk with us for they engage us to every one, and if they happen to break off and not walk a day or two, why then they are juwaubed or in plain English refused. We are quite independent of such reports now and only laugh at them. We warn new comers of their danger and find out if there is any one to be made jealous at home, for these reports do not rest here, but take wings to America, for they often rebound.

21 Went to Church this morning. Heard a very good sermon from Mr. W[imberley]. Wrote some letters today. Walked after dinner with Higginson and D. and they took tea with us.

22ᵈ Got letters from Uncle this morning, which discomposed me for the day. After dinner however I received letters from home per *Panama* which drew my thoughts in another channel. The accounts of Uncle Daniell's [Low] return [from Paris], Susan's [Orne] long letter, her troubles, etc., all of which I truly sympathize in. Thankful to hear you are still all well. I ought to be very thankful for such good accounts. Went to walk with D. & H. Read the papers when we came back. Mrs. Macondray took tea with us. We played whist. Was glad to go to my own room to meditate. Felt gloomy and sad.

23ᵈ Went into Aunt Low's room, had a long talk. Set there from 10 till 1, talking and settling the affairs of the nation. Don't know that I ever felt more wretched. Had a letter while I set there from Canton.
    What a world of trials and disappointments this is. Money seems to be the one thing needful, the *sine qua non* of existence. Oh romance, where dost thou dwell? Our dearest and fondest hopes are often dashed for the want of the filthy lucre, our fairest schemes defeated, our plans broken, and even our affections have some times to be sacrificed for the want of it.[36] Walked to the Gap with our usual escort. Returned and spent the evening with Mrs. Daniell, 9 ladies and 2 gents there, the bipeds of the genus homo are scarce now. There was two new arrivals, a Mr. & Mrs. Luke from Bombay.[37] Had a stupid evening, my whole amusement was in watching one of our beaux and making fun of him, for he is nursing a pair of horrid mustachios, his face is white and sickly. He is as large as a knitting needle, and the most conceited puppy you ever saw. To make himself look ferocious, he lets the light hair grow all over his upper lip, to which he has to pay great attention else he stands a chance of chewing it. It is quite

amusing to see him <u>poke</u> it on one side that he may find room for his food. He caught me several times looking at his maneuvres and almost laughing. He almost hated me before, and he will <u>quite</u> I suppose as I do not approve of such <u>ornaments</u>. I fancy he heard me when I was laughing at him with Mrs. Morrison, for she helped me out. I intended he <u>should</u> at any rate. He goes by the name of "<u>Don Whiskerando</u>." Now I am at home and just going to bed. Hope I shall not dream of him. Mr. Luke looks like Mr. Walsh of Salem.

24 Mrs. Morrison was in this morning, also Mr. Dumaresq, Chay Beale, and Ibar. Had a long dissertation on engagements and the display of the tender passion with its effects, & etc. Walked with D., Beale, Ibar, & Calvo, with Higginson & spent the evening with us. Played <u>old</u> <u>maids</u> and had some sport with it.

25 Mrs. Donolly called this morning, a little <u>wee</u> bit of a woman. Is said to have been a great belle on her first appearance in Calcutta, but four years residence in that climate has destroyed all appearance of beauty, and there is no trace of it left. She has very pleasing manners however now. Those will never <u>fade</u>, and how much even beauty is indebted to manners. Mrs. Thornhill called on <u>official</u> business. She is really Irish, <u>such</u> a temper. Mrs. Wimberley, too, truly <u>Scotch</u>. They all seem to possess in perfection the national characteristics. She is a very pleasant woman and has the Scotch accent. Mrs. Daniell, Higginson, and Dumaresq spent the evening with us.

26 An invitation to spend the evening with Mrs. Pereira, but had invited company at home, of course refused. Walked after dinner with H[igginson] and D[umaresq]. A fine cool day with a northerly wind. Had some proofs this evening of the <u>insincerity</u> of one who has <u>asked</u> to be called a <u>friend</u>—but knowing his character pretty well, I neither accepted his proferred <u>friendship</u>, nor am I by his late conduct at all deceived, and though he has now turned his back and is trying all he can to injure us, yet I think he carries it too far, and will let those who have <u>hitherto</u> respected him, know he is not worthy of their slightest consideration. <u>Nor is he</u>. 'Tis a pleasant thing to know our friends from our enemies. These things all conspire to make me feel uncomfortable, but the time will come when I shall laugh at their ever having given me a moment's uneasiness—and serves to make me suspicious perhaps.

27 Mr. Dumaresq came in this morning and said Mrs. Macondray was going to Lintin tomorrow morning in his Ship. Ibar and Higginson in and spent an hour. Had a long dissertation upon Spanish ladies and Lima beauties, who Ibar says are called the Circassians of S. America. Their manners are very fascinating, but their morals are at the lowest ebb, I should say. They wear the "<u>Manta</u>" which covers their face all but one eye. Their dress fits tight to their bodies and is very <u>expensive</u>; this dress enables them completely to disguise themselves, and they sometimes carry on intrigues with <u>their</u> <u>own</u> <u>husbands</u>. They are excessively ignorant, and one of the <u>belles</u> of the highest class and consequently as well informed as any, asked a Frenchman if he came from Paris to Lima <u>by</u> <u>land</u>? which does not say much for the cultivation of their <u>intellect</u>.

Walked over to Mrs. M[acondray]'s with Dumaresq. While there Mr. M. came from Lintin[38] for his wife, and urged me to go up with them. I went home, asked Aunt Low, and she thought it a good opp'y, and as I longed to change the scene and get out of Macao for a while, I consented to go very gladly. Packed up my things accordingly, and was all ready to start the next morning. Dr. Bradford with his brother just arrived in the *Morrison*,[39] come in this morning, came from Lintin with Mr. M.

Walked after dinner with Higginson and Dumaresq, they all spent the evening with us. Wrote a long letter to Uncle on <u>special</u> <u>business</u> which I shall probably write you in a letter.

28 Got up at 5 o'clock this morning. The party for Lintin consisting of Mrs. Macondray, two Bradfords, Higginson, breakfasted with us at 6. We started in the *Sylph* at 7 and got on board the *Martha* which anchored in the roads at 8 with a pleasant breeze. Our party on board was Mr. & Mrs. Macondray, Mr. H., Dr. Bradford, and Dumaresq <u>Skipper</u>. The *Martha* is a fine little Ship. Reminded me very much of the *Sumatra* and our departure from home, excepting the feelings. It was a beautiful Sunday morning just like the one we left our own dear shores. It was very still and very little motion, but notwithstanding I was so unromantic as to be <u>sea</u> <u>sick</u>. Was bright at intervals however and able to enjoy our pleasant sail. Our party was all very agreeable till toward night when Mrs. M. being delicate, was afraid to stay on deck and went below, leaving as *triste* a trio as you ever saw. My head ached most dreadfully, and there sit Bradford, Higginson,

Lights and Shadows of a Macao Life

and my Ladyship all as deeply wrapped in our own meditations as we were in our cloaks, and not a word was spoken for some time. The moon was shedding her clear and beautiful light upon us and not a cloud was any where to be seen. The breeze had strengthened and we at 8 o'clock anchored at Lintin. Just at that moment I was again taken sick and I felt wretched enough, for there is nothing so depressing to the spirits and the strength as sea sickness—such a feeling of loneliness and utter hopelessness as you never feel in any other sickness.

We were "<u>whipped</u>" into the Long Boat and were soon landed on board the beautiful "barque *Lintin*."[40] I do not mean by <u>whipping</u> my dear sis that they took a rope end to us, but we were put into a <u>chair</u> and <u>hoisted</u> over the side, the most <u>genteel</u> way of getting over the Ship's side. Mr. Dumaresq and all the other passengers were as attentive as possible, and anticipated every wish. And with the exception of the times of sickness, I enjoyed the day very much. After getting on board the *Lintin* I was again sick, but after laying about an hour on a couch, I recovered my strength and was able to prepare for bed. Took some hot peppermint and felt better. Slept well, and got up in the morning, dressed me, astonished myself with a dose of salts which would not stay upon my <u>perturbed</u> stomach. The gentlemen came to breakfast with us but I could not eat any. Went on deck, the Peak of Lintin close on our side, and about 23 other ships around us. It is a very pretty sight I assure you. The *Lintin* has a fine round house on deck and fine accommodations.

Lintin October 29th 1832 B.que *Lintin*

29 Dumaresq, Bradford, & Higginson breakfasted and spent the day with us.

After dinner we went on board the *Red Rover*, expect to be quite a connoisseur in Ships before I leave. A lovely evening, a beautiful moon, were sitting on deck. Capt. [William] Mackay[41] and Capt. [Benoni] Lockwood came on board, spent the evening. Brought their little band of music which sounded very well. We danced a <u>quadrille</u> upon deck and the gents <u>waltzed</u>. Finished the evening with a game of Old Maids.

30 Was sitting in the cabin this morning reading and Capt. M. brought me a letter from Abbot dated Philadelphia per *Commerce* now anchored in sight of us. I need not say how glad I was.

The same party spent the day with us. After dinner went on shore with our party, had a pleasant walk. The Island of Lintin is rather barren, though there are some fertile spots, the rice plantations on the level ground look very pretty. Went through the village and saw women, <u>pigs</u>, and children all eating together, and inhabiting the same place. The great fat dirty pigs have the *entrée* of all the houses, to say nothing of fowls, & etc. Perfect pictures of filth and all uncleanness.

Saw the stuff they make the grass cloth of preparing; it is a large <u>stock</u> which they dry and beat till the fibres all separate. We had a delightful pull home to the Ship. Had the same band we had last night, and some fine singing from Mr. Gilman, mate of the Ship, who has a most delightful voice and sings with great taste. Capt. Lockwood also give us some amusing songs and we had one quadrille. Expect 'twill be reported all round the fleet that we are having <u>Balls</u> on board—every thing here is so exaggerated.

31ˢᵗ Busied myself all the morning making myself useful to Capt. Macondray, writing and performing the office of <u>Clerk</u>. All around me gentlemen, chattering and talking with me. [Charles S.] Bradford at one elbow criticising, Higginson at the other. Dumaresq and Dr. Bradford join, in the round house. Dumaresq bid us <u>good bye</u> at 2, and got under weigh for Canton. The passengers, 2 Dr. B[radford]s and Higginson dined with us and said Adieu at <u>3</u>. We shall miss them very much, H. particularly. He is a nice creature and so open and frank in his manners that we cannot help liking him. Very droll and keeps us laughing all the time—but he's gone.

After dinner read aloud to Mrs. M. Commenced *Waverley* and intend going through all Scott's novels. We spent the evening alone, very pleasantly.

Novʳ 1ˢᵗ Fine morning, got up at 7, had a fine bath, dressed, dispatched letters to Macao with <u>dirty</u> <u>clothes</u>, then set down and brought up my journal which was a week behind hand. Just had an interview with a Mr. Greene who came out in the *Morrison*. Says he saw Father a few days before he left. Says he carried H. Davis on to Brooklyn. Read the rest of the morning.

Capt. [Williams] Howland[42] of the *Florida* dined with us. Went on shore after dinner and walked half way up the Peak with him— poor man he was quite exhausted. Sailors are poor walkers on shore, they have so little practice. I am so used to it that I was not much fatigued—it was rather steep and the grass very slippery. Came home, walked a while and played Whist in the evening. A most lovely evening. The weather could not be pleasanter than it now is. Just cool enough to be comfortable any where.

About 10 rec^d letters from Macao, one from Aunt & Caroline and one from Canton, of which you will probably know the purport one of these days. It made me _triste_ I assure you and disturbed my night's repose. Some advice contained in Aunty's which is very hard to follow, for it goes much against my <u>inclination</u>, but I must follow it I believe and I hope it will prove for my good. But it is nevertheless very trying to the feelings.

2^d Wrote most of the morning to my Canton correspondent [W. W. Wood], then worked a little. After dinner we saw the Ship *Lion* from S. America come in and anchor, proud of having reached her port in safety. No news. Then commenced reading *Newton Foster*, a novel,[43] very amusing. A happy mixture of the grave and gay.

We spent the evening in the round house. Mr. Gilman sung to us most of the evening, accompanied by Mrs. Macondray, who has a very sweet voice.

3 Spent part of the morning in writing, then read the rest of the day. Several calls, but I did not see them. After dinner we were <u>whipped</u> into the Long Boat and were pulled round among the Ships. The sun had just set and the moon appeared to have borrowed an uncommon share of light, and <u>my</u> stars were shining brightly above us. The waters were still and it appeared impossible that a cloud could ever appear to obscure that brightness. It was too lovely. I was lost in thought and longed to soar somewhere where I cannot. It seems at such times as though one <u>ought</u> to divide the material from the immaterial and not be chained to [so] small a sphere. However the material must be attended to and gets much more attention to its wants than the immaterial, for in spite of myself soon after we got on board the *Lintin* I set myself down to a huge bowl of bread and milk which I relished exceedingly. Then I was weighed and find this <u>mortal body</u> weighs 115 lbs., which is 7 lbs. more than I ever knew myself to weigh before, but it is the first time I have been weighed for 5 years. I am now in very good care and look almost as fat as when I first arrived. Read awhile, then walked the remainder of the evening. A perfect night, seems too pleasant to go to bed.

4th Sunday morning. Have been reading in the cabin all the morning, feel dreadfully sleepy though. Mr. & Mrs. Durant called, very common sort of people. She's a <u>half</u> cast[e].

Had a fine pull towards night.

5th Wrote several letters, recd one from Macao & one from Dumaresq. Read part of the day as usual. Had a delightful pull in the evening. Every night is so still and delightful, not a cloud to darken, and all calm and "all save the spirit of man seems divine." [Byron, *The Bride of Abydos*, Canto 1, St. 1] Several ships coming up. Hope is arraying visions of happiness in placing before me budgets of <u>letters</u>. Mr. Howland spent the day with us. Went on board the *Florida* anchored near us, a pretty ship.

6th This morning wrote letters to Macao & Canton. Capt [P.] Tonks [*Lord Castlereagh*] called and we went in his boat to visit some Ships and the ladies. Went on board the English Ship *Caledonia*, a magnificent ship, and accommodations of a <u>palace</u>, really worth going to sea for. Then went on board the *Castlereagh*, another splendid ship. Saw Mrs. Tonks, Mrs. Rickets and her mother, Mrs. Lathrop, an American Lady. Came home. After dinner Mrs. Macondray and I had a pull in the wherry [a row boat]. Wrote a letter for *Italy*.

Mr. Gilman and Mrs. M. sung to us this evening.

7th *Flora, Sabina, Howard,* and several other ships arrived, but no letters for me. Letters from Macoa this morning. The *Lancaster*, the "laughing Capt. Jennings" in.

The *Lion* from Boston in. Young Sturgis[44] in her, about as big as our Willy [aged 13] when I left. Company for dinner. After dinner went on shore. A Mr. Morrel breakfasted, dined, and went on shore with us—a youth from New York, a rather pleasant young man. Played Whist with us this evening.

8th Mr. Morrel brought us some new books. Left for Canton. Letter from Higginson, D[umaresq] and Macao. Beautiful day. Busy at work all the morning, after having written divers and sundry letters for Macao & Canton.

Read a novel after dinner called *Romance & Reality* by L. E. L[andon].[45] Capt. Evans of the *Clematis* spent the evening with us. The C. is in sight of us. Always makes me think of Uncle David [Low, master of the *Clematis* before his death].

9th Had my breakfast and here I am in the Cabin leaning [on] the transom, looking ever and anon upon the blue water and the forest of ships that plant it, endeavoring to think what has happened for the last week. The incidents are fun, though there are many things happen that I do not put in my journal, partly from laziness and partly from prudence. Now I have just been interrupted by letters from Macao from my Aunt and Caroline. Poor girl she has heard the awful news of her mother's death. She wrote me however and is composed. She says she is frightened at her own apathy and feels as if she should go mad. I expected she would be just so. She exerts herself too much to control her feelings. I have wept for her, yes bitter tears. Would I could alleviate her sorrows, but nothing but time can soften them. What can be said—words are a mockery. I wish I was there now, but I know not how to go. No mail stage, no steamboat. Aunt Low wishes me to come too.

About 2 o'clock the [US] Sloop of War *Peacock* arrived here, anchored pretty near. Capt. M. boards her, and Capt. Guysinger [David Geisinger],[46] Mr. Roberts [Edmund Roberts][47] and the first Lieut, Mr. Cunningham [Robert B. Cunningham],[48] came and dined with us. Very pleasant & gentlemanly men. Mr. Roberts, a fine look-ing man, looks like a clergyman, a statesman, or any thing great you can name. They all made many pretty speeches at the pleasure of seeing ladies, meeting their country women, etc.—but oh I am sick of professions and pretty speeches. After dinner we had a delightful perambulation on shore, and a still pleasanter pull off to the Ship. The water was so still and the moon so bright and clear,

> it seemed to say that sorrows ceased
> In the calm sphere where she was burning.

We came home, had several other gentlemen and a band of music after tea. Dancing was proposed. How different our actions are from our feelings. Tonight I would gladly have spent alone in my own room. The thought of the affliction of Caroline and other things combined made me feel much more like crying than dancing, but it will not do to indulge our own feelings at all times, and when there are but two ladies it would never do for me to leave. Besides we cannot obtrude our sorrows upon others. So dance I did. Every one seemed in great spirits, but how little can we tell of the feelings of the heart by appearances. They kept it up till 12 and then retired.

10th Busy at work all the morning. Some of the gentlemen of the *Peacock* went to Canton. Mr. Cunningham spent the evening with us. Invited us to come on board to Church the next day, but as he told us they had the Cholera on board and had lost 7 men with it, we were afraid to go. They got it in Manilla, they say; that Ships were laying all around them in Manilla and none had it <u>but</u> their ship. They say it was in the atmosphere, and say it is only in a particular current or draught of air, but I cannot conceive of that.[49] They say it is not contagious, for many of the officers stood by when their men were seized with it and watched the progress of the disease, which must be <u>really</u> <u>awful</u>—but none of the officers ever took it.

11th Wrote letters most of the morning. Ships going [home] <u>thick</u> soon. Several gentlemen called. Read some. After dinner we had a delightful pull in the gig—went round the *Peacock*. A lovely evening. Almost inclined to be <u>sentimental</u>.

   Sung Psalm tunes in the round house with Mr. & Mrs. M. and Mr. Gilman.

12 Busy at work all the morning making a blue crape dress. Mrs. Ricketts and Mrs. Lathrop called; did not see them. Mrs. R. was born in Boston. Mrs. L., her mother, is a sister of one of the most respectable gentlemen in Boston, Mr. Motley. This morning Capt. [A. A.] Ritchie called and said good bye. He tempts the broad ocean tonight and steers toward the land of <u>liberty</u> in the *Italy*. Give him <u>two</u> letters.

   Mrs. M. went to a party tonight on board the *Good Success* [invited by the captain's wife], Mrs. [Euphemia] Durant. I did not feel like it and sent an excuse. Spent the evening in writing home. Went to bed about 12 before the folks came home.

13th A lovely morning. Went on deck. A smuggling boat alongside. Such a sight you never saw. They contain generally about a 100 men, when <u>alongside</u> they generally take this opportunity to eat or "<u>catchy</u> <u>chow</u> <u>chow</u>" and they form in little groups of 4 or 5 each round 5 or 6 little messes of fish and oysters cooked in divers ways. Each has his bowl of rice in his hand chop sticks in the other which each one dips into the <u>public</u> bowl and from these into their mouths. Having none of the delicate ideas of more refined people, they then <u>shovel</u> as much rice into their mouths as they can possibly <u>crowd</u> in. They appear to eat with <u>glorious</u> <u>appetites</u> I assure you. They sit on their

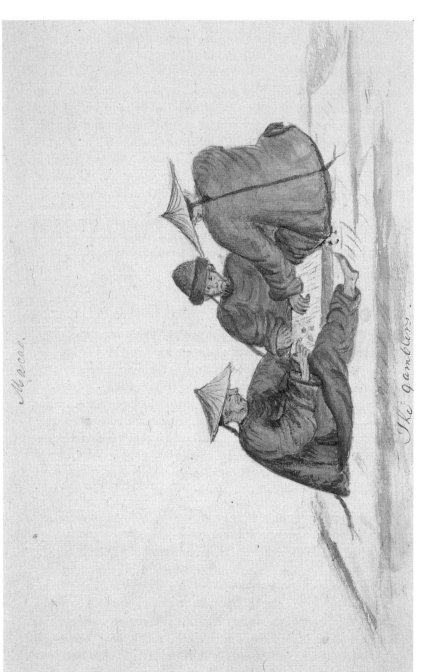

Macau.

The Gamblers

The Gamblers, Lucy Cleveland's Sketchbook (Peabody Essex Museum)

feet, and are <u>dirty</u> and <u>ugly</u>. They are generally the lowest class of people and as to morals, I will not say. If they have a moment's leisure, they commence <u>gambling</u> and I see them generally as soon as they have crammed down their food either have cards or dominos, each playing with all the interest possible. It is a curious sight to watch the expressions of their faces and if by chance they have any expression at all, it is an expression of avarice and love of gain. You see one laying on the side of the boat smoking his long pipe with apparent indifference to every thing in this world and the next. I often wish to ask what they <u>do</u> <u>think</u>, or if they think at all.

Spent the day in working, reading and writing as usual. Evening I wrote invitations for Mrs. M. for a party tomorrow night.

14th Mr. Grant & Mr. Calhoon [James Colquhoun, according to *Canton Register*] and several other gentlemen called. Had letters from Macao, want me to come home as soon as convenient. Caroline is very calm and resigned, but feels her loss deeply. In the evening we had our party. There were about 20, only <u>three</u> <u>ladies</u>. Danced and <u>waltzed</u> all the evening. I mean the gents waltzed. I am <u>too</u> <u>light</u> headed for such <u>evolutions</u>. We had the officers from the Sloop [USS *Peacock*] and the Capt. of the Ship, a band of music, and a nice supper. Was very much tired for it was two o'clock before they departed, and being no spring to the deck it was very fatiguing.[50]

15 Kept pretty still today, in fact could not move for we were quite done up. Nothing new.

16 Feel stiffer today than usual. However after dinner we went on board the *Peacock*. Very politely received, and liked the Ship much, every thing in good order and very neat. Most of the officers in Canton.

17 Feel better today, recovered mostly from fatigue. George H. Williams called this morning and Capt. Abbot [*Flora*]. Mr. W. reminded me very much of his sister both in manners and appearance. Suspect he is a little odd, like the rest of the family. Asked him a good many questions, but he made only a short call. Wrote a letter to Macao, as he leaves tomorrow morning. No arrivals and no news. Was half inclined to be melancholy and sentimental tonight, but thought it was not worth while. So eat my bread and milk and commenced writing letters home this evening.

18 Dressed myself and set down to reading. Was soon interrupted by company. Capt. Durant & Crockett called, then Lieut. Cunningham came and dined with us. Now here I am expecting every moment to be summoned to take a <u>pull</u> in the *Peacock's* cutter. <u>Still</u> <u>afternoon</u> <u>no</u> <u>motion</u>,—think there is less variety here than at Macao. No events, lead a quiet and steady life, indeed I find it best suits my disposition of late. I am getting <u>old</u> and <u>sedate</u>, not so fond of gaiety as when all was bright and fair. When I was young and unsophisticated in the ways of the world I was easily amused and believed all gold that glistened.

Mr. Cunningham left us early, thinking the sea <u>too</u> <u>high</u> for a <u>pull</u>. I was quite astonished, as you see I thought it was very still. I went on deck and found the wind had sprung up and <u>kicked</u> up a little sea at once. However I told Capt. M. I would go with him. He manned the gig and we started, and you would have considered me very courageous had you seen me dancing over the waters in this little thing—indeed I considered myself so and should not have trusted my precious <u>carcass</u> to the treacherous waves in so frail a bark had I have been aware the sea was so high. I however think there is very little fear in a row boat; it is only the sail boats I fear. I got back to the ship safely and we spent the evening conversing. Mr. M. read prayers in the cabin after we returned. It reminded me of our Sunday evenings at home.

19 Had just made up a bundle for Macao and got comfortably fixed to my book, when a note was handed me saying the Company's Ships were in sight and Capt. [Alexander] Grant sent word he would call and go on board with us when they anchored, as he promised me a few days before. In about an hour Mr. [Joaquin Ybar] Ibar, a passenger to England in the *Orwell*, and Capt. Makay [McKay] called and escorted us to the Ship *Orwell*. Capt. Grant was engaged. We were delighted. The Ship is very near as large as the Frigate *Potomac*, her accommodations very fine, and they may well be called "floating Castles." There is a great deal of style and etiquette to be observed. They appeared to be bountifully supplied with every kind of stock for the passage, and must be as comfortable as it is possible to be at sea. Mr. [Charles] Millet retires this year with a <u>fortune</u> I suppose, dearly earned by <u>20</u> years residence in this country. He has grown old and grey headed in the service, his habits fixed, and he is no doubt unfitted for living happily and comfortably in any country but this. He has a fine cabin and every thing neat and in bachelor style. He leaves China without a sigh of <u>regret</u> however. We stayed on board an hour and a half, had a nice Tiffin and returned to our little Barque, which is very comfortable though a <u>mite</u> compared to this. We bid all good bye, wished them a pleasant passage, and parted with Ibar and Millet probably <u>forever</u>. Ibar particularly we have spent many happy hours with.

Mr. Makay and Capt. Howland spent the evening with us. Capt. H. and I walked deck a long time. He asked me when I expected to return to America. I told him, and like every body else he seemed to speak in a <u>pitiable</u> tone of my situation in China, thought it must be very unpleasant. I wish people would keep their pity for those who wish it, for I do not for one. I told him I was as happy now as I ever expected to [be], I lived very well at Macao, and was not unpleasantly situated. You perhaps would have thought to hear me talk that I had no wish to return, but you have no idea how unpleasant it is to have every one think you need their <u>pity</u>. This man looked at me with astonishment and said my feelings must have changed very much. I told him they had not, that when it was right and proper for me to go home I should and till then I should endeavour to make myself contented, and that my feelings for every member of my family remained the same.

20 This morning a Circular was issued for a party to Lintin Peak, from 15 to 1800 feet from the sea. At 1 o'clock we started from the Ship. Mr. Macondray, Dr. Ticknor [Benajah Ticknor][51] of the *Peacock*, MaKay, Crockett, Wilson, <u>Dailey</u>, Tish, & myself, with about 15 attendants, carrying provisions, and a <u>band</u> <u>of</u> <u>music</u> and proceeded up the hill. The sun was rather hot and the roads rough and steep. We however reached the Peak at 1/2 past 2. They give three cheers, I have the honour of being the <u>first</u> <u>lady</u> that has reached the summit. When I got up there I could have walked a great deal further, just began to get my limbs in walking trim. We had found a very good appetite on our way up and were very glad to shelter ourselves from the sun behind an immense mass of granite with which the summit is crowned, and finding a table formed by nature for the purpose, we assembled round it and drew forth the contents of each ones basket and had quite a <u>sumptuous</u> <u>repast</u>—the music playing at

the same time, altogether would have made a most interesting group. I was the only lady of the party, and every thing was conducted with the most perfect decorum. Capt. Crockett arose and <u>palavered</u> a little about my <u>honoring</u> Lintin with my presence and drank a toast which was, "May Miss Low attain her wishes, how high ever they may be." I think that was it, upon which I bowed and begged Mr. Macondray to make a <u>speech</u> for me upon the occasion. He returned <u>many thanks</u>. We finished our meal and made preparations for descending, after having admired the view which is very extensive. This Island as well as all the Islands with which these seas abound are excessively barren, and capable of very little cultivation; there are many wild monkeys upon the Island, we saw one on our way up.

We descended on the opposite side, where the grass was very long. Some of the gents sat down and slid from the top to the bottom of the first ridge. I slipped down supported by two gentleman.

About 1/2 way down we came to a little cottage, just big enough to hold the <u>ancient</u> Darby and Joan [from a ballad (1735) written by Henry Sampson Woodfall] who were busying themselves about the door, their <u>faithful</u> dog and some fowls seemed to compose their worldly stock, with a chair or stool and mat. They kindly invited us to enter their humble mansion and eat some <u>rice</u>, which is the <u>one thing needful</u> with them, which we <u>politely</u> declined. The old woman of about 70 handed me a stool and I sit down under the shade of a tree to rest myself. The old woman seemed much pleased with me. And my hands attracted her attention, she saw my gloves were ripped and she looked upon them with an eye of pity; as they were of a flesh colour I fancied she thought it was my flesh. When I took it off the astonishment was very great, she chattered something in Chinese and tried to put my glove on but she could not succeed. She then motioned to put her hand upon my face to see if that was covered, but I did not like to have her touch me, and made signs to that effect. She shew me her hands to shew me they were clean. I gave her my gloves and bid her good bye. I moralized upon her situation and concluded she was just as happy there as one rolling luxury and refinement—she looked contented and happy, and having never known better, she appeared satisfied with her lot.

We arrived safely at the Ship about 6, after having had a delightful time and quite satisfied with having accomplished my visit to the Peak.

The gentlemen of our party took tea with us. Having a band there, more from <u>Brava</u> than any thing, I stood up in a <u>quadrille</u>, but for once my strength was gone. I sneaked away to the Cabin below and reposed my weary limbs upon a couch. Soon after went to bed. And Mr. Macondray thought then he should prefer going to Macao with me Thursday to tomorrow as I had expected. I agreed to wait.

21st Wed^y. Before I was out of my cabin this morning Mr. M. came to my door [and] said if I would like to go to Macao he would go today. I told him I was ready if it suited him, so I packed up my <u>duds</u>, eat my breakfast and bid Mrs. M. <u>Adieu</u>. In less than an hour was on board the *Flora*, a fine little schooner, and on my way to Macao. Being so long an inhabitant of the floating habitation, I was not at all sick and enjoyed our sail much. Set on deck all the time, feel a little stiff from yesterday's walk. About 2 arrived in Macao, found Caroline and Aunt well, and delighted to see me. It is really worth while going away for a time for the pleasure of returning. I was chief speaker that day. Caroline <u>seems</u> in good spirits. I got dreadfully burned coming down.

Walked out after dinner to Casillas. Met several of the ladies. Our house looks so magnificent after being cubbed in a cabin that I do nothing but look round in amazement at its <u>vastness</u>.

22 Had a great deal to do this morning, putting my things <u>to rights</u> and <u>talking</u> too. Aunt Low says every thing smells of <u>cockroches</u> and I should not wonder for there were many in my cabin. I never went into it without having to sing out to the Steward to came and kill two or three and sometimes more. So I tumble all into the <u>wash</u>. I have become quite <u>accustomed</u> to them now.

Walked this afternoon. Aunty spent the evening with Mrs. Whiteman, a musical party. C. & I stayed at home.

23^d Nothing new today. Wrote letters all the morning to send per *Martha*. Fixed up a box of <u>traps</u> to send per *Martha*. Walked after dinner. College walked with us a "<u>piece</u>" as they say at Weare. He is the <u>best</u> man I know.

24th Had letters from Canton and Lintin this morning which disturbed my peace of mind and oblige me to act <u>decidedly</u> and against my <u>inclination</u>. How often that is the case—more in a letter. Answered it and sent them off. Spent the evening in talking and listening to the music of our sweet organ. Oh I forgot the <u>bit</u> of <u>sun-shine</u> in today, Mr. College called upon <u>me</u>. Sent me a book of maps done by his sister and book of drawings for me to copy, and some Columbian Balm for my hair which he recommends as mine comes off dreadfully.

25 This morning after breakfast was sitting in my room cogitating, head on my hand, and saw the servant go to Aunt Low with a packet of letters. My heart went pit-a-pat. I hoped yet hardly dared hope it contained some for me. I waited patiently till I heard the sound, "H. letters for you." Then I flew and rec^d a good package per *"Romulus."* Your interesting journal, I followed you through all the operations of cleaning with great interest I assure you, the different arrangements are all noted, and I think I know just how every thing is placed. I had quite a "feast of reason and a flow of soul" [Alexander Pope, *Imitations of Horace; Satire*, II, Sat. 1, l. 127] in Brother Nat's [N. P. Knapp] epistle, and happy in all the others. Josiah [Low] is a strange boy. I sometimes think his letters must be borrowed. Does he compose them himself, and yet I need not ask, for they are just like him.

After dinner I read a sermon and then Caroline and I read a book together. Took tea, then I wrote letters till I was tired to go by the *Martha*.

26th Got up this morning, finished my letters, signed and sealed them with another journal, and sent them to Lintin for *Martha*—very glad to get them off my hands. Commenced copying Mr. College's pictures this morning. They are views of Macao and I take great pleasure in them as I shall one day have the pleasure of showing them to you I hope, scenes to which I have been so long familiar. Commenced the history of Napoleon's *Court and Camp*.[52] Walked after dinner and read all the evening. About 10 we all got into an argument upon Fatalism, Caroline against me and Aunt Low half inclined to be— neither of us convinced. I went to my room and read till after 12. Having Beattie on *Truth* upon my table, I took it up and exactly agree with him upon the subject.

If we are not free agents or have not some power over ourselves, how are we accountable creatures? And if we are not accountable creatures, why are we to be punished or rewarded for our good or evil deeds. And while I believe in a good, wise and benevolent God, I must believe we are free agents, and although we cannot always discover the justice of every thing, yet we believe it. Caroline says she believes we are accountable, she believes that is one of the feelings given us that balances the others, but still we have no power ourselves. But what can we know; at least we cannot decide. We must be fully persuaded in our own minds.

27th This morning I was busy in superintending my little garden, having fresh earth put into the pots, and cutting slips for new geraniums, throwing away old plants. Read a little and then drew some. Am copying some of Mr. Chinnery's sketches of Macao. After dinner went to walk, the evening seem like one of our delightful spring evenings, warm and clear. We had a shower of rain this morning, the first one since the 10th of September, and the very sky or atmosphere looks <u>cleaner</u>. The trees look bright and shining, and the sky was so clear and beautiful. All nature seemed dressed in her liveliest dress. The moon and the stars were looking newly polished. We went to the gardeners and bought some flowers.

28th This morning again superintending in the garden; got lots of new flowers. Wrote a letter to Aunt Cleveland and one to Mrs. Macondray. Read history aloud to Caroline, reading Queen Elizabeth's reign. It's well she does not live nowadays. She would find she could not impose upon people as she did then.

This morning we were talking of postages in America, revenue, etc. We all come to the conclusion they do not pay the government officers enough. Here our president to begin with has not so much as the Chief of the British Factory, not half the sum. His generally amounts to 60,000 dol[lars], and our Chargee's are not half paid. Then the Navy officers, poor creatures. How do they ever support a family—and if they die no provision of widows. It makes me cross, to think with such a revenue thing should be conducted in such a miserly manner. I wish if you think <u>my</u> <u>opinion</u> will have any weight with <u>General</u> Jackson you would make it known to him, but alas *pour moi.*

Read *The Court and Camp of Bonaparte* this evening. Aunt worked and Caddy listened. Rather interesting, some of the characters, indeed <u>all</u> of them very interesting, the sketch of Murat quite a romance.^{53}

Now I have just left Caddy's room where we have had a long "<u>consu</u>," a very rational conversation, and all are asleep but me. As

I sit here writing last night till 1/2 past 12. I will go earlier tonight or I shall hear Aunty striking her repeater [a watch that strikes the time when a spring is pressed] presently, and singing out to know if its the rats or my ladyship. Good night.

29th Did as usual this morning. Got up, washed, dressed, and performed the usual ceremony of eating my breakfast, which was very unsatisfactory inasmuch as we had no butter. Report says Mrs. Cow who has usually supplied us has just produced a "son" to use the China men's expression, and her *accouchement* has occasioned us some regret. But such things must take place so we must wait patiently. After this operation was over of eating, I went to my room. I finished the *Court and Camp of Napoleon* and tried very hard to read some French, but my mind is in such a state I read to no purpose. My eyes wander over the pages without taking in tow my thoughts. I long to return to my composed state, which has not been the state of my mind for a long time. I recd a letter from Mr. Dumaresq this morning saying he should leave on the 6th. He hoped and intends being home in 104 days.

Caroline got letters from her brother saying he should be up as soon as the letter. Had taken passage in the *Cowper* and may be expected every moment.

Mr. Seaver came from Lintin spent the evening with us. Mr. Daniell & Mr. Dalrymple, Mr. Wimberley, and Mr. Morris called.

Went out early after dinner. I never saw a more lovely night. So clear, so purely bright, the moon and the stars all so bright, so brilliant, as a correspondent of mine [W. W. Wood] says. "We look upon the stars flashing and sparkling like 'a jewel in an Ethiop's Ear' and sigh to think how much happier may be the tenants of those distant spheres. We sigh to leave this earth to revel in the happiness of another, figuring to ourselves the bliss which may reign in each of those distant worlds, too often without thinking that the star we gaze upon with such inexpressible longing instead of the habitation of the happy may be only the prison of the condemned." This was in one of his melancholy moods. Can you guess my friend? My dear sis, would he could have been with me tonight. He is so rich in his ideas, and so keenly alive to the beauties of nature and all her works. I sigh of such an evening for one who can help me to think, to admire with me, and for me. He can amuse, instruct, and entertain; he is gay with gay and grave with the grave. In a mixed company you would think him the greatest <u>rattle</u> that ever existed, but take him by himself, let him feel interested, then he shines. Will it ever be my lot to be <u>with</u> him? I fear! Anxiety, hope & fear are the predominating feelings now. Tomorrow <u>must</u> bring me a letter. Then my fate may be decided. Well whatever it is I will bear it <u>patiently</u>. I have had examples of patience and fortitude before me, and I will copy them in every situation. Good night again. How short time it seems since I said it last.

30th Wandered about in a very unsatisfactory manner most of the forenoon. My mind is in such a state, I cannot read, in fact I can do nothing at all. My ideas all seem to have vanished. My thoughts are all centered on one event just now. Went to walk early after dinner—a most perfect evening. The sky so <u>intensely</u> blue. It seems as though we could see beyond the stars. I cannot describe my feelings on such an evening. It appears to me I must have the <u>feelings</u> of a poet, though they will not come out in words. No one can feel more inward delight than I at looking at beautiful scenery of such an evening. I long to put it upon paper, that others may enjoy it too. Ah but where shall we get the colours? It is glorious and seems to lift us from earth and make us think of <u>heaven</u>.

We went to Mrs. Daniell's this evening where we met Mrs. Whiteman, Mr. Jackson, Sir Charles Grey,⁵⁴ Mr. Inglis & Dalrymple. Had a very pleasant evening, endeavoured to make myself <u>very agreeable</u>.

December 1st No letter for me again today. I am almost worn out waiting so long. Dressed this morning and Aunt and I sallied forth to see the world. First called on Mrs. Morrison, discussed <u>matrimony</u>, the ceremony and fashions. Called on Mrs. Luke, <u>discussed</u> the weather, climates, etc., then to Mrs. Wimberley, had a good joke about one of our <u>American Capt[ain]s</u>, a variety of subjects on the carpet. Left our cards at Mrs. Ploughdon's. Called on Mrs. Donolly, a sweet little woman, improved much in her health since she has been here. Then went to Mrs. Thornhill's, had a glimpse of College. Then went to Mrs. Grant's, then to Chinnery's. Saw the picture* an elegant likeness, and very handsome picture. She is sitting at her harp, a full length figure. She has a most <u>classical</u> face, and of <u>herself</u> makes quite a picture. Has a sweet little figure. Several other <u>very interesting</u> pictures there.

Went to walk with Capt. Seaver. Had to exert myself very much for Caroline was not in spirits. About 1 went to Lady Robinson's. She had a large party and some good music. Mrs. Underwood played and sung very sweetly. Mr. Jackson on the violin, Hudleston on the hautboy and Inglis on the flute, all superior players. Mr. Hudleston played very well upon the musical glasses. Wonderful to relate, Mr. College was there. I amused myself with a <u>small</u> <u>flirtation</u> with Mr. Jackson and Mr. Dalrymple, made but to pass the evening rather pleasantly. Talked a great deal of nonsense, heard as much in return, and came home. Went to bed.

*A picture of Mrs. Underwood.

2^d This morning rec^d the long desired letter from Canton. It was all I could wish. My mind was so much discomposed that I could not go to Church. After I felt that I could attend, I read an excellent sermon. After Church Capt. Grant and [Capt. Thomas] Larkins,[55] <u>Jackson</u> and <u>Dalrymple</u>, Sir Charles Grey, and College called. Did not see them, stayed in my own room. Wrote several letters and dispatched them tonight in divers ways. Mr. Seaver spent the evening with us and has bid us good bye for this year.

Caro & I have been having a chat while brushing our hair, and conclude that <u>duels</u> are necessary evils to keep society in a wholesome state. This place needs something, you see the necessity fully proved here* for people do give the greatest license to their tongues of any place I ever knew. Some of them ought to be called to an account for what they say, for they actually make stories without foundation. Oh I am tired and so good night.

*Do not be shocked my dear sis at this remark regarding duels. You know I have, as well as every one else has, a horror of them, but in some cases (particularly where there is no law to protect one as in this place) they are necessary. If a man hears his wife or sister's character attacked by an unprincipled man, what recourse is there left but for him to be called out. This is an extreme case. In the present state of society a challenge cannot be declined without an apology to the challenger, unless the challenged has a great share of moral courage and a moral and religious character well established. Under any other circumstances he would be branded as a coward and wanting in <u>physical</u> courage. If it were not for this check upon the tongues of men, what mischief might they not do. Therefore I say they are <u>necessary</u> <u>evils</u>, though I trust but rarely to occur.

Fortunately people here very seldom give credence to flying reports without very good authority. Our friends have most brilliant imaginations and are always ready to embellish and enlarge upon trifles. The gentlemen certainly employ their minds in a very trifling and unprofitable manner. It is true they have great opportunities for displaying their wit on the variety of people who come here and they are not spared.

3ᵈ I endeavoured this morning to give my mind to my studies and do as in days of yore, but alas my thoughts strangely wander and it is the greatest exertion to fix my thoughts upon my book. I read aloud to Caroline part of the time, then drew a little. Am copying some of Mr. Chinnery's sketches, fondly hoping that one of these days I shall I shall show them to you. I did not walk this afternoon except upon the terrace with Caroline. I spent a pleasant evening at Mrs. Morrison's, set round the table and chatted. Mrs. Davis was there. Before we left I had to defend my country from some of Mrs. Trollope's imputations, and endeavoured to represent correctly what she has so grossly misrepresented. She tells some truths I grant and many the <u>reverse.</u>

'Tis astonishing how ignorant most of the English ladies are regarding America. It is impossible to make them understand the geography of our country. They ask the most simple and absurd questions you can imagine.

4ᵗʰ This morning exerted myself again to study. After dinner went out to walk. Saw Mr. College. Went to the garden and bought some flowers. Came home and I never felt more *triste*. The organ was playing beautifully all the evening. I <u>bore</u> it as long as I could, and had to ask aunty to stop it. 'Twas too much for my <u>nerves</u>. I had one of those <u>freaks</u> you used to have my sis, <u>vulgarly</u> <u>called</u> Hystericks, in which I laughed and cried, and behaved very foolishly, but could not help it. I know how to pity you now. It's an awful feeling.

5ᵗʰ Was reading aloud to C. this morning and had a packet of letters and papers handed me per *Franklin*, in which I find you all well to the 7th of July. But oh the Cholera. I shall dread to hear again and yet I hope the precautions will be effectual. Cannot feel thankful enough that you have thus far been preserved. Did not walk this afternoon. Mr. Macondray made us a call this afternoon. Says *Martha* went out last night. We spent the evening in working. I worked till near 11. Now, as it is near 12, I will say good night my dear.

6th This morning received a large musical box and a letter requesting my acceptance of it from Mr. Dumaresq. It made me quite <u>wrathy</u> as he has gone and left me no chance of returning it till he comes back. I shall however write him a note by Capt. Seaver and tell him I shall not accept it. It plays most delightfully and is fine music. I wish he had it in his cabin. I was admiring his disinterestedness this morning. But Aunt L. and C. do not seem to think it deserves the <u>name</u>. Well, I dinna ken. I am no great believer in disinterestedness myself.

Charles Bradford called this morning, he is about sailing in the *John Gilpin* for South America.

After dinner went to call on Mrs. Fearon, found her out. I sit on the hills about an hour on my return and enjoyed my own meditations, "far from the busy haunts of men." [Felicia Hemans, "In the Busy Haunts of Men," *Tale of the Secret Tribunal*, Part I, l. 203] I then walked home *à la solitaire* and who should I meet but Sam Sturgis and his little brother George. They turned and went home with me and spent the evening. George is a nice lad, reminds me of William Henry.

I sit in Caroline's room talking till the clock struck <u>one</u>, which warned me that it was time to retire. We conversed on many different subjects, both <u>grave</u> and <u>gay</u>. You may judge we were very much engaged by the lateness of the hour. We truly "take no note of time but by its loss." [Edward Young, *Night Thoughts*. Night I, l.55] It passes away and seems like a dream. My mind has been in such an unsettled state that it appears to me I do nothing to any purpose. I exert myself day after day and try to apply myself to my books, but not with the same pleasure I did. I feel gloomy and *triste* enough at times and yet I laugh and seem the <u>gayest</u> of the <u>gay</u>—for I will not be laughed at.

7th A cold North wind this morning, a little bit of rain last night. We have had no cold weather as yet this season. I hope it is coming now. Some person or persons attempted to get into our house and took a very unpleasant method too for they burned the door <u>1/2 way</u> up. They must have got over an immensely high wall. Fortunately the smoke was smelt, but the thieves were not caught. They are very busy now, stealing all they can get hold of. We were very glad they did not <u>burn</u> us up. As all the gentlemen are in Canton, they would not have had an opp'y to show their gallantry.

Sir Andrew Ljungstedt called this morning, also Mrs. Grant. Poor Mrs. Ploughdon who came out in August is to leave in a few days for England. Her health is so very bad she cannot stay. Mrs. Underwood also goes in a few days. Spent the day in reading and writing—wrote to George [Archer], Mr. Russell, and Uncle, and despatched them to go per first ship. Being alone this evening, one of us read aloud Russell's *Modern Europe*,[56] while the others worked. It's a very delightful book, the style very interesting.

Now it's almost 12 oclock, my doors are closed for the first time this year, and I must go to bed to get warm, so *Buenos Noches mi querida hermana*.

8th A rainy, drizzly, cold gloomy day, spent as usual. C. Bradford and Sam P. Sturgis called to say Adieu, and Mr. Lindsay and Jackson. Did not see them. Mrs. Underwood sent her cards P.P.C [*pour prendre congé*] tonight—so it goes; they come, we meet and say good bye. I have kept my resolution this year and have hardly become acquainted with any of the strangers. Although I have had a strong wish to become better acquainted with some of them, yet I think if you do get interested in them the pain of parting probably forever overbalances the pleasure you receive from their society—so they may come and go and I will care not. In fact I sometimes say I never will decidedly love another person, male or female—but I dare say I shall, for I've a great propensity that way. But alas I have been sadly chilled in my attempts at friendship but I have had warm and sincere ones too fortunately.

> And what is friendship but a name,
> A Charm that lulls to sleep?
> [Oliver Goldsmith, A Ballad. A *Vicar of Wakefield*, Chapter 8)]

Well it's Saturday night again—and what has passed to remind us that it has been. What have I done? either good or bad? An unprofitable account is I fear to be rendered. How small my reward will be if it is in proportion to the positive good I do! 23 years of my life gone—and what have I accomplished to merit reward. I am a mere passive being, floated along with the stream. And yet with so little apparently to do, I have more than I can do, or more than I do, do, to take care of my tongue and my thoughts. How often that little member offends. How my thoughts run to waste—

Well, well, well

Let us walk <u>thoughtful</u>
on the silent solemn shore,
Of that vast ocean we must sail so soon;
And put good works on board, and wait the wind
That shortly blows us into worlds unknown:
If <u>unconsidered</u>, too, a dreadful scene!
                    - Young [Edward Young, *Night Thoughts*. Night V, l. 669–73]

9 Went to my room directly after breakfast, read three sermons. All excellent. Reflected on each and feel that I spent two hours of my day in a profitable manner. I was then called to the drawing room to see Capt. Benjamin, who spent two hours with us. I then received a letter from Canton which occupied my thoughts for the rest of the day. I feel miserable, wretched, and what shall I do—but this is not for the journal. I went out to the barrier this afternoon with Caroline to get warmed and try and cheer our spirits, but all is gloomy, the sky cloudy and air chilly. We were both wrapped in our own meditations and hardly spoke a word. We returned unmolested and I spent most of the evening in writing.

10 Cold, gloomy day again. Most of the morning was spent in writing to Canton. I have endeavoured to explain all and have been as clear as possible. I despatched it and also a letter to Grandmother. After dinner took another long walk—Mr. Lindsay and Jackson joined us. Mr. L., Caroline and I; me, and such a <u>goose</u> [Jackson]. Oh dear it is enough to <u>destroy</u> one's <u>nerves</u>. He came in and I was very much afraid he would stay to tea, but fortunately he had not been to dinner, so we were spared his <u>presence</u>. Mrs. Pereira called this morning and invited us to go to the <u>Opera</u> tomorrow night. Fancy an opera in Macao. It's the same one we had before of Cinderella, but we partly declined, and now I am sure I will not go for Mr. J. asked to <u>escort</u> me and <u>I</u> <u>won't</u> <u>go</u>.

We spent the evening very delightfully in reading aloud while the others sewed. It is a rational way of spending an evening and far pleasanter than to have to meet people you care not a farthing about. After the folks had gone to bed, I sit up till one reading a novel Mrs. Macondray sent me, called the *False Step*.[57] Some scenes of great interest in it, but on the whole think it not worth reading. But I did think I should like to put it into the hands of a lady of my acquaintance. I did not regret reading it as I <u>stole</u> the time—the only justifiable theft I suspect.

10 [11] Wrote a letter to you my dear sis and Mrs. Macondray. Had my carpet put down. Studied a little, worked a little, eat my dinner, and walked to the barrier. Returning met Mr. Jackson. What a bore! We schemed in all ways to avoid him, but alas the unlucky moment came. He was sillier than ever. Oh I forgot, Mr. Inglis called this morning, a very pleasant man, but very much inclined to be satirical. He has seen a great deal of the world, travelled all over Europe, America and India, and I suspect is a little bit disgusted. I think does not much <u>respect</u> the <u>fair</u> <u>sex</u>, thinks them very pretty <u>play</u> <u>things</u>, and not fit companions for <u>lordly</u> <u>man</u>. Hum! Was once desperately in <u>love</u> with an American Lady, a Bostonian, his <u>first</u> and <u>last</u> love! He speaks highly of American ladies. But the ladies in India he cannot abide, and indeed they are but toys. They are designed by their parents when children for the Indian market. They are taught to dance, play and sing; that is, they are taught to <u>tinkle</u> upon some instrument. They are then fitted up and sent out in <u>ship</u> <u>loads</u>, and disposed of to the <u>highest</u> <u>bidder</u>. You perhaps will think I joke, but it is a fact. More than half their marriages turn out unhappily, and from people who have lived there, I have heard the most melancholy description. The climate renders them unfit for anything and they lead a listless, vain, and useless life. There are exceptions of course but this is the general view. There has just left here a beautiful young woman, possessed a great <u>genius</u> for music, plays and sings divinely, has a good husband and one who doats on her. But alas with all her outward beauty, who would envy her either these or her accomplishments to have the name she has, a <u>flirt</u>, and more still more. She is ten times worse than a <u>flirt</u>. I was told today that her husband was obliged to fight a duel on her account in India, and there is now a young gentleman come on with her who is her <u>slave</u>. "Oh woman, woman, thy name is frailty!" [Shakespeare, *Hamlet*, Act I, Sc. 2, l.146] 'Tis strange a woman who has a good husband, one who is worthy of all her heart, cannot be satisfied, possesses the greatest earthly blessings and yet so abuses them. It makes me wish to deprive her of them that she might be sensible of them.

I have just returned from my walk, quite tired. Aunty is playing the organ. It is delightful music.

11 [12] Mr. Inglis in again this morning and introduced his friend Mr. Bridgman, a young <u>sprig</u> from India. Did not see them. Did not walk this afternoon, for I could not run the risk of having Mr. Jackson's <u>agreeable</u> company. We spent the evening very pleasantly in reading.

12 [13] Spent the morning as usual. Endeavoured and succeeded in giving my thoughts to my books. <u>A great effort</u>.
    Did not walk. Read Goldsmith's *Animated Nature*.[58] We read aloud in the evening.

13 [May be a continuation of the above entry **12** since the dates are out of order] Did the same today. Rainy, cold, and drizzly today. I feel about as forlorn as I wish to, without one bright thought to cheer me. Nothing interests. Oh for some excitement. I am glad to go to bed and sorry to get up.

14 This morning Caroline was made happy by the arrival of her brother [John Shillaber], so long expected. How I wished he was my <u>brother too</u>. It made me long still more to see some one I loved, some one in whom I feel interested. How long since I have seen any one that would feel sorry if they were to hear I was dead. Though I was delighted to have Caroline made so happy, yet I never felt more wretched. Oh Molly you cannot know the feeling of <u>loneliness</u> that comes over me at times. With so many around you, to love, and in whom every feeling is interesting—neither do you know my dear sis the value of your situation. You cannot appreciate it. I sometimes feel that I should be happier to be with those who cared nothing at all about me, if I could not have <u>my own</u>. Well patience. I wonder how Job would have behaved had he been sent to China. Well I will try and exert myself. I am ashamed of myself, I ought to have more <u>energy</u>, and I will, so *allons*.
    I received a letter from Susan [Orne] too, dated Northboro. Dear girl, she was happy among all her friends, and I fear not entirely happy in the thought of leaving them forever. Had a letter from Nat [Knapp], too. I set down and answered them immediately and sent them to Canton. Mr. Tuckerman [Joseph Tuckerman, Jr.][59] of the *Cowper* called and dined with us. Son of Rev. Dr. Tuckerman.
    Went to the barrier after dinner. Fine cool weather now, gives me <u>roses</u>.

15 "<u>Doing</u> <u>one</u> <u>thing</u> <u>and</u> <u>another</u>" this morning, but the most of <u>another</u>. Drew considerable. Mr. [M.] Pereira called. Going to Calcutta [in the *Isabella Robertson*]. Did not walk after dinner. Was troubled with the Chillblains, first time since I left the ship. Hope I am not to have them all winter.

Spent the evening very pleasantly with Mrs. Whiteman, had a quiet little party. <u>Sewed</u> <u>our</u> <u>gloves</u>, always the work in Macao, and had some good music. Mr. Hudleston played on the Hautboy, Clarionet, flute, guitar, and the ladies on the Piano and Guitar. Had a very merry time, people all making a great fuss about the cold weather, and I was saying we should call it very warm at home with the thermometer at <u>60</u>, but the English admire to <u>play</u> winter. But it really is very chilly, we feel it much more having had such warm weather. Now a fortnight ago, muslin dresses were worn. Now it is cold enough for fires and flannel petticoats.

16 Sunday morning. How I should like to go to Church today, sit in my old place and hear a good sermon from Mr. Upham—and the sound of that organ would carry me back three years at once. But I must read my own sermon and think my own thoughts, and the service of the heart will be acceptable to our Heavenly father. Read my sermons and did as usual. Mr. S[hillaber] dines with us every day. We walked out, and it was a lovely afternoon, every body out. Such a group at Casillas.

Wrote part of the evening, then we gathered round the fire and talked of something that will take place soon. Shillaber came in about 1/2 past 9, stayed till 11. It makes me wish for a brother too, to see Caroline with one. They are a strange family and puzzle us.

[Harriett wrote the following letter, supplied to Arthur W. Hummel by her granddaughter Elma Loines]:

Sunday evening. Macao. Dec.ʳ· 16, 1832

When the heart is sad and sighing for sympathy what greater re-lief is there than to fly to a dear sister. Thus I approach you, but at an awful distance. And you wish me to tell you all my feelings even if they are sorrowful.—You say right, my dear sis, sorrows we must all have in this world, it is a checquered scene and though I am sad now, I may be joyful tomorrow—and by allowing me to bestow a little of my tediousness upon you you will remove a weight from my spirits—

and was I by your side every cloud would be dispelled. Here Aunt Low is kind and Caroline is kind, but they are neither of them sisters. I have written you several times of late, and respecting a youth [W. W. Wood] who had become very dear to me, but I have never given you any particulars of him, so I will now. The youth came out here two years this next February [February 12, 1831]. He called upon us soon after his arrival. He paid me every little attention but I thought nothing of it, for it is so much the custom for people to come here and being no other American ladies in the place, we see much more of them than we otherwise should. He draws very well; and he immediately took me under his protection and became my <u>teacher</u>. I received many little *billet doux* upon the <u>fine</u> <u>arts</u>, but it never occurred to me that he cared at all about me till last winter. He was down several times, as soon as Mr. V[achell] ceased his attentions. I always took great pleasure in his society and enjoyed it more than anyone I knew, but I treated him as a mere acquaintance, and <u>if</u> I ever did think that he cared about me I thought of it as an <u>impossibility</u>, and treated him with still more coolness. He wrote me several times upon the <u>drawing</u>, to which I of course replied, till Uncle requested me to stop the correspondence, which I immediately did. He then gave up all <u>hopes</u>. But in the summer there was another person who paid <u>particular</u> <u>attentions</u>, which I have mentioned before. Mr. W[ood] came down about the same time, and he very soon found the other person had no encouragement. Mr. W. made himself very agreeable. I found his conversation, tastes, sentiments and feelings all corresponded with mine. His character and principles are unexceptionable. I did not wish him to propose for I knew how Uncle would feel. But it came and I could not say <u>No</u>, and I did as I have told you before, desired him to keep it secret till we went to America. But we afterwards thought it best to make it known to Uncle. The result you know already. Now I must live on. He says he cannot <u>change</u>, the spring which impelled him is now broken, and though he may perform his duties as before, he shall do it with an unwilling heart. He is too proud to go [away?]—but he will never be happy. I wrote him the other day as fully as I could—as yet I have had no reply. He is very busy assisting Uncle now. He gave up his own business which perhaps was small and served [several words illegible] and all for my sake. Now for his personal appearance which is a small part, but you may think he has a handsome face and that has won your sister's heart—but it is not so. He is not handsome, though he has a most intellectual face—high and noble forehead, blue eye and brown hair, a turn up nose and a sweet smile. Full face he is tall and a good figure. His manners are those of a perfect gentleman. He talks a great deal, but always sensibly, wise, witty or grave as suits his hearers. His talents are first rate, and various. He can do anything with the pen or pencil. He understands business too. So that whatever he applies himself to he can do. His morals are excellent. Such is the man of my choice. Now for his faults. He is hasty, impetuous, and rash, the consequence of strong and ardent feelings. But though quick to anger he is quickly cooled and ever ready to make concessions when he is wrong. His disposition is excellent, he is <u>proud</u> as <u>Lucifer</u>—but pride is necessary in this world. But this same pride has <u>offended</u> me and I now think that I cannot overlook his treatment. I do not think he has treated me well, so my dear sister, do not grieve for me, for I shall <u>survive</u> it, I have no doubt. I feel hurt and sorry and half inclined to be miserable, but I will soon conquer that. There is nothing like <u>resolution</u>, and I will exert mine. You know once decided on the course I am to pursue, I am very persevering and will conquer, if possible. If I do not become quite disgusted with human nature, and settle into a <u>misanthrope</u>, I may find someone I shall like quite as well. If I do [not] I can but live my allotted time, a <u>spinster</u>, and if I ever return to my native country, I will try and do some good by assisting my friends—at any rate I will endeavour in some way or other to make myself useful. There is precious little happiness here below, for the best state the great secret is to be <u>contented</u>. But alas, I am not the thoughtless, contented being I used to be. It appears to me my nature is wholly changed, my mind is ever restless, and I sigh often for tranquillity of mind, or great excitement. For discontent was once a stranger to me, though I think I always had a roving, restless disposition, but if I could not wander I made the best of it. Now my dear I have said all of this person that I ever expect to. I shall try to think it <u>all for the best</u>. I know Uncle and Aunt are very glad it is all off— But I had no wish to change. I feel that I have done <u>right</u>—and that is a great consolation. I feel that he <u>compelled</u> me to act as I did— Oh my dear sister, these men are faithless creatures — professions and vows are empty sounds often. He declares he loves me the same as ever, that his heart is and will be unchanged, that there can be no second love—but I am no great believer in all these pretty things. And yet I do not doubt that he feels all this now and I am sure I wish he might forget me and be happy. I can conceive no pleasure in having a person miserable for my sake and he has my best my most sincere wishes for his happiness.

17 Spent most of the morning in my room. Doing little or <u>nothing</u>, time passes but to little purpose. I walked after dinner with Mr. S[hillaber]. Mr. Inglis joined Caroline and Sir Charles Grey Aunt Low. I had a long conversation with Mr. S on different subjects.

18 Mrs. Ploughdon, Sir Charles [Grey], Dr. Pierson [Alexander Pearson] and another embarked this morning on board the *Charles Grant* for England. I could not help pitying Mr. Ploughdon who was obliged to part with his wife and child.

I was busy writing letters all the morning. Walked after dinner and spent the evening at home.

19 This morning studied a little but interrupted by visitors, Mr. [Thomas] Beale & Pereira, Mr. & Mrs. Fearon, Mr. & Mrs. Thornhill. Mr. Shillaber left for Canton at 4. We went to walk. Mr. Jackson joined me, and was rather <u>more agreeable</u> than usual. We spent the evening with Mrs. Thornhill. The two Mr. Beales there.

20 Trying very hard to do something this morning, but could not give my attention to my books, so I took my drawing. Walked after dinner and spent the evening at work. Aunt Low had a long *tête à tête* with Mr. College this morning. No ideas for you tonight, so I will go to bed. I hope to be more interesting soon.

21 Had our feelings much excited today. Perhaps not being acquainted with English customs, strange manoeuvers which we cannot understand. Well you scold me for such sentences, but it is other peoples's business, so you know my dear I cannot mention it. Time will clear up many mysteries.

Did not walk. Read or finished *Waverley* [Sir Walter Scott]. I intend now to read them all through. Set up till near one reading.

22 Still more strange and incomprehensible. The man [Dr. Thomas R. Colledge] whom above all others I thought perfect, or the one who for the last three years I have thought not capable of a dishonorable act, has sunk in my mind to the level with the <u>rest of his sex</u>. And yet I suspend my judgment, for there must be some mistake— when every act of his life has been the reverse, every feeling would oppose it, it cannot be. No I cannot yet let him fall. If it does prove so, I shall never put faith in mortal man more. I never shall believe one. I hope to be mistaken, for I cannot bear to be <u>mistaken</u> in this person, for he has been my model for character and nobleness and goodness of heart. It <u>cannot</u> be. It <u>must</u> not be. But every circumstance is against him, every appearance condemns.

Did not walk. All our feelings absorbed in this <u>event</u>—all dissatisfied and unhappy. Speculating, conjecturing, wondering, and completely *égaré*.

23 As yet no light upon the subject at least not before noon. When the <u>sun</u> appeared from behind the clouds, all was cleared up and we find it untarnished by the clouds which have dimmed it. I thought so, I knew it would prove so. Yes! how careful ought we to be in judging a person. Here the highest principles of duty were exerted, and every thing was sacrificed to it, but fortunately it is cleared up. It was impossible almost to see through the veil, but now we understand all. It should teach us to be slow in <u>condemning</u>.

I wrote a letter to Father and Samuel Low. Went to Church this morning. Heard a very good sermon from Dr. Morrison upon the Lord's Supper. He is very liberal in his sentiments.

Am afraid the Dr. will die of apoplexy, he grows so stout. Went to walk after dinner with Caroline; Inglis joined her and Jackson me. Jackson is I believe a little <u>mad</u> or something else I believe. I never knew a man <u>act</u> as he does—he's a droll specimen. He is said to be very clever, but I cannot discover it. He either thinks me not capable of comprehending, or else he has not common sense; <u>which</u>, I have not yet determined. At any rate, all he appears to have in his brain is "will you go up that hill? will you go here or there?" Thank heaven he is going to Calcutta in a few days [left December 26 in British ship *Ann*], and then I shall not be bothered with him any more. We <u>dodged</u> him this afternoon several times, but he was determined we should not escape. If he does not make himself more agreeable the next time he joins us I shall just tell him he is <u>very</u> <u>stupid</u>—or cut him direct, I don't know which. Well fortunately he had not dined, so I did not have to ask him to tea. Spent the evening in writing. Caroline made me read some of this journal to her. She has had a good laugh at my <u>leaps</u> from the <u>sublime</u> to the <u>ridiculous</u>. I think you must have many a laugh at my nonsense.

24 Today has been rather gloomy. Most of the morning I spent at my French and drawing. The day is dull and gloomy so that we had no walk. After dinner I took the second volume of *Guy Mannering* [Sir Walter Scott] and finished it, find it very interesting. "Dominie Sampson" a very fine character, and amusing—if such a term can be applied to so grave a personage.[60] There are some capital scenes in it.

Mr. Roberts from the *Peacock* spent the evening with us. He is called the naturalist, but I suspect if the truth was known he is a diplomatist. Think I understand the whole business—they are going to Siam to form some treaties with the government. It seems Mr. Shillaber took a great deal of trouble to enlighten our government on the state of affairs in those quarters. And he was promised the commission if it should take place—but they have said nothing further to him.[61]

A year ago tonight we were about this time going to the Church of San José. What a change a year has made. My friend Mrs. Cartwright was then here, but I fear now she has gone to her long home. Mr. V[achell] who was also here is on his way to England [sailed October 25, in HCS *Canning*]. And then how our feelings have changed.

Now the bells are ringing, the people are all again assembled saying masses and singing, and tomorrow will be a day of rejoicing that Christ our Saviour was born—he whose example it should be our study to follow. And if we imitate it we shall have the reward he promised his obedient followers—everlasting life.

25 A rainy unpleasant day—nothing pleasing or at all cheering. One thinks of the happy family groups assembled round the "festive board" on such a day and sighs for such a scene. We dined alone very quietly, were reviewing the different anniversaries of this day passed in China. The Changes are quite astonishing from year to year, and yet here we sit in the same places, without any visible proofs that any time or events have passed between. But Memory, "fond memory brings the light of other days around me." [Thomas Moore, *National Airs. Oft in the Stilly Night*, Stanza 1] I hope next year will find us preparing for a voyage.

My friend Mr. Jackson called this morning to say Adieu. Stayed an hour. If he is as clever as the English say he is, he chooses to conceal it under a veil of stupidity.

R[ebecca] Morrison came in after dinner just as I had commenced the *Antiquary* [Sir Walter Scott] and spent the evening. Made herself very agreeable. We had a variety of subjects of conversation. Now I hear the clock striking 12, the witching time of night, and I do not want to go to bed. I have just left Carry's room. We have been anticipating the time when we shall be <u>ancient</u> <u>spinsters</u> having become almost disgusted with the <u>genus</u> <u>homo</u>, and almost determined to live a life of <u>celibacy</u>.

[Marginal note, written the following March 20th] How soon she has deserted me

We were thinking we would live together and do all the good we can. However I think if it is not Hobson's choice I shall yet espouse some poor unfortunate man, just to be the <u>torment</u> of some body's life. But Good Night.

26 It seems I went to bed in a particularly Christian spirit last night, by the conclusion of my last page. Cold enough this morning, drizzly too. No one in but Dr. Morrison. Nothing new. Oh yes, Mrs. Davis and little Helen came in after dinner. Spent the eve'g as usual. Sit up till one o'clock reading the *Antiquary*. Read it with just as much interest as though I had never seen it before. I find myself quite in love with old "Oldbuck" only he is a little too <u>prosy</u> sometimes.[62]

27 Terrible cold. I do not like cold weather in this country—great barns of rooms, great <u>cracks</u> under the doors and the floors you can see through. The carpet does not seem to do much good. And it is so rainy now we cannot get a walk, and one's limbs are almost stiff with the cold. It makes me shudder at the thought of encountering our winter, though I know you have more comforts at home, that nice warm basement room. I wish I was in it.

The Chinamen all look as thick as they are long now. So many clothes on. The Portuguese, many of them go to bed and there lay.

Mr. Inglis in this morning—give us the history of several widows who have been on here. Upon my word I do not wonder that men get disgusted with our sex. They do behave so, particularly the ladies of India. I have no respect for them <u>generally</u>. It is enough to sicken one of marriage I think. I sigh and groan in the spirit as tint after tint of the romance of my <u>youthful</u> days is obliged to become

extinct. "All is vanity and vexation of spirit." [Ecclesiastes 1:14] Mr.
I. I believe is completely disgusted, and I do not wonder.
   No walk today. We roasted over the fire all the afternoon reading. Worked a little this evening. Finished the *Antiquary* at 10 minutes before 1, then went to bed and slept soundly. Rather like sitting
up late. Feel brighter in the morning, for the room is tolerably comfortable at night and cold enough in the morning.

28th Rainy, cold, gloomy, cheerless, uncomfortable weather. The
mind and body seem equally torpid. We hover over the fire and try
to keep comfortable. At dinner time received letters from Uncle,
and Mr. Shillaber has just come down [from Canton]. Spent the
afternoon and evening with us. Nothing new. Caroline and I set over
the coals till nearly one again. It seems like the ghost of last winter
returned—to be sitting in the same place in the same way. At this
hour one's thoughts seem to flow more freely and if one has a kindred spirit to talk to it is very pleasant.

29 Oh how cold! I assure you it requires a great deal of resolution
to jump out of bed into a tub of cold water. But we do it every
morning, because it gives the blood a start and we fancy we feel better
all day. Obliged to keep in the drawing room all the time, so my
journal will I fear be neglected. Every day passes alike—we have but
little company, and are very quiet. Mr. Shillaber spends much of his
time with us, and we find him very agreeable and pleasant. Commenced *Rob Roy* [Sir Walter Scott]. Compare my friend Caro to Die
Vernon.[63] Think in spirit and independence she is very like her. Many
traits of her character are very similar. The brother and sister are
very much alike. After dinner walked to the barrier. It's awful cold
and though the Thermometer only stands about 40, yet to our feelings it is nearly at Zero, either because it comes so suddenly upon us
or because we have been so thoroughly heated this summer.

30th Went to Dr. Morrison's this morning, shivering and shaking.
Heard a very good sermon, requiring us to review the past and make
good resolutions for the future, resolutions that are (alas) too often
made but to be broken. He reminded us of mercies received, of the
use that should be made of afflictions, and exhorted us to live holier
and better lives. And may I attend and remember. Another year has
gone, and again the question returns, am I any better than at the

close of the last. Alas, I am still in the balance that is found wanting. My account is always against me.

Walked home from Church with Mr. College and Chay Beale and found Mr. S[hillaber] at the house. Mr. Van Basil called, a stupid Dutchman. Mr. Shillaber and I had quite a <u>philosophical</u> <u>discussion</u>, such a one as I hate, and subjects I never enter upon when I can help it, for we end just as wise as when we commenced. He reasons deeply and thinks deeply, which is dangerous business I think. And yet why was the power for reasoning given us if we were not to use it. And is it wrong for us to use our reasoning powers to their extent? And if we do where shall we find ourselves? Who can answer satisfactorily even these simple questions.

This afternoon did not walk, stayed at home and wrote to A. A. L[ow], N. P. K[napp], & S. Allen. We spent the evening in talking and reading Mrs. Heman's *Poems*.

31st Spent the morning in reading Goldsmith's *Animated Nature*. Mr. Daniell called. Very cold day again.

Mr. Shillaber dined with us. Poor Aunty feels gloomy. The anniversary of this day brings with it many unpleasant thoughts and associations.[64] Oh that she could drink of the waters of Lethe and drown those sorrows in the cup of forgetfulness. These feelings will always be a damper upon her happiest hours. I have been thinking over the events of the past year and feel that I have had <u>many</u> useful lessons which I hope will prove of use to me. I trust the year has not altogether run to waste.

Took a long walk with Mr. S. He read aloud to us this evening. I finished the first volume of *Rob Roy*. We set the old year out and the New Year in and wished you all many happy years, and prayed sincerely for you all my sis.

January 1st 1833 I must commence with the compliments of the Season. Suppose you are receiving your <u>bevy</u> of <u>beaux</u> today with your <u>cookies</u> and wine. How I should like to be there, and share in the sport.

Mr. & Mrs. Luke called on us this morning and our little Josepha went round administering her kind wishes. To the maidens of the family she wished rich husbands and long life, to the married <u>wealth</u>.

The Caffres were all dressed in most fantastic dresses parading the streets, singing and enjoying themselves—seem the happiest creatures in existence. Animal pleasures alone constitute their happiness however. I have commenced this morning anew with French and intend to apply myself more closely to it. It is necessary to apply myself to the attainment of a definite object and I know of nothing else I can do just now. I devoted most of the morning to it. After dinner we had a little bit of a frolic. I did not walk, stayed at home and read *Rob Roy*. It is almost too cold to enjoy a walk, the wind is so strong.

I have just got thoroughly heated through and have left Caroline and her brother in the drawing room. It makes me almost envious and I sigh deeply for a brother too, that is one near me. I am almost heart sick of this kind of life. I dare not think of it. I sigh and smile. All say, "How complacent and serene you always look." I sometimes long to say

> The ray that tips with gold the stream
> Gilds not its depths below

but I do not wish any one to know how I feel, and the effort to conceal is the best for me.

I should feel happier could I look into the heart of <u>one</u> person [W. W. Wood] I think, if I could but know its state and the <u>cause</u> of certain actions. But alas I shall never know perhaps, and perhaps from misunderstanding I may always be regarded as heartless and deceitful. Oh what can I do?

2^d Mr. and Mrs. Donolly called this morning and Chay Beale. Studying French all the morning, find it very difficult to commit to memory with my head full of other things. Went to walk after dinner with the Shillabers. It was a lovely evening for a rarity, moderated a little and clear tonight.

We spent the evening in reading aloud Russell's *Europe*. Ended by singing songs. We <u>all</u> <u>joined</u>.

3^d Took to my grammar this morning and studied till I became thoroughly sick and <u>cross</u>. Nothing disturbs my <u>serene</u> temper more than a grammar. There I sit all the morning hammering verbs into my head which seemed to resist the pressure with unusual force. Oh if I had children this should be drummed into them when they were susceptible of such impressions, and it is so provoking when I can take up my French book and read it without any difficulty and yet cannot conjugate a verb without all this trouble. I got sad and *triste*, perfectly dissatisfied with myself and my capability, think myself the most stupid of creatures and wonder that any one has any pleasure in my society. Indeed I do not believe they would for any length of time, and I think I shall never get married lest my husband should get sick of me. I am unfortunately fond of gentlemen of sense and could not abide one <u>wanting</u> it; I cannot therefore marry a fool and a sensible man would soon be sick of me. Therefore I think it most wise and sensible in me to join the venerable class of spinsters and never become acquainted with any one particularly. Here I try, endeavour and exert myself to learn something, my brain does not seem to expand, but fully proves that two things cannot remain in the same place, for I never can keep but one thing in my head at a time. Oh woe is me! I do feel sad enough at times. And this is all from want of memory which retains only what I would forget. Now my dear I know you will think <u>verbs</u> have a very bad effect. *C'est vrai*, but they must be learned.

After dinner I read *Rob Roy* to bring <u>myself</u> back again. I did not walk, but after much wise cogitation between daylight and dark, and having finished *Rob Roy* I regained my spirits in a great degree. We made out to go to bed at 12 tonight, the first time for a long time.

4th A lovely morning as ever shone. I am going out to make calls now, so bid you good bye.

I <u>adorned</u> myself and sallied forth as proposed. Went first to Mrs. Davis's and joined her to go to Mr. Chinnery's rooms. Went to Mrs. Thornhill's and took possession of her parlour till Mr. College and Mrs. Whiteman joined us to go to C's. Then we went; saw his picture of Dr. Pierson [Alexander Pearson] just taken, true to the life. I then went to Mrs. Grant's where I heard an observation which in connection with some made by Mrs. D[avis] during our *tête à tête* roused my indignation, and which must not stop here. Being 3 o'clock I was obliged to postpone it till tomorrow. It's a lovely day, the ladies all flying round.

After dinner took a walk with Caroline. We sit on the hill sometime and became rather *triste*, but it is useless to say why or wherefore. Mr. S[hillaber] joined us soon after and we walked home and spent the evening alone.

5th I studied as usual this morning till about 12, then <u>proceeded</u> to <u>business</u> very quietly and in a very dignified manner. Cleared up satisfactorily the observations made yesterday. Have discovered how easy it is for some people to misunderstand and how <u>dull</u> of <u>comprehension</u> some people are. There is one lady here who is <u>French</u> [Maria Teresa Grant] and in speaking English she makes great <u>blunders</u> and thereby causes much mischief. I have also discovered the maneuvers of a certain gentleman, so much so that I expressed my sentiments very freely. Said I <u>despised</u> him, which I do most heartily. If he comes to me for my reasons, I shall give them to him, without retracting what I have said. It is quite astonishing the ill will existing among people here and all from this cowardly practice of <u>backbiting</u>. We have many things to annoy us my dear sis. Forbearance has every opportunity of being practiced here and poor me who would feign be the most quiet person in the world cannot remain so. Insignificance is far preferable I think, but alas the most insignificant are brought into notice here. It is a queer place.

I stayed at home after dinner and read [Sir Walter] Scott's *Black Dwarf*, a very interesting study, and quite a treat. Oh how I should like his talent at description. He is inimitable.

6th Have been to Church this morning my dear and heard an excellent sermon read by Dr. Morrison. The subject was that the chief end of our existence is <u>to do good</u>. He says it certainly is not <u>to enjoy</u>, for the trials and troubles we are subject to in every stage of life goes to prove it. I thought his reasons and argument very good. But alas my dear sis if this is the end of our existence, by how few is the end answered. It appears to me many are born to no purpose at all, at least so it seems from the circumstances in which they are placed. But as Dr. M. says it is not <u>how much</u> but the doing as much as lies in our power, and the whole life of our Saviour set us this example. But why were we placed here as to require <u>good</u> to be done. It was the Almighty's <u>will</u>, is the only answer we can give. Why were we made to sin? The same answer, to all the numberless questions we can answer. How much need we have of <u>faith</u> in this world, and how useless it seems to reason deeply on things we cannot comprehend.

There is one person here who I think quite fulfils the object of his existence, and that is Mr. Colledge—he is continually going about doing good. He makes every one love him. He is so universally kind and obliging, and exerts himself to make all happy who come in his way. Every one go to him in their distresses and if possible he relieves them. He heals the sick, comforts the afflicted, and in his practice is really a Christian without any display—quietly and without ostentation he fulfils his duties. Cheerfully and happily assists all. We call him the "sunbeam" for every thing smiles when he approaches. His greatest pleasure is in doing good and his face speaks the goodness of his heart. He is open, generous, and possesses every noble feeling—without deceit, affable, cheerful, and entertaining. Mr. Chinnery called here after church and he was extolling him as every one does, and was speaking of his skill as an optician. He says a gentleman in Java hearing of his skill came on here on purpose to try it. He has been perfectly miserable for two years with his eye which he had stung by some insect. He had no peace of his life and his eye was in a horrid state. He came on here despairing almost of ever having it cured, and in two months C[olledge] has performed a perfect cure, and now the man has gone blessing him for his kindness and attention. He sent him a most excellent letter containing every expression of gratitude, but feeling that the strongest words cannot express his feelings, he sent C. a large sum of money but it was returned (as every gift of the kind is) with saying he could not take it. He was only too happy to have the opportunity of curing him. I hardly know which must feel the happiest, the restorer or the restored, but I cannot conceive of a more heavenly feeling than this of doing good. The contemplation of this after the sermon of this morning leads me to think that Dr. M. is right and that we should be happy if we exercised the best feelings of our nature. But then every one has not the opportunity, and the Fatalist will say why if we have feelings given us which overpower these good feelings, feelings which overbalance them, what can we do. But ah I am not a fatalist or I believe in free agency, and believe that we have the power of balancing those feelings, and if not, where is our responsibility? We cannot control events but we can our own passions if we exert the power that we have within us. At least so I believe and if I do not believe so, how can I believe in a wise, just, and benevolent God? But there I leave the subject. I only pray to be led in the right path that my thoughts and actions may be acceptable to him to whom I look as the disposer of all events, the judge of all hearts, and the rewarder of all those who diligently seek him. Do not think my dear sister from my thinking and reasoning upon this subject that I am skeptical. Oh no. But I know those who are. But heaven forbid. It appears to me I had rather lose my reasoning powers than lose the hope of Heaven. As Mrs. Hemans says

> What bright exchange, what treasure shall be given
> For the high birth right of its Hope in Heaven.
> If lost the gain [gem] which empires could not buy,
> What yet remains? A dark eternity!
>
> [Felicia Hemans, *The Sceptic*, Stanza 2]

Her poem to the "*Sceptic*" is all beautiful.

7th Prosing over French verbs all the morning—after dinner walked and evening sewed. Thus day after day passes. Nothing to excite, amuse, or instruct.

Oh how I daily sigh for home sweet home. It is wearing out our existence.

8th This morning studied a little, then went to Chinnery's room. There is now a great attraction, a picture of my friend [W. W. Wood], which I was strongly tempted to pocket. It is a perfect likeness. I shall probably not see it again as it is going to America—well I do not know why I should wish to. He is nothing to me.

Mr. Shillaber left for Canton at 4. We did not walk—a Dr. Burroughs[65] from Philadelphia called and took tea with us. He bowed and scraped like a Frenchman, talked and made himself very agreeable. After he was gone we began to think how different people are who come from the civilized world to residents here. They talk so much that it quite fatigues us old residents, for here we get in the habit of saying only what is necessary. It is quite dreadful, the stupid lazy habits we get. Caroline says when she first come she thought all the ladies were terribly stupid. The fact is we lose all interest. I am afraid I shall be quite stunned at home the first month. I would consent to be killed the first month however if I could but get there. How can I endure two years more.

9th After breakfast I poked about awhile, then dressed and was very busy enveloped in the intricacies of the French language. Begin to see through its mazes and by dint of application think one of these days I shall be able to *parler* and a trip to Paris will make me quite perfect. After dinner feeling satisfied with my morning's study I took *Old Mortality* [Sir Walter Scott] and finished it—works that will always interest. They are very useful too for they impress historical facts upon one's memory.

10th As usual, read, studied, and walked. No news.

11 Did just as I did yesterday. Do not remember that I had any <u>new ideas</u>. Suppose you will say it would be something quite new if you had. *C'est vrai ma soeur.* I cannot dispute it. I only am astonished that I have any old ones. As it is when I sometimes say what I think very smart—and I ask C. why she does not laugh? that my brilliant flashes would be more attended to by other people. She protests she knew what I was going to say, she has got so <u>used to me</u>. And it is a fact that we know so well the train of each others thoughts that we often anticipate.

Borrowed Miss Edgeworth's works today. Read the *Modern Griselda*.[66] Think there is some piquancy in it and is amusing, but unnatural. I think that a woman who loves her husband should treat him so. And another inconsistency, she makes Griselda a sensible woman, and none but a little simpleton would behave as she did.

12 At home all day. Studied till dinner time. Read Miss E[dgeworth]'s *Leonora*—tolerably good, though after reading W. Scott, appears insipid and tame. Must confess I am rather disappointed in her works. Do not think many incidents at all natural. Some of them I dare say are true to life.

Took a violent fit of <u>mending</u> about 9 o'clock at night. Caroline and Aunty say it is [a] complaint I generally have Saturday <u>nights</u>. Old habit you see, (the remains).

13 No church today all the padres are in Canton. I read an excellent sermon of Mr. [John] Brazer's aloud to C. The text was—oh I forget exactly—but every word of the sermon agreed with my ideas. To keep the spirit by the bond of peace. It was written in the true spirit of Christian Charity—allowing to every man the privilege of thinking for himself, and that he is not only <u>permitted</u> but <u>obliged</u> to examine his own heart to know what his own views are, and to abide by them, that thinking himself right, he has no right to say another is wrong, that he can no more rule another's faith than he can his practice.

Wrote a long letter to Uncle Porter giving him what information I could about the missionaries here as he requested. We spent the evening in talking. C. and I are making plans to go to Canton and surprise the people.

14 Studied a little, but Hudleston came in and stayed 2 hours. I then went and called on Mrs. Crockett and Mrs. Whiteman. Walked after dinner, met Hudleston, had a very pleasant walk to the barrier. Came home, spent the evening round the fire reading.

15th Studied this morning very diligently and find I can conjugate a verb now with reading it over.

Mr. College came in just as I had become engaged in one of Racine's plays, *Alexandre* [*le grand*], a fine thing. Did not tell us any news, but was as agreeable as usual. When he had gone we rec^d news from home, letters from the Knapps per *Emily Tailor* [*Taylor*]. I heard of my father and mother and you were all well then. I trust you will be spared from the pestilence—they write me that the people are all leaving the City [New York]. I feel anxious as you may imagine, but sufficient unto the day, etc. I hear Fisk Allen[67] is coming in here in the *Mandarin*—how happy I shall be to see him. Mr. [Joseph] Cooli[d]ge[68] has come out as clerk in the house of R[ussell] & Co.

16th Wrote to Mrs. Macondray this morning. Said my French lesson, walked after dinner, came home and read again. Thus go the days, unchangeable—one day certifies another. Dull enough. I sigh for the excitement of New York, but not of the Cholera. My journal will be dull enough now, for I can only sing of myself, and myself is dull enough. Well, well—we are going to have an importation of *beaux*, but none that I care for. And I am sure I shall be sick of the sight of them in a few days.

17 Studied all the morning. Cold, rainy day. We have most intolerable gloomy weather now, cold and cheerless. Coals scarce, wood brought by the catty, very dear. What would you think at home of buying wood by the pound? But so it is in this place. C. & I get into the fire almost. We have no exercise and it is almost impossible to keep comfortable. I am almost tired of poring over books and there is no other resource. If one leaves off reading one gets thinking unpleasant thoughts which is worse.

Tonight we had a thunder storm, the lightning very vivid. It seemed strange for such cold weather; it distresses the Chinese, for they think it portends some calamity.

The Chop Boat arrived tonight [from Canton] with the Sturgis's, our friends Blight & Wilkinson. They had a sad time coming down. Brought letters for Aunty and C. Oh dear if I only had some one to write to me there. (How provoking! dropped my pen and inked my book) Read aloud this evening Russell's *Europe*. Like it very well. After reading Hume [David Hume (1711–76), Scottish historian], think it a very good review.

18 Mr. [J. H.] Blight come to see us this morning, looking finely. I could not help exclaiming that it was the ghost of last winter, for here we all sit just in the same places and talking in the same brother and sisterly manner. B. is a good creature and seems more like a brother to me than any one here. He stayed till near three, and then just commenced an argument. Speaking of reading reviews, he said just to set Caroline and I out, that ladies were not capable of comprehending these works, comparing and reasoning, which we disputed. We instantly began to defend ourselves, but being three o'clock I begged him not to differ long for I was hungry and we should not get any dinner till he was gone, whereupon he took up his hat and run.

Rainy day. No walk. Stewed over the fire and very much inclined to feel miserable. But laughed off the blues and finished the evening in reading.

19 Cold and gloomy this morning. Sam Sturgis called. He is a handsome looking person enough, but no mind. He is really stupid. Cleared off after dinner, and we sallied forth and it was quite perfect—the air so bracing that we walked out to the barrier and over the hills without feeling at all tired. Mr. Daniell joined us and was very agreeable. The air and pleasant company quite revived me and I don't know when I have felt in such spirits. Came home and finished Goldsmith's *Animated Nature*. A very cold night, and I was very glad to get snug in bed. C & I sleep together and it reminds me so much of you, Molly, but she does not flirt [open briskly] the bedclothes as you used, for she does not think it necessary that one should know how cold it is to enjoy the comforts within.

20th Shall I say it is cold again. Am sorry to say I was up rather late. Have finished my breakfast. Aunty has gone to her boudoir, C. is dressing, and here am I sitting in the drawing room upon a little footstool in front of the grate, one side is <u>roasting</u> and the other shivering with cold. My book is on my lap and my inkstand in a chair by my side. Now I must turn round. I do hate cold weather.

It is Sunday today. No church to attend, I must read my own sermons. C. has just been in and we have been prophesying that J. H. Blight will go home and marry Miss Fulton, sister of his brother's wife.[69] C. wants to know if you will invite her to your wedding if she is in America, and if she shall be <u>Bridesmaid</u>? When are you going to [be] married my dear? I should think you would be tired of courting, and yet I know not how Mother would do without you, you dear little creature. I suppose you are trusting that I shall come home a <u>venerable</u> <u>spinster</u> and be just fit *pour ménager*. The first is most probable, but the second not, for when I come home I suspect you will condemn me as a <u>drone</u> and turn me out of the hive. I must confess I never desire to see a kitchen, (you know I never had a <u>penchant</u> for the place) but in any other way that I can make myself useful I shall be most happy. I do not think I shall ever be <u>espoused</u>, and beside I think there is nothing gives one more real happiness than making others happy. So that shall be my aim when I come home. If I cannot be a pattern of <u>conjugal</u> felicity, I can be a model for the heretofore despised class of <u>old</u> <u>maids</u>.

After all it makes very little difference whether one is married or not. If they are, ten to one they <u>repent</u> it and if not they are independent and can do pretty much as they please. After one's heart gets <u>callous</u> and our feelings too often thrown back upon ourselves, it matters little whether they are married or not. One should be very <u>unsophisticated</u> to get married I think. If they become old enough to look behind the scene, ten to one they never marry.

Wrote several letters today and took a long walk after dinner to get warmed.

21st Eat, drawed, studied and read as usual. Mr. Blight came in this morning. Mr. & Mrs. Hudleston called. Walked after dinner, with B. Came home and he spent the evening with us.

22d Did just the same as I did yesterday. I mind just ditto, ditto, now. By the by, Mr. Davis called; and Mr. Alexander, going to Calcutta. Wrote a letter to Mrs. Cartwright, also to Mr. Dumaresq and fixed up his musical box to send him. Wrote a letter to Uncle and sealed up some letters from home. Then wrote off some mottoes for a <u>seal</u> to send to Canton. Quite a busy morning. Strange I should not have remembered. Rec^d a letter from Mrs. Macondray. Got a bad cold in my head. Walked to the barrier. Spent the evening in reading.

23 This morning we made an alteration in our <u>system</u>; we are going to have dinner late and walk before dinner. Commenced today. So I must tell you how we managed. But to premise this morning, having moved from my usual course it is right and proper you should know it. I took a <u>dose</u> <u>of</u> <u>salts</u> before breakfast and eat <u>nothing</u>— wonderful to relate.

Well now we are going to have breakfast at 9, Tiffin or a little bread and butter and a cup of tea at 2, and then at 3 go out to walk; come back before the sun sets because its so cold, and then dine at 6. So we managed today and this is the plan for the cold weather. We liked it very well. Mr. Blight came in this evening.

24th This morning after breakfast took up *Patronage*[70] and finished it. It's very interesting, and the best of Miss E[dgeworth]'s that I have read. There is a great deal of talent displayed. And she must have had an amazing deal of patience if nothing else to have written such a work. There are some fine characters pourtrayed and some which give a very good idea of fashionable life, which for my own part I never wish to know except in novels. Mr. [J.] Hudleston & sister called, a very pleasing woman. Leaves in a few days for Madras [sailed January 29, in *Good Success*, Capt. Durant]. Mr Blight in also. Aunty & C. walked. I stayed at home and read *Arlington*.[71] Think it rather good. I am getting into a bad way or reading novels. It is the only excitement we have; we are all miserably stupid. Mr. Blight dined with us. Mr. Wilkinson called this morning. We had quite a <u>philo-sophical</u> conversation.

25 Mr. College came in, found us playing "Battledoor."[72] After dinner walked to the barrier. On our return we were joined by Blight and Wilkinson. I had W., a youth who has sense enough, but he is too lazy to talk. He however made himself very agreeable, and we had a pleasant walk.

26 Studied a little. Received a letter from C. Dean and Uncle Porter via Manilla per *Lotos*. C. sends her love to you my dear. I laughed heartily when I read it, such a <u>round</u> <u>about</u> way of sending love <u>via</u> <u>China</u>. All well 25th of July. Thank God.

Two Mr. Hudlestons called this morning & Blight & Wilkinson. Had a bad cold in my head and felt stupid.

Finished *Arlington* after Tiffin. Did not walk. Mr. & Mrs. Davis, Mr. [Thomas] Beale, & Mr. Blight took tea with us. Endeavoured to make myself agreeable, but it is such an exertion. I would not have believed once that I should ever have arrived at the state of feeling I am now in—I who was once so easily pleased. Now to laugh is the greatest exertion.

I could have sung "O Be Joyful" as soon as they were gone.

27ᵗʰ Sunday morning. I have been reading two very good sermons written by Dr. Paley. Did not go to Church, for I have had a bad cold and I did not like to sit in a damp church. Believe I must write some letters now per *Cowper*.

Wrote several letters. In the midst of writing received a soliloquy from a Bachelor [W. W. Wood] who professes to have been jilted by his faithless.⁷³ A droll affair to be sure, it was addressed to "Mesdames H. Low & Co., At the Palace of 'Sans Souci,' Celestial Regions, Merchantesses." In reply to which we wrote a long note—I do not think it worth copying. Perhaps one of these days you may find it among much other rubbish of the kind. The "tender passion" seems to exhibit itself in the most wonderful manner in these regions. It has served us much amusement I am sure. We do meet strange characters. C. and I took a long walk round the Penha this afternoon, and enjoyed it much. Met no one we knew.

28ᵗʰ Received a letter from Mrs. Macondray this morning by Capt. [William C.] Little, who has returned again from the Coast and the Sandwich Islands. He called to see us this morning. He is a very handsome man, only too thin. His face answers to Byron's Conrad in the *Corsair* I think. His manners are very pleasant and gentlemanly. He came and spent the evening with us. He says reports reached the Islands and the Coast that I was to be married to three or four people. I told him I thought one quite enough. It is amusing to find what a notorious person my ladyship is. Really I ought to be very vain. He says my fame has reached from pole to pole, and all forsooth because I happen to be a spinster in a distant land. I might have remained in America till the end of my days and never been known beyond my own fireside. And even now should I only take unto myself a spouse, I should forthwith sink into insignificance. Well it is the fate of spinsters to be the subject of speculation. So I must be content till I have arrived to a <u>clever</u> age, then, what then? Why I suppose I shall be laughed at. I am almost tired of this notoriety and wish, heartily wish, I could see some one worthy of being I won't say worshipped, but there is always something in every one to make one get sick of them. I fear I shall never be suited. I do not mean to say there are not many worthy of being loved, but such will never see fit to love me I fear. It is strange. I feel that I am in a very "<u>bad</u> <u>way</u>" my dear and am afraid I shall be a misanthrope before long.

Mr. Blight came in this morning. He amused us a while. Verily think the spirit of mischief is fully developed in us two girls. No stone remains unturned that will serve for our amusement. Our spirits are at a low ebb though I assure you and we have hardly <u>energy</u> sufficient to keep us alive. Rained after dinner, so did <u>not</u> walk, a pleasing variety for you. Studied my French a little and finished the *Heart of Midlothian* [Sir Walter Scott].

29 This morning Mr. Blight and Sturgis came in and played Battledoor with us. Mr. Whiteman called—an invite for tomorrow evening. Accepted. Received as a <u>novelty</u> a letter from Uncle.

Also one from a gentleman [W. W. Wood] in Canton, very interesting. Gave me his opinion of me and my character, frankly and candidly. Told me some of my <u>faults</u> and also my good qualities—he was partly right I think—but no one knows me so well as I do myself I think. It is not many years since I thought of myself at all and it is but a short time since I have been fully convinced of the necessity of self examination. But having been convinced, I have searched my own heart and no one can know me better than I know myself. I know my weakness, and I know it is great in some respects. Knowing it, it shall be my task to guard the weak parts, to <u>strengthen</u> the <u>strong</u>, to guard against my most besetting sins, and in future to live and act more wisely, more reasonably and more as a rational being should act. I have been guilty of many follies in <u>my</u> <u>day</u>, I have committed many errors from thoughtlessness and indecision, and from not being acquainted with myself. But these I hope will serve as warnings in the future. I replied to this said letter at once and pointed the causes of these faults pointed out, for I see the <u>source</u> of these mentioned. I returned my thanks and shall endeavour to improve upon the hints.

30 This morning wrote several letters, studied, read, etc. After Tiffin was reading the travels of a German Prince in England, France, and Ireland,[74] translated into English. Some of the remarks and reasoning I like, on the whole rather interesting. While reading I received a letter from E. W. Ward. Interesting, as usual. Tells me of lots of new matches, among others Eliza Sprague.[75] She was a good girl and will doubtless make a good wife and I hope she has found one worthy of her. How the girls are splicing and "nuptifying." Upon my word when I go home I shall find a quantity of wives and Mammas I suppose. It appears to me there are but few left now. Well they have my best wishes. E. says her brother Henry is in the *Lotos*. A little rogue, I should like to see him. [Henry Ward was born December 31, 1816, hence slightly over 16.]

Well I went to walk and about 8. Sam Sturgis called and waited upon me to Mrs. Whiteman's—a small party, but pleasant. Some fine music. Piano, flute, and voice—enjoyed it much. Beside that, at this house you know all is harmony—perfect specimen of conjugal felicity. Oh if there is an Elysium on Earth, it is this, it is this.

31st Had a letter from Lintin this morning. Says the *Mandarin* F[isk] Allen is not coming. A disappointment. Well I am used to these things. Therefore I quietly say I am extremely sorry and endeavour to forget it—but I had hoped to have a chat with Fiske. But patience! Called on Mrs. Fearon and Miss Pereira this morning. Walked after dinner with ourselves and Mr. & Mrs. D[avis?]. Mr. Blight spent the evening with us, and so closes this month.

Adieu January

February 1st 1833

1st Warm day. Doors all open, and a little rain. Sam Sturgis in this morning; played Battledoor with him. College came in about 2 and we had some rational conversation. He is a pleasant creature, so frank in his manners that you cannot help liking him. He is thoroughly English, somewhat aristocratic, and fond of old customs. The English resemble the Chinese in this respect. Even though their reason tells them they are wrong, they stick to old habits. We talked a little upon the Unitarian religion. He is prejudiced like all others, not at all knowing what they do profess. To me a creed seems a small part of our religion. I like his feelings, he possesses a Christian Spirit and acts like a Christian. He prophecies we shall before many years have to <u>indent</u> for a <u>king</u> for America, which we all opposed with a true republican Spirit.

Finished The Travels of the German Prince in England, France, and Ireland. A liberal minded man and writes well. I like his reasoning and ideas much. He cuts up English aristocracy handsomely. Dislikes the people apparently but likes the Irish character much.

Speaks often of Lady Morgan [Sydney Owenson (1778–1859), the novelist], and says as every one else does that she possesses most consummate <u>vanity</u>. What strange inconsistencies in people's characters. Now she certainly has talents and yet good sense seems incompatible with such weakness.

2 Felt <u>miserable</u> this morning. Spent most of the morning in the interesting employment of <u>weeping</u>. Had a little <u>misunderstanding</u> which I have at last happily settled, and will be a lesson for the future. [See February 19] How experienced I am becoming. Well experience forms the character. I have been a most thoughtless <u>child</u>, have acted too much from <u>impulse</u> all my days. Now I am going upon reflection. I see the error of my ways and I will try to improve.

I went out to walk after dinner and Sam Sturgis joined me, College, Caroline. She, no doubt, had a very delightful walk. I cannot say so much for myself, for S. is no companion. He is one of the most amiable creatures I ever saw, but one wants something more than that in a man. S. "is handsome, too handsome for any thing."

Sunday 3ᵈ Went to Church this morning, had a very good sermon from Mr. Wimberley. He is far superior to his predecessor [George H. Vachell]. In fact he seems to know what he is about and enters with some feeling in to his duties. His sermon was upon the Spirit of Christianity, upon the State of mind we should cultivate—"that the same mind should be in us which was in Christ Jesus." That we may observe all the outward forms and be punctual in performing them, and yet not be accepted, for the religion of Jesus is of the heart. That religion is not to be put on and off at stated times or seasons, but is a spirit to be with us wherever we are. In every moment of our lives, every action we perform is to be done with reference to the end of our existence. And these are just my ideas. Religion seems with some to be an <u>excrescence</u> which interferes with their plans of a Sunday morning, and can be put off again after church, but to my mind it is not so.

How much purer are one's feelings, how much holier, when admiring the beautiful works of Nature, when contemplating the wisdom and magnificence of <u>his</u> works, how much more ardent than the often constrained feelings of a prayer, merely because it is <u>the</u> hour. Yes let them be the out-pouring of the soul when it is actually felt, as it must be by all who have any feelings of the kind. Yes religion is to go with us where we go, dwell with us where we dwell. It is to soften the asperities of our character, to console us in the hours of affliction, to be our guide in prosperity, our guard in youth, our support in age. We have an example familiar to us all. <u>There</u> is our rule, and happy they who follow it. It is my constant prayer. My standard is high. Heaven grant I may attain unto it. Alas how far I have to climb.

It was communion day, and so it was with you I presume being the first Sunday in the month. My reflections were serious and I hope the effect will be lasting.

Caroline and I took a walk to the barrier and were both wrapped in <u>meditation</u>. Came home and dined. Now my dear Sis having nothing more to say at present I say Adieu. My song is all of myself or chiefly. If I could tell you all that happens here I should have <u>such</u> a book. But I cannot, it would never do, because others are concerned. So Good Night.

4 I got out of bed at the usual hour, eat my usual quantum of toast with its accompaniments. Felt in unusual spirits all day. Why or wherefore I cannot say unless it was the weather, for in spite of Dr. Johnson, and my regard for <u>him</u> on <u>nature</u>, the weather does have an effect upon our spirits, or upon mine I am very sure.[76] After I left writing last night it was 12 o'clock, and C. sung out to me to come into her room. Her brother had just arrived and threw stones up at her window. He came in and stayed till near 2. I set talking till after 1 then went to bed. Mr. Blight came in this morning and we played Battledoor. I was reading over your letter last night and find you kept it up 2000 times. You beat us <u>all</u> <u>hollow</u>, for our Battledoors and birds [shuttlecocks] are <u>constructions</u> of the Chinese and the bird goes any way but the right.

I took a walk after dinner with Blight. College in. We dined <u>ourselves</u>, a <u>quartette</u>.

Spent the evening with Mrs. Davis, a small party, mostly gentlemen. I was very much amused listening to a political discussion between Mrs. Davis, our <u>parson</u> [Wimberley], and Capt. Gaston,[77] the latter being a thorough <u>radical</u> and ably supported his arguments, and to use their own expression "floored" the others. The "Parson" of course taking the side of the Church—he waxed <u>warm</u> and looked a little displeased—whereupon the spouse sympathized, as a good wife should. I enjoyed it very much and learned something.

5 The morning Caroline, Mr. S[hillaber], and I sallied forth to see the world. We made the circuit of Macao, Caroline's first calls for sometime. And beside there is something <u>brewing</u> for the public, which will astonish them. We found most of the ladies at home. Had the pleasure of leaving our cards at a number of places. When we went home found J. R. Latimer[78] there, just from Canton, the first time for nearly 3 years. He is a pleasant man, and one of our best friends. He came and dined and spent the evening with us. Capt. Little, J. M. Forbes, and S. P. Sturgis came also. John [Forbes] is going home, his health is so miserable. Passed rather a pleasant day. Some little variety.

6 Latimer & Forbes in, F. to say Adieu. Wrote a letter to you this morning. Today my friend Mr. College offered himself to my Caroline, and she has accepted him. I have given you his character before. She will make him an excellent wife. There is strong affection on both sides and will no doubt be happiness, at least it remains with themselves to be so or not. She is capable of being just what she pleases and I have no doubt will be all that he can wish. She has my best wishes and he too—for if I cannot be happy myself, I have no objection to seeing others so, indeed I am not so selfish as not to delight in the joy of my friends. But notwithstanding it does make me feel melancholy and more lonely than ever to see every one having some one worthy of loving, and poor I no one. I seem doomed to this and so I must bear it patiently, seem happy, lest those around should think me <u>envious</u>. Well if I can't do <u>better</u>, I'll do all I can to promote the happiness of those around me. Perhaps my turn will come, but I see nothing in the future worth living for—nothing that I most wish for that there is the least prospect of my obtaining. I should like to shut myself in my own room and die a sort of temporary death till the time comes for us to leave this detested place. You can have no idea how tired how sick I am of it—time's wheels I once wished to <u>stop</u>, but now I say roll <u>swifter</u> on, for till I change the scene Life is almost insupportable.

[Marginal note] You must not mind these <u>azure</u> <u>spots</u> in my books—
they come and go.

We dined at home and spent the evening in talking and thinking of the <u>electric</u> shock the people will have tomorrow. No one in
the place out of our own family had any idea of such an event.

7 Latimer came in this morning and I had the pleasure of <u>electrify-
ing</u> him. His astonishment was <u>great</u>. He could hardly realize it. I
enjoyed it much. College is beloved and respected by <u>all</u>, there is
not a dissenting voice. All wish to see him happy. In all the three
years we have been here, there has not been a word said against him
in any way, and every one knows him and speaks of him highly. He
is not a <u>negative</u> character, liked because he does no harm, but positively <u>beloved</u>.

Latimer forthwith dispatched a boat to Canton to set the news
afloat there, which will no doubt suspend all business for a time.
The bachelors will feel they have lost one of their most worthy members, and the married men rejoice at such a <u>convert</u>. He had for-
sworn <u>matrimony</u>, but the charms of Miss S. has overpowered his
resolutions. It would have been a shame that such a man should
not have been married, and happy <u>must</u> be the woman who marries
him. Well it will never do for me to go on at this rate, for you will
think I am in love with him myself. But no! understand me. I admire him and hope I know how to appreciate his character. I feel
for Caroline as a sister and would be as glad to see her happy as to
be happy myself.

College came in while Latimer was here and the congratulations
were very <u>fine</u>. L. is one of his best friends. College appeared "shut
up in measureless content," [*Macbeth*, Act II, Sc. 1, l.17] looked perfectly complacent and happy and looked as though he would say "Let
him laugh who wins." A <u>rival</u> was <u>thunderstruck</u> this morning at the
announcement. It certainly could not have been very flattering or
pleasing intelligence.

Rainy day, and we had no walk. I have been reading Godwin's
St. Leon.[79] He is supposed to have found the <u>Philosopher's</u> <u>Stone</u>,
has drank of the *Elixir vitae*, but alas it only makes his misery. A
very good moral, very well written. Requires some imagination and
is very interesting.

8 Rainy day again. Latimer in, give me some very good anecdotes of the surprise of every one, the exclamations of others, and the doubts of which of us it is before they tell them. Funny times. Mrs. Davis came to pay her respects to the lady. Finished *St. Leon*. College in this evening.

12 o'clock and I have just come into my room to give you a few of my thoughts. Do you know my dear Sis what it is to feel alone? No you do not—you cannot, surrounded by a host of brothers and sisters, interested in each one, watching the development of their minds, caressed by them. And then the chosen of your heart always near. It is not possible for you to know the feeling. But let me tell you what it is—it is to be in a <u>far off land</u>, separated from your kin, in a place where the society is too small, the interests clashing, petty <u>feuds</u> existing, where the voice of friendship is seldom heard, where none feel interest in each other's happiness, in a word where all are strangers to each other, to be put into <u>such</u> a place, left there three years, and you will know what solitude is—these are the outward circumstances. Now to be more particular, and come to myself. Here I am with an Uncle and Aunt who *sans doute* feel an interest in my welfare, they wish to see me happy and would do all in their power to make me so—but it is not in their power. They are happy in themselves, there is a sympathy of feeling between them which is worth all the world. They are all in all to each other. Their world lies within themselves. They cannot understand my feelings and therefore they cannot fill the void. To set them aside then, we all know how kind and good they are.

Then here is my friend Caroline. In the first place she has a brother here who idolizes her—every thought of heart can be told to him. He tells her of her faults and assists her in correcting them, he explains to her what she does not understand and enters into all her feelings. Her wishes are laws and not a sigh escapes unnoticed. Now to add to her happiness, she is to be doubly blessed in being permitted to marry the man of her choice—and one who is worthy of her whole heart. She is quietly and positively happy. I do not envy her. That is I would not deprive her of the smallest particle of her happiness, but I cannot help feeling. I have expressed it tonight, but dear girl it made her feel unpleasantly, so I will endeavour to say no more upon the subject. But I now feel like one

Who treads alone some banquet hall deserted
Whose leaves are dead, whose garlands fled
And all but me departed—
[Thomas Moore, *National Airs*. *Oft in the Stilly Night*, Stanza 2]

that is I feel as though I was the only one who has not some one to
lean upon, some one to care for me, some one to feel with me and for
me. But no I must still be what I am, the receptacle of cold and un-
meaning compliments, the cypher, nay worse for a cypher adds value
to the other figures and I do not. Yes a girl, the object of speculation
and a subject of criticism, yes a girl, who is expected to walk in the
path of a Chaperon and because she does not happen to be married,
has no right to give her opinion, and indeed is of no consequence.
Yes my dear this is to be alone. To see those around you loved, caressed and made of consequence and to feel yourself as belonging to
no one,—in a word "going upon my own hook." Now my dear I have
preached till my hand aches. I think I feel a little better, knowing
there is one at an intolerable distance who will read this with patience, and with the hope that one of these days I shall have the
felicity of resuming those dear and delightful feelings which used to
be so pleasant in our own family circle. Yes the hope that, that pleasure is in store for me and the joy I shall then have, supports me now.
In those days of happiness, I shall look over this perhaps and wonder
that I could ever felt thus. I dare not reverse the picture.

Good Night my dear Sister. Caroline says come to bed.

9 I closed my book last night feeling dismal enough my Sis, but I
must fight against these feelings. They are of no avail and there is
no help for them. Therefore

I must be resigned when ill betide
Patient when favours are denied
And pleased with favours given.
[Nathaniel Cotton, *The Fireside*, Stanza 11]

This is said to be wisdom's part, so I will try. But alas my nature is
social and formed for sympathy and I cannot alter my nature—and
yet there are few who can more readily find resources for amusement than myself, but there are times when books, work and amusements fail, when nothing is required, but the society of one dear
friend. But you must be tired, so I'll tell you who has been here.

First came Mrs. Fearon, then Mrs. Whiteman, Mrs. Grant & Mrs. Wimberley. All come to offer their kind wishes to Caroline. I was the only one among the number who had not a friend to speak of one. Some were anxiously waiting the arrival of their friends, one had just come, and one was fearing the departure of hers. Certain it is that <u>husbands</u> are more thought of in this place than any other. Rainy weather no walk.

10 The first thing I heard this morning was Uncle's voice, came quite unexpectedly. He is looking pale and very thin, but says he feels pretty well.

Mr. College, Mr. Shillaber, Caroline & I went to Church this morning. C. walked <u>betrothed</u> as I told her. The English always think it necessary to go to Church before they do any thing else. After every event, say marriage, *accouchement*, or the like—they have some odd predjudices—they "strain at a gnat and swallow a camel" [Matthew 23:24] often I think. Spent the afternoon in talking to Uncle. It does seem good to see him again. Read him one of Buckminster's excellent sermons—speculations upon the future life, and agrees perfectly with what, since I have reasoned at all, I have thought of a future state—that is that we go on from one world to another gradually progressing. It cannot be it appears to me that any one leaves this world in a state for perfect blessedness. We are none of us perfect nor are any <u>all</u> evil. And I firmly believe that we shall all of us be rewarded according to our deeds. As we make use of the talents committed to our charge in this world, accordingly shall we be rewarded in the next. If we have been faithful servants, we shall be trusted in future & vice versa.

This morning we parted with one of our family, Caroline's English servant. She was called up yesterday and told to pack up her duds, she would be off for England in the *Reliance*, starts perhaps in a few hours. She dared ask no questions having a guilty conscience. She has turned out very like our "<u>Nancy</u>"—not <u>exactly</u> a "Nancy case" but very near. She is quite notorious here, we find by a certain gentleman. European servants will not do in this place. They seldom keep their characters—deceitful creatures.

Lots of calls to C. after church.

11 Latimer, Wilkinson, Capt. Gaston called this morning—I did not see them. Went into Carry's room after breakfast, found her in great

distress, cutting or trying to cut a dress. She will need her woman
more than ever now. I took her dress, cut and made it for her in
Mantuamaker style. I shall be quite accomplished in the trade before long.

Cold, rainy weather. No walks, and we are perfectly miserable,
or as the English say, we seem as though we should starve with cold,
an expression which will sound as odd to you as to me when I first
heard it.

We had College, Latimer, & Shillaber to dine tonight. Had a
very pleasant and social party.

12 This morning I received very unexpectedly a letter from my friend
[W. W. Wood] in Canton, to which after mature consideration I replied, as I have told you in a letter. Oh that I could look into his
heart and see its workings. I have become so distrustful of words now
that the warmest expressions fail.

The weather still cold and gloomy. Believe I should be quite con-
gealed was it not for a game of Battledoor with Mr. Latimer every
morning.

Mr. S[hillaber] dines with us. Mr. C[olledge] in this evening.

13th The *Red Rover* back again this morning. Seems but a week since
she left here for Calcutta. Brings news of the failure of Alexander's
& Company [of Calcutta] which will involve great number[s]. Riches
will take to themselves wings. The news of the death of the Duke
de Reichstadt[80] so there will be no danger of him any more, indeed
I believe he did not inherit his father's spirit at all. I had letters
from home too, a number. Set down and answered them to send
per *Emily Taylor*. Played with Latimer, Whiteman called, and Capt.
Jennings. The latter dined with us with Mr. S[hillaber]. Like dining
late much. It is very social with a small party. Uncle is troubled with
a racking cough which I do not like; he has had it for some time.
He is obliged to go up again tomorrow, a flying visit after an absence of 5 months. I hear some little news in my letters. Have been
writing most of the day.

14 Spent this day just as usual, but my mind I fear is in a bad way.
I do not give my mind to my books as I did. Caroline's engagement
I suspect has unfitted me. Went to a dinner party at Mrs. Davis's
made for Caroline. Only 10—rather pleasant.

15 Had a *tête à tête* with Mr. Latimer this morning of an hour and 3 quarters, played Battledoor. After dinner it cleared up a little and we had a walk, the first for over a week. Very cold, but feel all the better for it. Now we have just had dinner and tea, and College is here, so Aunty has gone into her little room, and thinking myself *de trop* I have very kindly absented myself for a while. Suppose Caroline will scold, but I do not like being in the way—it is very <u>kind</u> in me, for my room is cold enough. So I shall go back again soon. I believe I will read over my letters received yesterday and so bid you good night. Then I shall feel they have courted <u>long</u> <u>enough</u>. Do you remember the <u>cranberry</u> sauce & firebrand? What a time. Ah those were my youthful days.

16 I went back to the drawing room last night but found myself, or thought myself very *de trop*—but as it was 11 o'clock I would not go again, so I made myself comfortable. This morning I spent in reading till I was interrupted by Mr. Latimer who comes regularly to play Battledoor with me. But our <u>affairs</u> are so poor that we do not keep it up very well, but as they answer the purpose, which is exercise, we keep it up. The Miss Ullmans called and Latimer made his exit. Had a delightful walk after dinner with Mr. Shillaber and our family. It was a perfect afternoon and one could not help feeling in spirits. College came in this evening to "*bebe cha*"[81] as the Portuguese say and Aunt Low & I very <u>sagaciously</u> left the room—that is we had <u>sagacity</u> enough to suppose we should be more agreeable in <u>another</u> room. Well I hope they will quarrel soon, for I do not like this <u>turning</u> <u>out</u> business.

17 Walked to Church this morning with Caroline & College. We got half through the service and then the Clergyman thought proper to <u>withdraw</u>, as the Caffres it appears have a holiday and they were dancing and singing and making a great noise in the next yard and disturbed Mr. Wimberley so much that he could not read. It seems the Governor is to be married and it was on this occasion that his slaves were liberated for a day.

Being a pleasant day and losing our sermon, we walked along the Quay & into the Franciscan Church, a very neat pretty place, beautifully situated as is also the monastery attached to it. They were just in the act of filling up the grave of a person just consigned to the dust. They bury the people in the Churches always, and the manner seems to us very shocking. The body is exposed in the coffin through the streets. It is taken into the Church and put into the ground <u>without</u> a coffin, it is then covered first with <u>quicklime</u> and then the earth is beaten down hard upon it by the <u>black</u> <u>boys</u>. When the flesh is decayed the bones are sometimes taken up and burned. No female friends ever follow the corpse. The padres chant and read prayers in the Church and the bells ring most furiously, from the time the person dies till he is buried, which generally follows in a very short time. The priests as in all Catholic countries exact large sums from those who are able to pay for their prayers and extort grievously from the poor I am told.

They have great power over the minds of these poor ignorant creatures, and from all accounts many of them are very unworthy of their charge. I was told the other day by Mr. College, who knows more of them than any one else, that he was called to visit a woman who was very ill indeed and had quite lost her reason, and the father confessor had been the sole cause of it. It seems she has received great kindnesses from the English residents here. She is a poor woman and they had assisted her and one day some of her friends were abusing the English as they are in the habit of doing, and this woman said she thought them very <u>good</u> people, and expressed her gratitude to them. The padre either heard her or was told of it. Whereupon he thought it necessary to chastise her and for <u>this</u> <u>heinous</u> sin as he pretended to consider it he told her she must confess her sins, going back to her seventh year, (she was now 40). The poor woman thought it impossible I suppose, and it preyed so upon her mind that she actually went <u>mad</u> and College says it will no doubt be the death of her.* Is it not horrid? Many such instances of oppression occur and it seems dreadful that such creatures should have such power. I wonder if the time will ever come when this Catholic <u>religion</u> (if we can call it so) will be done away. Yes by degrees I think it will; think of the time when all Europe was in the same state, but as the world becomes enlightened, this bigotry and supersition will be done away. The mighty fabric is gradually decaying—the foundation will soon be undermined and a new one will be erected. The religion of Jesus Christ will overspread the earth, the mild spirit of Christian Charity is growing in <u>America</u> and it cannot fail of spreading itself. I should like to look upon this little planet 2000 years hence and see what <u>mind</u> will be then. See if people will not think for themselves, and consider themselves the keepers of their own consciences and God their only master, their best judge. How different the world is now or the state of society from what it was in the 15th century and shall it not go on towards perfection? We certainly have not retrograded since then,—I prophecy it will! We shall, or others will see these <u>Chinese</u> exalted in the scale, their turn must come I think— the barriers must be broken down, ignorance must give place to knowledge, and slavery to freedom. Females will then be exalted; what a state they are in now, poor degraded beings, mere toys for the idle hours of their oppressive masters—crippled, tortured, merely to please them.

As I was walking this morning I saw a poor creature toddling along on her little feet. Oh the hours of torture she has suffered for this barbarous fashion—I am told that the agony they endure is beyond conception. They commence <u>swathing</u> the feet at the age of two and for years they suffer excessively. The poor child does nothing but scream from pain and all to gratify the pride of the mother who thinks her child will not be beautiful without. And yet I am told that the men do not like it, though they think it necessary to have their <u>first</u> wife with small feet. I was one day talking with a very intelligent compradore upon the subject, who seemed to think the custom of <u>nipping</u> in the waist was quite as barbarous and cruel as to pinch the feet—it seems to be a matter of astonishment with them "how we can <u>catchy</u> <u>chow</u> <u>chow</u>." That is how we can <u>eat</u>, which certainly would be a greater grievance to them than not being able to walk.

A short time since [October 18, 1832] there was a wedding in Canton. Young "Minqua" <u>was</u> married and the gentlemen were all invited to call upon her on that day. They were all rejoiced at the opportunity (which is very rare), and went. They were asked to sit down and the Lady was <u>tottled</u> into the room. Supporting herself by putting her hands on the shoulders of her two <u>bridesmaids</u>—she walked round and curtsied to the gentlemen and they were not permitted to stand up to receive her. After having performed this ceremony she was <u>backed</u> out of the room, looking highly delighted that she had finished the task. She was very richly dressed and had strings of pearls hung all round her face, coming from the comb behind. She was painted and looked pretty. The presents were all displayed, some of which were very <u>substantial</u>, being cakes of <u>Sicee</u> <u>Silver</u> of good size—and every thing else. The bridegroom is obliged to take a <u>bumper</u> with all his friends and *sans doute* feels very merry before the day is over. Ought we not to be thankful that we are so much further advanced in civilization? For although refinement and civilization bring with them their evils, they are of a more <u>refined</u> and <u>civilized</u> kind—though I dare say, never having known better, the China woman is just as well contented with her situation as we are with ours. And indeed I am sometimes inclined to believe that she is to be envied when compared with a woman of <u>fashion</u>, who is "tortured with envy, malice, and all uncharitableness."[82] When I think of all these things my dear, I can <u>sympathize</u> with Solomon and say "<u>all</u> is vanity and vexation." [Ecclesiastes 1:14] If it were not for a <u>hope</u> of a better world, a something beyond this, should we not despond with this feeling in our hearts and these sentiments on our lips? And it is when we feel thus, that we most sincerely thank our father in Heaven that he has sent his Son into the world to <u>assure</u> us of a resurrection—to add this to all the proofs his works give us, that there is an immortal germ within us, that will again spring up and put forth, as the seed sown in the ground. Were it not for this <u>faith</u>, it appears to me the trials and disappointments of this world could not be borne. Vanity is so legibly engraven on all our brightest prospects that they would not be thought worth the taking. We might be too ready to cast aside the ills we have without fearing the consequences. . . . . . .

Upon my word I have been thinking on paper for the last half hour—I hope the ideas are not as disconnected as my thoughts often are. I must review, I had almost forgotten I had a pen in my hand. As you do not rouse me by your replies I go on without them and alas how long before I shall receive a reply.

Since I came from church I read a sermon to Mr. S[hillaber] and Caroline, had some Tiffin and here I have been in my room ever since. Now I will not prose any longer, so adieu for the present.

Read one or two more good sermons, dined, and spent the evening in reading and talking.

* The woman has since died.

18 Mr. [Thomas] Allport arrived this morning and called upon us. How delighted I should be to see his wife. She is the jewel after all. Had a long walk after dinner with Aunty. Nothing occurred today

worth noticing. <u>Tom</u> [Colledge] came, in the evening and Aunty and I very <u>kindly</u> <u>withdrew</u>.

19 This morning Mr. and Mrs. Thornhill arrived—came to congratulate Caroline and settle <u>accounts</u> with me. She is real Irish inasmuch as she cannot live without quarreling.

- At Midnight -

At midnight I left you and at the same hour I resume my subject. And to proceed with my friend of the <u>belligerent</u> disposition, for such she has and a proof of it is that she has been trying to pick a quarrel with me the most <u>peaceable</u> creature in existence.

About a fortnight since she sent a note accusing me of <u>cutting</u> her and resuming her acquaintance at my pleasure, accusing me of caprice, & etc, all of which was very foolish and not worth repeating. It certainly astonished me much as I fancied myself on very good terms with the lady—but I see wonderful proofs of the power of imagination daily and this must be one. However she came this morning with her poor h-- p----d [hen pecked] husband and after stating the case and making herself very ridiculous she told me she was sorry and we shook hands, and are now apparently in good terms. However I would as soon put myself into a nest of hornets as to be intimate with her again. I shall have to play the hypocrite when I meet her, for I must confess that I have lost all regard for her, and if she ever commits the like offence I will not keep any terms with her. But in such a place it is unpleasant to meet people and not speak. Oh how sincerely she made me wish to be with my own friends. She said many disagreeable things which I <u>pocketed</u> for peace sake. She is not the woman I thought her. She has no resources within herself and having but little <u>occupation</u> she frets herself dreadfully, and I should think would worry her poor husband's life out. But there enough for her ladyship. I could tell you such stories of her.

Soon after they had left and I had hardly recovered possession of my nerves (for an Irish woman completely deranges them for a time) and Sir George and Lady Robinson came in—a perfect contrast to the former couple—she all kindness and amiability, a devoted wife and mother, making all happy around her and happy and contented with each other, their own home contains their world and they are independent of the world. And what can one wish for more; than to have a devoted husband and fine children around. But what's the use of dwelling on such pictures? It is like

> The [Peri] at the Chrystal gate.
> We gaze on heaven and mourn our hapless fate!

I then went to see Mrs. Morrison whom I found very agreeable. She has just been confined and has another boy. A happy circumstance, the Missionary Society allow them something for every child they produce—why or wherefore I cannot say. Methinks it will cost them a pretty penny if they go on in this way one a year.

I did not walk for I felt too *triste*, too unhappy to bestow my tediousness upon any one. So I stayed at home and read.

20 China New Year commences today. Mr. Latimer and Rieves called, and L. kept us laughing for 2 hours, then he departed. We had Tiffin. Had just finished and were on the terrace "Sky larking" and the bell rung. I heard Latimer's voice again. I went racing into the drawing room and crying "Why J. R. Latimer why are you here again?" and came pounce upon a stranger who was no other than Mr. Labouchère,[83] a Frenchman by birth. Has been in America and all over the Continent. They in just from Canton, he and Chay Beale both called. They went—and we went to the Campo.

21ˢᵗ Studied all the morning or till one o'clock. For a wonder I give my attention to my books. The fact is I am in a bad way. My mind I fear is not in my eyes.

Mrs. Crocket, Latimer, Labouchère, and College in this morning. Mrs. Davis and Mrs. Allport dined with us. After dinner in came Latimer, Labouchère & Chay Beale *sans cérémonie*. Labouchère's a very pleasant fellow and good looking. Now they are gone and here I am writing, waiting for Colly. If I don't give her a scolding, letting Tom stay so late—it is more than 5 minutes past 11 the usual hour with you, you know when I made enquiries in old times. The clock has begun to strike little ones and it is time he was gone. If I was as mischievous as I used to be I should walk in and disturb their *tête à tête*, but I believe I am a little more compassionate than of yore. Well I'll go to bed at any rate so *Bon nuit, ma chère*.

22ᵈ C. has promised to be married in 3 weeks from this time. Short work of it. I think my mind will not be regulated till she is "nuptified."

So I shall be glad when it is over and I tell her will do my best to get her out of the house. This morning I went to work and cut out a satin dress for her—consider myself No. 1 at the trade.

Took a short walk. Had a dinner party in the evening, made for Labouchère; but his Ship came about 4 and he went off. We had T. R. College, J. R. Latimer, two Mr. Beales, Chinnery, Capt. Jennings, Mr. Shillaber, and ourselves. Oh and Mr. Allport.

Had a very good dinner and as pleasant a party as one can have in this place. The people are all <u>stupid</u> or get into a very bad habit of talking <u>nonsense</u>. It would astonish you to know the trifles that the gents interest themselves in. What they shall eat and put on seems to be the ends of their existence. Oh it's tiresome, very, to have parties here, I am sick of seeing the same people.

23ᵈ Uncle came in this morning just before we got up. Is looking much better. Mr. Latimer and Allport in this morning and I am astonished to find a joke Caroline and I had upon the *tapis* last night was all taken for fact and Latimer came here looking very serious at me. They were all quizzed completely. I joked him again this morning for not having sagacity enough to <u>understand</u> it. However I at last asked him to forgive me, but he says he cannot quite yet. But he cannot hold out long I suspect.

Went out to walk with Uncle after dinner, it seems delightful to have him here to walk with and talk to, some one that belongs to me. He says going to Canton they picked up part of the crew of a China boat, very near perishing. They had been capsized or run afoul of the fishing stakes the night before, 5 were drowned. I can hardly account for the indifference we feel regarding these creatures. We hear of their being killed and drowned and misfortunes of divers kinds occurring but not with the feelings that we should have in parallel cases in our own country or Europe. It must be that we have no sympathy with them, they appear to me to be a connecting link between man and beast, but certainly not equal with civilized man. And you see the different grade and links in all the rest of nature's works is it not reasonable to suppose there are higher and lower orders of men? They certainly do not possess the sensibility and feelings of other nations. And when we hear of these accidents, our imaginations never picture distressed and bereaved families, and happy families destroyed—for knowing their brutal customs we cannot think

such distresses exist. "More is given us, and of us more will be required." [Luke 12:48] Therefore how anxious we should be to be able
to give a good account of our stewardship.

Had a fine walk to the barrier, head wind coming home which
was very disagreeable, we arrived safely notwithstanding and Capt.
Jennings dined with us.

24ᵗʰ Mr. Latimer and College come to wait upon us to Church. Mr.
L. is coming round. Wanted to know if I was penitent. Told him <u>no</u>.

Went and heard a good Sermon at Dr. Morrison's. A new <u>spin-
ster</u> come—she is very ugly and rather <u>common</u> looking. She stays
only a few days and I think I shall not make her acquaintance.
Clifton, Capt. Gaston and Morris called after church.

After dinner I read Aunt & Uncle two of Mr. Buckminster's excellent sermons. Sermons which make you wish to be <u>better</u>, make
you wish "to be perfect as our father in Heaven is perfect." They
exalt your feelings and invite us to make good resolutions and to
reflect upon our errors and desire to mend them. A lovely afternoon.
<u>We</u> <u>three</u> went to walk, had a delightful time it was so pleasant, the
weather warm and clear. We sit upon the rocks and mused. The town
was busy (while we were enjoying the beauties of nature) in performing some ceremony relative to this particular Season (Lent). They
carry Christ upon a cross through the streets, a dreadful mockery it
seems to me. I did not see it for it is not pleasant.

We met young Henry Robinson walking, a victim of consump-
tion— a perfect picture of it, the brightness of the eye, the hectic
cheek, the attenuated form. All bespeak this melancholy disease,

> Yes, 'twill be over soon. This sickly dream
> Of life will vanish from his feverish brain.

It is melancholy to see a youth cut off so quickly and when I say this
I ask myself Why? What is there here below to make us desire to
live; nothing but a succession of disappointments, vexations, and
cares. And if our father sees fit to call us from them, to relieve us
from the burthen, if he shortens our probation, why should we complain? We should rather be thankful. A few tears may be shed by the
survivors and then all will go on as before.

I came home, reflected awhile on the vanity of this world's possessions, eat my dinner, then Latimer & Clifton came in. L. & I had

a little "<u>spat</u>" and then forgave each other. He is a good creature as ever lived. He said good bye and leaves for Canton tomorrow morning. Clifton leaves for Calcutta again. So they come & go "like the old woman's soap." C[aroline] would say your <u>steps</u> from the sublime to ridiculous and the grave to the gay are very great. But so it is our lives are made up of it. Inconsistencies and <u>caprice</u> are found in large <u>quantities</u> in every human breast I believe. Well I think I have moralized enough for tonight and as it's 12 o'clock I'll bid you good night my dear.

25th And your birth day my dear Sis. Methinks your 25th year. May God bless you and give you many happy returns of the day. We are growing old, my dear. I should think it was almost time for you to be married [Mary Ann Low married George Archer in Brooklyn, March 14, 1833]. I have thrown aside my once cherished theories of long engagements and think it best they should be as short as possible. Don't ask me why? for I am sure I cannot say. C. intends being married in three weeks, and I am very busy aiding her in the cause. She seems quite happy. And there is nothing negative in the feeling, it is <u>positive</u> <u>bliss</u>. Too rich to last it appears to me.

We thought we had parted with Latimer and Shillaber last night, as they were to leave for Canton this morning but they sent word before we were out of bed that they should come and breakfast with us. They accordingly did and left about 12.

Last night a Shipwrecked Capt. arrived here. Wrecked on Lord North's Island—lost his vessel and every article of clothing—they were treated very kindly by the natives who built them a canoe and supplied them with food, setting an example to more civilized people of hospitality and kindness. They went in their canoe to a neighboring Island where they would be likely to be taken off.

Stayed at home this afternoon and read while the others walked. College in, got a terrible cold and had to go home and nurse himself.

26th Busy all day in assisting Caroline. Am astonished to find how very <u>capable</u> I <u>am</u>! A long time since I have made such a speech. Think I have rather been going upon the <u>modest</u> lately. A gentleman [probably W. W. Wood], who professes to be a great observer of human nature, wrote me a letter the other day telling me what he thought of <u>me</u>. One thing was he thought me <u>too</u> <u>modest</u>—that is he thought me too diffident of expressing my own opinion. In an instant the <u>look</u> of my dear father's came to my mind, accompanied with the anecdote of a friend of his, a lady, who said a certain degree of "modest assurance was necessary to show a lady to advantage." I remember father used to think I possessed a good share of this "modest assurance." I wonder what he would say now. I think the lady perfectly right, and am sure nothing makes a person appear so well as a little self-confidence, it should not <u>border</u> upon <u>conceit</u> but should express herself with sufficient boldness to have some effect. Well to go back to my <u>capability</u>. This of which I am speaking is in the dressmaking line. I make nothing of cutting out a Satin or lace and making them up. This is a dreadful place to get married in—no shops to go to. Must pick up such things as you can catch, "asking no questions for conscience sake." You would laugh to hear us tell the Compradore send and "<u>catch a Tailor</u>" and then to see a great long tailed fellow trot in, impregnated with tobacco smoke to take your work, which after much trouble you get <u>stuck</u> together, often in a manner that would little suit our particular ladies at home. But to get them done is the thing. If they have an exact muster they sometimes do pretty well, but the <u>grievances</u> are many, and one has to <u>bear</u> and <u>forbear</u>.

Poor "<u>Tom</u>" is quite sick today and can't go out.

The *Water Witch* arrived today and brings news of another terrible failure in Calcutta, Mackintosh and Co. They seem to be falling like a pack of cards. One gentleman here (Portuguese) loses by them about 200,000 dol[lar]s. Quite a fortune for most people. But they say it is not much for him.

No walk today, a little unpleasant.

27 Busy at work all the morning, helping Caroline. Have read a little this afternoon, but my mind is full of the approaching event, and I shall not feel settled till it is over. Capt. Jennings dined with us, and College has been here all the evening, and there they are in the drawing room, Caroline and College. Yes, happy? But will it last? Can such happiness endure? A little while ago I had almost the same feelings (only we never met, after the engagement). I thought I had found one [W. W. Wood] on whom I could lean. I thought—but there it is vain, let it pass. It was but a <u>dream</u>.

It makes me tremble though, and yet I am sure C. can never <u>change</u>.

I do believe, though I have found them not
Words which are things,—hopes which will not deceive.

[Byron, *Childe Harold*, Canto 3, l.1061]

But I am getting prosaic, so good night my own dear sister. There is happiness yet in store for me I dare say, and if not, what boots it? It would be but short at best.

28 Another wet gloomy day and here I am again in my room all ready again to consign myself to the arms of Morpheus who watches over my slumbers regularly. Then I forget all my sorrows, and suppose I shall rise to do the same as I have done today—ply the needle and read by turns. My ideas are already asleep so I will compose my carcass. So good night my dear. May you be blessed with every blessing is the daily prayer of your sister H. who though she sometimes repines is not ungrateful for the very many blessings she receives.

March 1st The English Factory all arrived last night. A lovely day today. Had a present of a beautiful shawl and dress this morning.

Hudleston and Lindsay called this morning to congratulate Caroline. It seems to me a very odd custom to congratulate a lady upon such an occasion. One would suppose that she had accomplished some great enterprise or that she had been endeavouring to win the gentleman's affections (and you know, the lady is never supposed to do any such thing) and had at last accomplished her designs. They may offer her their kind wishes, but in my opinion I think the gentleman is the only one to be congratulated. I forget whether it is common with us. Lindsay and I had a game at Battledoor. We have some good new ones and served very well but have not reached your number.

After dinner Uncle, Aunt & I went to walk. The afternoon was quite perfect. Felt in fine spirits and felt equal to any thing. Mr. Daniell joined us and we had a very pleasant walk. He is a very agreeable companion, not too lazy to talk, like most of the people here.

2 Busy all the morning making C. a muslin dress. We are beset by Tailors, and such torments. Hope in mercy I shall not be called upon to be married in this place.

Visitors too all the morning and but little can be done. Mrs. Pereira, [Thomas] Beale, & Allport, Young & Donolly, and last of all the Chief [W.H.C. Plowden of East India Company Select Committee]. I did not go to see them however so I kept to my work like a good child. After Tiffin we three went to walk. Caroline was engaged with C[olledge] and did not go—I have quite lost her for my walking companion. This dining late I do not much like it, for it makes me sleepy. My friend Somus lays violent hands upon me and I cannot do any thing.

3 Went to Church this morning with Uncle. Mr. W[imberley] preached or read (I do not know whether it was his own or not) a very handsome discourse. That is the composition was good, but the sentiment I did not like. He did not represent our father in heaven as the God of love, but made him such a one as we could never love. Excites very different feelings in our minds towards him from what our good Unitarian preachers do at home. He would make you fear him, and not fear to offend him because you love him, but a mere slavish fear, which is not in my opinion the feeling that should be cultivated. The text was "Flee from the wrath to come." [Matthew 3:7] Do not much like English Clergymen as clergymen. Now Mr. W. is supposed to preach his own sermons, but last Sunday or a few Sundays since he preached one of Dr. Paley's. It was found in a printed volume word for word—he had it in manuscript too. If he had have taken the book into the pulpit and give people to understand he was not preaching his own sermons every one would praise him—being assured he cannot write so well as many others— but it is a literary theft and dishonourable I think.

After dinner I read aloud to the family two of Mr. Buckminster's sermons. Those are delightful. Make one desire to be better, they have always a good effect, they exalt your feelings. Mr. College dined with us, he is a most engaging person.

4 Up again this morning and at work in the good cause. One would imagine by my zeal that I was to be the happy bride. I am only too happy to be of any use. I called at Mrs. Thornhill's today but had to leave my card. They said she was out. Raining this afternoon, had no walk, so played Battledoor.

5 This morning heard of the *Boston's* arrival from England. Does not bring much news. The death of Sir W[alter] Scott, who has done so much for the amusement of the world—and not only amused but improved the taste of the age. How different the style of novels since his time, to those before. It is true there is an immense deal of trash comes from the press, but the good novels are certainly of a higher order.

Beside his novels impress historical facts and characters upon our minds, which we might otherwise forget. They incite us to read history. And it is not only the good they have done, but the evil they have prevented. Where fifty might have employed their time better than in reading novels, 100s would have employed it worse. Beside how much scandal and malice they have prevented, for they certainly serve for conversation every where.

I think he certainly has not lived in vain, his private character is said to have been an example for the father, husband and friend. It is no doubt selfish to wish he could have lived longer, for I trust he is far happier in receiving the reward of a well spent life.

I went to Miss Morrison's today to ask her to officiate as Bridesmaid at C.'s wedding, but she declined. She is very diffident and thinks she has not <u>resolution</u>. After dinner we were sitting reading, in came a large packet of letters via Manilla per *Eclipse* but not one for me. Dates 15th Sept. Nothing being said to the contrary conclude you are all well. More vessels expected daily so I shall have some soon I hope.

6 Miss Morrison called to <u>retract</u> this morning, but we [had] invited Miss Pereira and she accepted.

Mr. and Mrs. Donolly called this morning to say Adieu. They leave for Calcutta in a few days [in the *Jamesina*, March 16]. Mr. Young came too. Rainy gloomy day. I am now snug in my <u>dormitory</u> and Caroline and <u>Tom</u> are in the room talking "soft nonsense" I dare say. At any rate they are there and I do not believe these conversations are ever very <u>sage</u>. They are both happy so I suppose it does not matter much. But I am cold, so my dear goodnight.

7 This morning busy as usual of late in cutting out work. A note from College says there has just landed here a company of Italian singers, 4 gentlemen & 2 ladies. It seems they have been driven from South America [Chile] and came here on their way to Calcutta, but they propose staying here a few months. It will be delightful to hear some good music. I hope they will give concerts.

Aunty had a splendid Cashmere Shawl given her today by Mr. Heard, Uncle's partner. Am afraid Uncle will be obliged to go up [to Canton] again.

Read the *History of France* by "Crowe," one of Lardner's collection.[84] It is extremely well written and very interesting. I have just
got to the reign of Louis 13ᵗʰ or rather Richelieu's reign for Louis
was a mere cypher. R. was a tyrant, but with such talents you cannot
help respecting and trying to attribute to necessity many of his un-
godly acts.
    We commenced dining at 3 again. We feel so sleepy after late
dinners. Felt bright and worked all the evening in consequence.

8 Dull, dismal, foggy, damp, drizzly weather. Uncle waiting for it to
clear that he may be off again. Been busy as usual all the morning,
working for myself. After dinner read and worked the evening. And
now my dear as I have not an idea for tonight I'll now say good night,
where fortunately ideas are not needed. It is now the witching time
of night so *ma chère bon nuit.*

9 "Another six days' work is done!" Yes another week is gone, never
to return. The weather is perfectly calm and foggy. Have not been
out of the house for a week. Uncle had been trying to leave us all
day, but the weather is so bad and the water so calm that it is useless
to start in a European boat, and the Chinese demure at taking foreigners in their "fast boats"—it is partly for the sake of extortion I
suppose. A ugly, wicked looking creature came here this afternoon
and had the audacity to ask 40 dol[lar]s to take him up to
Whampoa,[85]—a creature that any where else I am sure one would
be afraid to trust himself with. And to think of paying that sum, to
be put into a little miserable hole where you cannot stand up, with
15 or 20 of these ugly creatures, who resemble more what we imagine evil spirits than any thing I can compare them to. He did not go
tonight however. We hear of the arrival of the "*Roman*" tonight so
I shall have some letters I hope.

10 The first thing I heard this morning was "Harriett your letters
per *Roman*." I seized them greedily and first thanked God for his care
of you all. I am quite relieved I assure you. I did not go to Church.
Uncle left about 9. The fogg cleared up a little, and a bit of wind
blew up and he was off. Read several sermons. Looked over the papers.

11 Cut out a gown for myself. Thick fogg again. This visitation is
really very distressing. No walk and every thing so damp and nasty
as the English say. You would be astonished to hear how common

this word is. It is applied to every thing, both people and things. It sounded very odd at first for I remember it is never used with us except in <u>nasty</u> <u>cases</u>. I think they cannot laugh at the Americans for odd expressions.

This evening dined at Mrs. Daniell's. Had a pleasant time rather. Sir George & Lady Robinson, Ploughdon, Lindsay, [Thomas] Beale, Inglis, Wilkinson, Gaston, College & ourselves there. The host & hostess are <u>elegant</u>, have an elegant house, <u>elegantly</u> furnished, <u>elegant</u> children, and all together in <u>elegant</u> style. Stayed till 11 & just come home. Now my dear good night.

A gentleman asked me tonight if the sacrament was ever administered in America. Only think what a question, one would suppose they thought the Americans perfect heathens, to hear the questions they ask.

12 This morning Mr. and Mrs. Daniell called. We are all endeavouring to get the marriage ceremony performed in the <u>evening</u>. It is so awkward in such a place as this to have it before 12 o'clock. The Daniell's are going to Mr. W[imberley] to find out his reasons for declining.

Had a little walk this afternoon in the midst of fog for we were tired of staying in the house. Rich weather for vegetation. The Chinese will get a fine crop of rice I suspect. As we go out on the Campo in the valley there are gardens which produce two crops of rice and a crop of vegetables a year. They take great pains in cultivating the ground, as indeed they are obliged to or they never would produce any thing from such soil.

C's brother arrived tonight from Canton. Brought me a letter from Blight.

13 Had a letter from Mr. [Samuel] Russell this morning, written the evening he called on you. Says you all seem as happy as possible. How happy I am to hear it. Am afraid our poor country is in a <u>bad</u> <u>way</u> from all accounts. I think I shall <u>weep</u> if <u>Jackson</u> is re-elected.

Letters from Uncle too, says he arrived safely, but a long passage. Am sorry to find I have only one leaf more and no other book ready, so good night my love.

14 Mr. Ploughdon called this morning and invited us to come to the Company's tonight as the Italian singers were to be there for the first time. We declined going to dinner, but went about 9 and heard some very good music, though they were suffering from colds. The Italian music requires some little time to get accustomed to it but before they had finished this evening I began to feel its power. I shall say more of these hereafter as they are to give concerts through the season, which will be very pleasant we think. <u>Dr.</u> [Richard H.] <u>Cox</u> accompanied me. I cannot by any stretch of imagination transform him into such a person as my old friend of the same name.[86]

15 Making preparations for the wedding. Have been writing cards all day. I shall send you a <u>muster</u> to show what the English custom is. If it comes in season you had better adopt it. I think it very pretty. Took a walk after dinner as it was nice and cool though cloudy. The sun has not been visible for many, many days. We however get accustomed to it—creatures of habit indeed! Mr. C[olledge] spent the evening with us arranging matters.

16 I have been so busy all day. It really has seemed as though I was of some consequence—helping C. all the morning—writing notes to <u>all</u> the people in the place to come and breakfast at 12 on Monday morning to meet the <u>bridal</u> party. Sent out about 65 invitations— something of a party. The Company's steward will arrange it.

Uncle, Latimer & Gover arrived about 12. Left Canton yesterday at 4, had a delightful passage down. Latimer dined with us. Feel tired and cold. Nothing new for tonight so I'll to bed, my dear. Uncle has brought me another book, I am happy to say.

17 Spent the day in making some preparations for tomorrow. College dined with us. Is quite happy in anticipation of course.

18 This morning soon after breakfast I dressed the bride in white Satin with a lace handkerchief over her neck and veil on her head. She looked interesting of <u>course</u>. Dressed myself in white muslin and at 11 our party consisting of Mr. & Mrs. Low, Mr. College, Miss <u>Shillaber</u> & brother, Mr. Plowden, Mr. Lindsay, Mr. Gover, Mr. Latimer & Hudleston groomsman, Miss Pereira & self bridesmaids, proceeded to the church or chapel, where the ceremony was read in a most solemn & impressive manner by Mr. Wimberley. There is much in the English service that I should think better omitted, but however we got through very well and returned to our house, where the tables were all elegantly laid for about 70 people. They all came in and were introduced to Mrs. Colledge as at our evening parties at home after a wedding. The Governor [Senhor Joao Cabral de Estifique] thought to make himself of consequence and kept us waiting an hour, so that we sat down to <u>breakfast</u> about 1. Latimer engaged a band of music to play to enliven the repast and play as we entered from Church. Every thing went off well. The Italian Singers volunteered to sing and they were a great acquisition. The party broke up about 4 and the bride & bridegroom went to their house at 6. We had the groomsman and bridesmaid to dinner at 7 with several other gentlemen. All together the day was passed in a very satisfactory manner. And feeling that the parties were well suited to each other and the proper affection existing we could but feel happy that they were thus united. I thought at the time that you my dear Sis might possibly be performing the same ceremony—if so may God bless you and make you as happy in your choice as I think Caroline is. There is no mistake in Colledge. Nor do I think there is in George. Therefore I resign my <u>two</u> <u>sisters</u> with the greatest cheerfulness. Now my dear as I am coming to the end of my book 5th it is time to give a few parting words. But <u>now</u> good night.

March 22^d Uncle starts for Canton in about an hour and if I am quick I can send this by Green. So my dear make all due allowances for all the errors that may be found here, and do not I beseech you let this or any of my others by seen out of the family.

> What is writ, is writ,—would it were worthier—
> Farewell a word that must be and has been,
> A word which makes us linger, yet farewell—
>
> [Byron, *Harold*, Canto 4, l. 1667]

Volume VI
March 19–August 23, 1833

The <u>Lights</u> and <u>Shadows</u> of a Macao Life
by A <u>Travelling</u> <u>Spinster</u>
Dedicated to her beloved Sister

Macao March 19th 1833   No. 6

For the sake of variety I will have no prelude, but endeavour to think where I left my other [book], as I must look some days back.

I closed with the wedding day—that memorable day! A day which has witnessed the union of two people, who two years ago did not know of each other's existence, how strange! Meeting in the uttermost parts of the earth and linking their interests for life and <u>perhaps</u> <u>longer</u>. What a change in their manner of living. How delightful to find one on whom you can bestow all your affections, with a certainty of its being reciprocated. That their horizon may be always as cloudless as at the present moment, is my earnest prayer.

Tuesday 19th Was very busy all the morning in arranging my room and putting things to rights, for everything was disarranged, for yesterday's entertainment—so that I have had not time for feeling the loss of my "<u>better</u> <u>half</u>." Several people called but I could not see them. Went to walk after dinner, got caught in the rain & had to run into Mrs. Davis's. Latimer spent the evening with us.

20th Had a note from the <u>bride</u> this morning, wishing me to come and see her, which I did about 1. Found her looking <u>blooming</u> with every thing comfortable and elegant about her.

All the people think it necessary to call on us after the party, thought I should never get out of the house. Latimer went with me to Mrs. Colledge's. Dreadfully foggy and damp—scarcely ever see the sun now.

21ˢᵗ Tried to read a little but was <u>summoned</u> to see Caroline, so jumped into my chair and stayed there till near 4. Had a very severe thunder storm while there.

We dined with her at 7, the bridal party. Had a very pleasant evening. The bride does the honour handsomely, for a beginner.

22ᵈ Latimer came to breakfast with us, & Uncle & he started for Canton at 11 with a good breeze and appearances of fair weather. We shall feel gloomy now Uncle has gone—the house seems so still and quiet. We can get no walks either, the weather is so bad. A stupid journal this will be, for I assure you I have had no ideas nor thought of any thing it appears to me but <u>the wedding</u>.

Colledge came in to see us after dinner and found us nearly asleep upon the couches. Mr. Cox called this morning. Also Mr. [Thomas] Beale & Inglis.

23ᵈ Busied ourselves this morning cutting out work for the tailor. After dinner finished the *History of France* by <u>Crowe</u>, one of Lardner's collection. Beautifully written and very entertaining. His remarks appear to me excellent, and his ideas of Napoleon just. He exhibits him in his true colours.

What a series of crimes and wickedness one reads in reading history, what contrasts in Character. One cannot help wishing when reading of a man of great talents that they are hereditary, though the men of the greatest talents seem to do the most mischief. You seldom meet with a <u>great</u> and <u>good</u> man. They seem incompatible almost.

I am exceedingly fond of reading history, but yet it always disgusts me with human nature. What a strange propensity we have to admire men of great and powerful mind even if every page of their history is blotted with crimes. Now Richelieu the tyrant one cannot help respecting him while at the same time we cannot help detesting him—and <u>many</u> others of the same kind.

Went to Caroline's after dinner and then in my chair to the Campo. Came back feeling *triste*. The weather is so <u>stupid</u>, so dismal. Colledge came to see Aunty. Not very well.

Sunday 24th Went to Church this morning. Called for Caroline. Did not much like Mr. Wimberley. Came home and read several other sermons of Buckminster's. After dinner wrote letters for home. Spent the evening with Caroline—Chinnery & Cox there. Mr. Chinnery was very entertaining.

25th Cutting out work again this morning. Commenced after dinner the *life of "Frederic the Great" King of Prussia*[1] by Lord Dover—rather interesting. His father Frederic William treated him in a most unnatural manner without any apparent cause. After dinner cleared up a little and we want to Casilha's. Came home and went to Caroline's, where we spent the evening.

26th Have been reading most all day the *Life of Frederic*, a great and in many things a good king. He had some strange inconsistencies in his character, his kindness to his subjects and <u>humanity</u> was remarkable, but the military in times of peace suffered by his severity. It could hardly be accounted for, it seemed so averse to the general display of his feelings. It's now 12 and I believe I am <u>asleep</u>, so I'll to bed. Good night.

27th The "pea soup" as Chinnery calls the fogg has cleared up and no rain today, though not clear. The sun is very sparing of its cheering beams at this season. Suppose it is fully aware of the power of <u>contrast</u>. Reading & sewing most of the morning. Sir Andrew & Gover paid us a visit. Heard of Uncle's arrival in Canton. Aunty & I sallied forth after dinner. Met Mr. & Mrs. <u>Colledge</u>, joined them. <u>Tom</u> & I walked together and Lindsay & Huddleston joined the others on the beach. Went to the barrier. Rather warm and <u>muggy</u>. Read aloud to Aunty the wonderful exploits of "Frederic." He certainly was an able <u>general</u> in battle and Napoleon says the only one of Modern days who he had any respect for & Voltaire says he was greater than Charles the 12th, for he was a Statesman as well as a hero.

Now I have closed another day's accounts (which alas have little merit in them) and it only remains for me to go to my bed there & spend a few hours and to rise to the same thing probably. No by the bye a dinner at the Company's ahead, which is not half so pleasant as reading aloud at home, but suppose as it is made to the bride I must go <u>officially</u>. Well, well, *Bon nuit ma chère*.

28th To my book, to my book to tell my distresses. It is the receptacle, the depot of what, shall I say <u>miseries</u>? I dare say you will think
and perhaps rightly that they are all <u>imaginary</u>— but to begin at the
beginning of my day. I spent an hour or two in reading, then went
to Chinnery's room where I sketched till 1/2 past 1. Then I went to
Caroline's & then home where I took my very particular friend a
<u>book</u> again, and read till it was time to dress for dinner—in the mean
time, having tried very hard to make the boy understand that I
wanted some flowers to adorn *mi cabeza* (<u>vulgarly</u> <u>head</u>)—but all my
bad English could not accomplish it. He said "no could catch, could
catch in Canton," this being the state of the case at least not thinking it of consequence to trouble myself about it further, I said <u>Masque</u>
[never mind] and told him he was a very stupid boy, which was all
the satisfaction I could obtain. Soon after I was supplied by a friend,
made myself <u>very</u> <u>beautiful</u> and at 7 went to the party from which I
have just returned, having had as pleasant a time as possible here.
Laughed and talked a great deal, heard some music and was apparently the gayest of the gay. But alas they were only skin deep, for the
moment I got home I could have had a good cry, & indeed I could
not restrain my tears, for I do feel so <u>lonely</u> to be the only one in the
room <u>alone</u> the only spinster. It is no doubt very foolish to feel thus
but I cannot help it. I wish I could stay at home, then I am <u>con-
tented</u>, but to be dragged to these places night after night, it is too
much. I think I am a little <u>bilious</u> now, therefore I'll say no more. I
dare say you laugh at me. You must excuse my writing it, for I cannot speak my feelings to any one, and so <u>you</u> get them. I am sick,
sick of all. Would that I could find a good excuse for staying at home.
Now you will say if this is the amount of my <u>grief</u> it is imaginary and
perhaps will say with an author I was reading the other day, "that
there is nothing like <u>real</u> evils, to banish imaginary ones, and matrimony is a <u>sovereign</u> <u>cure</u>." A very true observation I dare say.

It is not that I wish to be married that makes me feel so. I only
hate to be the <u>only</u> <u>one</u> in a party, to see all others have someone to
call upon, some one to care for them. The <u>many</u> that I can have I do
not want. Beside there is not one among the many whom I wish to
care about me, no one here whose <u>friendship</u> I covet. That is the
worst of it. Now my dear I feel better and you no doubt will call me
a foolish girl, and that's all I shall get. Never mind I am at a good
distance—but hope ere this reaches you I may be thinking of pack-

ing up to move from this. I care not much <u>where</u>, Good night my dear my head aches.

29th I seem to have been in a very dismal mood when I closed my book. The <u>weather</u> is my excuse, <u>in spite</u> of <u>Dr. Johnson</u> [vol. 5, n. 76]. For such a spell of nasty, dirty, drizzling weather is enough to make one gloomy. But several days have elapsed since I wrote and I now feel better. But the next morning I arose with the same gloomy feelings that I carried to bed and they continued through the day. I took a short walk just to keep Aunty company. Some calls this morning, but I did not like any one well enough to speak to them today. I was engaged to Caroline this evening, a small party, but I sent an excuse—and stayed at home all alone. Read the *History of the Crusades* by "Mills"² rather interesting and well written. Went to bed feeling much better.

30th A lovely morning, like our delightful spring mornings. The very air reminds me of <u>home</u>. My spirits revived at the sight of the sun and I feel quite myself again. The house was opened to dry up the damp and <u>mould</u> and a regular "Saturday's cleaning going on." I mended my clothes a little and before I had finished had all the letters per *Beta*, Capt. [William] Cleveland handed me, and glad enough was I. Had quite a feast. Abbot quite come out with his 20 pages.

Suppose before this, my dear, you are Mrs. Archer. Would that I could have been there on that occasion, but it is useless to regret. I think you were wise to defer it no longer. How much I could say, but before you receive this, you will be an old married woman—and having no experience in this line I can give no advice. I believe you are both firmly attached, therefore I doubt not you will have all the happiness you can have in so dear a friend—and I feel happy in the thought that you are thus united. All the observations in all your letters of the children are very gratifying and read with great interest.

After I had read my letters we went to Caroline's and with her and some others to Chinnery's to see Colledge's picture.³ It is a most interesting thing. It is a group of 5 figures. But first for the likeness, which I am sorry to say is not so striking as many others of his pictures. It is taken in profile, which is perhaps the reason. It should have been a full face I think. The figure a full length is perfect; he is resting one hand on the forehead of a China woman whom he has restored to sight from being <u>totally</u> blind—he has lifted the spectacles and is turning to Afun, his China servant, and telling him to explain to the woman how she must proceed in future. Afun's likeness is excellent. The 4th figure is the son of the woman on his knees before C. presenting a Chop, (or letter) of thanks for his kindness to his mother—(which are always written on red paper). The [5th] figure is a poor old man sitting on the floor in a corner with his eyes bandaged up waiting for attention. It is a most interesting and touching picture. I hope to have the pleasure of <u>bringing</u> a copy engraved from it with me. The Chinese likenesses are all excellent, and it is beautifully grouped.

Mr. C. has cured an immense number of Chinese of afflicted eyes. It is a very common complaint among them. Some have thought that it must be something in the rice they eat that produces a disorder in the eyes. But Colledge thinks otherwise and thinks it is because they pay no attention to these complaints in the first instances, and often use medicines not at all suited to the disease. It is not uncommon to meet 4 or 5 blind people together some days in the streets. The deformed people too about is quite shocking sometimes. I never saw any thing to equal the distortion of limbs that I have often met here.

As I came out of Chinnery's today, I met one a perfect object of despair, suffering and misery. I could not help asking myself what feeling or principle it was within him that could induce him to bear such loads of misery. It cannot be the <u>fear</u> of death appears to me in a Chinese, for the most intelligent have no idea of a future state.* It appears to me this poor wretch never could have looked beyond the present. And it seemed quite impossible that it could be the <u>love</u> of <u>life</u>. But it is so ordered that we have feelings implanted within us, all to suit the circumstances in which we are placed. Poor creature he could not walk but was obliged to crawl on the rough pavements with scarcely clothes (and indeed they were nought but rags) wound round his body. He was <u>singing</u> in the streets to get a few cash, which certainly would be given him because of his importunity more than for the pleasure of hearing him. Every note bore such sounds of distress—indeed you would hardly call it singing. The other day I saw another whose legs were turned and twisted up to his back, and he was <u>rolling</u> along. But I will not trouble you with hearing such misery.

After I left Chin'ys I went to Caroline's a while and then home to Tiffin. We had a lobster (or a Craw fish as they are called here) which I am as fond of as ever. Read till time to dress for dinner. Went to Mrs. Grant's at 7 to meet Mrs. Colledge. A party of <u>sixteen</u> and very pleasant—music in the eve'g.

*This reflection is made without reflection I think, for many of the Chinese believe in <u>transmigration</u> of souls.

31ˢᵗ Another pleasant day. We both went to Church this morning. Came home and read two more excellent sermons, one of Dr. Channing's which I would advise you to read. It is in the *Liberal Preacher*.[4]

Wrote a letter to Father & Mother & Gr. Mother and dined with Caroline at 7.

April 1ˢᵗ This morning Caroline come to us and young Calvo who is kind enough to come and hear us read French that we might get a good pronunciation. We intend to study hard now. We commenced reading the letters of Madame de Sévigné.[5] And he is kind enough to say he will come twice a week. This took most of our morning and when we speak well we shall find great pleasure in it. After dinner Aunty & I walked—a lovely afternoon, came home, had some tea and then I read aloud the Life of that <u>wonderful</u> man "Frederic the Great." Went to bed about 12.

2ᵈ This morning dressed and called to see Caroline a minute or two, then went to that amusing man's, Chinnery. Stayed till after two sketching. There is a great deal to be gathered from his conversation and his <u>similes</u> are most amusing. He is a man who has been a great observer of human nature, having had great opportunities, his profession having brought him in contact with [people] of high & low degree. He has been in Calcutta 20 years and has seen a great variety of characters as you may suppose in that changing place. He has excellent sense and "<u>plumes</u>" himself upon being, "though not handsome excessively <u>genteel</u>." His personal appearance I think however rather against him, being what I call <u>fascinatingly</u> <u>ugly</u> & with a habit he has of distorting his features in a most <u>unchristian</u> manner, and with taking snuff, <u>smoking</u>, and <u>snorting</u>. I think were he not so <u>agreeable</u> he would be <u>intolerable</u>—but to give <u>him</u> his due, he is <u>really</u> <u>polite</u>, and speaks well of every one. I being one of his especial favourites I must say something for him—to use his own expression "he <u>buckles</u> to me."[6]

We were asking him if Afun in Colledge's picture could keep still enough to be painted. "Mam, (he says) the Rock of Gibralter is calves foot jelly to him." He (Afun) considers it No. 1 good luck to be put in the picture.

After coming from Chinnery's I dined, then went to Caroline's awhile, from thence to the Campo in search of Aunt Low. And where do you think I discovered [her]—why upon the tip top of one of the highest hills. Should not have seen her with my eyes, but fortunately some of the gentlemen had espied her and pointed her out. She is remarkably well just now and takes very long walks. I read aloud to her all the evening the "Life of Fred," and find it very interesting—he was certainly a most wonderful man.

3 Did not feel well this morning, and was very stupid. Tried to read, write, study, but all in vain—I was not in the humour. So wandered about the house.

Finished Fred last night. He died of dropsy. He had no religious feelings. Though very little is said upon the subject, I should judge he was skeptical on those points. Some say he was an atheist, but from one observation he makes I should think not quite so bad. Though Voltaire was one of his intimates at one time, but they were both too satirical to live in harmony together long.

Commenced a History of Greece and read all the afternoon and evening—very interesting.

4th Calvo came this morning and we passed a very pleasant morning. Nothing like employment. Had letters from Uncle and one from Uncle Daniell. Very much amused with his description of his visit to Weare, and the mistake Aunt L. made in not wearing her best bonnet. The old lady is as proud as ever—think she beats her children & grandchildren.

Thundered & rained in torrents this afternoon. Wrote a letter to Susan Orne, and then read & worked a little this evening.

5th Good Friday. Again the same dreadful procession which I have seen before and described. Went to Church and heard a sermon which I did not much like—a sermon which in my opinion would produce a bad effect. Oh that I could hear some of our good preachers. Some that speak their own thoughts and show some reason in what they preach. This man is what is called a "new light."[7]

Caroline and her husband come to see us after dinner. We had a long discussion upon religion produced by the sermon this morning—which if I could remember I would tell you, but I cannot all. Beside I often regret having <u>spoken</u> my thoughts as I have in these books, thinking they are so detached that you may not understand me, but I hope you will make due allowances.

Took a walk after dinner. We came back and worked a little this evening, and read some. Have commenced a *History of Greece* by Gillies.[8]

6th Went to Chinnery's this morning. Spent a pleasant morning in sketching. Came home and went to Caroline's a little while. Came back and dressed and dined with her at 7, a small party. College was called away professionally just before dinner. We waited till nearly 9, a genteel hour for dinner, and the gentlemen feeling very <u>voracious</u>, having eaten nothing since 9 in the morning. He did not come back the whole evening, he was with a lady—the <u>delights</u> of marrying a physician. When we got up from table it was after 10. The party consisted of Mr. & Mrs. Fearon, Chinnery, Huddleston, Shillaber, <u>Dr. Cox</u>, & ourselves. Had rather a pleasant evening.

Sunday 7th Did not go to Church this morning. A very severe change in the weather. Yesterday warm enough for all the doors to be open, and today cold enough for a fire. A cold northerly wind. I read my bible & Buckminster's sermons. I find I feel much better than by hearing Mr. Wimberley, at least when he preaches doctrinal sermons. His practical sermons are good.

After dinner I walked a little with Aunty. A <u>constitutional</u> walk. We find it necessary, particularly on such a day. It is so cool and bracing.

Now here I am back again. Have been reading over some letters by way of comfort. We have been talking of going home. I get very impatient—fear this will be the <u>longest</u> year.

8th Up and busy at my French till Calvo came and then we had our lesson till two. Spent the time very pleasantly and hope by perseverance I shall yet speak well. He says I read *très bien* now. After he left I spent an hour with Caroline. Saw Mr. Lindsay. He says the Opera will most likely be performed next week. They are to have the "*Father & Daughter*" by Mrs. [Amelia] Opie[9] dramatized and translated into Italian. Say it is a fine thing. Fancy an Italian Opera here. Well wonders will never cease.

Came home and dined, and read till it was time to dress for Mrs. Davis's. Spent a very pleasant evening there. Mrs. Whiteman & ourselves were the only ladies, and several gentlemen. One Capt. Garstin from India—who has travelled an immense deal and knows a little of every thing—he <u>will</u> talk and seems happy to get a <u>listener</u>. He does not find it difficult however as he is a man of good sense. The party was just large enough for the conversation to become general and the subjects were various—Ramonhen Roy[10] and Indian customs were among the number. Mr. Chinnery & Garstin, both old residents in India, were the chief Speakers on those subjects. Wish I could remember all the good things I hear to tell you but I am afraid I shall forget them. They would not do written, because they want the manner. Chinnery gives us some rich treats. He has a face made on purpose to tell stories. Nothing wonderful has happened I believe within my knowledge today, so as it is near the witching time of night I will lay by the goose quill and say pleasant dreams & sweet repose to you my dear.

9th Spent part of the morning in translating English into French. Am very much in want of a Dictionary, wish I could go into <u>Buffins</u> [a store in Salem]. About 12 Caroline & Chinnery came here. He is going to take her picture and he wished to have her on our couch with skreen, fireplace & etc. He is going to take a full length for, <u>Papa Colledge</u>. When he had done we went to Chinnery's room to see Aunt Low's likeness, which is excellent. Then I went to Caroline's and stayed till dinner time. Took a walk after dinner and came home again. After tea I read a Tragedy to Aunt Low called *Francis the 1st* written by Fanny Kemble—when she was 16 years old.[11] It is very, very good, very well written, and seems almost impossible that she could have done so well at that age—but she is said to be a young lady of great talents.

10th Went to Chinnery's myself this morning to have my <u>phiz painted</u>. Great presumption on my part I think, but it was at the request of Uncle & Aunt and the thought of the pleasure it would give you all, that induced me. I sat there an hour looking at one of the ugliest men in existence, but he makes himself so agreeable that you quite forget how ugly he is. He requested my <u>mouth</u> to be open, a thing which I abominate in a picture, but he says it will never do to have it shut, for I generally have it a little open.

Oh wad some power the giftie gie us
To see oursel's as others see us. [Robert Burns, *To A Louse*]

Now I am sure I was not aware that I was in the habit of it—it is the ugly formation of it. Well there I set with head screwed and twisted in a strange manner. Then after he had finished the first sketch I looked at it. Oh ye powers! what a thing. And yet I think it must be like because I saw Mother's look about the eyes, also Cousin Forster's, whom I was always said to resemble. But such a <u>fright</u>—I have laughed 51 times since to think of it. The head appeared about ready to take leave of the neck. The mouth open as though I was snoring—a little something yclept <u>nose</u> and a place where eyes should be. I suppose I must wait with patience for a few more sittings but I think it will rather lower my <u>vanity</u> though on the subject of personal appearance I never had much. *Nous verons* how it will turn out. Came home, found the table covered with cards and <u>billy</u> <u>duckes</u> [a play on *billet doux*].

Evening I spent in working, now and then laughing at my <u>picture</u>.

11th Aunty went to C's [Chinnery's]. I was not very well and stayed at home all alone. Had an industrious fit for a rarity. Found I was too stupid to read so I sewed with all my <u>might</u> & <u>main</u> till 3 o'clock, fixing for summer which is threatening its approach. Some days very severely. After dinner read "Grecian History." You see I have nothing to tell you now a days, one day is just like another. Aunty & I walked the verandah, talked of going home, the feelings we shall probably have, the changes that had taken place, etc. till we both got quite melancholy, she with retrospection I with impatience to be there. We were comparing our blessings and troubles—hers I see has been all positive mine mostly negative. She has certainly tasted and deeply too of affliction. Yes the bitterest sorrows, but in all of them she has had her husband who is her <u>all</u>. While he lives she can bear any thing, I verily believe. She is certainly blessed in such a husband, and while she has suffered the keenest sorrows she has also tasted positive happiness. He has been proved and found faithful. She is an extraordinary woman, & indeed I never knew any one to possess so much fortitude. If all the world were like her, there would be much more happiness in it.

Now I pass along as with the current. I have never as yet had either positive happiness or positive misery. I have thousands of vexations and annoyances, but in comparison with her afflictions, not to be mentioned. For my part I think happiness is very equally divided throughout the world. We are all suited to the circumstances in which we are placed, either by nature or habit which is second nature. If we all rightly estimated the blessings we enjoy daily the amount of happiness would be much greater than we are apt to fancy. 'Tis true I have been disappointed, defeated in my fondest wishes. Hope has flattered but to deceive, but I bow thinking it is "all for the best," hard as it may seem.

12 This morning Calvo came and we spent the morning very pleasantly with our French. I translated some English into French, with which he was highly gratified—said it was exceedingly well done which will encourage me much. We find him a very pleasant teacher. Caroline came in and took Tiffin with us. Read till it was time to dress for dinner. Then went to Plowdon's to dine. It was very hot and every one stupid. A small party made for Caroline. Came home and declare I will not go to any more parties at present except to Caroline's for I am sick of every one we meet.

13 A very hot day. Thermom. at 80, it comes so suddenly that it is really quite overpowering. I found it necessary to look at my white dresses to get them in order, so I worked most of the morning. After dinner the little Daniells came to hear the organ. Fine children and very smart, but I should think troublesome, they are so full of life and roguery. The eldest is a coquette in miniature by nature I might say for she has been so ever since she could speak. If she lives I am sure she will torment some poor man, for she will be handsome and her manners are so formed now that I am sure she will be always <u>elegant</u>. She is the facsimile of her mother. They stayed an hour and I was really glad to have them go for I was not sure that any thing would be left in place. I am now so unused to children, and I am always afraid they will break some of their limbs.

We dined with Caroline, a pleasant party of 10 or 9. The evening was cool and pleasant. Played Whist with <u>Dr.</u> [Richard] Cox. He did not <u>fall</u> back in his chair however. Do you remember that turn over? Poor Dr. [Benjamin Cox].

14 Wrote a letter to Uncle this morning. It rained hard and blew 1/2 a gale and I did not go to Church. So read some excellent sermons at home and the *Unitarian Miscellany*.[12] Like that work much. I have been reading upon the Atonement. I find all my sentiments which I have formed from my own reason and as I understand the Scriptures agree when I compare them with the Unitarian writers. It appears to me as the world becomes enlightened these sentiments and doctrines must be come universal. The Doctrine of the Trinity with its numerous inconsistencies must vanish when men begin to listen to what their reason and common sense teaches them.

It is quite shocking to my feelings to hear the being who we are taught to love & adore, one who we call our Father, so represented as we do here Sunday after Sunday. They make him a cruel tyrant (and as the writer in the *Miscellany* says) "actuated by some of the worst passions of men and possessing no other virtue than vindictive justice" & "The glory of the Father is totally eclipsed behind the blazing luster of the Son." I believe our ideas upon this subject are the same my dear Sis & you will understand my feelings.

I read over my dear father's letter [vol. 1, June 7, 1829, n. 12] which he gave me when I went to sea. I now fully comprehend it all and find he anticipated much that I have since encountered. But thank God my faith is yet firm, what was instilled into me in youth is sanctioned by reason in later years and every day I find my faith strengthened, and I pray my father in heaven daily for the assistance of his Holy Spirit that I may rightly understand his word, that I may lead a life consistent with the rules there laid down and the example there set for us. Now my dear Sis I will bid you good night, for I must get up and study tomorrow morning.

15 A glorious morning this. Air so delightful. It smells like home. You may think this a foolish idea but you have no idea what a trifle brings home and its endearments before us. Seems to me Byron says something *a propos* in *Childe Harold*. I'll see if I can find it. Yes, I have. "It may be a sound—a tone of music— summer's eve, or spring, A flower, the wind, the ocean which shall wound, Striking the electric chain wherewith we are quickly bound," etc.

And how and why we know not, nor can trace
Home to its cloud this lightning of the mind.

[Byron, *Harold*, Canto 4, l.204]

Say what you will of Byron, he could write Poetry. Follow him alias Childe through Italy, go with him to the Coliseum, his description is beautiful. His Apostrophe to Time or invocation is truly delightful, beginning

> Oh time! the beautifier of the dead,
> Adorner of the ruin, comforter
> And only healer when the heart has bled -
> Time! the corrector where our judgments err,
> The test of truth, love - sole philosopher,
> For all beside are sophists, from thy thrift
> Which never loses though it doth defer -
> Time, the avenger! Unto thee I lift
> My hands & eyes and heart and crave of thee a gift: etc.
>
> [Byron, *Harold*, 4, 1.1162]

Then his description of St. Peter's is perfect—not a word too much nor a word too little. When reading his poetry you wish almost that nothing of his character had ever been known. He was a creature of impulse and no principles at all and therefore you cannot respect him, or think with any pleasure of the man, but mourn that he did not make himself all that he might have been.

However I have sadly digressed from my subject. If I can find my way back again I will tell you in plain prose what I did with myself yesterday. Every moment I had before I went to Chinnery's I studied French. At 11 I went there and looked at the man till 2, when I found myself in better humour with my portrait which I think will be an excellent likeness and a little paint will make it I fear better looking than I am. But if you see the likeness you can make allowances for paint. Chinnery said some good things and we passed the morning very pleasantly. He compares aristocracy to <u>Laudanum & Salt</u>, which taken moderately have a very good effect, but take too much of either and you know the consequences—exceedingly dangerous & extremely disagreeable.

After dinner I went to Caroline's and we all went to the Campo. Colledge lent me an English & French Dictionary and <u>now I am made</u>. Worked all the evening and now it is near 12, which is my hour for bed.

16 Calvo came to us this morning. We had a very good lesson and I find I have already made progress. I get great praise for my translations. However these <u>gentlemen</u> <u>teachers</u> are so polite that it does not do to mind all their compliments, though by the corrections that [have been made] those have been good.

I read after dinner and walked the terrace *à la solitaire*. It was a lovely afternoon but the Campo seems so *triste* now I do not like to go. The people seem to have given up walking. This evening Caroline, Mrs. Whiteman, Chinnery, Don Gabriel, Hudleston, & Calvo have been here, so that I have had to do my best at Spanish & French for neither speak English—but I make poor work at it. However I do not despair. We have had a very pleasant evening. Now it's after 12 and the mosquitos are busier than bees and buzzing about at a terrible rate, little insignificant creatures. Does it not seem odd that we can be so annoyed by them. But so it is, and it is very sartain I must go to bed so my dear good night.

17 Went to Chinnery's this morning with Aunty, and amused myself with sketching. Have commenced Mrs. Opie's Tales.[13]

Walked after dinner and spent the evening with Caroline. Went home and studied till 12 and neglected my journal as you will know by this days work.

18 Studied hard this morning till 12. Then I went to Chinnery's to see him paint Caroline. He has got a splendid likeness. Hudleston & Colledge saw mine & think it excellent.

Passed the time very pleasantly till three, then went home, dined and read till 7. Then went to Caroline's, 4 or 5 gentlemen, 3 of which could not speak English. Blundered at French & Spanish. Played a game of whist.

19 Calvo came this morning and we had a very merry time. He is a very pleasant <u>master</u>. Blight came from Canton & called but we did not see him. Had a kind letter from Uncle. He is the best of men. Happy woman that gets such a husband.

After dinner Aunty & I went to walk, on returning met Tom & C[aroline] and went back with them to the bay where we sit till it was quite dark. Came home and spent the evening in altering gowns that the Tailor made. Now my dear Sister here I am in my room wishing yes, sighing to be with you again—but why do I. The clock says 12 o'clock and I think it is time to leave sighing for tonight and go to sleep. So I will my dear and say Good Night.

20 Studied a little this morning then went to Chinnery's with Aunt Low at 11. Drew all the time. It is not very pleasant sitting there, for it is a little bit of a room and no windows open it. We stayed seeing him paint till near 4. I came home with a headache, read till dinner time, when I went to Caroline's at 7. A small party of gentlemen. We had the singers there in the evening and had some fine music. The party increased after dinner.

21 Did not go to Church. Read some excellent sermons at home and then wrote letters for the *Beta*. Cannot have my picture ready for the *B*. Am sorry as it will not be able to go before the Autumn.

22 Caroline and I went to Chinnery's this morning, where we stayed till 4. I went and dined with Caroline, then went home and dressed to go to an evening party at Mrs. Daniell's where we met *tout le monde et sa femme*. It was a very hot evening, but their house is so pleasant that one does not much mind it. They had dancing, but I would not dance but once. Mrs. Pereira sung beautifully. Had a supper and came home about 12.

23 Calvo came this morning and we had a pleasant lesson. The hot weather is coming and makes us rather lifeless. After dinner read *History of Greece*. Believe I walked and spent the evening at home, but I am sure I almost forget for I am near a week behind hand with my accounts. Oh Blight took tea with us.

24 Aunt went to Mr. Chinnery's. I studied part of the morning, then took Mrs. Opie's "Tales of Temper"[14] and read till she came home which was after 4 but I had forgotten I had had no dinner. I have been reading all her stories lately and like them much. Read after dinner till tea time, then went to Caroline's to read a <u>Comedy</u> Mr. Hudleston lent me called *The Hunchback*.[15] Is thought to be very good, but must confess I did not think there was much wit in it though some fine parts.

25 First thing this morning wrote to Blight to ask him to go to Chinnery's with me—we went at 11—I set three hours. He has made a little alteration, put a book in the hand, and I like it much better. Caroline came at 1 and we stayed till 4. Had some <u>fun</u> with Blight, as we generally do when we three meet. He has to cry for <u>quarters</u> often.

I dined with Caroline and walked with her but spent the evening at home, reading aloud to Aunty. (Oh dear I have inked my pretty clean night gown. What a shame) Oh the mosquitoes are so thick I must to bed.

26 Hot sultry morning. One feels <u>no</u> <u>how</u>. Feel like laying on a couch with a book or I believe if I acted as I felt, I should lie down, fold my hands, and do <u>nothing</u>. It is just that listless feeling weather, particularly when it first comes on. But it will not do to give way to them. So I dressed and took my books to the drawing room to study, expecting young Calvo but he was engaged and did not come. So I studied a while, then sent to the Library & got Madame Genlis' *Lives of La Duchesse de la Valliere, & Maintenon*.[16] The first I read with great interest, the second I have not yet read. They were mistresses of Louis 14th. It shows the corruption of the age and the Court and although we condemn we cannot help <u>pitying</u>. For who knows the strength of their virtue till they have been tried, it certainly is but <u>negative</u> when there has been no temptation. Beside when to <u>err</u> is an <u>honour</u> it requires the greatest virtue and the strongest principles to withstand temptation, indeed it too often proves too much for human nature. It is well written and the facts taken from history. What a curse <u>beauty</u> proves in such situations. The Duchess went into a convent at the age of 28 when she found herself superseded in the affections of the King and lived a life of rigid piety. She joined the Carmelites which is the Strictest order. Poor thing she was taken from a life of retirement and carried directly to the fascinations of a corrupt and lascivious court. I read this till it was time to dress for the <u>Opera</u>. Called for Caroline when we proceeded with our party to the Opera.

<u>Our</u> <u>box</u> holds 7. It is 7 chairs placed in a row which we dignify by the name of <u>box</u>. Aunt L., Chinnery, Hudleston, Caroline, & Self and College & Blight in front. The Opera was called the "*Father and Daughter*" [*Agnese* by Ferdinando Paer]. It is one of Mrs. Opie's tales dramatized and translated into Italian with Italian music. The Heroine was Madame <u>Scheroni</u>, Ernesto her seducer was <u>Madame</u> Caravaglia who took the part of a man, both good singers but the first the best and appeared to more advantage being in better health than the other. They all did very well and we were very much entertained. The music was very good. Much better than we anticipated. It is really quite a treat.

It was over about 11 when we went to Mrs. Daniell's and had a *petit souper* which relished very well.

27 This morning studied and finished *La Vallière*. Very much pleased with it. I stayed at home and read till dark. Blight came and took tea with us—and we resumed our old seat upon the terrace, it was a lovely night. We talked over the changes of the past year and divers and sundry topics. Then I bathed and went to bed.

28 Sunday morning. Went to Church today, hoping to hear something less revolting to my feelings than I heard the last time. I have not mustered courage for the last three Sundays but today I went and heard an <u>excellent</u> sermon—a practical discourse, showing us that godliness is profitable in this world and the next.

Mrs. Colledge dined with us and her *sposo* at the Company's. It seemed quite like old times to have her here.

After dinner we sallied forth to enjoy the pure air of heaven which is delightful at this season. We seated ourselves on the rocks at Casilhas and a lovelier view was never beheld by mortal eye. The broad ocean rolling at our feet, seemed the sabbath for that, as well as human beings. It is a place where one can sit and reflect without wishing for company, for

> There is a rapture on the lonely shore
> There is society where none intrudes
> By the deep sea, and music in its roar—
> [Byron, *Harold*, 4, l. 1595]

but now we were not alone. On Sunday evenings the Noñes all turn out, and such a display of <u>figures</u> you never saw. It is really very amusing, they <u>smoke</u> as they go and generally walk in groups of 10 or 20, and it is quite dreadful to get in the rear of one of these groups with a head wind for you are in danger of being suffocated with smoke and fumes of <u>garlic</u>. Beside these all the English seemed assembled here. But they formed in different groups and we were joined by Hudleston, Inglis & Mr. Allport. It was a most lovely evening. The sun was setting gloriously, making every thing look cheerful and serene and having his place filled by his sister the moon who filled well her sphere, illuminating our little planet with a softer light. We went home about 8 and Mr. & Mrs. Colledge & Inglis took tea with us. We sit upon the terrace & enjoyed the delightful breeze from the ocean.

29 Had to go to Chinnery's this morning where I stayed till two. My picture comes on famously, but will not be finished for the *Beta*. Mr. C. and I had a great variety of conversation. He makes himself very agreeable. Caroline came at 1 and then I went home with her till three. Then to dinner. Did not walk in the afternoon, spent the evening at home.

30 Had our french lesson this morning, think we make progress. Allport and van Basel called. I wrote several letters in different directions. Walked after dinner. On our return met the C's [Colledges] and Blight, we sit upon a China <u>tombstone</u> for sometime chatting and laughing. I could not help thinking with what different feelings to what we should have set upon the graves of an unknown countryman. It is strange, but I suppose it is because we have no sympathy, no feeling in Common with the Chinese. As I passed along I noticed some Chinamen about <u>Chin Chinning</u> their fathers as they term it. I walked up to the grave to see what they had prepared. They had an immense quantity of gilded papers which they were about to <u>burn</u>. Then I counted 15 different messes of "<u>chow chow</u>" or food which they were to place there I believe with the idea that they come forth or the spirit and eat it and find they are still remembered. I noticed in the *Evangelist* (a paper just published)[17] a prayer offered at these times which I will copy thinking you may not see the paper. At these times you see all the graves with a piece of red and white paper put upon the top of the mound and two fresh pieces of turf dug from another place to keep it down. There is something written upon these papers which of course I cannot read.

Mr. Blight took tea with us.

1ˢᵗ of May All New York in a bustle today no doubt. I think it must be terrible confusion. Mr. Ploughdon despatched the Cutter to Lintin with letters for the *Beta* and some *Chinese Repositories*[18] published in Canton in which you will find many interesting things.

Caroline & her husband called upon us today. Did not walk, finished the Life of *Madame de Maintenon* whom de Genlis makes little short of a perfect character.

We have delighted to hear of the arrival of the *Sylph*, a Ship which has been to the North to explore and sell and get gain, the great end of all mankind. They have been missing some months and reports have been circulating here that she was burnt and every other

horrid thing, but it seems they have been suffering from the opposite, extreme cold, and have been frozen up. But the expedition has
been successful and very interesting. The Chinese have treated them
with great kindness, assisting them in every way in their power, sup-
plying them with provisions but insisting that they should not pay—
a most extraordinary instance of Chinese generosity, for they are
generally (or in these parts) extremely avaricious. I have not yet heard
much of the expedition but I suppose [Charles] Gutzlaff will publish
something as he was of the party.[19]

2[d] A very hot morning but we had made up our minds to call on
the ladies as we have been very negligent of late, and we went at 11
to Mrs. Morrison's, then to Mrs. Davis's, not at home. Found her at
Mrs. Whiteman's where we had a pleasant chat. Then to Mrs.
Wimberley's, "no could see," Mrs. Grant's ditto—*Ces dames sont tous
deux grosse!* [Harriett more easily described pregnancy in French than
English.] Then to Mrs. Daniell's where we met [William] Jardine[20]
& Grant. "The great man" of Canton, Mr. J. 'case he's rich. Then
went to Lady Robinson but could not see her. Then to Mrs.
Thornhill's where we were very graciously received. Then to Mrs.
Fearon's & Mrs. Pereira's and our work is done for some time. We
called on all, found all very pleasant, although it was a hot day. Read
after dinner St. Pierre's *Studies of Nature*[21] till it was time to dress to
go to Caroline's, where we met Don Gabriel, Calvo, & Blight. A
lovely evening. The monsoon has set in strong and the evenings are
delightfully cool.

3[d] Expected Mr. Calvo this morning but he sent an excuse, so we
were obliged to give up our lesson for today. I read many of Madame
de Sévignés letters, which are very interesting. We had a call from
Jardine & Grant. He entertained us much with some anecdotes of
the expedition to the North. The circumstance I mentioned on the
last page of the unheard of generosity of the Chinese, was done from
fear, they said they would give them any thing to leave the place.
They appear to have the same character there as here. Governed by
fear and interest, it is I know too much the case with all mankind
but appears to me never so unadulterated as here. They seem to have
no feelings of pity or compassion in their nature.

Mr. Gutzlaff being so good an interpreter was a great assistance.
He was obliged to carry the laws of the Empire with him, and when

they objected to ask them Why? If they said it was against the Emperor's order, he would then show them they were wrong, and that the laws were immutable.[22] By thus reasoning with them they made out to succeed, but Mr. Jardine thinks there is no hope of forming any commercial treaty with them as they are so jealous of innovation, and so immutable as their laws certainly are. Mr. G. will I suppose publish his adventures and I will say no more upon the subject at present at any rate.

I read all the afternoon. I get mulled over books all of them and yet am not happy without having one in my hand.

Aunt Low went to a musical party at Mr. Plowden's. I stayed home alone. Sit upon the terrace and enjoyed my own reflections —read a little, but there is no peace in reading or writing hot evenings. The mosquitoes are so busy that you lose all patience if near a light. All the world at Plowdens' tonight. They had some fine music Aunty said.

4ᵗʰ Expected to have gone to Chinnery's this morning but he could not wait upon me. The Opera is postponed tonight on account of the sickness of the Operators till next Tuesday night.

So you see we make plans for a day, but they are all defeated without our having the least power to prevent it. What passive creatures we are! And how different this day has passed from what I anticipated in the morning. Wonderful to begin with I got up at six after which should have been expected some great change. Did a little work before breakfast, then studied, got tired, and went to see Caroline where I spent 2 hours. Met there Inglis, Plowden & Thornhill. A tremendous shower while I was there. However held up at three and I went home to dinner. We are expecting Uncle and Aunty always gets in a figit afraid he will not come. Long to see him. We have both got dull and want to see him. Well we dined got up from table and walked on the terrace as usual. Saw the *Sylph*[23] just arrived from Canton. Run for the glass and had the felicity of seeing the dear soul just coming on shore in a Tanka boat.[24] We were delighted of course. He's looking well and now I hope will stay with us some time. He had no sooner got into the house than he espied a Ship coming in which looks like an American, perhaps the *Hamilton*. She has gone to Lintin.

Then Caroline come to see Uncle, and we walked home with her. Uncle brings us dreadful news from America via S[outh]

A[merica] & Sandwich Islands, that is the re-election of Jackson and
the Declaration of Independence of the S. Carolinians.[25] Well it is
"truly awful" I think that the <u>people</u> should choose such a man. It is
a disgrace to the country and I shall be prepared to hear any thing.
The dissolution of the Union will follow I dare say. And the next
thing Jackson will be declared King, Emperor or something of the
kind, and about the time we are ready to come home there will be
civil war and all sorts of evils may be anticipated. Well I shall no
longer fight for the happiness of our government, when such a man
as Jackson can fill the highest station, by consent of the <u>people</u> too.
I have been scolding furiously about it. Even stopped on the Quay
several times by the sound of Miss Low, "hope you have recovered?
Thank you I have quite but was not aware I had been ill. Why you
did not patronize the Concert last night." "Well," I said, "I did not
send word I was sick—I said I was <u>lazy</u>" which certainly was my excuse
and no disposition to go to their concerts.

So I shall be bothered. "There's no peace for the wicked." [Isaiah
48:22] Mr. Blight & Allport took tea with us. Aunty's picture came
home, which Uncle is much pleased with.

5th Rainy day. Uncle & Aunty gone to Church, and I have read a
sermon to myself, quite as good as what they will hear. Mr heart goes
pit a pat every time I hear a step thinking I shall see a heap of <u>let-
ters</u>. Now the boy has come and brought us some delicious Mangoes
from Don Gabriel—they are from Manilla. I think I have described
them to you before.

Eve'g. We hear the Ship is the *Ninus* from Boston in November
last from Batavia, but no letters. The Ships from all parts of the world
come tumbling in with the southerly monsoon. Rumours of war in
Europe, and alas I fear what may be the next news from our own
happy country. Dr. Bradford came down yesterday and called on us
today. Had no walk as it had rained so hard, as a sort of <u>treat</u> I read
over some of your letters my dear. I am thinking of putting them in
some order, but I almost despair of doing it, for now they are all mixed
up together and I fear I shall never find out <u>which</u> is <u>which</u>.

Bradford spent the evening with us. I exerted myself to make
Harriett Low agreeable. Succeeded tolerably well I think.

6th Studied all the morning till near 2, then dressed and went in to
see Sir George & Lady Robinson. They have been to see my picture

and say it is to the life. So does every one, and I only hope you will think so too. I long to have it go to you. Uncle has been to see it and likes it much. Bradford dined with us. A cold northerly wind today and a great change in the temperature, cloudy and a little <u>misty</u>.

Braddy & I walked after dinner. Fine air but a little rain. An arrival from Manilla and I had a letter from H[enry Parkman] Sturgis in answer to one I wrote him with some wedding cake. Says he is going home via China next year, so we shall see him.

We talked most of the evening. I read a little of Mrs. Heman's *Poems* aloud to Aunty and Uncle. And now I am going to bed, for the mosquitoes are so troublesome they cheat me of an hour every night.

7th Up at 6 this morning, an event that should be put down in black and white for its rare occurrence. The wind still keeps cold and the gentlemen have found it necessary to put on coats again. Such sudden changes I should think must be trying to invalids, but thank heaven I have such good health that I feel well in all. Chinnery & Bradford breakfasted with us. As Mr. C. says, he "<u>goes</u> upon breakfast" meaning he likes good breakfast. He gets up at 6 o'clock and goes out and makes sketches and earns his breakfast certainly. Uncle set for his picture today. We had our French lesson but were interrupted by company, Mrs. Fearon and Mr. Tuckerman, and it was shortened very much to my annoyance. Mr. T. is son of the clergyman of that name in Boston. I went to Caroline's at 1/2 past 1 and stayed till 3. We pinned up <u>Turbans</u> to wear to the Opera tonight. Went home and dined and went to her at 7 and went with her. *Our <u>turbans</u> were pronounced elegant. They were made of Benares muslin scarfs. Hers, is blue & silver, mine white and silver. They were both presents. They are such as the higher class *natives [marginal note: *of Bengal] wear. The same opera was performed to a full house. The singing was very good, but I do not much like the play, though they <u>act</u> very well. Madame Scheroni was not quite well, but sung beautifully.

* That was by partial eyes. You will observe what follows regarding them. Aug. 17th

8th Do not feel very well. However read and studied all the morning. Uncle & Aunt at Chinnery's. Don Gabriel & Plowden sent cards, but I told them to say "Mrs. <u>have</u> go <u>out</u>." But Mr. & Mrs. Wimberley would come in. They wanted to see Aunty's picture which happened to be at C's undergoing operations. Mr. W. is raised two or three pegs in my estimation by declining the Opera. They had tickets given them for the Season but they do not go. It appears as though he took some interest in his profession and can make some sacrifices for it, which I fear would not have been the case with my <u>friend</u> [Vachell].

I did not walk after dinner, but Caroline sent for me to come there to her and sent Bradford for me so I went and had a pleasant time. A number of gentlemen there. We played "old maids" and had <u>fine</u> <u>fun</u>. They were speaking of our Turbans. I find [mine] was not <u>generally</u> thought becoming. Indeed they begged me not to wear it again—the fact is the house was not lighted enough to display its beauties. Beside it was a Turban that belonged to an <u>ancient</u> spinster. So you see how we are deceived. I went away perfectly satisfied with myself, not having a <u>doubt</u> but that I should be the "<u>observed</u> of <u>all</u> <u>observers</u>" [*Hamlet*, III, Sc.1]—<u>that</u>, perhaps I was but not the "<u>admired</u> of all admirers." Well I don't care much. I generally have the credit of dressing with taste! Hum! "The American ladies are said to be the best dressed ladies of the place"—because we are always <u>neat</u>. The clothes of many of the ladies, the gents say, look as they were <u>thrown</u> on with a <u>pitch</u> <u>fork</u>.

After dinner we saw the *Beta* go out. "Homeward they steer to the land of their loves." Well may they have a pleasant passage and safe return.

My little Ellen's birth day too, 6 years old. Oh dear how she must have altered. God bless her. How impatient I am to see them all.

9th A lovely morning and so continued through the day. At 11 we all went to Chinnery's, we all are there also in <u>effigy</u>. He will have an excellent likeness of Uncle. I drew while Uncle was sitting. When we got home we found letters from England and one from Mrs. Allport. She is a dear soul and she is expected here again this summer. She appears delighted with England.

After dinner went out to the hills. I went mostly in my chair not feeling quite well. Blight joined me coming home and amused me very much with his <u>sentiments</u> as usual. He is a strange fish. Generally makes me his <u>mother</u> <u>confessor</u>, quite an <u>unsolicited</u> <u>honour</u>. He has been much too long in China. However I believe he is about as contented as most people. His self love makes up for a deficiency of other people's and having a pretty good disposition he appreciates the blessings he does possess—which is more than every one does. Miss "Laura" alias <u>Bradford</u> spent the evening with us and I had to entertain him. I miss Caroline very much at these times, for together we used to have great sport.

10 Went to Chinnery's this morning to have my own face painted. Set there with all the patience I could muster from 11 till 3, in hopes it would be the last, but there is one more to come. The room is so hot that it is almost insupportable, not a breath of air allowed to enter from out of doors. But there is one satisfaction that it must give you pleasure (the likeness I mean) for it is said by every one to be <u>perfect</u>. They think I must have run against the canvass and left an impression—so I think of the pleasure with which you will see it and it consoles me for all the exertion I make in this hot weather. Blight was kind enough to go with me and Bradford and Uncle stayed part of the time. I was quite exhausted before I left. However had some dinner and stretched myself upon the couch and felt better. Had a walk, met Caroline, so we had one <u>old</u> party. Set and chatted at Casilhas Bay and then returned to our respective domiciles, where Blight gave us his company at tea.

11 Hot calm morning, but the wind changed to the North before noon and it was quite cool. Calvo came at 11 and we had a very good lesson. He is an intelligent fellow and very observing and we have great sport with him. He & I are obliged to <u>dispute</u> for the sake of conversing. He has the advantage speaking in his own language. He is quite French in manners and feelings.

We had a dinner party consisting of Mr. & Mrs. Colledge, Mr. Inglis, Bradford & Blight. All Americans but <u>two</u>, and as Colledge has married an American lady we take him on our side and Inglis has been there considerable and is a great <u>lover</u> of it, to say nothing of having lost his heart to one of our Boston belles, which is said to be the cause of his being still a bachelor. <u>She</u> is now married. We had a very pleasant party indeed. Had torrents of rain today. Vessels have arrived from Calcutta, bringing some unpleasant intelligence for some of our friends. Also brought papers from America and letters from home to the 30th of November but none for me alas. There were packages immense for others, but I had none. Well there is one comfort, I have been become accustomed to these feelings now and

I make the best of it and patiently endure what I cannot cure. So I eat my dinner and tried to forget them. The evening party was Caroline, Bradford, Inglis, Hudleston, & Chinnery. Had a very pleasant evening.

12th A rainy day—however went to Church and heard a pretty good sermon. The text was "Be ye not only hearers of the Word but doers also." [James 1:22] That being the text you will conclude the purport of the Sermon. As Mr. W[imberley] always sticks to the text, there was nothing new said upon the subject, but was well written, reminding us of our duty, and very much to the purpose, for it certainly is a great failing with all of us here, that we are <u>hearers</u> and not <u>doers</u>.

Bradford dined with us. After dinner it was tolerably pleasant and as Aunt Low nor Uncle were neither very well I took my chair and called for Caroline and we had a quiet walk to the Peña to one of our old haunts where <u>Miss</u> <u>Shillaber</u> and I used to walk. We turned our thoughts upon the past and painted some fancy pictures for the future and talked of the present, a time which we are too much disposed to undervalue. I took tea with her and then went home. There is no comfort in writing you nights now my dear for the mosquitoes are so troublesome that I am glad to put myself under the curtains for a little repose. For I must confess, insignificant as they are they ruffle my temper and discompose my nerves. And it is the more annoying, their boasting so loudly of their triumphs. I would not grudge them a living from my <u>person</u> if they would take it quietly and go off, but that seems not to be their aim. And much as I often feel inclined to write at night when I am still and every thing else beside, I am obliged to acknowledge myself conquered and retire from the field. So my dear you do not know what brilliant <u>ideas</u> you <u>may</u> lose and what fine <u>sentiments</u>—the collection of a day which may all <u>evaporate</u> before the next morning.

13th This morning about <u>2</u> we were awoke by the guns, drums & Bells all proclaiming in their different <u>languages</u> <u>fire</u>, a very rare occurrence here. Indeed I hardly remember it at all, so that it did not occur to me that it could be fire. I heard a great noise, but thinking or supposing it must be daylight I concluded it was some <u>feast</u> day which is certainly not rare, so I turned over and went to sleep. It seems it was a <u>salt</u> merchant's establishment in the bazaar. In consequence the price of salt has risen 20 cash on the "Catty." So you see they make the public pay for it.

After breakfast I went to my room where I stayed till three o'clock undisturbed (except by a short call from Mr. Plowden) and Uncle & Aunt were both at Chinnery's. I busied myself turning English into French. Rather difficult at first but I succeed tolerably well. You may think I spend a great deal of time learning languages and so I do, but I do not feel that I waste the time, for independently of the pleasure and benefit of learning the language, or rather of knowing it, I think it is of advantage having some fixed occupation. It fixes the attention too. I might spend a great deal of time in reading but in the warm weather one is apt to fall into a dreamy state over a book. You become weary of constant reading and require some stimulus to make any exertion. So I think it far better to divide the time as I do, and I always feel that I have not a moment to waste. It requires an effort at times to study, but I exert myself and I find I always fret less. If I think much of home and other things I become discontented & unhappy, thereby making myself uncomfortable in the present time and when I seriously reflect I am obliged to reproach myself for ingratitude for the many blessings I do possess. And perhaps the time may come when with more positive miseries or troubles I shall have to look back upon the time spent in Macao as at any rate the most quiet and most free from troubles, if not the happiest portion of my life—but it does not seem to be in our natures to enjoy the present. I bitterly sigh for home in spite of all my endeavours to the contrary. Time passes rapidly and yet I am continually wishing [it would] quicken its flight till I shall be again with my friends—but enough of this.

After dinner I read the travels of a German Prince in England, part of the same I mentioned a little while ago. [vol. 5, January 30, 1833] Very interesting. It is a fine offset to Mrs. Trollope's, and some parallel cases, which I shall take for my weapons of defense the next time I am attacked on that score. He seems to be an inveterate hater of English people and manners. It seems he was affected with a "Parkomania" and went to England to visit the Parks which are unrivalled in the world. Think you would like it if you can get it. I think many traits of English character must be true as it suits very well most of our friends here and the idea I had formed of them from other books. I must confess I am not an admirer of them. He is very sarcastic, and whips them well in some parts. At 6 we went out to the Campo and set at Casilha's where we were joined by Plowden, Caroline, Colledge, and Bradford. Talked till nearly dark, enjoyed the fine breeze, delightful sunset and *par* contrast were tormented all the way home by the <u>cock chafers</u> which buzz about at this season and every now and then give one an unceremonious box in the ear or nose so that keeps one warring continually. They are short lived, they come out of the ground, take wing, devour the bamboo, and die. It is singular to see what network they make of the leaves of the bamboo in a short time. Came home and Bradford saw fit to "*bebe cha*" with us.

14 This morning up early and went to studying. Made the most of my time till 11 when Calvo came. Had a good lesson and says my translation is very good, which pleases me.

Went to Caroline's at 2. Came home and dined. Read the travels [of a German prince] till dark. We have walked and talked by turns, and read this evening, and as there is a tolerable draught through my room I have made out to bring up my journal. Now here comes a great long cooly walking like an elephant to shut up the house and I shall bid you good night and rest awhile.

15 Went to Chinnery's this morning for my last sitting. The likeness is said to be perfect, but I think it is a very ugly person. It has not raised my vanity in the least. I sit till near three till I was quite exhausted, very glad to leave the "Studio." Walked a "<u>short piece</u>" (as they say in Weare), sit upon the hills and as usual enjoyed the breeze. Then came home and did *comme à l'ordinaire*, which I think you must be very tired of hearing. There is nothing here now to interest. Everyone seems more dead than alive. The only exertion made by any one is to keep as far from all others as possible. I suppose when the strangers come on and the Ships come in [about September 1st] the good people will mix a little more but at present it is <u>atrociously</u> dull.

16 Mr. Chinnery breakfasted with us this morning. He is particularly disagreeable at breakfast, being something of a <u>gourmand</u> and not particular in his <u>manner</u> of eating.

Capt. Little called after breakfast. Our "<u>Conrad</u>"—fine looking man, except being too thin. He dined with us. Uncle and Aunt went to Chinnery's. I remained at home and studied till two when Caroline came and we had a frolic as usual when she comes here. Soon after the <u>folks</u> and Bradford came in.

Walked after dinner, joined by C. & Bradford. Just got comfortably seated and it commenced raining, so we had to move. Did not get much wet however. I spent the evening with Caroline. We read a Tragedy called *Fazio*,[26] one played by Miss [Fanny] Kemble lately in New York. It is very good and it is said she performed the character of "Bianca" perfectly. Came home feeling very *triste*. Why, I cannot say. I do suffer more from low spirits than I ever did before. What a light hearted thing I used to be. Now I hardly find any thing to make me feel really merry. I laugh of course, but I have lost the feelings I once had. 'Tis <u>introspection</u> I think. The past year has been I can truly say the most melancholy that I ever passed. At least I may say there has been more positive feeling of both kinds, both pleasure and pain—but would that it had never been!! But it is against my principles to murmur for what I cannot avoid, at least to murmur <u>loud</u>. So I forbear. It is useless to recall the past events. *O monde! O monde!* as Napoleon used to exclaim. I sometimes feel quite sick of it, but I will now bid you good night or I shall become <u>sentimental</u>, and that is out of fashion.

17 Engaged all the morning with Calvo. He says we make progress daily, which is encouraging. Bradford dined with us and Caroline, Calvo and Bradford spent the evening with us. I found it difficult to keep awake. Thus has finished my 23d year. Only think, it expired tonight—how shocking! Well it cannot be helped can it? I see I am looking much older than I did.

18 Bradford breakfasted with us. Felt very miserably today. Had an <u>oppression</u> which has kept me sighing. You know my old complaint of wanting to <u>draw</u> a <u>long</u> breath. However went to Chinnery's with Uncle as he was to have his last sitting. Drew a little but I do not take the same interest in this amusement as I did <u>last</u> year. The change of <u>masters</u> [W. W. Wood was her drawing master] makes a great difference I find. Besides it recalls many circumstances which were as well forgotten.

Bradford was there also. It was hot and uncomfortable and I was quite tired. Went home and finished the "Travels of the Prince" in England. He gives a shocking idea of English fashionable Society. He is a very pleasing writer. At 7 Bradford came and we went to the

Opera at 8. Had some fine music. The play was called the *Italians in Alg[i]ers*.[27] The dresses were rich and most of the characters well supported. It was very amusing. You would laugh at our stage which is 10 feet high, 16 wide, and 20 deep. The tallest man, Pizzony [Signor D. Pizzoni] nearly touches the ceiling, but the music is the thing, and we laugh at the rest. It was over about 11. Thus has ended my birthday!

19 Heard a very good sermon from Mr. Wimberley today. The text was "Come unto me all ye that labour and are heavy laden and I will give you rest." [Matthew 11:28]

Do not feel quite well today. Have become Bilious and that causes depression of Spirits and Sleepiness. It is with the greatest difficulty I can keep awake. Went to sleep twice before dinner. Caroline and her brother in. Uncle went to Lintin this morning, but coming back tonight. Nothing to say for I am too stupid to have an idea so excuse me my dear. I should like some letters better than any thing, for it seems an age since I heard from you. After dinner I took a book and went to Casilha's in my chair where I ensconced myself behind some rocks with the broad ocean before me and out of sight of the numerous parties around me. There I really enjoyed about an hour and a half undisturbed. Saw the Cutter coming in slowly. Also a Ship to bring us news from distant lands, but from whence I could not tell but hope. I then joined a party just below whose voices I could distinctly hear without their being aware that I was near. However I did not listen. They were astonished to see me spring up as they thought they were above every one. I walked home with Sir George and Lady Robinson. Uncle came soon after.

20 Studied part of the morning, then went to Caroline's. Torrents of rain daily. She invited me to dinner, was going to have a spinster party, but I would not go. Told her I would come in the evening. She had Miss Morrison, the Misses Pereiras and the Misses Ullman, and all the bachelors in the place—quite a turn out. It was very hot and rather stupid.

21 The Ship on Sunday was the *Peruvian* from England, bringing an American paper to the 5th of December. No news. The Carolinians seem to be taking a decided stand. I fear for the peace and quiet of the Union—a division seems to be at hand. She spoke the *Gaspar* from America. Now if any one had have written by her I should have got them. She was bound to Batavia. Inglis in this morning. Calvo did not come. Shillaber dined with us. He is not a favorite in Canton or Macao.[28] Went out after dinner, met Caroline—but strong symptoms of rain. Bradford spent the evening with us.

22 This morning Josepha did not call me and I slept till 8 o'clock very much to my annoyance. Read one of Moliere's Plays before Calvo came. He is not a favorite writer of mine however though some of his Comedies are good. Calvo came at 12 and I had my lesson alone as Aunty *était un peu malade*. I wrote a French letter which was pronounced *très bien*. I think I progress daily—it is quite an amusement too. C. is a fine young man and makes an excellent <u>master</u>. After he left I wrote my exercises for the next lesson. Torrents of <u>rain</u> last night and today.

After dinner read History a while. I have now reached the reign of George the Second of England. I turned from this to St. Pierre's *Studies of nature*. I love to contrast the discords of man with the harmony of <u>Nature</u>. History lessens your respect for men, the study of nature leads you to admire more the author of all. In the evening as we were alone I took *Woodstock*, one of Sir Walter's,[29] and got quite interested in it. It is written or at least the scenes are in the time of Cromwell just before the restoration of the Monarchy. As I had been reading this lately, I thought it would come in well and I allow myself a novel now and then as *sauce piquante*. I read till 10 when I was so tormented with mosquitoes that I thought it best to undress and screen myself inside the curtains, for it was a hot sultry night and no wind any where. So I did and read till 1/2 past 11, when the tempting pillow could no longer be resisted. Beside my eyes ached. I am afraid to try them too much for if I was to lose them what would become of me. <u>Little</u> as they are, they add more to my happiness than any of the other senses I am sure. So you see all my vanity consists in a change of books. I am generally very contented with one however but perhaps should take it with more zest if I was to meet some <u>dear</u> <u>friend</u> to converse about it. But we must submit to fate whatever it may be—mine in comparison to some is perfect bliss. And I ought to be grateful rather than repine for the many blessing I enjoy.

23 Four years ago today I was with you my dear, but feeling *triste* enough. I can hardly look back to the three months before we left with pleasure, for it was a species of <u>torture</u>. I never shall forget the variety of feelings I had—inclination drawing me one way and duty another. To resign for such a length of time all the delights of home and to sever as it were the dearest ties for a strange land and strange people is no trifling event, though I must confess I have much greater respect for my character and my <u>resolution</u> than I should have had, had I yielded to its <u>weakness</u>. I have gained a world of experience in the time which I hope will not be lost.

Bradford dined with us today. Almost forgot about it, for I left my book a week ago and have not written since. The mosquitoes are so busy at night that I find it impossible to write, and therefore I neglect it.

24 Four years today since I said Adieu, since I bid "my native land good night." In less than two I hope to be hailing it again.

Spent the day with my French. Calvo came and we find we make progress daily. After dinner I read English—History generally. And in the evening if we have no company I treat myself to a novel. Read *Woodstock* this evening. I had never read it before, and as I have been reading about the time of Cromwell I felt interested though I do not think it is one of Sir W[alter]'s best.

Went to see Colly awhile.

25 Caroline in this morning. I went and dined with her at 4. Mr. Robertson & Shillaber there, no one else. Went home after dinner. Aunt Low and Uncle and all the people went to the Opera, but I took it into my head that I would not go, so stayed at home and read by myself.

26 Went to Church this morning. Think I never heard a more simple sermon. The text was "And they were all with one accord in one place and there came a sound from heaven like the rushing of a mighty wind and filled all the house [where they] were sitting" and the next verse. [Acts 2:1–3] He divided [it] into four parts, dwelt long and in a very simple manner upon their (the 12) being in one place and made out that the noise was a sudden mighty wind, whereas the text says no such thing. I do not [know] what the good people of Boston would have said to it—to write one sermon a week, and such a one as that. I stayed to communion.

I hear there is a ship to sail for home soon so I shall have a chance to send my picture and write again.

Took a quiet walk after dinner. Evening we were alone. I was descanting on the miseries of an idle life—anything is preferable. To feel that you have nothing to do from morning till night. Were it not for my love of reading I should be miserable, but how much more I should enjoy it if I took it at intervals. I thought of Mother and said I believe with all the cares, pains and troubles she had had in bringing up her family she has been far happier than though she had been idle. For my own part I would rather have a host of children I think. But it's no use to complain.

27 French as usual. Finished a letter for home. Shillaber and Bradford dined with us. The "duke of Gordon" called, just arrived from Canton. Caroline and the others spent the evening. Finished *Woodstock*. Like it very well.

28 Calvo came this morning. Our lesson lasted till two. Then I went to Caroline's till 5. Came home and dined and then read till it was time to walk. A lovely evening as ever was. Went out, set on a rock, which by the bye was very hard, a property which you are probably not aware rocks possess. Lindsay came and had a chat—finding me alone, as Uncle & Aunt had gone round the hills. He is going home this year via Bombay, and over land to Egypt, Alexandria, Jericho & Jerusalem, etc. He has the spirit of adventure most fully developed. Came home, changed my shoes, and spent the eve'g with C. where I found her delectable *père* [Dr. Colledge].

29 This morning studied and took a dose of salts, for what I cannot say. Fancied I was Billious or ought to be from the quantity of cucumbers I have eaten of late. It is astonishing what good health I have, and always eat just what I fancy. And other people are mincing and fearing to eat this, that, and the other. I verily believe it is of the imagination. But I suppose it is wrong for me to be so uncharitable. I only ought to be thankful that mine is so much better.

Calvo dined with us and we talked French, made out very well. We had a delightful walk to the Peña, went to some of our old haunts. Some consecrated rocks, and I sung, "But oh there are so many things, recall the past to me" and so there are. There is not a hill in the place but that has some event which I always think of.

It was a perfect evening, cool and pleasant. Came home and spent the evening in reading *Brambletye House*,[30] written at the same time

Woodstock is, and the same subjects for its story. It was rather a singular coincidence. It is very well written and worthy of Walter Scott. Now I have brought up my book and shall bid you good morning. I do not like to neglect it because I always have to be very <u>concise</u> when I do, and I like to be "<u>copious</u>" as Haskell [a younger brother] says.

30 Sometimes. The above was written before breakfast. Quite a merry day for us. Mr. Latimer & [John C.] Green arrived last night very unexpectedly. He and Bradford called first about 11, then Inglis, Bradford, and Greene last. They came down for the <u>Opera</u>. Green has not improved in appearance I think. He spoke of having seen you all but it is so long since, now over a year.

The first thing I heard from Latimer was about the <u>Turbans</u> C. & I wore to the Opera. I tell you this to give you an idea of the trifling things these people talk about. One has only to do a little different from other people and you are talked of from Macao to Canton. I told him I did not wish to hear any thing about it. I felt <u>cross</u> to think they make such a fuss about nothing. I could not tell whether he was laughing at it or not, for I stopped him. I was quite indifferent whether it pleased or not.

Dined alone, read after dinner, and went to the opera at 8. The house was very full—all the "beauty and fashion" of Macao was there. A perfect night, cool and clear. We were however very much scandalized at seeing enter <u>a</u> <u>certain</u> <u>lady</u> (whom no decent lady would associate with, and whom no <u>gentleman</u> would have sent there, *savez vous?*) covered with <u>diamonds</u> head, neck, and ears, looking as impudent as possible with the servant behind her. When I come home "I can a tale unfold concerning this which would harrow up your very soul," [Shakespeare, *Hamlet*, Act I, Sc. 4,] but I cannot <u>disgrace</u> my book with it. I came from the Opera and begged Uncle the next time she comes into the house to <u>hiss</u> her.

Now to the singing. Scheroni [Signora T. Schieroni] as Almenaide [Amenaide in *Tancredi* (1813) by Gioachino Rossini] was quite enchanting. The dresses one and all were <u>splendid</u>. But what appears to me almost a miracle is the compass S. screws herself into to come on to the stage. And then to sing laced in this manner it is quite <u>shocking</u> to think of. Caravaglia in the character of Tancredi did very well, much better than usual. But poor thing she is quite *passé* and not fit to sing. Her lungs appear affected and it distresses you to hear her sing at times. I begin to admire the Italian music very much. It is quite an acquired taste.

31 This morning I read the Opera in Spanish. Shall enjoy it more next time. Had a bad cold in my head. Could not study so went to see Caroline awhile. Explained the play to her and came home and read *Brambletye House*, a capital thing. Commences during the time of Cromwell, takes in the restoration of Charles the Second, gives you a description of his dissolute court and the favourites of the times and the plague and great fire. It is very interesting and impresses these historical facts upon your memory.

At 3 we went to dine with Plowden, a party of 12, no ladies but ourselves and Mrs. Colledge. Had a very pleasant party. After dinner we jumped into a boat which [was] waiting for us in front of the house and went to the Lappa to see or hear a sounding rock which from its peculiar situation and the metals in it sounds like a Church Bell. Indeed there are a number. It appears very curious. The walk was delightful. The scenery on that side is quite perfect, much prettier than in Macao. All the way at one side runs a clear stream of water called the river "Inha." It is about 2 ft. wide most of the way, but in places widens into a lake where the washing is done of the Portuguese and English in Macao. The rocks are their scrubbing boards and you may judge what work they make. But this said stream forms in some places pretty little falls, which contrasted with the green around is beautiful. Then the high hills on either side with the full moon in the heavens and the broad ocean seen through an opening of the hills in the distance is quite lovely. I always feel better for going here, it is so charming and such a relief from going daily to the Campo. We got back about 8 and went into Plowden's to tea and stayed till after 9 and then I went home with Caroline and set talking in her verandah till 11. Then came home and went to bed. Quite a day this has been.

June 1ˢᵗ Latimer & Bradford stayed an hour this morning. L. will laugh about the Turban. At last I said, "Do hold your tongues about that for I am sick of it." So he quoted the old Antiquary, who you remember used to plague his nephew about the Seal till he became very impatient. At last the gentleman said he never would mention the Phoca again even if he wished to seal a letter.[31] You will remember it I dare say. And Latimer says I never will mention the covering for the <u>head</u> in any way. Now they make all manner of fun. It is a standing joke here. Only the word <u>Turban</u> must not be used, so they go the most round about way possible to ask for their <u>hat</u>. Bradford told a Parsee he wished to introduce him, but he must not wear his <u>Turban</u>. The poor man was shocked beyond measure at the thought of appearing without his head dress.

Green, Latimer and Bradford dined with us, had a very pleasant time. Walked after dinner with Bradford. We all met at Casilha's— Aunt & Uncle, Caroline, Green, Bradford, Hudleston, & Campbell. Enjoyed the breeze and then went home and dressed for the <u>Opera</u>. *Tancredi* was repeated. I never had a pleasanter time, that is I never enjoyed the music more, it was rich. They were all in fine voice to-night. I begin to love it. I was thinking how father would enjoy it if he would allow himself to go. I am sure I can see not the least harm in it, at least in such a place as this. The <u>effects</u> in other places I have never been able to judge. I had a book and followed them tonight. The Italian language seems made for singing, and they articulate every word so distinctly that [it] is very pleasant to hear that alone.

2ᵈ I found by chance that May had 31 days. [Refers to renumbering the dates from May 31 to June 2.] Did not go to Church this morning. Stayed at home and read first a review upon <u>revivals</u>, then some of Buckminster's excellent sermons, which from all accounts was much better than what Mr. W[imberley] give them. It was today what is called Trinity Sunday and the creed of St. Athanasius was read, which I cannot fancy that a man in his senses could have <u>written</u> in any age, and much more a man of his senses read in this enlightened age. I believe it is not common to read it, but Mr. W. is [a] thorough going Church man. Shillaber & Latimer came in after Church. We walked after dinner—went to a retired place behind the hills, but were joined by Latimer, Bradford, Gordon, Greene, and a Mr. [Henry] Lawrence³² to whom I was introduced while <u>fighting</u> a <u>small</u> <u>battle</u> with Mr. Latimer. They all spent the evening with us.

3ᵈ Mr. Green gave us the <u>pleasure</u> of his company this morning, he had been at Chinnery's. Does not seem to like my picture. After dinner Uncle, Aunt & I had a long discussion upon wealth, happiness, & etc. I told Uncle just what I wanted, and he says I shall never be happier than at <u>this</u> <u>moment</u>. Woe is me if I am not! As I did not feel quite well I did not walk. Shillaber came in and walked the terrace with me. Went to Caroline's and passed the evening. Mr. Inglis there with our family. Mr. Inglis, S. & myself were talking together all the evening—we commenced with lady's dresses, large sleeves spoiling the figure in Mr. I's opinion, from that we somehow or other went back to the days of chivalry and ended in battles. Passed a very pleasant evening—Mr. I. can be particularly agreeable. He is a delightful person. I walked home with him and S. The evening was very fine. Caroline's house was very noisy tonight. There was a fresh breeze and the sea came tumbling in so that it was with great difficulty that we could hear each other. Our house seemed so delightfully quiet when we went home that I was quite enchanted. It stands back and we have just as much of the sea as is pleasant.

4 Mr. Calvo here this morning—passed very quickly and very pleasantly. Went to Caroline's about 2 and translated to her the first act of the next play, *Edouard & Christine*.[33] Found I had passed our dinner hour so I stayed there. Went home after dinner and dressed and went to walk with Uncle. Came very near being carried away by the wind—made a great display of "feet handles" vulgarly called legs, however persevered. Mr. Inglis saw me in distress and offered me his arm. My hair without a bonnet was blowing in every direction, but the *dégagée* style is all the go here for every one sits in a draught of air, the more the better.

We at last anchored under the lee of one hill and were soon after joined by Shillaber. He and Green took tea with us. I got into a great chair in the evening and took no part in the conversation. I listened. It is not what I often do but I felt like it tonight.

5 This morning went out to breakfast and heard an American "Barque" had gone up. After breakfast saw another Ship very like an American. Both gone to Lintin, so I must have some letters in the course of the day. Studied all the morning.

Caroline in just before dinner. Latimer, Bradford, Green, Shillaber, & Gordon dined with us. Had a very pleasant time. They came back to tea and we all went to the Opera together. I fully expecting on my return to find a packet of letters, but it does appear that I am never to have any more. Uncle received one at the Opera from Capt. [Charles] Pearson of the *Gaspar* and the *Rome* arrived this morning, both from home the last of December, and not a letter. Well, I must bear it I suppose, but I should like to know the reason.

Uncle's mentions the war in Europe, the loss of the French at Antwerp, & etc.

We were highly amused with the Opera—the play was the *Barber of Seville*. [*Il barbiere di Siviglia* (1816) by Gioachino Rossini] And all appeared well acquainted with their parts and performed with great spirit. The music was fine. We hear by this arrival of War in Europe, the taking of the Citadel of Antwerp, & etc.—10,000 French reported killed.[34]

6 Studying in my own room all the morning. Green, Latimer, and others in but did not see them. Had a delightful walk after dinner with Uncle, and in the evening we had a little party—Mr. & Mrs. Daniell, the Davis's, Whiteman, & 7 or 8 other gentlemen. It was very pleasant, but after they were gone I had the treat. Uncle had received the letters from the *Gaspar* and would not tell me about it till they had gone. I had only 2 but they were both delightful, one from the good Mr. [Charles W.] Upham, and one from Mr. N. P. K[napp]. I was highly delighted I assure you. I shall answer them immediately and thank Mr. U. for his kindness. It seems father shewed him my letter on the subject of joining the Church, but he misunderstands and thinks they scrupled at my partaking of the communion which was not the case. I suppose that that letter must have been written while or before I had concluded upon the subject. I recollect Mr. V[achell] wished me to wait until I had read some books, which he sent me. Mr. U. thinks my views correct which pleases me. I think I could write a much better letter now upon the same subject as I have thought much more upon it and it is now much clearer to me than it then was. I feel exceedingly obliged to Mr. Upham for the apparent interest he takes in me.

7 This morning I dressed and set down to read papers received last night. Was exceedingly pleased with the President's Proclamation with regard to Carolina[35] and think with him that they ought to be <u>whipped</u> if they do not behave. I do not give the old gentleman the credit of writing this spirited and elegant production, but that he has had the good sense to subscribe to such sentiments has raised him some degrees in my estimation. I do not feel very anxious now about the division as I think the Carolinians will certainly yield. There seems to be terrible times in Europe too, rebellion here and rebellion there, and all about this said <u>independence</u>, a spirit which is placed in every human breast. Did not find much in the papers except <u>politics</u> to interest.

George Jenks arrived in the *Rome* but I suppose we shall not see him.

As Mr. Calvo sent an excuse this morning I had a holiday and at 1 went to Caroline's, stayed till 3. Read to her awhile.

After dinner went to walk. Saw every body! An importation of six from Canton. Came home and at 9 went to a musical party at Mr. Plowden's, had the Italians there and some amateurs. Had a very pleasant time and enjoyed the music much. Think I am becoming quite music mad.

8 Set down in the verandah after breakfast with my book and there I sat till dinner time in my morning dress, feeling quite mulled and half sick, all because I drank a glass of Champagne last night at Supper. Latimer and Bradford spent an hour with us.

After dinner went to walk as usual. B[radford] and Gordon joined me and we set upon the hill till nearly dark and then went home and had the <u>critters</u> to tea. Braddy & I were very <u>agreeable</u>.

9 Went to Church this morning. Did not much like Mr. W[imberley]. <u>Silly</u> sort of <u>sermon</u>, begging his pardon. After Church C[aroline] came home with us. Mrs. Davis called, Latimer & Bradford. Got no time to read before dinner. Since I have read two sermons upon the "Government of the Thoughts,"[36] both excellent— a subject I fully feel the importance of, but which I fear I am too lazy to attend much to, which doubles the evil. I make many good resolutions, but the watchman is often drowsy at his post. Now I have brought up my book and I shall commence a letter to Mr. Upham.

Eve'g. Did not feel like writing to Mr. U. when I commenced, so give it up. Latimer did not go to Church this morning because he <u>lent</u> his <u>coat</u> to Mr. Allport—an odd reason and would astonish people out of this place, but it is very common here. They are obliged to wear a coat to Church and wearing a jacket at all other times, they often leave their coats in Canton. I took a cup of tea at home and another cup with Caroline and spent the evening.

10 Read all the morning. Some gents in but I was in my room and I did not see them. Latimer left at 4 o'clock. 3 Bombay Ships arrived today, which will take them all up. L. waved his handkerchief as he was going round the point. We went out to the Gap and set upon "Martyr [Francisco's]" tomb. It's a beautiful spot and the evening was <u>delicious</u>. Shillaber spent the evening with us and I came very near going to sleep.

11 French lesson this morning. Capt. Wemyss and [Capt. George] Melville[37] called. The former has such a <u>loving</u> wife. She calls him her "<u>blessed Bob</u>." John Morrison called, just returned from his expedition in the *Peacock*, A Sloop of War. Succeeded in their treaty at <u>Siam</u>.[38] Rainy day and I had no walk. Finished St. Pierre's *Studies of Nature*. I do not like it <u>all</u>. Evening we were alone.

12 In my room this morning till 3. Very busy writing or translating one of H. K. White's letters. Find it very interesting and the morning is gone before I am aware of it. Bradford, Gordon & Shillaber dined with us. Rainy day and no walk today. I got Memoirs of Rossini[39] from the Library and amused myself with them till it was time to go to hear one of his best Operas, *Il Barbiere de Seville*. Shillaber waited upon me. It is a capital play and some of the music very beautiful, but on the whole I prefer the music of *Tancredi*—that has made a lasting impression. Rossini had certainly a genius for music with a great knowledge of the science. He would compose music as fast as he would write letters almost, adapt it to the voices and instruments of the performers. He was excessively indolent and put off till the last moment always. He imposed often upon the Italians by sending them old music when he had delayed too long the new, and it is instantly detected by an Italian who knows his music by heart. Musicians are certainly troublesome people to deal with.

13 Another rainy day. Uncle was going to Canton but the wind is North and he cannot go. Gordon, Bradford, & Inglis in to say <u>Adieu</u>. We are very <u>melancholy</u> of course. Mr. I. was very entertaining as usual. Music and composers was the subjects. He was giving us anecdotes of "Rossini" whom he saw daily at Naples. He says he was the most indolent person in the world, reckless and extravagant. He says after the Opera in Naples they used to assemble at the house of one of the principal <u>patronesses</u> of the day for a <u>petit souper</u>. He says after the first performance of an Opera the Italians would come from the play and one after another would go to the piano and play different parts of the Opera they had been hearing. Among them the whole was often played from memory. They trusted to that altogether, as there was no printed music in Italy. Oh the Italians have certainly the souls for <u>music</u>. If I was any thing but an American I should choose to be an Italian with an English education after I was 12 years old. I admire their <u>natures</u>, do you understand what I mean. I admire their <u>enthusiasm</u>, their strength and warmth of feeling, their love of music which I think must be innate. After dinner read R[ossini]'s *Memoirs* and finished them. Some interesting anecdotes in it. Rainy day, no walk. Caroline came to see us towards night.

14 Rainy morning, no prospect of Uncle's starting. Went out to breakfast, found Capt. Gregerson[40] there, a person to whose house I remember having gone once with Grandmother many years ago. I did not remember him at all except in name. He says he used often to quarrel with my mother when he was a boy. Says he saw Father in Boston a few days before he left.

It cleared up after breakfast. Uncle & Gordon started from our house about 11, went in the *Sylph*. Beside them was Allport and Inglis. Bradford and Shillaber both took leave this morning, going in other boats. So you see we clear all off at once. Now we shall probably have no one to come for some time. Never mind, we get rid of good, bad and indifferent and if we are at peace with ourselves there is some chance of our being happy and peaceable.

After they had gone I took a Spanish book for the sake of variety to see if I had not forgotten it, but I find I read it with as much ease as ever. I got very much interested in *Numa Pompilio*.[41] After dinner I commenced Marshall's *Life of Washington*.[42] I want to <u>review</u> the proceedings of our own Country; I intend to read it attentively. I read till it was time to walk. It was a most lovely afternoon, a fine breeze for Uncle. We sit upon the rocks to "muse o'er flood and Fell"—rather to watch the glorious setting of the sun than "to trace the forest's shady scene" and it is difficult to find a spot in Macao "where mortal foot hath never been" but we can "hold converse with Nature's charms and view her stores unroll'd"—but this as Byron says "is not solitude!" [Byron, *Harold*, 2, l.224] The sun was just tinging the clouds above and they reflected their light upon the <u>foot</u> of the Islands which gave them the appearance of being all on fire at the foundation, and the blue peak of "Lantow"[43] raising itself into the clouds with its <u>fiery</u> base was quite magnificent. "Filled with the fire of heaven, which, from afar, Comes down upon the water; all its hues, From the rich sunset to the rising star, Their magical variety diffuse, And now they change; a paler shadow strews Its mantle o'er the mountains; parting day <u>Dies</u> <u>like</u> <u>the</u> <u>dolphin</u>, whom each pang imbues With a new colour as it gasps away, The last still loveliest, till—'tis gone —and all is gray." [Byron, *Harold*, 4, l.259] <u>Then</u> we went home, were joined by Caroline. Had our tea *tête à tête* and the mosquitoes drove us to bed by 10 o'clock, rather reluctantly on my part for I can never depend upon my lazy person for finding the lost hour in the morning.

15 Read, wrote and etc. all the morning. Wandered about like a distressed pigeon as my room was taken by <u>Coolies</u>, being Saturday, and a regular cleaning day. How I do hate it. About 2 I made out to get dressed and went to Caroline's till 3. Eat 2 mangoes in Indian style. How delicious! Read an article in a Magazine about a new fashioned beds for Invalids, called the "Hydrostatic Bed." It is made upon <u>water</u>—an odd idea! But I should think [it] must be very comfortable. People certainly stretch their imaginations now for comforts, but I doubt if any less people die now a days than in old times when they had not all these comforts.

Came home to dinner, went to walk at 6. We were joined by young <u>Calvo</u>. Had to muster our French, got on very well. Lovely evening again. C[aroline] sent for me to come and take tea with her, but I was too lazy. So after tea undressed and put on a loose gown and set upon the terrace and <u>star gazed</u>. Saw the <u>Southern Cross</u> set and saw a most splendid <u>meteor</u>. I meditated upon the past and anticipated the future. Built *Châteaux en Espagne* and destroyed them. Sighed "all is vanity and vexation of spirit," [Ecclesiastes 1:14] took a warm bath and went to bed, where I laid till <u>8</u> o'clock the next morning—quite abominable.

16 Asked Josepha why she let me sleep so long. She said she went to *Misa* or mass at <u>5</u> o'clock and she did not come home in time—said she thought it was Sunday and Miss Harriett would not want to <u>study</u>. You may think her getting up at 5 to go to Church is an instance of <u>piety</u>, but I think far otherwise. Much as she goes to Church and as many prayers as she says there is no more religion in her than there is in a <u>Bamboo</u>. As to <u>virtue</u> among them there is no such thing.

The other night I came home late and I asked her if she went to sleep evenings when we were out. She said No. I said what do you do evenings. She said she read prayers. Said I do you read prayers two or three hours. She said sometimes she did not get time to read any for two or three days and then she made up for <u>lost</u> <u>time</u>. I said "do you like to read them Josepha." She says, "Must, <u>liky</u> no <u>liky</u>!" She give me to understand that it was not at all agreeable but she was accountable to the padre for a certain number, which she must either read or suffer the consequences! Oh it is a vile system!

Stayed at home this morning and read some of Thatcher's excellent sermons. Then wrote a letter to Mr. Upham. Was in my room from breakfast till 6 o'clock at night with the exception of dinner. Then dressed and spent the evening with Caroline.

17 A stormy blowy and miserable day. Saw no one from morn till night but Aunty. Sent to the Library for some books but could not get them, and so had to read Molière. There are very few French books in the Library. About 3 Aunt Low received a letter from Uncle, he arrived safe in 24 hours. Mr. Wood came down in the *Sylph*. I do not know whether he will honour us with a call, he dined with Caroline. Read all the morning and afternoon the *Life of Washington*. Had to read some pages over a number of times before I could take the sense. *Savez vous pourquoi?* Oh dear—

18 Another blowing miserable day. Have been out attending to my Geraniums notwithstanding, for the wind has broken them I am sorry to find. Now we have just had an excuse from Calvo I am so sorry, for I don't know what to do with myself. Think I will write a french letter. Oh Idleness thou art the bane of happiness.

I read awhile then went to Caroline's as she had something to say to me. It was a message from Mr. [Wood], he does not intend to call. So be it!

Came home at 2 and felt *triste* enough, did nothing all the afternoon, had the blues in good earnest. However before night made some good resolutions and intend to act upon them. Commenced this evening. Took my book and by dint of exertion became interested in it and went to bed satisfied that for once I had conquered my feelings, for there is a satisfaction in conquering yourself, to feel that you have some power over your own mind if you have not over other people.

19 Well I had to get up again with very little more prospect of pleasure through the day than yesterday. However I took my books and employed myself which is the great antidote to <u>Ennui</u>.

After dinner we had a walk too. Met Mr. and Mrs. Daniell at the Bay, had a pleasant chat, came home and spent a pleasant evening at Mrs. Whiteman's. They played beautifully together on the piano and flute. The *Red Rover* arrived tonight. I went home hoping I might find some letters, but was disappointed.

20 This morning I was busy doing some odd jobs. A terrible hot day. About 12 Capt. Gregersson of the *Nile* [*Ninus*] came in and seemed quite ill—he wanted to lie on the couch a while—it seems as though strangers here were mad. He says yesterday he took a long walk in the heat of the day up the Montana,[44] which would be quite enough to addle the brains of any man I should think. He seemed feverish and I prescribed a dose of <u>salts</u>. Mixed him a powerful dose and told him he had better go to sleep. So left him. He made his escape and I have seen no more of my <u>patient</u>. He met Colledge going out, who told him he had better go to the tavern[45] and keep <u>quiet</u>. I went to Caroline's about 2 as she was not well and chatted till 3.

Came home and dined, read till 6, then went to the Peña. On the Quay we saw <u>my friend</u> [W. W. Wood]—he saw us at a distance and "<u>right about</u>" at once. We went into Caroline's to get rid of [Temple Hillyard] Layton[46] and saw him pass while we were there. Went to the Peña. It was very hot on that side, as the wind was behind the hill, and beside we had to go <u>shying</u> about to avoid company. You would laugh to see our exertions to keep from people and we are generally <u>bored</u> in some way or other. We succeeded in getting home however and I read all the evening to Aunt Low.

21 Hear that my patient is convalescent, the <u>salts</u> cured him. I expect to hear of this all over the town as it is I have heard of it from 2 or 3 different ones. Every thing flies like <u>wildfire</u> here, the more trifling the quicker it goes. This man is a great talker and tells every thing if he can find a listener. We were all prepared for our french lesson today but Calvo was *très occupé* and sent an excuse. Soon after the bell rung and who should walk in but our old friend [Thomas] <u>Fox</u> whose name you will often have seen in my books. He is a great ally of mine. He has been half over the world while we have been here still & quiet. He went home to be <u>married</u>, but <u>the</u> lady to whom he was engaged did not love him well enough to leave <u>Papa</u>. Therefore they dissolved partnership and he remains an <u>unhappy</u> <u>bachelor</u>. He was very much attached to her and had been for many years. All his plans and ideas of happiness for the future were connected with her, now they have vanished and he will probably remain a <u>celibate</u>. He is an excellent man and I think she has <u>missed</u> it. So the world goes. Disappointments is the lot of all, a <u>trite</u> but true saying. One builds castles but they are soon demolished even if built upon a good foundation, at least <u>apparently</u> good.

He came from Bombay in the *Fort William* with Mrs. <u>Neish</u> whom I have often spoken of before. The strangers begin to come in and we shall shortly have the place full.

Went out to the Gap toward night, were joined by Shillaber, soon after Caroline, College & Fox. Went home and S. spent the evening.

22 Josepha routed me out at 6 this morning (as ordered) to wash my hair—it is a dreadful operation but must be done. So I wanted to get all done before breakfast—had to sit with it over my shoulders all the morning to let it dry. Caroline came in and dined with us as her <u>hubby</u> was going to the Company's.

Read a French novel today, *Hélèn de Toumon*, very interesting. Rebecca Morrison called after dinner. Fox and Shillaber came in to tea and waited upon us to the "Opera" where was performed Rossini's Opera of *Edouard & Christine*. The music very fine, but they do not excel in the [*opera*] *Seria* here. With a comedy every thing is in <u>keeping</u>, but Tragedy or *Seria comica* will not answer. <u>My</u> <u>friend</u> [W. W. Wood] was there but did not <u>speak</u> to me.[47] I am more and more convinced that all in regard to that affair is as it should be. My feelings were very much hurt this evening as I may tell you in a letter but this book I am afraid of. It seems as though I was doomed to have all the <u>annoyances</u> possible and little things that one must bear quietly and submissively, which without gaining me any credit are ten times worse than one great event which is seen by every one and if conducted with dignity gains you some applause. I recollect seeing an observation in one of Mrs. Opie's works the other day, that struck me as being very correct which was much to this effect, that it was very easy to perform a great action now and then when the eyes of the world are upon you. Must it is the little petty every day occurrences which try the person and which makes the happiness of yourself and those around you. I went to bed in a very unhappy humour tonight, only wishing I could have an opportunity to give the gentleman a piece of my mind with my own lips. I would not spare him.

23 Went to Church today, heard a sermon but cannot say much for it. Read some of Buckminster's which are worth a dozen of his.

I went to Caroline's a few minutes. Felt sad at heart and withal a little angry. Went home and wrote a letter to you detailing my troubles. After dinner as Aunt Low would not go out, I took the chair and went alone, hoping <u>behind</u> some <u>rock</u> to dissipate the gloom. I went to <u>our</u> <u>hill</u> and ensconced myself where I could see every one but not be discovered, where the soft wind blew upon me and I was in spite of sadness enchanted with the beauties around me, the setting sun, the green forest just behind me, the ocean beyond me beaming with <u>sunny</u> <u>smiles</u>, <u>literally</u>. All seemed quiet and if there had have been no thought within I should have been as perfectly comfortable as it is possible for a mortal <u>body</u> to be. But I felt sick at heart. I had been seated about 1/2 an hour when a gang of Chinamen and boys came up and surrounded me so that I run down the hill 1/2 way but was determined they should not disturb me more. They saw I was alarmed and followed me, but I took no further notice of them and they got tired and went off. I knew there was no danger as there were people about on the other hills. I did not know but they might give my earrings a <u>twitch</u> which would not be agreeable, but a Chinaman is a great deal more civil than I fear the same class of my own countrymen would be.[48] I am sure had these been English or Americans I should not have dared sit there.

Well in removing from the top of the hill I was discovered by Mr. W[ood] who came to my rescue and made a very humble apology for his conduct last night. I was perfectly astonished at my own apparent coolness, while he was <u>choking</u> and <u>stuttering</u>, but it is astonishing what pride will do and for the <u>few</u> <u>moments</u> you would [have] thought me perfectly <u>indifferent</u>. Well I was satisfied with myself and came home feeling much better. As I have given you the whole story in a letter I will say no more.

We spent the eve'g alone and went to bed early.

24 A dreadful day, hot as possible—got tired of reading about 2 and went to Caroline's. She had been making some <u>gingerbread</u>, and not having any butter the servant brought her <u>mutton</u> <u>tallow</u>, which she put in. The Chinese think any thing in the way of <u>grease</u> will do. For their own cooking [they] use <u>lamp</u> <u>oil</u>.[49]

I did not go to walk, stayed at home and <u>mused</u> upon the terrace. Read till it was nearly dark. A lovely evening, which quite compensates for a hot day. Turned in early but it was hot.

25 Hot. Wrote letters again this morning and read the rest of the time. After dinner went out to the Gap and enjoyed the breeze. Spent the evening with Caroline where I met Mackay and Shillaber. C. told me my friend W[ood] went to her in the morning and told her with how much coldness I received his apology. Seemed quite <u>piqued</u>. Well I am glad he could not see <u>inside</u> as the Chinese say—he might have been too much flattered.

26 An intolerable hot day. Wanted a French book. Sent to the Library for the Memoirs of "Cardinal de Ritz."[50] They sent me a 1/2 dozen old worm eaten vols which I am sure I shall never read. Beside I do not care about knowing about all the intrigues, I am not enough of a politician. I am sure by the looks of them they must be very tedious, so I shall send them back forthwith. Set in the verandah with as little on as I could be decent in. We told the servant to say "<u>No</u> <u>could</u> <u>see</u>" and made ourselves comfortable. Closed my letters to send to Canton tonight.

After dinner proceeded with my American history which is very interesting. Did not walk, but took a warm bath and dressed for the <u>Opera</u>. Enjoyed the music very much and quite forgot the heat. Saw Mr. W. there but he did not speak. Reminded me of the song, "We met, t'was in a crowd," he left soon after with Shillaber for Canton, perhaps the last time I shall ever see him [Wood sailed in the brig *John Gilpin* for Manila on October 15]. Well God bless him! These things must be borne although they are grievous, all is as it should be I am convinced and could I but <u>forget</u> I should be glad, but "Time! the comforter and only healer when the heart has bled" must be my friend. Saw them start about 12, the moon shining on their sails and the breeze wafting them on. A dreadful hot night, expected I should dissolve before morning.

27 Another hot day. Find it very difficult to keep off my <u>back</u>. Think if I had any complaint in the <u>spine</u> should certainly earn it. You would think I had a very lazy life could you see me, and I fear I do. I sometimes get very tired of books.

Caroline dined with us today as her hubby was going to meet [Lancelot] Dent at the Company's. She went home about 5 and we did not go to walk as had engaged to go to her to tea. Spent a very pleasant evening, no one there but Calvo, so we had to *parler Français*.

28 A melting day again, or rather baking. I feel very well however except a listless, lifeless feeling which makes it a great exertion to do any thing, even read, and unless the book is interesting one is in great danger of going to sleep over it. If I followed my own feelings I should lie down on a couch and pass my time in a sort of reverie without thinking even if I could help it. That is I should let the thoughts come and go and use no exertion to detain them. It must be the weather and the quiet way in which we live. However do not think I give way to this. No I make the exertion and study all I can.

This morning Caroline sent us "Mrs. Trollope's *Refugee in America*,"[51] a novel just arrived here. It is a very interesting story and pleasantly written, that is the style is amusing. I dare say she touches upon many of the foibles of our countrymen, but I think she caricatures all she touches. She certainly uses a great deal of language I never heard of, but I only say in reply to the many queries on that subject that I never heard such words before. I do not know what they do in Rochester. You will read it no doubt and I dare say the words many of them will be as new to you as to me. I hope however where "she does twit upon facts" they will be improved upon, as I notice in the papers that her hints in her travels were not lost. I have no doubt such books if taken in the right spirit may do an immense deal of good. I should like to know who this said Mrs. Trollope may be. I do not believe it is a lady. I read two volumes before dinner and about 6 I went out in my chair and set alone upon [a] rock meditating and enjoying the fine breeze. A little distance from me was a heap of married ladies, but as I have no feelings in common with them I would not join them and no doubt they thought me very unsociable.[52] When I was tired I got into my chair and met Caroline on my way home and she made me go to her house to tea. No one there but Mr. Plowden, laughing about the book which he has been reading. Says he does not believe they are so bad in America. Had a very pleasant evening.

29 A dreadful hot night the last, could not sleep in comfort till I got on my couch this morning. Do not know when I have suffered so much from heat as the last week. I think because it has come on so suddenly. Every expedient is resorted to to make myself comfortable, and you would laugh at my ingenuity sometimes. This forenoon we could not dress to see any one, as we were going to dine with Caroline at 1/2 past 3. We thought we would enjoy ourselves till that time, and we had a ratan carpet from Canton this morning to cover the verandah. It was nice and cool there. So out went my sofa cushions and in a few minutes there was I with my book stretched upon the carpet with a delightful breeze blowing upon me, and following General Washington through his glorious cause. Finished Mrs. Trollope too this morning. Was very much interested in both and it was time to dress for dinner before I had thought of it, so I had to hurry which is not pleasant of a warm day. However got there in time. The party was made for Mr. Dent. It consisted of <u>ourselves</u> to begin with, Mr. Hudleston, Gover, [Thomas] Beale, Rieves, a very pleasant party. Hudleston handed me to the table. The *Refugee* is the subject now. They think as I told them that we have a capital offset in the travels of the German Prince which they say is almost invariably <u>true</u>.

After dinner we were sitting in the verandah and saw 4 ships come round the point one after the other in rapid succession, all from Bombay, with opium. How I wished one might be an American.

We went out to Casilha's in our chairs and then home to dress for the evening—quite a large party of gentlemen and Mrs. Clifton. A Mr. [William] Dallas[53] whom we saw over two years since here came in one of these Ships. It seems but a week since he left. *Que le temps passe!*

Pleynell was there and performed beautifully upon the violin. Came home, took a warm bath and went to bed.

30th Letter from Uncle this morning. Says Father's letter says one of the boys will come out in the Autumn. He says Abbot but I think it must mean William as I think A. means to remain in New York. That he will probably be here in the Autumn. I wish I could get some letters to tell me what you are thinking of. However I shall set to work and write a letter and send it to Lintin to wait his arrival whoever he may be, as I think he may come with Dumaresq. I hope it may be so. So my dear I will leave you and write now I am in the humour.

I wrote the letter after leaving this and gave all the good advice I could think of. Then I was not very well so I did not go to Church but sent to the Library and got Priestly's *Memoirs*[54] and sermons and read them through the day, having placed myself upon a couch in a good draught of air, so that I found my <u>body</u> and <u>mind</u> in a very comfortable state and enjoyed the book much. I find every day and every day feel more convinced that I am a thorough Unitarian, for in comparing my sentiments and feelings of Christianity they accord perfectly with all the Unitarian writers I read. And having in a manner my own ideas upon this subject, I am delighted when I find myself supported by greater and <u>wiser</u> people. For though I may have heard the same over and over again with my <u>outward</u> ears yet I am very sure the beauty and truth of the Unitarian Sentiments never sunk deeper than that. And though when I left home if any one had have asked me to explain the Unitarian Sentiments to him, I should perhaps have thought myself competent, whereas in fact I knew nothing of it. And I rejoice now that I have been placed in a situation which has led me to think of it and to form my opinions by my own judgment. And I earnestly hope the love of it will grow with my years and strengthen with my strength, for I am very sure it is the only true consolation in adversity and the securest refuge in times of disappointment and trouble and in all the events of life whether joyous or grievous it is our rock and our staff. This my dear sister I sincerely feel and yet at times I fear I do not act upon it. I am afraid it is not the rule of my life.

I did not walk this afternoon except the terrace. Aunty and I spent the evening in talking and reviewing past scenes, thinking how many funny things we might tell. We eat some peaches and went to bed about 10, but alas I could not sleep it was so hot. I began to think I belonged to the <u>Peripatetics</u> for I was wandering from the bed to the Couch all night and I also compared myself to a Typhoon, for I was pointing to all points of the Compass all night. I got up feeling more tired if any thing than when I went to bed. Violent perspiration and no sleep soon takes the strength away and a short walk quite overcomes one. But I ought not to complain. Such health as I have had is very rare.

July 1st Another hot day. Spent part of the morning with Caroline, then came home and read till dark. Not a remark to make for today, saw no one but C. and heard nothing. We were alone all the evening, talking of Mrs. Trollope's works and the <u>words</u> she attributes to American <u>manufacture</u>, many of which I never heard. The word <u>fix</u> which we certainly do use very often is one that she makes great sport of, as the English never use it but in the sense of making fast, settling, to transfix.[55] And we often find ourselves using it. Now as Webster defines it it is correct in many of the senses in which the Americans use it, but as Johnson does, not correct. One gets to be rather particular living so much with [the] English for they are always ready to call you to an account for such and such words—& though unwillingly, I must allow that <u>generally</u> they speak most correctly.

2 Had wind, rain, thunder, & lightning last night but precious little sleep. A most tempestuous night. We found ourselves breakfasting at 10, mistook the hour. Calvo sent an excuse for this morning. Sent to the Library and got *L'Hermite en Province*.[56] Very interesting, giving the peculiarities and customs of the Provinces in France—some amusing things. It amused me till dinner time with writing a little French. A dull day however no news no letters nor nothing to rouse one from almost a state of stupor. After dinner by way of variety I took Washington's *Life* and followed them through several battles, where <u>my</u> <u>friend</u> Pulaski [Count Casimir Pulaski (1748–79), Polish patriot in the American Revolution] was killed in Carolina. Read this till Caroline came in, and we talked till 7. And Calvo came and spent the evening with us, but one becomes too much exhausted after a hot day to make much exertion to speak aught but plain English. Quite tired out I went to bed the moment he had gone and for a rarity slept well. The night was cooler, and I managed to have a door opened at the head of my bed which made a good draught of air upon me.

3 This morning after breakfast having had a little molasses given me I undertook to make some candy. A delightful employment for a hot day—but upon my word I felt no hotter for the fire. Indeed I have not been so <u>comfortable</u> for some time. I had a little Fogong or furnace put on the terrace which goes out from my room and had the apparatus brought up. And there I sat and stirred, reflecting on the many candy frolics I have had at home and the work we used to make for the servant alias "<u>help</u>." I thought of Miss Melbourne, too and a thousand other associations. In spite of my reflections and my

attention my candy all of a sudden <u>burned</u>—<u>because</u> the fire was too hot. A very good reason, sure. So I sung out to Achow that he must take it down and bring me another kettle or (what ever name it might be dignified with) and some more molasses and I would commence on the remains of the coals and be sure not to burn it this time. Sundry and divers regrets, but of no avail, so I laughed it off and was soon under way again—thinking as I had less fire I might take it more comfortably. So with my bamboo in one hand stirring with all my might and my book in another, and a fine breeze upon my back, I began to think I should make candy often, when suddenly I looked at my candy the fire was <u>defunct</u> and my <u>lasses</u> had stopped boiling. Thinks I to myself this won't do. So I <u>sung</u> <u>out</u> to Achow that the fire was <u>defunct</u> and the molasses would not <u>walky</u>. So up he came, the cooly with some coals, and the boy with some <u>fire</u>, for it takes three to do any thing here. And you would have laughed to see me sitting there in the midst of them with my bamboo and book and their operations are very amusing. Finally I was in order again and succeeded, *à merveille*. The Candy was delicious and the only difficulty was, <u>once</u> <u>in</u> the dish we could not get it out again—for it was not well buttered. Well I thought I must do my best to get some out for I had promised some of it to Mr. Wimberley and Caroline. After much trouble I succeeded in getting some out for Mr. W. & Mr. Davis, which they thought very nice, and I had some very <u>facetious</u> <u>notes</u> in return. To Caroline I sent a dish as it was, and told her she would probably have to eat dish and all, for I despaired of getting it out. She wrote me word Ricarda (her ayah) was tilting at it like any knight in romance (not to unhorse it) but to <u>undish</u> it, and she thought there was some prospect of her succeeding. But alas, alas, the last remains to be told. In the evening I wanted to taste my Candy and lo and behold it had returned to that from which it came and I saw nothing but a dish of <u>molasses</u>. It reminded me very much of the "Old Woman's Soap" which comes and goes, but I fear this goes not to <u>come</u> again. Well I hope you will be edified, it has filled a page in my journal.

After dinner I had a letter from Uncle praising me for my spirit on a certain occasion upon the Campo.[57] I wrote you all about it in a letter. He tells me it is Abbot coming out. Now I shall be all impatience till he comes. Hope he will come with Dumaresq. After I heard it I found I could not read to any profit as my thoughts were wandering so I jumped in the <u>carriage</u> [chair] and drove to the Campo at the risk of a ducking, for it had been raining very hard. There was scarce a breath of wind "the blue wave to curl," and all was as still at Casilha's as night. No one out save Mr. Plowden on horseback. I set musing upon the pleasure it will give me to have one of my kin here, and for want of air turned my <u>horses</u> [chair bearers] homeward. Walked the verandah an hour feeling *triste* as ever a poor mortal did, thinking from Uncle's letters we shall be condemned to stay here another year. This <u>thought</u> is intolerable, but we cannot be positive yet. I tried to cheer up for I am actually tired of <u>melancholy</u>, but how can one be merry without one single circumstance to cheer them. I read all the evening.

4 of July The glorious birth day of our Independence! How much I should like to know if <u>Union</u> and <u>peace</u> is still preserved. Mr. [Thomas] Beale, Mr. Chinnery, & Mr. Dent called this morning to congratulate us on another return of the day. I dare say they have been making noise enough about your ears, the last 24 hours. Mr. C. sent me his Sketch book and I finished a Sketch I commenced at his room. Aunt Low went out to pay visits. Mr. Colledge called. Some odd things happen here, which I could write would fill many a volume, but prudence restrains my pen. Beside they might not interest you.

After dinner read Marshall's *Washington* and finished it before I went to bed. And then I retired envying Mrs. Washington. She was a widow when he married her. Am afraid she did not love him as he ought to have been loved, and yet how could she help loving such a man. Certainly he is the model for a good man. Fancy Napoleon's <u>genius</u> added to such a <u>heart</u>. Why he would have been more than mortal. Such patience, such perseverance, such energy, such firmness and decision of character are worthy of every praise and all the love that is bestowed upon him by his country and the <u>World</u>, for even his enemies must admire him. He appears to have been made for the circumstances. And his Army too, pity that every one who suffered and endured such hardships could not have his name set out in bold relief and enjoy the fame they richly deserve. And how many of the most deserving are never known or heard of. Well now the name of Washington will never cease to be heard and loved. "What title shall he have? he paused and said. His <u>Name</u> alone strikes every title dead."

5th July We expected Calvo this morning, but he had other employment which he could not leave. So we wrote a little French, read some, and then I drew till dinner. Caroline came in about 2 and spent an hour.

After dinner I commenced Spark's *Life of Gouverneur Morris*,[58] and read till it was time to walk. It was a lovely afternoon and I determined to make the exertion which is very great and take a constitutional walk, for I think I need it. I am getting too lazy, and moreover by poring over a book continually I fear I shall addle my brain. Met Calvo on our return so that we had a little chat as he turned about with us. Came home tired. Capt. and Mrs. Clifton spent the evening with us, the funniest little couple you ever saw. He is 5 ft. 2 just my height. She is 4 ft. and small in proportion. She would be a very interesting woman but for her deafness. She took a violent cold after one of her confinements. He is a droll creature as I think I have told you before, very independent, high spirited and withal good sense. He economises the truth so that we generally make a discount of 75 per cent on all his stories. If one repeats a story that they hear from him, they say Little Clifton told me. Ah! He says he had letters today from [Robert B.] Forbes in Boston as late as the last of January via Calcutta. Why will not some one write me by those opportunities. It is very strange I can not get a letter in any way. He says Forbes "is still a Bachelor and intends to remain so forever." "Another case" of *Jewaub*[59]—the girls seem to be cutting curious capers all over the world. I have made up my mind tonight that there are as few men bachelors from choice as there are old maids.

6 This morning I felt in remarkable spirits. Why or wherefore I cannot say, unless because I made my body so comfortable and the day was fine. Feeling so well. I merely studied till 12 and then I dressed and sallied forth in my chair. First went to Mrs. Morrison's. She is an invalid and going to England this year with her little tribe. Having a child a year is rather too much in a hot climate for the constitution and comfort. Think the old Dr. will die of apoplexy before many years. Then after confabbing with Madame a while I went to Mrs. Neish. She is a nice creature but looks tired of being a wanderer. We hear there has been a tremendous gale in Calcutta. Lost many Ships. Capt. Locke on his way to China lost his. They seem to have every kind of melancholy there now. Sickness, deaths, failures and gales—it must be in a dreadful state. Then went to Mrs. Fearon's, then Mrs. Grant's, where I met Caroline and as usual when [we] meet we got into a frolic. Made Mrs. Grant laugh so that I did not know but she would be sick after it, as it is the first visit since her confinement. Mrs. Wimberley has produced a daughter this morning.

Went into Caroline's and eat Pumelo till 3 when I went home to pay my devoirs to the wing of a <u>cold</u> <u>capon</u>.

Read after dinner till it was time to go to Caroline's to get some tea and from there we went to the concert where we heard some fine singing. And Pleynell upon the violin. Played beautifully upon <u>one</u> <u>string</u>. We call him Paganini; he is certainly a very good performer. We were quite delighted with our evening's entertainment.

7th A dreadful hot morning and here I sit in chemise and corset and still melting. I intend to made an effort and go to Church by and bye. Shall read a sermon first and get cool, to do which I shall bid you good morning.

Went to Church, only 9 people there. Had a very good sermon. The text was If ye keep the whole law and yet break one of the commandments ye are guilty of all. [James 2:10] At least that is the sense, I believe, not exactly the words.

After church I was quite exhausted and went into Caroline's and laid on her couch a while. Met her brother there—seems unhappy. Poor man, I pity him.

After dinner I went out in my chair, intending to pass an hour alone but I was waylaid by Mr. Shillaber who joined me so we talked <u>Sentiment</u> on the <u>top</u> of a hill and came home again. Caroline and he took tea with us.

8 Oh how hot. Sultry, no wind—however studied, read, and <u>drew</u> by turns this morning. Mr. Colledge called. After dinner read Gouverneur Morris's *Life* till dark. Did not walk, it was so warm. Mrs. Neish took tea with us. A very pleasant woman and we passed a delightful evening. She has just enough of the accent to make it pleasant. She give us several histories of people in India, some of whom have been on here, and they seem more like romances than real life. Indeed we have almost daily reason to prove that the "truth is strange, stranger than fiction." [Byron, *Don Juan*, Canto 14, stanza 101] She was telling us of Mrs. Urwin who was here a few years since.

Her husband died and left her a widow. It was 12 o'clock before I went to bed. Aunt Low and I got talking of things past.

9 This morning <u>being very hot</u> we chose it for paying a few visits. Called on Mrs. Davis. Found her very agreeable apparently, although I believe she cares very little about seeing us. That is she would much rather not. Oh the hypocrisy of this world! Then we went to see Mrs. Whiteman. She always reminds me of Cousin Ann Orne, her manner and appearance always pleasant and entertaining. Called on Mrs. Clifton but her husband is sick, stopped but a moment. Then went to Caroline's, which generally brings me up. Found her busy in domestic cares superintending the preparing of a fish for baking. She had all the <u>articles</u> in her dressing room. She makes a very good wife. I am sure I should not know how to manage such a thing.

Came home and dined. Undressed and read till it was time to go to the Opera. Went and was not at all pleased. The play was riotous and vulgar and the music not music to my taste. I laughed but was provoked that I should laugh at such trash. Shall certainly not go to see it repeated.

10th Oh how hot again, though a pretty good breeze. Read some French and then finished a Sketch. Mr. Shillaber and Blight came in and we talked for two hours. I was sitting drawing very comfortably in my petticoat when the bell rang. I had to fly. We discussed the merits of Mrs. Trollope's *Refugee*, of divers and sundry words in common use with us, which the English ridicule. In referring to Johnson, find we use some of them in as correct a sense as they do, others perhaps not.

Wrote a long letter to you per *Providence* and went to dinner. After dinner read Morris's *Life* and wrote a letter to Mrs. Macondray— and spent the evening in thinking of home and etc. Went to bed at 10 and went to sleep.

11th Spent the morning as usual in reading, writing, drawing a little and in violent <u>perspiration</u>. However as we said "No could see" to visitors I passed it tolerably comfortable. Mr. Young did us the honour to <u>call</u>. I was reading part of the time French history, the reign of Henri 4th and *L'Hermite en Province*. L'Hermite finds as many peculiar customs and as much <u>unheard</u> of language among the provinces of France as Mrs. Trollope does among the Americans. How foolish it is for one nation to laugh at another when each has its own follies. L'Hermite writes however with a much better spirit than the Trollope and in a very different style.

After dinner I read English always. I finished the "Memoirs of Morris." A man of great integrity, judgment and talents, whose principles and politics I admire, and who appears to have been consistent throughout his career, and the many trying situations in which he was placed were filled with dignity and honour. I do not think I should have liked his manners, as from all accounts they were such as I detest, but that is a trifle now. He seems to have been very much beloved by those who knew him and could appreciate his worth. Now comes two volumes of his correspondence which I shall proceed with.

Went to walk at 6, and Aunty and I went up to the top of the Peña hill and sit upon the church steps. A most splendid evening and a beautiful view from there as I have told you before. See August 2d [August 1]—last year. Well do I remember it. C. & I were sitting there with what different feelings from what I did today, but there it is useless to regret, so I will spare you the details of my thoughts as I sit there. We went into Caroline's on our way home and spent the evening there. She is "shut up in measureless content." [Shakespeare, *Macbeth*, Act II, Sc. 1]

12th Letter from Uncle this morning. Says they are inundated in Canton and cannot move out of their houses except in Boats. Must have been heavy rains in the interior to have raised the tides so very high, and they run down so strong that [it] is impossible for boats to get up. Says it is dreadfully hot and I fear after this it will be unhealthy.

I am grieved to hear from Mr. Shillaber dreadful accounts of the Ship *Mandarin*, Fisk Allen. He says she was spoken off the Cape and many had died, so that they must be in a wretched state, with losing so many men out of the small crews those Ships have and having others sick. I shall feel very anxious to hear, but it will be a long time first. T. Shillaber [son of John Shillaber] was on board and his father is very unhappy.

This morning I wrote Chinnery a flourishing note, give him a little "soft soap" which he says he cuts mutton chops out of, and returned his Sketch book and hinted that I should like another. Whether the soft soap operated well or what other motive he may have had I only can say 1/2 an hour afterward I rec^d the book brought by himself, but could not see him as we had given orders "no could see." Asked him to tea.

I set to work at once to draw, thinking I shall never have such another chance. A dreadful hot day but I stripped myself of all that I could well dispense with and drew till 3 o'clock, a sketch which I hope one of these days to lay before you.

After dinner I read the Memoirs of "La Vallette,"[60] one of the heroes of the French Revolution.

Received a note from a gentleman wishing to meet me on the Campo, wished to have a little pleasant conversation. Applied a little of the same article that I gave Chinnery in the morning, but it would not do, it did not have the same effect. "I knew a trick worth two of that" [Shakespeare, *King Henry IV*, Part I, Act II, Sc.1] and preferred staying at home. Oh what a humbug this world is.

Mr. Chinnery took tea with us. He is not a pleasant companion at table.

You will notice in some of my books Mrs. Beaucaut's name. [June 7, 1832, vol. 4] Now I can give you the finale. She went home to England, and from all I can learn from those who went in the Ship with her, she was there a disgrace to her sex, but let that pass. She went to England and has eloped with a hatter—the whole to conclude, with Mr. Beaucaut her husband and child, go into mourning for her. Yea verily they put on black. What a farce. Did you ever hear any thing so absurd?—but this is a finale no one expected, a high spirited, proud woman to elope with a hatter. No one would have supposed any thing less than a nobleman would have tempted her to such an act, as I believe she was thought to act cooly and deliberately rather than from impulse. But there is no knowing what a wicked woman will not do. It will be a lesson for people here, not to worship every pretty face that comes along without any recommendation beside.

13th Nothing new to day except that the new Governor [Bernardo José de Souza Soares Andrea] took the keys and went through the ceremonies, at which time they saw fit to fire guns. Read and drew a little this morning. Felt dreadfully sleepy; the hot weather produces such a lassitude and weakness that it is impossible to do any thing with any spirit. Caroline came in just before dinner. Read after dinner till 6, then went to the Peña. Called for Caroline and we went together. [Her] brother John discovered after a while. Walked home and I took tea with her.

14ᵗʰ Read two excellent sermons written by Thatcher. He is certainly a superior writer. A very rainy day and I did not go to church. After dinner read Zimmerman on Solitude.⁶¹ I like some parts of it much. I fully agree with him on the advantages of retirement, and the pure and delightful pleasures one may feel in Solitude, but for my own part really to <u>enjoy</u> Solitude, I would have one kindred spirit as the poet says. To say "How Sweet is Solitude." [William Cowper, *Retirement*, l.740] But for the <u>advantages</u> of <u>retirement</u>, when we wish to commune with <u>ourselves</u>, then we must be quite <u>alone</u>. When we wish to survey our <u>weaknesses</u> and put a stronger guard upon our fortresses, then let us examine them ourselves and trust no one's opinion but our <u>own</u>, for who can know so well as ourselves. A person may go into the world and hear on all sides other people's opinion of him, and smile to see how they may be deceived with regard to his real feelings. Yes we must examine ourselves and rebuild those parts which we find have not a good foundation, and we build where all before has been waste. But it is not in Solitude or retirement our strength is to be tried, no we must go into the midst of temptation. We must be tried in actual service before we can be pronounced strong, we must be tried in the storm, the rains must come, and winds blow, before we can feel sure. So that it is not a nun or a recluse who can be said to have a perfect character, in my mind, though she may pass her days in penance and her nights in watching and prayer. She does not fulfil the object of her existence, certainly, nor can she be called positively good, because she has no temptations to sin. So it is not that kind of solitude that I should either desire or feel that I was better for. It would only be when I had overcome any great temptation, when I had resisted some powerful pleasure, because I felt it was against my principles, after one trial I should feel better able to promise myself for the second. I do not mean to say that it is only in great acts that one can be positively virtuous, because I think often in little events of life you find the struggle even harder to make, because they have not the applause of any. Whereas a great event that many were waiting to know the result, from the pride or glory of it you might resist. Every one of any reflection must see and feel the advantages of retirement. It leads us to look at events and things in their <u>true</u> colours, unexcited by passion and with reason for our guide; we can go back to the gaieties of the world, prepared to enjoy its smiles, to value them at their true worth and undismayed by its powers. With a guard upon yourself and knowledge of your besetting sins you can face the danger, and every effort that is made will serve to give you <u>confidence</u>; but then too great a confidence in oneself is dangerous, it is always necessary to walk like a person in a dark room, always fearing that you may stumble. But when we come to the <u>enjoyment</u> of Solitude that is a different thing. It is not <u>every</u> <u>one</u> that can enjoy it I think. It must be one of a contemplative and reflecting mind, one who has resources within himself, who can admire the beauties of Nature, and who can feel that there is a God who has made and rules all things, and one who can feel that the miseries and afflictions of life are or will be eventually for our good. One who is willing to believe that what appears dark and mysterious to us now, is only from our shortsightedness, our narrow mindedness. One who can feel too, that this is not the <u>end</u> of our existence, but that we are to go from one state to another till we are fitted for perfect bliss. For surely none of us are perfect in this world, therefore we are not prepared for perfect bliss, we are "none all evil" therefore none fitted for endless misery. To enjoy Solitude too, one must be capable of feeling the finer feelings of our nature, for to go into solitude and brood over the follies and vanities and sins of mankind, would only be to indulge a sour and morbid melancholy. No, to enjoy Solitude, it must not be retiring into the woods and being a recluse, but it must be occasional, with a kindred spirit as I said before, who can feel with you, think with you and talk with you, independent of all the world beside, looking to <u>that</u>, for none of your real happiness, but entering merely to do your duty to society, by your cheerful and happy disposition, which you may have acquired in your moments of abstraction from it. Every one has duties to perform in society, and those are not to be omitted for your own selfish gratification, every one has a sphere to fill, and however small it may be still it is to be filled and <u>well</u>. "Act well your part" there all the honour lies. Oh dear how easy it is to sit down and say what one should do and to create your own little world, fill it with beings created by your own fancy, take one perfect one from the number, make him respond to every wish of your heart, take him to yourself, take him into the most delightful scenes you ever conceived or ever heard of—to be troubled with none of the cares or annoyances which constantly assail you in real life, and in fact to live in an ideal world of your own. Ah you will say that is the disadvantage of retirement, instead of coming back to the world prepared to encounter its difficulties you merely return to be again and more disgusted with its follies. But no with a good foundation and good religious feelings I do not think it would have that effect. But to reap <u>real</u> good from retirement, one must have their thoughts and affections fixed on another and better world, on a being who is always near when we call upon him. But there if I go on in this way you will think I am very piously disposed, and I am sure I do not wish to deceive you, for the only one whom it would profit me to deceive can see the inmost recesses of my heart and doubtless sees many a dark spot. I am a very naughty child I am sure and feel that I have very little power to resist temptation. But that I do often think of these things you may be sure. But living as I do here in Macao, if I went to bed every night feeling that the day had passed without any sinful thought, word or deed, that if I could lay on my pillow and feel that every moment had been well employed, I should say (I might have been much worse) I have had no temptation to do otherwise than I have. I have had no opportunity no desire to do otherwise. Now this is what I call negative virtue and merits very little praise.

Caroline came in to see us about dark. A rainy evening and no walk. It is a long time since I had one.

15 Went to drawing immediately after breakfast and was very diligent till near three. About 2 an officer from the Brig *Nabob*[62] was announced. Says he left Boston 12th of March. Brought me no letters. I could have cried but would not! I have still a hope that I may have some yet. I do not know who this man was but said he was from Beverley. Nothing new that he could tell us. Disappointments have become so familiar to me now that I bear them with all the composure imaginable. Naught but a <u>sad</u> smile betokens the inward feelings of my heart. However these are trifles and will appear far more trifling to you who have never felt the pleasure of receiving letters from friends in the midst of <u>strangers,</u> when feeling alone in the <u>universe</u> as I do sometimes. However let that pass.

A rainy day and no walk. Read the Memoirs of La Vallette after dinner till Caroline came in about 6. I read after tea till 10 to Aunt

Low and then went to bed and dreamed of Napoleon, Ney, Soult, and all those "critturs."

Oh Aunty had a letter from Aunt Eaton[63] in Weare. Think of a letter finding its way from the wilds of Weare to our house in China. How wonderful it seems. She mentions no one in the more civilized world, except that Abbot was coming out in the Spring.

16 Read a little and tried to draw, but was not in the humour. Am hoping for letters which always puts me out of sorts. I am constantly thinking what news I shall have and from whom I may have letters. After dinner I finished the Memoirs of La Vallette. Some parts of it are exceedingly interesting, particularly his escape from prison.[64] He had a most heroic and devoted wife. She dressed him in her clothes and stayed herself in his prison, and so planned his escape that he succeeded and got out of the country. It is told in a very interesting manner. You follow him along and one's feeling get wrought to the highest pitch for fear he may be taken. She poor woman has her feelings tried to such an extent that she went mad, so that for many years she could not live with the dear one whom she had liberated from prison and freed from a violent death. She finally recovered however so as to live with him but was always subject to fits of abstraction and melancholy. France produced many such examples in those days, and I dare say many women could be found in every country under the like circumstances, that would show as noble feelings, but they had better be kept latent than brought forth at such times I think—I mean than to have such circumstances to display in.

We went to the Opera this evening and were very much delighted. They performed *Agnes* [*Agnese* by Ferdinando Paer]. The music was beautiful, some duets that were worth any thing. They performed very well too.

17 This morning Mr. Heard sent us some newspapers in which I see Margaret Low has become Mrs. Huntington [March 22, 1832, vol. 4]. She has my best wishes for her happiness. She appears to me too young to be married, but I dare say her mother knows best.

Do not see any other news of importance except that peace is restored in America by the modification of the Tariff, so I hope they have done with nullification and that our President will presume no more upon veto's.[65]

Mr. Heard & Mr. Coolidge called to see us this morning, having just arrived. Heard has very altered, looks thin and ill. Close confinement in Canton does not agree with him and I think he will be very glad to make his exit. Coolidge I have never seen before. I should think might be a very pleasant companion when one becomes acquainted. He is well informed, having been a close observer of men and manners and a great traveller. He has the appearance of being very much depressed in spirits now, but perhaps it is his usual manner.[66] Heard says he sent a large packet of letters to Uncle and I think I must have some enclosed.

After they were gone went to Caroline's and stayed a while and she came home with me—*à la Espagnol*. If you call on a Spaniard in Lima he immediately orders his carriage and returns it the same day.

When I got home Mr. Stevens [Rev. Edwin Stevens], the missionary in Canton,[67] handed his card in and for the life of me I could not think who Mr. Stevens was and what to say to him I knew not. However I asked him to sit down and told him it was a <u>hot</u> day, which fact he seemed to be fully aware of, having walked through the streets. I told him it had been raining very violently, which he also seemed to be aware of. Finding he would not contradict me, and knew so well all I told him, and thinking I suppose that I of course knew his whole history, whereas I had not the slightest idea of the animal, finding he would not enlarge upon any of my sage observations, I said I would speak to Mrs. Low and fortunately she remembered his name, so I introduced her and soon after left her to entertain him. He is a rosy cheeked, bright eyed looking fellow, but something of a <u>Goth</u> I think—nevertheless Aunty asked him to tea.

Being rainy had no walk. And I commenced the *Works of J. Barry an historical painter*,[68] a book Mr. C[hinnery] lent me that I might get some new ideas upon his art. He was a very eccentric strange man, but a very worthy upright man and devoted to his profession.

Mr. Shillaber, Capt. Pearson [Charles Pearson][69] and Mr. Stevens took tea with us. We passed a very pleasant evening, conversing round a <u>table</u>. So you see how it is in Macao, if we see one person in a day, we generally have 1/2 dozen, and then no one for a week. Coolidge and Heard went immediately back to Lintin, as Coolidge sails tomorrow in the *Good Success* for Bombay.

18th Felt not quite well this morning, for a rarity. However took a little <u>Salaratis</u> [saleratus][70] and felt marvellously refreshed and comforted, so spent the morning in reading, writing & drawing. After dinner I went out to Casilha's in my chair. Rainy weather [so] there is no such thing as a walk. Had a good shower while I was out. Set at the bay some time with Mrs. Morrison, we chatted upon different subjects. She had her little <u>pet</u> boy with her who she considers as a <u>paragon</u> of perfection. All I can say for him is that he is the most disagreeable child I ever saw. He is intelligent no doubt, very inquisitive. Then American manners was our subject after having discussed the merits of the <u>prodigy</u>. I do not think it is right for mothers to select one of their children as a particular favourite. My lady went home and I sat musing still, and had a short chat with Sir George Robinson who came up waiting upon his son on horseback— a little boy of six or seven. I do not know what papas would think at home to be trotting after children in such a manner. Every day we meet Sir George running at the side of the pony which mounts one of his children. Three times in an afternoon he trots out to Casilha's and back again. I think if he knew the value of time he would hardly be willing to spend so much of it in tending babies— but "every one to their fancy" as the old woman said. <u>Titles</u> do not always bring <u>sense</u> nor always <u>cents</u>, as per example in this instance. Spent the evening in reading *Inheritance* [vol. 3, August 16, 1831, n. 79]. Made my eyes ache very much, which I suspect is all the good it will do me.

19th Calvo sent an excuse again, so I took to my drawing and drew all the morning. Was interrupted once by Mr. & Mrs. Clifton. After dinner read *Inheritance* and finished it in the evening. Thought it would rain, so did not walk but it proved a most lovely evening. Saw a boat come in from Canton and concluded I should get my letters, but *comme à l'ordinaire* I was disappointed. A large packet was handed to make it still more provoking but they were for Manilla and one for Caroline. I despair of hearing again but I smiled and said "My all was not laid there." Was not that heroic? I walked the terrace and asked myself if it was not a great weakness to feel disappointed at such trifles, but when I reflected that it was but the result of natural affection and that all my happiness comes from that quarter I concluded that it was not a trifle and that it was right and proper that

I should grieve and that it was not weakness. So you see how ready I am to excuse myself, and in this instance think I am justified, do not you my beauty?

Uncle says Abbot was to leave the 20th of March, so that I shall soon see him I trust, and he will be able to answer all the questions I should wish to ask. Now I shall be so impatient!

The Empress of China is dead,[71] and the people will all have to <u>mourn</u> for 100 days. The men are not allowed to shave for that space of time so we shall have <u>beautiful</u> looking servants. We hear Mrs. Allport is coming out in the *Waterloo* with Mr. & Mrs. Jackson, Mr. Astell & Clark so that we shall have quite an importation. I long to see Mrs. A., she is a pearl of price.

It seems it is the Mother of the Emperor who is <u>defunct</u>.

20th Took my drawing after breakfast and was employed till 2 in finishing a sketch which satisfied me and now only long for the time when I shall have the pleasure of showing it to you and bringing to your view the representation of places so familiar to my eyes. This one is a view of the <u>barrier</u> which I have so often spoken of. It will also recall to my mind many a long walk and agreeable conversations, as well as some dreary and desolate ones. After I had finished it I dressed and carried Mr. C[hinnery]'s book home as he is afraid to trust it to Coolies. I only went to the door and he came down to my chair, and I suspect from his appearance I roused him from a good nap—and I dare say he wished me and his book <u>any where</u>. He says he can do nothing the weather is so hot. It is the complaint of every one. For my own part I think the mental <u>laziness</u> is worse than the bodily and it is the result of living so quietly and in such a monotonous manner. No one takes the trouble to talk if they can possibly help it.

I went to Caroline's and found her just going to Mrs. Wimberley's so I went with her to see the new <u>production</u>. Then went home with her and dined.

Went home and called for Aunty after dinner and went to walk. Went up to our hill, were joined by Lindsay, Caroline and her brother. Walked home with Lindsay. He is so tall it made my arm ache awfully. He is the son of Hugh Lindsay, of the House of Balcarras, a nephew of the Earl. A very pleasant person of courtly and polished manners, has in his day been satiated with dissipation, but having been many years in China has reformed his plans, I suspect, perhaps from want of temptation, but that I cannot tell, so we will suppose it is from conviction of his errors. I should say he had very little <u>heart</u> and his sincerity is very much to be doubted. I am afraid I have not drawn a very enchanting picture, but he is no favourite of mine, though I would serve him better if I could. When we first came out he was very handsome, fine face and splendid figure, but he has been sick and has altered very much. He is always ready for <u>adventures</u> of any kind.

It was a lovely evening but I cannot say there was much pleasure in my walk although the youth tried to be very agreeable.

Mr. Shillaber spent the evening with us and I had a headache and was very stupid.

21ˢᵗ This morning felt quite unwell and was obliged to take some <u>salts</u>. Felt better before dinner so that I eat my usual quantum of Capon. Did not go to Church and was at home this afternoon, reading, & etc. A most lovely evening. We are expecting Uncle every moment.

22ᵈ Uncle came about 5 o'clock this morning, had a delightful passage. Gordon & Gillespie came with him. They called this morning but I did not see them. Was busy writing to Abbot. Uncle says he was to stop at Madeira so that I shall not probably see him for a week or two. I must splice my patience. Dreadfully hot. Can scarcely write. We walked after dinner and got very tired, for it seems to me I have no strength at all. I wish I could tell you how lovely this evening was. Appears to me you never have such at home, but perhaps I forget. We spent the evening *en trio*. No <u>intruder</u>.

23 Sent an excuse to Calvo this morning as it is too hot for any thing. I was reading Mr. Barry on Painting all the morning. I had no idea or at least never reflected how much the mind must be connected with the hand in this beautiful art. This Mr. B. had a powerful mind and was a great genius and with great industry and perseverance acquired a celebrity which it was his wish to obtain. He was very eccentric in his feelings and habits.[72]

Caroline spent an hour with us before dinner. Uncle brought me a long letter from my <u>friend</u> [W. W. Wood] in Canton, humbly apologizing for all that has passed, expressing his regret, and lamenting the dreary prospect before him, deprived of all hope etc. Having lost the <u>powerful</u> <u>motive</u> that has hitherto actuated him, he dares not hope that any of [his] good resolutions may be kept—a whole sheet full of this. But I say "it's all in my eye" as the boys say. I feel every day my heart grows harder my dear and I am perfectly astonished when I think how differently I view all that has passed from what I did a few months since and wonder what has produced the change. Why in this instance reflection and a thorough conviction that all is best as it is. I have brought my mind after terrible turmoils and convulsions, to a tolerably quiescent state and resolved to make the best of what I cannot avoid, and wait with patience and even cheerfulness the time when I shall be able to leave this place which I detest. Yes, I will be as passive as I <u>must</u> be <u>bon</u> <u>gré</u> <u>mal</u> <u>gré</u> and when I am called to act I hope I shall be <u>able</u> also to act. For circumstances I have no power to change therefore it behoves me to suit myself to them. There my dear is not that philosophical, does it not meet with your highest approbation? This happy frame of mind which I happen to be in is owing to a perfect state of bodily health which certainly always has great influence upon the <u>moral</u>—or mortal. How long it will last I will not pretend to say, but it shall be my aim to keep it so, for I am tired of feeling miserable and moping. Not that I have been out of health not to be sensible of it, yet I think we may often trace one's low spirits to feeling of lassitude and weakness of body, particularly when one has nothing to do but to think of one's self. This evening we went to the "Opera." It was very stupid and I was very much fatigued. It was *Il Baccanali di Roma*.[73]

24 This morning read till 2 then went to Caroline's, and the Dr. <u>ordered</u> me to dine there, so I did. Came home after dinner and went to walk with Uncle. We went to the hills round by the gap and you have no idea how pleasant it was—a breeze that was worth any thing fresh from the sea, and the "moon shining silvery bright" above us. The hills rise very abruptly from the sea and the foot of them covered with huge rocks so that a view of the <u>soap</u> <u>suds</u> (as Uncle calls it) right below us is beautiful. There is not a spark of romance in his composition and when I would fair quote a little poetry to express the beauty of the scene, he in plain prose calls it <u>soap</u> <u>suds</u>, which is you know the death of romance at once, for you immediately fancy a great washerwoman with a red face and <u>beefy</u> arms at a wash tub & etc. I will leave your imagination to finish the picture.

We saw a Ship coming in, which I dare not hope is the *Golconda*. I have been so often disappointed that I now see a Ship arrive with perfect composure, without even the hope that there may be any letters for me.

We came home from the Gap, had some tea, and spent the evening upon the terrace.

July 25th Now I have given you my account of yesterday I am going to work to make some molasses candy for *mon oncle*, and then I must go and see Mrs. Macondray as she came down yesterday.

Well I made my Candy, which was pretty good and at the same time read *Lara*, or the second canto, [Byron (1814)] stirring my "lasses" with one hand and holding Lord Byron in the other. Then I spent two or three hours with Mrs. Macondray. She has a beautiful child, but [it] is terribly troubled with boils as all children are in this place and at this season, and grown people too. I thought I should have baked going through the streets. It is much the hottest day we have had, a burning sirocco wind and looks something like a Typhoon. After laying on the carpet in the verandah and reading till 6 o'clock, I mustered strength to wash me, dress me clean and prepare for a walk which required no little energy I assure you.

[marginal note] Thermometer in the house at 93°

I sallied forth in hopes of getting more air out on the hills. Gillespie joined us at the corner so we had to be bothered with him all the way. Then coming home Calvo joined us and Shillaber and we had them all to tea. My mouth was sealed or appeared so and they must have thought me stupid enough. We sit on the terrace and Calvo talked to me and I said Yes & No. He told me I was very *triste* meaning stupid I dare say. I told him I was impatient for letters.

Thus ends a tedious day—and night. Oh horrible for sleep.

26th Got up this morning feeling more fatigued than when I went to bed for the heat was dreadful and such nights takes one's strength quite away.

[marginal note] Thermom. 93

I feel as though I had had a fit of sickness, so weak. I have been "located" upon the floor most of the day in different corners of the doors to catch every breath that was stirring. Have been reading very steadily all day and got through the day pretty well but had no strength to walk, so dressed and set upon the terrace. About 8 Gordon & Gillespie came in. I have no ideas for you now my dear for this weather deadens the mind more than the body if possible.

27 Another dreadful night the last but this morning there is a southerly breeze and a more comfortable day. Think the glass was not more than 91°. Spent the morning in reading *Le Solitaire*[74] for the beauty of the French, but a very interesting story, too.

    After dinner saw an American Ship go up, perhaps the <u>Golconda</u>. We shall not hear till tomorrow. No walk today for it looked like rain which came about 8 o'clock with thunder, lightning and wind, quite refreshing for a while but the wind died away and it seemed hotter than before during the night.

28 This morning the Thermometer is 10 deg. lower having fallen to 82°, which is quite refreshing. It rained very hard all the morning and we could not go to Church. Feel miserably having no sleep or at least such <u>tiresome</u> sleep. I spent the day in reading Mr. Channing's Works, sermons, etc. Spent the day rather satisfactorily. Meditated and conversed a little at dinner time which has not been the case for several days before, for no one has had strength to move even the tongue.

    Caroline and John [Shillaber] looked in just at night. Have not seen her since Wednesday. He took tea with us and she went home to take care of C[olledge], who she says is quite <u>done</u> <u>up</u> going out in the sun.

29th Received a long epistle from a <u>friend</u> yesterday in answer to a note I wrote in answer to his yesterday. It was a singular production certainly and I laid it aside without mentioning it. I was obliged to write a sheet in reply, but I only replied to the first part of the letter, which was a comparison between French & American ladies. I defended my countrywomen through thick and thin. We have had quite a <u>controversy</u> upon the subject. The latter part of his was chiefly regarding his own situation and feelings, wishes I believe to make me his <u>confidante</u> and I fight <u>shy</u>. I do not like to be in the confidence of gentlemen much, it is dangerous. So I made no comments upon his remarks, which filled a sheet. After I had finished this I

Chair at Macao, Lucy Cleveland's Sketchbook (Peabody Essex Museum)

read one of Mad[ame] Genlis' Moral Tales in French. It was *Le Mari Corrupteur*—a very excellent thing.[75] It applies the Philosophy of Voltaire, Diderot, d'Alembert to real life and shews the evil of it and quotes passages from all. I was quite delighted with it.

After dinner I proceeded with Morris's *Correspondence* which I read till six and find very interesting. Then we sallied forth the first time for a week, nice cool evening but damp. Spent the evening with Caroline—stayed till after 11. Promised to dine with them tomorrow.

30th Had a headache all night and this morning feel as though I had been mulled. Am impatient for an arrival and feeling exactly the reverse of what I did on the 23d. Attribute it, as I must having no other cause, to physical ills—for I am not well today. Tried to read but it was no use, tried to sleep but thoughts were busy and I was obliged to give that up. Rainy, dismal day. At 1/2 past 3 went to Caroline's. Met at dinner Gover, Melville and a Mr. Goddard,[76] two strangers to me. Had a rather a pleasant time. After dinner C. & I went to see Mrs. Macondray. She has a sweet little girl. Went back to Caroline's and spent the evening. Mr. Goddard was there, rather a pleasant person, an Invalid from Bombay. Got a dreadful cough.

July 31st It seems so foolish to take out this book every morning to write you such uninteresting accounts of my days. But in the hope of coming to something better I go through thick and thin as I do when reading a dry book. I go from page to page fearing I may lose something or that I shall find something good or why was the book published. So I go from day to day hoping to find for what I was created. It seems impossible it can be to pass my days in such a manner. But then I suppose there must be such beings in the world to fill up the chinks, but I do wish if I am for no more than to fill a chink I had had a quiet and contented spirit and not had so much ambition put <u>into</u> me—but "there what's the use of sighing since time is on the wing." Well since such is the case and dame fortune will treat me as she pleases, why I will even amuse myself as much as possible "studying to be quiet" as St. Paul tells us. [1 Thessalonians 4:11] And as nothing gives me more pleasure than writing you, I'll tell you what I do and how I pass my time. This I shall pursue pleasing myself, till a monitor within gives me a <u>twinge</u> and says think that your friends have better employment than reading such nonsense, so <u>forbear</u>—your Sister is busy mending her husband's stock-

ings or making her child a petticoat. Never mind, yesterday morning I got up, eat my breakfast, walked the verandah awhile, went to
my room, took the *History of France*, then Mad. de Genlis' tales and
read till interrupted by Gaffer alias the Duke of Gordon who was
very facetious and looked as fascinating as ever. I read the *Courier*
which contains a petty quarrel between "Plowden & Barretto."[77]
After dinner I read Morris's letters till 6, dressed and went to walk.
Mrs. Daniell called. Set on the Gravestones till time to go home,
and Gaffer spent the evening with us. There my dear quite a day.

A beautiful night, went to bed at 1/2 past 10. The Ship which
arrived was the *Liberty* from Cadiz. I am tired of waiting for Abbot.

August 1ˢᵗ July departed and not a tear shed by me for its demise.
A few reflections made and a new month commenced with a hot
morning, but a breeze came in about 11 bearing on its wings an
American Ship, exciting hopes but to deceive. It was only from Java
with rice, the *Jubilee*. I looked at it with longing eyes but to no purpose. Read Mad. de Genlis most of the morning. Rather like some
of her stories. After dinner read Morris's letters. Another Am. Ship
passed up right in our teeth as the saying is; it seems so provoking to
see them come directly before our eyes and to have to wait to know
who and what they are. This is most likely the *Eliza* from Cadiz, so
after a half a dozen more have come, hope Abbot will pop in.

We went out to the Peña church this afternoon. Met all the
people coming back, all driving home expecting rain. Met little
Clifton and his wife in <u>one</u> chair. Met Mr. Lindsay, said they had
just made a calculation that 2 Cliftons were equal to one <u>Gover</u>. Every
one anxious for Ships now, husbands expecting wives, brothers, sisters, and sisters, brothers and other friends. This is the return season
as all who went home two years since must come back. Our friend
Mrs. Allport is daily expected. Moreover all are anxious (I mean
English) about the renewal of the <u>Charter</u> [the Company's charter
ceased April 22, 1834]. A time of excitement verily.

2ᵈ A rainy day—but Calvo came this morning and we resumed our
French lessons. I almost despair of ever <u>conversing</u> well in it. I find
there are so many ways of making mistakes that I have hardly con-
fidence enough. Mrs. Fearon made us a call preferring rain to sun.
After dinner read Morris's letters. So rainy we had no walk. Mrs.
Davis made us a visit, and we spent the evening alone.

3 Rained incessantly all night and all this day. Seems as though it could not stop, a year today since Uncle was in such danger in the Typhoon. Reading from morning till night and walking the verandah by turns by way of digestion. These rains make the walls crumble. There is an old house next to us that keeps falling and making a tremendous <u>crash</u>. We have some fears that it may take one side of ours with it. Have seen nor heard nothing today but "patter, patter, patter." This evening we discussed Napoleon and several other great characters and the more I hear of Napoleon's character, the more I reflect upon it, the more I am delighted that I never sympathized with him in his adversity. He was great I acknowledge, he was made for the times and the times for him. But he was too heartless for any admiration, too ambitious of fame, too reckless of the comfort and happiness of others.

4 Sunday. Went to Church this morning, heard a pretty good sermon. Text "Without me ye can do nothing." [John 15:5] Went home after church and read Channing's Sermons. Mr. Allport called—every one stretching their vision to Cabarita point. Lots of Ships expected and a fine breeze today for them. Two arrived from Bombay, but they bring nothing but <u>opium</u>, which is the most interesting article to merchants and speculators. It is amusing to see how many of their thoughts they give it. It seems to be a never failing source of conversation.

After dinner about 1/2 past 5, I went to Mrs. Macondray's and stayed chatting with her till nine. Came home, walked the terrace a little and went to bed. Thundered, lightened, blew and rained all night most tempestuously.

5 Still raining in torrents by spells. No such thing as walking. I went to Caroline's and spent an hour this morning. Came home and read the rest of the day. Straining our eyes for Ships, every now and then see one coming round the point. Our hopes are raised but they prove nothing interesting. Gordon spent the evening with us.

6 Has hardly ceased raining today till towards night. Mr. Gordon sent me a nice Morocco Skin this morning. Wrote an excuse to Calvo, Aunt Low was not well. Read all the morning.

Tonight it held up raining a while and Uncle and I went to the Opera. Were very much pleased with the music. The play was interesting. But when it was time to go home we looked out in despair of moving for the night. It was raining in torrents and nothing was to be seen on the ground but water and the chairs appeared to be swimming. The coolies with their enormous hats wading up to their knees with lanterns in their hands formed a curious picture, this was the scene below. Above, the heavens appeared to be one sheet of flame, for the lightning was incessant, showing immense clouds in every part which appeared to deprive us of any hope of change. What to do we did not know. It seems the house has sunk and the drains were closed up, so that all the water stood around it as far as we could see. It reminded me of the descriptions of Venice and I converted the chairs into gondolas. At last as we despaired of the rains ceasing, the gents thought they could bring the chairs up the steps and back us down. They were made in this way. [Harriett inserts a small sketch of a chair and two bearers at the top of the steps.] I must confess I rather trembled at the prospect, knowing the steps were so wet and slippery. However I presently heard "Miss Low's <u>chair</u> <u>stops</u> <u>the</u> <u>way</u>" and I sallied forth with two gents, I forget who, to meet my fate whatever it might be with all the courage of a <u>heroine</u> in the midst of thunder, lightning, rain and darkness—and the roaring of Chinamen which exceeded the thunder, for they all hollow together and thereby hear nothing. I presently found myself shut up in my <u>box</u> and going down the steps backward. Rather an awkward predicament, but I knew I must make the best of it and I kept perfectly still, and when I got into the streets I got on pretty well till I found my lanterns had gone out. Here I was with three China coolies in the midst of the streets. However they lighted them again and I arrived at home safely, after much tribulation. My face was the colour of scarlet and my head ached violently, but I undressed and went to bed. But it was a long time before I could get composed. It was certainly an awful night. The thunder & lightning were very severe and the rain, it came in <u>torrents</u>, for there is no describing it in any other way. I had a very pleasant time at the Opera and notwithstanding the troubles I was not sorry I went, for a little excitement now and then is not bad even if it is not pleasant at the time.

7 Am happy to inform you that the sun has appeared again and the air is quite delicious this morning. Went to see Caroline this morning. She is not very well and feels some of the troubles of matri-

mony. [An oblique reference to Caroline's pregnancy.] If you will believe me I came home quite satisfied with single blessedness. Aunt Low has been married 10 years today, and seems as happy as on that day. It is happy to [recollect] such instances. She has been a fortunate woman no doubt in her selection—but few have such good reason to be satisfied.

This afternoon started for the Peña, the Campo was too wet. On the way we were stopped by a group of gentlemen to enquire after my health and success after the last night's frolic. In this group was a *ci devant* admirer of mine [W.W. Wood], who had the politeness (when he discovered who it was) to turn his back directly round without speaking. This is the one who last year about this time vowed he would be my friend for ever if he could be no more. So this is the friendship of rejected lovers. Well there is one comfort. I wish neither his love or friendship—they are not worth the keeping. I was exceedingly amused at his folly for he gave every body reason to suppose what had happened.

We came home and spent the evening in conversation. Uncle was telling us of the report Arthur Tappan made of the Magdalen Society, which you no doubt heard about. It must have been a scandalous production. From that we came to Chinese punishments, their cruelty, their recklessness of life and their belief concerning a future state, of their motives for taking such care of the dead bodies of their parents and superstitions concerning them. It is almost impossible to know what they do think of these things. There is a great variety of sects. Some believe in transmigration others do not, some believe in punishment according to their deeds and others that they are to be annihilated. Uncle says all he has ever spoken with upon the subject have scarcely any ideas upon the subject. Indeed I do not believe they trouble themselves much about it. If they live honest and decent lives it is because it is for their interest, that is the only feeling I can discover in them. What makes me think that some believe in transmigration is that I saw some letters to Colledge in which they said that although they could not pay him for his services in this world yet they could serve him as a horse in another, and many expressions of this kind. But it is difficult to determine what they mean. I recollect too hearing a Hong merchant say that "if he should live again, if he was to be a man he would be a Chinaman, but if a woman an English woman." This is in our (?) favour.

The other day I asked Achow where that Empress would go that had died recently. He says to a good place. I asked him if she was a bad woman if she would go to a good place, he says no, more good, more better. Then again what does their goodness consist in? They are very superstitious respecting the place in which they bury their dead. "Cumwa" a merchant in Canton whose mother died two years ago has just found a satisfactory place to bury her in, having kept her above ground during that time. And it seems he was not very successful after all for the late inundation of the rivers came up within two feet of her grave, so that he was in great trouble and obliged to have her taken up again. They endeavour to get the driest place possible and have samples of the earth brought to them that they may judge of it. The rich about Macao bury them on the tops of the highest hills, and around them an immense deal of stone work. They are a strange people and you can perhaps gain more correct information from the *Chinese repository* of their manners and customs than I can possible give you as I have no means of knowing them.

Coming home we passed three Chinese padres who have it is said been converted to Catholic religion. They dress in European costume, but with the exception of their being bipeds they bear no resemblance to the *genus homo*. To meet them any where else you would be extremely puzzled to know in what species they might be classed with any propriety. I have very little respect for converts of this kind, either for their faith or their works, though perhaps and no doubt it is quite as difficult to judge of their goodness or their sincerity as it is of one who calls himself a Christian in a more civilized country. It is foolish to pretend to judge either.

8th of August passed and no Ship yet. The Flag Staff [at the wharf] has not even been raised today to even excite a hope. A lovely day, was reading all day as usual. Aunty went out this morning. Gordon paid us a visit—the Duke is unfortunately ugly!

After dinner we went to the Campo and found a delightful place behind the Guia, an armchair in the rock which for very many years past has been called the "Yankee arm chair"—having been occupied by many of them evenings to smoke cigars and spin long yarns. Mr. Russell, Cushing, Forbes, Sturgis, Talbot, etc. I admire their taste for it is a most lovely spot, rather a scramble to get to it. But once there we have a fine breeze fresh from the sea, the broad bay before us and the hill to screen us from all intruders behind. We sit there and built a little chateau on the North river, with a lawn running down to the water and I fancied myself a picture of contentment, enjoying in a reasonable manner the pleasures of life, and having seated myself after my wanderings, glad to be retired and in my own country. Oh yes there is happiness to be found yet I dare say. At any rate it throws over one's spirit a pleasing melancholy to contemplate these things in the distance, and with the hope that they may one of these days be within our grasp adds to the pleasure. But if ever restored to one's country and friends after a long absence it is bliss of itself.

We came home about dark and spent the evening alone.

9th Got up in fine spirits this morning and commenced my capers soon after breakfast. A fine cool morning. Calvo came at 11 and we had our French lesson and a good deal of sport as we generally do when he comes. He is truly French in his manners, full of vivacity and esprit as the French say. Mr. Van Basel and Allport came in and interrupted us and I managed to have a good laugh with them. It seems the other night the three Miss Pereiras' each had a gentleman wading home beside of their chairs. Van B. was one of them. We told him nothing but love could have tempted him. Teazed him a great deal.

Caroline came in before dinner, and Gaffer dined with us. Walked with us and we went to the arm chair. Came home and he and Caroline took tea with us. C. and I ended the evening with one of our old fashioned frolics. I do not know when I have laughed so much.

10 More rain this morning. In the midst of it looked upon the water and saw two ladies coming on shore in an open boat. The Marquis of Huntley had just arrived with Capt. Hyne [John Hine], his sister and servant, and Mr. [James] Matheson. Now the ice is broken, hope some more will come in. I began to think the Straits were filled up.

Cleared off after dinner and we had a delightful walk to the Peña, fine pure air. As we passed Caroline's saw the new arrivals at her house, suppose they dined there. Hear she is a spinster of 30 or 40, or of that uncertain age ladies are when they have the misfortune to have arrived at 30 without having espoused themselves. Suppose we shall have them coming in thick and threefold now.

Came home a minute after my walk and then went to Mrs. Macondray's and spent the evening there. Hear Capt. Duncan is dead.

His poor [wife] is with him and is left a widow in a strange land. How melancholy. Hear she heard it with very little fortitude. They are at Mrs. Fearon's.

    As I was coming from Mrs. M's, my chair could scarcely get along for the crowd of Chinamen who appeared to be listening very attentively to a lecturer who was holding forth in a very audible voice, but I could not tell the subject of his discourse. They all appeared very grave as I passed, I conclude it must have been some tragedy. I asked Achow when I came home what it was, whether "he talky sermon all same Mr. Wimberley." He said, "No, it was a play." This was probably the recitative that I heard and I suspect he sings between whiles, as they often do.[78]

    Got home found all in bed, the only thing I could do was to do likewise. So I took a warm bath and went to sleep.

11th Sunday Another week gone and who knows where, or what is there to show, it has been. To look upon the three or four months past, it seems to be a perfect blank or like a voyage at sea, nothing that I remember with any particular pleasure or moment that I would wish to recall. It seems as though every feeling but hunger and a desire to sleep had been extinct and I almost fear that every other is—for I have almost done hoping that I shall ever have any thing to give me pleasure again, or that I shall be capable of feeling either pleasure or pain. For it appears to me it is only by the constant exercise of the feelings that they can be kept alive. They must die for a want of nourishment.

    Did not go to Church this morning. Soon after breakfast took up my book which led me to reflect a great deal upon original Sin but I am too lazy now to give you the result of my reflections. I read a good sermon upon the subject, and several others, and upon the whole felt tolerably satisfied with myself, though I must confess once or twice found my thoughts wandering very far away.

    Mr. Allport came in and regrets very much having to go to Canton before his wife arrives. She is expected daily. I find the lady that arrived yesterday was not the said spinster, but a Mrs. Bartlett, sister of Capt. Hyne and the other is a wife for the Capt. of the Cutter. She has come out to marry him—after the fashion of the English. Considering the nature of man or his disposition to change (be it natural or acquired) I should say a lady run some danger of finding herself underceded in the affections of the swain. It requires more faith in the constancy of man than I possess to be willing to undertake such an undertaking. However 'circumstances alter cases' and there is no knowing what necessity or love will not compel both men and women to do.

We went to our couch behind the Guia after dinner but could see no Ships. Coming back met Sir George & Lady Robinson, walked home with them part of the way. We spent the evening all alone, that is us three, and discussed the merits of republics and monarchy's.

12 Monday. Sent Trollope's *Refugee* home this morning which Uncle has been reading. Hope you have read it and if you have the memory of it will not be "obliviated" from your mind from "July to Eternity."[79] It is very amusing and a complete caricature. The *Quarterly* cuts her up beautifully, and the *Edinburgh Review* also.[80] I got from the Library *Memoirs of the Duchess d'Abrantès*[81] which will be amusing I "reckon"—though it is a repetition of the same times that I have so often read about. I am almost tired of the French Revolution. Finished Morris' *Life* this morning and *Correspondence*. Have been very much interested.

Had quite a levée this morning. The arrival of Mrs. Bartlett brings the lady's out and then they go the rounds as it is nice & cool today. First Allport came in and arranged how Uncle and he should go up, they start tonight. [Then came] Sir George & Lady R[obinson], Mr. & Mrs. Wimberley, Caroline and Gordon.

After dinner we did nothing but walk about and talk with Uncle as he was to leave us at 6. I walked down to the boat or very near it with him and bid him good bye. Called on Mrs. M. a few minutes and went home expecting to find Aunt a disconsolate widow and lo and behold when I went in there he sat by the side of her. It seems the "Chop" was not ready. He was going up inside and there is such a bother, the most provoking delays and impositions you can imagine. He and Allport took some tea with us and started again at 8 and we were left alone.

13 Calvo came this morning for the last time as he goes to Manilla tomorrow. I am very sorry as we shall lose our French lessons. He stayed with us till two. He is a very remarkable young man, very intelligent, enthusiastic feelings and character far more formed than youths of his age generally, for I suppose he is not more than 19 or

20. His manners are quite French, and he has lived just long enough to be bewitched with its amusements and gaieties and unfit him for every thing else. He is very discontented here and says he never shall be happy till he returns to *la belle patrie*. He has a fine face and will I think make a very good or very bad man. As yet his feelings are very strong but refined and good, but now perhaps it will depend upon his company and the examples he has set him whether he turns out well. I shall always feel interested in his welfare. Poor boy he has early felt the reverses of fortune. His father was a very wealthy man living in great style in Paris, but failed a short time since.

About 2 I went to Caroline's and found her busy in <u>domestic</u> cares. I heard nothing but <u>Catties</u> of <u>Oil</u>, and <u>Taels of Fish</u>.[82] I laughed at her and rejoiced that I had nothing of the kind to bother my head and came home to dinner. I admire to plague her. I dare say she thinks its all envy, but it is a fact that part of the business I should hate as much as she does.

Mr. & Mrs. Daniell and all the children came to our house this afternoon to see a procession. Mrs. D. stayed till dark when we dressed and were attended to the Opera by his Grace, "the Duke of Gordon." Had a pleasant time and some good music. My chair was stopped on its way home with old Golatti beating his slaves.[83] They misbehaved and he took his stick to them and gave them some <u>awful</u> thwacks, and I was made an unwilling witness of it, for my bearers would not go on, thinking I suppose they might come in for a <u>share</u> in passing. These streets are so narrow.

14th Rather a hot day again. I wrote, studied, read and drew by turns this morning and kept the spy glass at my side ever and anon sweeping the horizon to try and see a Ship, but nothing comes from any where. It is really very strange. Ships are expected from every where now, but some days the signal staff is not hoisted. It is so tiresome I get almost out of patience.

I was reading this morning de Genlis' *Palais de la Vérité*.[84] People were put into a Palace of Truth where they spoke all their thoughts and their real thoughts. They were all diverted of politeness and dissimulation of all kinds when there, and appeared in their real characters, undressed and unadorned by art. It is very good and very well told and gives a very good idea of what the state of affairs would be if every one spoke the truth and the whole truth.

After dinner I read the *Memoirs of the Duchess [d'Abrantès]* and was so much interested that I would not go out to walk. Caroline came in and made me go home with her. She had Capt. Dallas, Gordon, and Young there.

15th Amused myself an hour or two this morning in filing your dear letters, that is folding them all up even. I am sorry to say that I have not done it as I received them and now they are all mixed together and I must leave them so till in some future day your biographer chooses to arrange them in proper order. In future I intend to do better and file as I receive them. I had a good laugh over some passages that I had forgotten, and found when I had finished it was 12 o'clock. Then I dressed, took my book, and read till dinner time. The play of the Spy glass served as interludes. But I watch in vain for Ships, nothing comes.

After dinner I read till it was time to sally forth. Being a lovely evening, we walked. Saw no one to speak to. Came home and I passed a pleasant evening with Mrs. Macondray. Coming home I passed the same crowd in the streets as before [August 10]. The performance seemed to be comic this evening, if loud laughter betokens it. I discovered that the performer was blind. Came home found Aunty had had a letter from Uncle. He had a good passage up.

16th This morning dressed early and took my book into the verandah. The Duke [Gordon] called and Van Basil. Mrs. Macondray, and Lucy spent the day with us, and I by way of variety cut out two little dresses, one for Lucy and one I intend to send to another lady [Caroline Colledge, who was expecting a child]. It was quite an amusement. I know not when I shall finish it.

After dinner I was watching for Ships, at last spied an American Barque which I concluded must be the *Tartar*, but it proved to be the *Harmony* from Liverpool. I saw the Co[mpany]'s Packett landed and all waiting on the Quay for letters. She left the 25th of March. Caroline spent the evening with us. Colledge and Mr. Dallas came about 10. The ship brings no news. No more monopoly after next year. [A reference to the end of the East India Company's charter.]

Sarah Elizabeth's birth day. She must be quite a different looking person from the little girl I left. I hope she is as good as she was pretty then. I think she bid fair to be a smart, intelligent girl and think she had more every of character if I may use the expression

than either of her Sisters, begging your pardon my dear. As for myself
I am quite ashamed of my <u>mental</u> laziness. I actually think it a trouble
to <u>think</u>, much more to accomplish what I often think would tend
to my advancement in knowledge. I hope Sarah will be more active
than my ladyship and I think she is far superior in every respect from
what I remember.

17 We intended to have made some calls this morning, but alas we
were made to feel our <u>dependence</u>. We called for <u>chair</u> <u>bearers</u> but
they were not forthcoming—"No could catch." <u>You</u> would fancy from
such a speech that they were wild beasts or birds, but no poor creatures, they are far from that and under bodily fear of every petty
mandarin who has the <u>honour</u> of wearing a <u>button</u>. It seems they
have come short in meeting their expenses so they have come with
an extra squeeze upon the poor bearers and until that is paid they
forbid their carrying the chairs. And they would sadly fear for their
poor backs were they to disobey the order. We cannot help pitying
the poor wretches who are subject to such tyranny, and feel annoyed
also that we are obliged to be so dependent. So we lost our visits
and the Opera this evening.

So I read all the morning Memoirs of Madame Junot or the *Duchess d'Abrantès* and was very much amused and entertained with it,
though I cannot put confidence in many of her opinions and state-
ments because they are at variance with every thing I have ever read
before. For instance she speaks very lightly of Josephine and says she
had no influence over "Napoleon."[85] Now every book I have ever
read upon this has given us to suppose the reverse, and as I find they
were not very great friends I make allowances for prejudices of this
nature. I get quite provoked sometimes in reading lives of great
people. If you read <u>two</u> <u>sides</u> you are sure to be puzzled regarding
their character. And how often you find that while the one makes
it an exalted and glorious character the other party makes it below
the common level, more especially a political character. I read this
all day till just at night Mrs. Morrison came in, and the play of the
<u>spy</u> <u>glass</u> was again the amusement and recreation of the day. I dis-
covered that something was outside the point by the movements of
the Cutter and Gordon came in to tea and told us that the officer of
the Ship *Superior* had just been at his house—she is only 104 days
from New York. So I must have some letters now. I cannot be disap-

pointed again I think, but I must wait a <u>few days</u> first. Well I will be patient. The stupid men could tell no news. I forgot my disappointment of the Opera and was only thinking of what we shall hear about. We shall hear of the arrangements regarding our going home etc. Had a good warm bath and went to bed and slept at the rate of 10 knots till 8 o'clock this morning, which now happens to be

Sunday Morning 18th of August Not being able to have a chair today was obliged to stay at home. Find being a prisoner by my own will or another person's is a very different thing. Self-inflicted imprisonment and with a feeling that you can go if you please is not grievous but I find now it is impossible. I have a great desire to go, but it is <u>impossible</u>, the sun is so hot. So I was a very good child at home and read good books and reflected all day. Before 10 o'clock at night I got violently sick of myself and was glad to go to bed. I was thinking this evening what a different summer this is from the last, for then we were <u>tormented</u> with the number of beaux and now a body has not a solitary <u>one</u> to call upon. So it is in China always in extremes either too many or none at all. Might have Gaffer but I'd rather stay at home. Never mind I shall have Botus [her brother Abbot] soon for a while I hope and then I can go where I please. Must wait two days more for my letters.

19th About 6 o'clock this morning Aunt Low got out of bed to go to her dressing room and found to her great surprise (by being called to a side window by some noise) the boy in her room hiding himself behind a screen. She awoke me by angrily asking him why he was there, to which he made no reply. Told him to go out, but he moved not. She went into her room to take off her night cap, came back to see if he was gone, but there he stood and stared at her as though he was stupified. She at last succeeded in getting him out. We strongly suspect he smokes opium as we have noticed several times lately, symptoms of <u>aberration</u> from some cause or other. We cannot fancy what sent him there or how long he had been there. He must have gone through my room to have got there, and he had a door to open which opens so hard that Josepha never can open it without awaking us, although she always tries. I cannot fancy what possessed him unless he was under the influence of that horrid opium. He is a youth of 18 or 19. Our headman is gone and we feel anxious to have him return.

Was delighted after breakfast to see our headman Achow walk in. He never met with so kind a reception from me before for he is not a favourite, but we feel so undecided regarding the conduct of the boy or rather the <u>cause</u> that we are very happy to be no longer under his <u>guidance</u> and <u>protection</u>. Aunty immediately related her grievances which Achow seemed to think a very great offense. Said it was very bad "<u>pigeon</u>." He forthwith went to examining the offender, but he could not extract a word from him. Says "sorry, no <u>savy</u> what he have got <u>inside</u>." However before night they had called a <u>jury</u> of Uncles and China doctors and pronounced the boy <u>delirious</u>, having a violent fever, or as he expresses it "too muchy <u>fire</u> inside." The verdict having been given <u>non</u> <u>compus</u> [*non mentis compos*—not in possession of sanity] by these said <u>savants</u> our anger changes at once into <u>pity</u> and a good dose of the <u>all</u> <u>powerful</u> <u>epsom</u> <u>salts</u> was at once dispatched, and if this is true he may be better in a few days. At any rate it would be hard to turn him out of the house. I should like to have Colledge see him, for it may be a <u>hoax</u> after all.

Having no chairs no one can go out in the day time, and I was of course at my books all day. Am very much interested and amused in the Memoirs of the Duchess, but she is so perfectly French in her feelings and style of writing that I laugh heartily at times. It is truly a woman's book. That is, she is so minute, dwells a great deal upon <u>pretty</u> <u>white</u> <u>hands</u>, <u>pearly</u> <u>teeth</u>, <u>curly</u> <u>hair</u>, and <u>white</u> <u>foreheads</u>.— A great deal of nonsense in the book, but upon the whole gives you good idea of the state of society.[86] It is more a history of private life than of public events. She is a woman of strong predjudices, but I should say pretty good sense, though nothing uncommon, with the education of a Frenchwoman or a French <u>lady</u>.

About 6 this evening we went out a little way and called at Caroline's. Came home and His Grace, the Duke [O. H. Gordon] give us the pleasure of his company to tea.

20th A very hot day and nothing new, no arrivals, no letters as yet and nothing to do but read. I this morning made a translation of the Argument of the Opera for this evening. Don Carlos the interpreter of the Musical Society undertakes to translate them. I will try and think to put one in here as a specimen,[87] for they are rich. We have as much fun with these as any thing.

His good <u>for nothing personage</u> the Soton[88] has not yet recalled his order respecting the chairbearers, but not choosing "to trust our charms to the perilous keeping of Caffre men's arms" we made ourselves quite independent and with the aid of Mr. Gordon we sallied forth at the hour and got there very comfortably. It was a fine evening. But the pavements of the streets are horrible. They remind me often of "Old Paved St." in Salem in days of yore, but perhaps worse. The whole width of the street is but very little wider than the sidewalk there and paved in the same way.

We had some fine music. Scherona really sung beautifully. I enjoyed it much. Mr. Hudleston and Gordon walked home with us. How you would stare to see the exhibitions that we see in the streets—they are literally lined with Chinese and Caffres asleep. They make the 'cold flinty rock' their pillow and lay there at the mercy of cockroches & mosquitoes, though I much doubt whether the latter could make any impression upon their <u>well tanned hides</u>. It seems to us impossible that they can sleep in such situations, but they appear as quiet and no doubt they are enjoying as delightful dreams as their <u>imaginations</u> will permit, for it appears to me that that must influence people's dreams, but "<u>I no savy</u>" as the Portuguese say.

Colledge came in today. Says the boy is no doubt sick, but he had best be sent away at any rate. For my part I shall have no peace till he has gone.

21ˢᵗ What can I say for today my dear Sister. It seems as though I could say nothing but I am well and hope you are the same. I studied, read, and etc. very industriously, but the morning seemed double the length of mornings in general, for I fully expected to get some letters this morning. I fear I am not to have that pleasure. I read a little Spanish this morning by way of variety. Was afraid I had forgotten all I know of it, but I find I can read it as easily as ever though having no practice I cannot speak at all.

After dinner Aunty had a letter from Uncle. He says Dumaresq and several other ships had left home before the *Superior*. Where can they be. Nothing comes. Only one of the Company's ships. Every one is so anxious to hear their fate respecting the Charter. We hear the *Cabot* had passed Anger 5 days before the *Superior*, but she has gone to Manilla. About 6 we went to Caroline's and spent the evening with her. She and her husband walked home with us at 10.

22ᵈ A hot morning, no wind. Aunty has had a letter from Uncle
and I have received another book. Really I hope the next will be
filled with something beside <u>howlings</u> and <u>lamentations</u>. Uncle's
letter gives us a most distressing account of two young ladies in Salem.
I am sure I shall be ashamed to acknowledge myself as a native of
that place. These are Miss Page and Miss Shepard who have made
themselves notorious. It cannot be our friend Lucy Ann. It must be
the next I suspect. What is it my dear Sis, what does possess them to
behave so. <u>We</u> know that they have excellent parents who have
instilled good and virtuous principles into them, who have indulged
them in all amusements to make home agreeable, have set them a
good example, and in part Brought them up in the fear of the Lord
and in the way they should go—and yet how soon, how lamentably
she has departed from it. How can a child repay a parent's care by
such conduct, mortifying them, her brothers and sisters, ruining herself and disgracing her sex. How lost, how depraved! It grieves me
to think of the poor family. What bliss (comparatively) it would have
been to have buried her.

   This is the error of allowing girls and boys to be <u>trapsing</u> about
the streets evenings. They have a great deal too much liberty in
Salem. I shall begin to be an advocate for French Seclusion almost.
If girls have no respect for themselves, no power of controlling their
evil propensities or if they will not use that power, they had much
better be kept to themselves.

   None are apparently so prim and prudish as the Salemites in their
manners before strangers, but appears to me there are more *faux pas*
there than anywhere. If people in respectable and good society set
such examples, what can be expected from the lower classes who
can cite such instances? Oh I could cry for them all. For what can
you depend upon, if education kindness and example are all defied—
and here in this instance I know the parents. Oh my dear little sisters, may you never repay your parents care with such conduct with
such disgrace. It seems quite intolerable enough for a son to offend,
but a girl seems ten times worse. You know boys are more exposed to
temptation and more likely to come in contact with wickedness in
all shapes. And youth, thoughtlessness and strong feelings may sometimes be alleged as an excuse and the follies of youth in a man are
often forgotten in the more serious and sedate conduct of riper years.
But a girl if she sins, it must be the promptings [of] the wickedness

of her <u>heart</u>. (I mean in the deliberate and shameful cases now before us.) Once gone she is ruined for this world. Thorough and bitter repentance cannot remove the finger of scorn and contempt, that
will always be pointed to her through life. Nothing can erase the
stigma upon her character.

And then the workings of remorse and the stings of a guilty conscience. Oh who that possesses one spark of reflection can throw
themselves into such a <u>hell</u>, for can it be less? Oh wicked, heartless,
cruel, sinful man to bring such misery upon a female. But it appears
to me this young Putman was but a boy. How cruel it seems that he
may after all his wickedness, still go into the world and by future
conduct <u>may</u> make himself either respected or despised <u>as</u> <u>he</u> <u>pleases</u>.
Oh that the same disgrace could be entailed on man that there is on
woman. There might be fewer such instances to lament.

As usual I spent the whole day at my books, a shrine at which I
lay all my sorrows. I spent the evening in thinking (very uselessly I
grant) how my days are running away. I got so _triste_ by 1/2 past 9
that I went to bed feeling cross and almost weary of existence. You
can have no idea appears to me just how we are situated. Aunt Low
was sick today and so _bon gré mal gré_ I must stay at home, for the
idea of a <u>spinster</u> walking out <u>alone</u> is an enormity one never could
be supposed guilty of. And there is no gentleman here that I can
call upon and even if there was that would be another crime, for me
to go out unattended by a <u>Chaperone</u>. Oh hard is the lot of <u>Spin-
sters</u> in Macao. As we can have no chairbearers why we must e'en
make the best of it. So we poor solitary things are compelled to stay
within four walls and neither see nor be seen. Oh I am so sick of it.
Well I went to bed and there I laid till 1/2 past 7.

23ᵈ Got up and eat my breakfast and then vented my indignation
upon every thing. Aunty & I fully agree upon these points and I
cannot enumerate the thousand little ways in which we are compelled to surrender our own wills to that of the people. I verily think
if I was condemned to live here for 10 years I should go crazy. Oh
dear, oh dear. I hope I shall never be put into such another place.

After dinner I had the pleasure to receive my letters. They were
satisfactory inasmuch as they assured me of your health and that you
were all alive, for which I thanked God most sincerely. But they refer
to old letters and you do not at all seem to feel that it is a long time

since I have heard. From October to May is a great space. However I wait patiently for Abbot. You tell me you are married with as much indifference as though you told me you had dined. I should be most happy to know when Abbot left but that I cannot find out. All tell me of dreadful capers in Salem and all suppose that others have told me. So I do not get a word of the truth. Our boys all seem to be separating to seek their fortunes, here, there, and every where. I was not exactly pleased with my dear father's letter. It was short and appeared to me as though it was written in displeasure at me or my sentiments, which grieved me to the quick. Inasmuch as I am at such a distance I cannot explain. I should rather not have received it. A word or look of displeasure for him is quite enough to make me unhappy and always was and I do not find I feel any differently from what I did when I left in this respect. It seems he thinks I have caught the <u>immoral</u> <u>contagion</u> that prevails in China and mother thought my heart was gone and my <u>brain</u> turned. No wonder you feel anxious for me to return. However you cannot be more so than I am, for I long to find myself in S--- [word illegible] and among people more congenial to my feelings. Oh how I long for it! But can I, could I with any sort of feeling leave my aunt who has been so kind to me here <u>alone</u>, as she is nearly all the time. No I cannot do it. If she should be sick after I had left I should never forgive myself. Beside I should not like the idea of going home without a lady. It would be considered here very <u>indecorous</u>.

I long to have an opportunity to write. I wish it might be so arranged that Uncle could leave this January, but I fear it will not. Hope we shall know by this Ship. After I had read my letters I felt considerably revived and we went out to make a few calls. Paid our first visit to Mrs. Bartlett, found her a very pleasant woman. Then went to Mrs. Daniell's where we met Lady Robinson and Mr. & Mrs. Wimberley. Staid there till nearly dusk then went home. We felt quite independent going on our <u>own</u> <u>feet</u>, and got home very well. Aunt Low suffers dreadfully from corns so that she cannot always walk.

Now my dear I have come to the end of another book. I tremble for some of the last, as I know I have expressed my sentiments often and perhaps not <u>fully</u> enough to be understood. I have regretted sometimes since as I think they may lead my dear father to suppose my morals are more <u>corrupt</u> than they really are. Not that I should care that you all know every sentiment of my heart if I could talk and explain but in writing one often gives a different sense, or at least it appears different because you cannot explain fully. But I hope you will all make due allowances and believe that I mean well whatever I may chance to write. I often write thoughts that under different circumstances would never enter my brain.

Volume VII
August 24–November 17, 1833

Continuation of the <u>Lights</u> and <u>Shadows</u> of a
Macao Life by a <u>Travelling</u> <u>Spinster</u>
Containing the Grand Finale and an
<u>Affectionate</u> <u>farewell</u> to China

August 24th 1833   No 7

August 24th Another yet another. Are you not tired my dear of my <u>importunity</u>, for such it may be called I think when it comes to the commencement of the 7th vol. And now all the delightful <u>cares</u> of matrimony are coming thick upon you. I sadly fear I shall not receive such patient attention as heretofore. But I am very selfish in writing thus, for it gives me pleasure and when I return if that happy day ever arrives I shall recur to it with still more pleasure, for the recollections of Macao will like the <u>view</u> of it appear best at a distance.

This morning at breakfast I rec'd a budget of news from Mr. Gordon and some newspapers, so that my thoughts were wandering all day. I find every arrival recalls all my home feelings and makes me wish more and more to be there.

It has been a burning hot day and no wind, and appears like a precursor of a Typhoon but the Barometer is high and people are not anxious. After dinner we dressed in spite of the heat and went to pay some visits. Left a Card at Mrs. Clifton's, and then went to Mrs. Macondray's, Caroline with us, and left a card at Mrs. Fearon's. All the world gone to the Opera tonight but us. About 6 o'clock a strong breeze set in from the N. E. and cooled the air beautifully. It was a most lovely night.

25 This morning commenced as the Sailors say squally and rainy, so that we could not go to Church. I was reading all the morning "Faber, *on the Prophesies*."[1] Was quite interested. About 2 o'clock breeze strengthened and [there was] every prospect of a visitation from one of the Typhoon family. At 7 very little doubt about [it], as Achow says, "it's Typhoon he own," that is himself. It is to be hoped he will not be followed by his wife and family. We were watching the destruction of our comforts which were vanishing like chaff before the wind. One after the other of our mats flew off and all we could do was to look on and see them go. The tile came tumbling from the roof and destroyed our grotto the monument of our industry. The unsparing hands of the coolies pulled down my pretty vines to spare the pots from destruction. But this is not the worst. Where are the Ships? Who can say. We can only trust to the wisdom and goodness of a kind providence. I trust they are all out at sea and will not experience it. There must be whole fleets near. The severity of the gale was over before 10 o'clock and I hope it was not so bad as last year. Poor Mrs. Thornhill must be suffering the same as Aunt Low did last year, for her husband left last evening in the same boat.

26th Had a note from Mr. Gordon this morning telling me the news. Rained in torrents all the morning. Contrived to make the day pass quickly away by varying my employments, reading, writing, drawing and sewing a little. But I feel so anxious about Abbot that I cannot feel easy. He has been out now 5 months and it is quite time he was here. After dinner I commenced Bigelow's *Travels in Sicily and Malta*.[2] Very interesting but he is too strongly predjudiced to be always just. He seems to hate the English. From his description of Gibraltar I should think it was little better as a residence than Macao. It has this advantage—it is nearer the Christian world.

Gordon spent the evening with us. Cleared off beautifully tonight.

It seems people do not call the gale yesterday a Typhoon. The wind was wholly from the Eastward. We appear to have suffered more than any one.

27th A beautiful pure air this morning and clear sky that seems to refresh one. The *Scaleby Castle* arrived this morning, the first direct

Ship [from London]. Suppose all are busy, reading letters from home sweet home. Had letters from Uncle but give us accounts not very satisfactory. I feel anxious, miserable, and sad. I do wish Abbot would come. I long to see some one that belongs to me.

After tea we walked up to see Mrs. Macondray. Came home and spent the evening. We did not feel disposed to go to the Opera, so sent our tickets to the Miss Ullman's. The most lovely evening and night I most ever saw.

28ᵗʰ How fully today has proved the words of the Poet "All that's bright must fade, the brightest still the fleetest." [Thomas Moore, *All That's Bright Must Fade*] Who would have thought such a night could have been followed by such a squally tempestuous day. Raining in torrents and we are obliged to shut venetians and glass to keep the rain out thereby making the house look like night. Dismal enough it would be without the thought that my dear brother may be exposed to the fury of these squalls and many, many others. We two poor solitary beings shut up in a dark house have a resource only in books. I am half tempted at times to give way to my feelings and give up in despair, but then I rally again, and say what is the use, take my books and try to forget every thing. I make a variety by commencing after breakfast with french exercises—then study a Page or two in Dufif,³ then I read French. I am just now reading Madame de Genlis' Moral tales. Some of them are very good and the French is said to be good, but they are not what I should choose if I could have my choice. But there are so few French books in the Library that I find it difficult to get any thing worth reading. After I have read French enough I take a little Spanish book and read that. It is Florian's William Tell⁴ translated into Spanish and very pretty. I am rather precious of it as Spanish books are more rare than French. Then I have arrived at 2 o'clock, the other hour till dinner I generally draw. I have got one of Chinnery's books. Then after dinner I read English. Read all this afternoon and evening Mr. Bigelow's *Travels in Malta & Sicily*—like them much. His observations upon the Catholics will apply to them in all parts of the world I suspect. And it seems that it has the same effect upon morals. The confession and absolution has a very bad effect. It does not appear to have any check upon their wicked propensities to know they must tell their sins to their father Confessor. The same processions and worshipping I may say images is noticed here as well as there. He speaks of the Misericordia or Foundling Hospital in Malta and doubts whether it has a good or ill effect. The same thoughts have often occurred to me—whether it is not encouraging vice by taking such good care of illegitimates. The same rules respecting that Society are established here. The mother has but to deposit her child when an infant in a basket upon the step of the door, ring a bell and no questions are asked and her child is provided for. Now in Catholic countries where the sin is so easily absolved and the child provided for and damsels have but little respect for themselves, I am inclined to think such Societies do more harm than good. For often the trouble and care of supporting a child might possibly and would often I dare say deter a woman from such wickedness even if no other feeling influenced her. But my dear Sister you can have no idea of the State of morals in this place—it is melancholy. And while the Catholic religion prevails it appears to me it must be so.

[Marginal note] There is no question but there should be some provision for such poor unfortunates, but I think the means of disposing of them should be more difficult and more shame attending it.

Oh that all nations could know and appreciate the beauties, the purity and holy feelings of Christianity!

I was much amused by Bigelow's description of the growth of the fig. He says the wild fig is brought to perfection by the assistance of a little gnat or ichneumon, which inserts its eggs into the fig which become in time little black shining worms. And that the domestic fig when growing, fills the branches so closely with its fruit that the tree cannot nourish them all. To assist their arriving at maturity, the natives hang branches of the wild fig in among the branches of the domestic fig. These little gnats go from one to the other, and by the fermentation they produce or the juices they circulate in the fruit it comes to perfection and in great abundance. I will say nothing of the manner in which it is packed and sent to America—this [is] enough. You perhaps will not thank me for enlightening you upon this subject, but I cannot get any myself and I felt a little <u>mischievous</u>—but never mind. Remember my dear if you took a microscope you might even refuse a drop of water. So ignorance is bliss and I think I shall never use a microscope for any thing I wish to eat. Eat the figs and say if gnats are there they are very sweet and no doubt improve the fruit wonderfully.

I read till 10 o'clock and was very much interested.

29th Went to bed last night but not to sleep, for the house seemed like a perfect Babel. The wind blew a tremendous gale from the S.E. and although the windows were lashed and bolted and fastened in every possible way, it seemed as though they could not stand the force of the wind. We could not sleep any all night. My thoughts were of the ships near. Now this morning it continues, the house is dark as <u>Erebus</u>. I have got my Venetians tilted a little so that I can just see to write. The wind has not abated at all and <u>such</u> a sea. Oh dear, Oh dear. The Chinese say it will be worse tomorrow. Am sure the house will hardly stand, it rocks now like a cradle.

The wind continued to blow violently through the day, but moderated a little at night and we hope the predictions of the Chinese will fail. They say there will be a Typhoon tomorrow. It is dismal enough to be shut up so, but we made up to keep the Venetians of the windows open so we both got near that and fortunately our books were interesting. I was very sorry to find I must bid Mr. Bigelow Adieu just as he was leaving Sicily to go to Naples. I should have liked much to have followed him there and through Italy. I closed the book at 1/2 past 10, sincerely hoping I may one of these days have the pleasure of finishing his travels. I like his style and observations much, all except his predjudices and his <u>display</u> of <u>patriotism</u>. Do not misunderstand me. I do not dislike patriotism, *au contraire*, but I do not like people's praising their own country and drawing comparisons at all times. I seems to me like a man's praising his own children to all strangers.

It is too much like the English I think, they make themselves disagreeable wherever they go by jesting and laughing at every thing that is not English, and seem to think nothing can be good that differs from them. Now this same spirit nourished among Americans will lead to the same effect, which is quite intolerable I think. Therefore it is best to keep one's thoughts to one's self I <u>think</u>.

30th This morning we found ourselves in bed at 1/2 past 9. Having had no sleep the night before and the house being dark as midnight we did not awake. The wind is still blowing furiously and raining in torrents, though not quite so tremendous as at first. I sent my books back to the Library after breakfast and got a new supply, for I live upon them. I begin to get accustomed to the weather and feel pretty contented. Aunt Low and my little bird and I sit in one corner of the room at the only window in which we have any light from morning till night. Our only interruption is the cooly coming with his tub and cloth to save us from drowning. For windows in China are not made to keep out rain, and every now and then we find ourselves in a pond of water, but the cooly discovers our situation by its dripping through and comes to our relief. I can fancy very easily a person in prison becoming attached to a spider after a time. I am sure I should feel quite melancholy without my bird. He seems to get very <u>pensive</u> now and then, but then again he says like his mistress "What's the use of sighing" and cheers us with a merry song. To think my dear Sis of your sister living without a care but that of <u>feeding a bird</u>—she who spent the young days of her life in making button holes and shirts, etc., one of the most diligent of her sex. Well I look back to those days with pleasure and would willingly have much to do now. There is nothing like employment. My books afford me great pleasure, but one wants something beside to take some interest in. But I will harp no more on this note. You must be tired of it.

I got several vols. of the Family Library this morning, and after dinner commenced the "Life of Peter the Great."[5] He was a wonderful man. There is a similarity in the early days of Catherine & Josephine I think. But alas their end, how different. You may suppose we got through the day pretty well when I tell you we were up till 1/2 past 11 reading. We walked the room from six to seven, talking of what we had been reading, of prisons, sudden death, and wound up with the education of children. If you had been near you would have said "Old Maids' children," etc.

August 31st This morning we had the pleasure of opening our windows and welcoming the sun which deigned to smile at times through the clouds which surrounded him. The wind still blows a fresh breeze, but this will bring the Ships, so I say, "Blow, breezes, blow." I need not say I took my book after breakfast for that is as much a matter of course as possible. About 1 Caroline came to us, she succeeded in getting Chair bearers again. I do not know when I have passed a pleasanter morning. It was cool and C. brought her work. Aunty & she worked while I drew and we talked of the late news from home and she amused us with her drolleries till 3 o'clock when she left us to take care of her *caro sposo*.

After dinner I finished the Life of Peter. He richly deserves the name of Great and appears to have had the good of his country at heart. But to accomplish his desires he waded through oceans of blood.

As to goodness I have done looking for that in <u>great</u> men. After I had finished this I commenced *Six Months in the West Indies* by Coleridge.[6] It is written in a light easy style and the marks of a Poet are upon it. He stops on his way at Madeira. Every word of which interested [me] as Abbot has been there, and if I ever see him, I can talk to him of places. He gives some ludicrous descriptions of adventures there.

We had some tea and then to our books again. About 9 the servant handed us some letters per *Sumatra*, Capt. Roundy. I had one from Mrs. [Lucy] Cleveland, and a few lines from Brother Nat [N. P. Knapp], all I rec^d from <u>all</u> my friends in my native town. I begin to feel that there are none but my own dear family who will hold out to the end and remember me. Aunt Low had a number of letters, out of which we gain nothing but dark hints of horrid occurrences, and some which concern one who has been a member of our family. We suppose they have written particulars by Abbot. I know not where he can be.

I assure you these letters make me very unhappy for I cannot bear that there should be any <u>slander</u>, for such it must be, about one with whom I have lived in such close communion for so long a time. I do not know what will come next. Salem seems to be the sink of iniquity and I shall be ashamed to call myself a Salemite any longer. What evil spirit reigns there? We hope to get at something by Roundy, for it is dreadful to be left in the dark so. Mrs. Cleveland remains the same dear creature. I hope I shall have the pleasure of meeting her again. She mentions George Orne was dying at Cousin Ann's [died February 18, 1833, age 33].

My friend Nat's engagement is confirmed by himself— consequently I am cut out of my letter there, at least only a few lines. Oh my dear Sis such heaps of wickedness coming to one's ears at once almost distracts one and sickens me of my species almost. I sigh in the spirit and say what is there in this world worth possessing and almost wish to fly away and be at rest. It makes me think of the importance of laying up our treasures where moth nor rust doth not corrupt, of fixing our affections on something more stable than this world or its enjoyments and praying that I may in every thought, word and deed do all to the glory of God.

When I think of the misery and mortification and anxiety children give their parents and in return for the most tender care, I say Happy is she who has none and better is it to remain in single blessedness than to bring little beings into the world, to so much wickedness and sin. I went to bed but could not sleep for my thoughts were too busy. How dreadful to have such tidings reach you in a distant land.

September 1st 1833

1st Awoke this morning to the same gloomy feelings after a most restless and disturbed night. I could not go to Church but I read my sermons at home and tryed to spend the day profitably. Mr. Inglis made us a call after Church and Sir George Robinson and Caroline. Every one seems to be singing the same tune. I am very anxious for such & such a Ship for my letters refer me to others that I have not yet received. That is the cry of all and well may the English feel anxious, for their fate almost depends on the next arrivals.

After dinner I went to see Mrs. Macondray to find out more about the *Sumatra*, but could not gain much. Can hear nothing of Abbot's having passed through the Straits.

2d This morning I had just dressed and was reading my Bible when I heard strange voices in the drawing room and a knock at my door. And I run thinking it must be Abbot but it was Uncle James [James Low][7] & Sam Sturgis just arrived. I was delighted as you may suppose, and seemed like drawing the chain shorter which has so long been stretched between us. He gave me a letter from you my dear, but I expected packets. One short one from Abbot. My dear mother too wrote me a few lines, in which as ever the same dear kind Mother is visible. Oh she asks me how I feel at the thought of coming home. Tell her it is too much to think of. I dare not—the thing now I consider impossible. It will grieve me beyond every thing to think you will be disappointed but when you think again I hope you will all see the propriety of my determination. Uncle James has already said that he thinks it best for me to stay another year.

You may be assured I had enough to say all day. Mr. Perit [J.W. Perit] called this morning and I liked him very much and should like making a voyage with him. Think we should be great allies, but I doubt whether he goes home in the *Cabot*.

They saw a dismasted Ship outside, but could not go to her. I fear there are many sufferers and my dear brother may be among the number. I cannot help feeling very anxious. They say the gale was tremendous.

Mr. [William] Dallas called this morning, Caroline after dinner. Uncle Low has got a bad cold but is looking pretty well.

3ᵈ This morning took my walk and sit with Uncle James. I have got all the satisfaction I can from him and it only makes me long to be with you more. I am very glad to hear from him that Margaret Low is well married.

Mr. Whiteman called. Says there is an account of the *Grand Duquesne* having been burnt at sea. How horrid. But fortunately the people were all saved.

This evening I went to see the Opera of *Othello* [Gioachino Rossini, 1816]. Aunt & Uncle being invalids did not go. I went with Caroline. The dresses were splendid, but the music not so good as usual. You cannot trace Shakespeare's play in it. Of course it was got up here under great disadvantage.

Had a very pleasant time. So long since I have seen the people here that it really seemed pleasant. Sam Sturgis waited upon me.

4ᵗʰ A pleasant day, the first for a long time. We spent this day in reading, drawing and talking. I have been very stupid. My [mind] seems in a maze if I am put out of my usual way at all. I do not know what will become of me when I come home with all the excitement and bustle of a city and seeing so many people. After dinner I took Uncle James out to walk, and I have not had such a one for a long time. We went to the top of a high hill where we could see all over the town. Came home and he give us an account of his and his wife's trip to Spain, Holland, & France. I should like to have been one of the party. She has been quite a traveller. Uncle James has not altered at all. It must be six years since we saw him.

5ᵗʰ The *Waterloo* arrived this morning bringing Mr. & Mrs. Jackson, Mr. Clarke [Henry Matthew Clarke], & Astell [John Harvey Astell] who went home two years since. Another delightful day. The Miss Ullmans called this morning and I then went to Caroline's to hear the news, but did not get any. Then went to Mrs. Macondray's and brought up at home about 3. We had a delightful walk after dinner, us three. The air was so soft and balmy as it blew fresh from the ocean that it seemed to give one new life and to soften the asperities of one's feelings. For when all nature looks so calm and delightful it seems a sin for any but the most holy, pure and delightful feelings to be at work— yet how often one finds this discord, which sometimes seems in mockery of our feelings.

We came home from our walk, found Caroline there. She spent

the evening with us. Uncle James seems pretty well but seems to have lost his spirits. He has not any of the <u>roguery</u> he used to have. Seems to like the quiet, still life we lead. I was afraid he would soon get tired of it, but it seems to suit him very well.

6 I have nothing to say today my dear, except that we had a delightful day. Had a letter from Uncle [W. H. Low] this morning which did not much please me. He tells us more sad tales of Salem, really I never heard any thing so shocking. Mr. Clarke and Astell called this morning. Seem just the same as ever. Say they have been making the most of their time in England. Mrs. Allport I am glad to hear is on her way out.

After dinner Aunt Low & I went out. Called at Caroline's and Mrs. Macondray's. Uncle James was too lame or lazy to go and he stayed at home.

7th Was reading all day the Life of Bruce and James the 1st of Scotland.[8] You will see my reading is very promiscuous, perhaps not the best way for improving the mind, but I have to read just what I can get.

At night I went out to walk with Aunty, we went to the Gap. Caroline joined us and I went home with her to tea, stayed till 11 o'clock. Her husband had gone to the Opera and she was alone. I read aloud to her one of Mr. Channing's elegant sermons. It was upon Immortality.[9] Such Sentiments do honour to human nature and excite the desire and a strong one to possess such pure and holy feelings. The only fault one can find with his sermons is, they are not suited for <u>vulgar</u> <u>minds</u>. That is common, uneducated minds would not appreciate them and they would appear cold and lifeless to any but the refined and enlightened hearer. But how much more to be envied is a man of his talents possessing such sentiments than a Byron, a Scott, a Napoleon, or a <u>Peter</u>.

8th Sunday Mon'g. Mrs. Macondray has a fine little boy this morning and is comfortable as can be expected. She sent for me after breakfast and I went to get my orders. Found her quite smart. She wanted me to write to her husband. So I did and came home and despatched it. As I went through the streets I could not help reflecting how different every thing appeared from what it would at home on this morning—every one at work and going on with the dayly work as usual, instead of the quiet still street. As I returned however the bells of St. José were chiming and by shutting my eyes I could find myself in a more civilized land where the one only true god is worshipped by <u>some</u> in spirit and in truth. But alas how few of the many who assemble in his courts really feel in whose presence they are. How many take his name upon their lips while the heart is far from him.

I came home, despatched my letter, and went to Church. Heard a sermon upon original Sin, "or the total depravity of the human heart." I have thought much upon this subject lately but I am puzzled. I have not yet made up my mind. I do not believe as Wimberley does that is certain, but I leave the subject for the present. I hardly know what I do think. I intend to try and put my thoughts on paper at some time. I went in to see how Caroline was a minute, then came home and read a sermon to Uncle James. Then commenced the *History of the Jews*.[10]

After dinner I read two more of Channing's excellent sermons.[11] They were the 10th & 11th of the new book, and most excellent. About 6 Aunt Low and I took a short walk on the Campo, were introduced to Mrs. Jackson and met a lot of people. Campbell and Layton joined us and walked home with us. We spent the evening in talking with Uncle James of all the good people at home, and Uncle seems like a sort of connecting link, for I know a <u>great</u> <u>deal</u> about you now.

9th This morning while we were at breakfast who should come in but Uncle William, looking like death.[12] Poor soul I never saw a person so much altered in so short a time. Uncle James says he should not have known him to have met him in the street. He has been dreadfully troubled with <u>boils</u> and some fever, but I dare say Macao air will soon restore him. He had taken a long walk this morning. He got so impatient in the boat that they landed a long way out. He was quite faint when he came but before night he looked better. Colledge came to see him and I hope will soon cure him, but I tremble for this winter's work. His health is not good and such close application is too much for him and he will make his money and what will it avail with ruined health. I wish he could go [home] this year but I fear he will not. Indeed he <u>cannot</u> unless he is so sick that he cannot work. If I had ever thought of going with Uncle James, this sickness would prevent me. I would not leave him for any thing.

Canton is now in a terrible state. The river has risen so high that it has completely deluged villages above Canton and the poor Chinamen are driven from their houses without a place to go to and their houses have fallen and many thousands killed. Their rice is ruined and they are in great trouble, but all these things are right we cannot doubt. There must be something to thin the populations of all countries. We see pestilence and disease in one country, wars in another, earthquakes and inundations in others, and I am sure it is a mercy for this abundant people to be thinned. They cannot move out of their Hongs in Canton except in Boats. Uncle says the water was up to their door and or course every thing must be wet and damp and sickness must ensue unless it dries up very soon. Our family now seems more homeish than I ever have known it in China. If Abbot would only come now we should have five Lows.

After dinner I went up to see Mrs. Macondray, and from thence went to the Peña and mused upon a variety of subjects—that was the hour particularly dedicated to Eliza Ward [Harriett's teacher in Salem]. The 9th of September at sunset 4 years ago today I was at anchor in Manilla Bay. Where shall I be 4 years hence? Who can say.

10th A dreadfully hot day but I spunked up and went to pay my respects to Mrs. Jackson. Called first on Mrs. Morrison, found her comfortable. The old Dr. complaining—wants to get a sick certificate to go to England with his family. Then went to see Mrs. Jackson, a pleasant, unaffected little creature. May be called pretty. I liked her very well. Then I called on Mrs. Wimberley, found Mrs. Grant there. Of course we had a dissertation upon children and the expedient way of nursing them, with divers and sundry comparisons of one child with another, the number of teeth, and etc. All very interesting of course to a Spinster. From there I went to Caroline and stayed till 3, from thence I proceeded home where I spent the afternoon in trying to read, but it was awful hot. I could scarcely breathe. Just as I was dressing to go to Mrs. Grant's, Roundy came in and so I did not go till 9. Stayed and asked all the questions I could think of. At 9 started, found a herd of women assembled in the midst of which was one gentleman Mr. Wimberley. I told him he had established his character as a man of courage. The conversation appeared to be general, the subject duelling and soon turned to ghosts and dreams. I stayed an hour. We had a little music and came home.

11th Roundy breakfasted with us and I spent most of the day in catechising him. I have become quite acquainted with the Salem folks through him and am very sorry to hear they have become so wicked there. The very demons of crime seem to be reigning there with full power.

After dinner I went up to see Mrs. Macondray with Roundy and we took a walk to the Peña. I find he heard all Macao reports at Batavia, respecting <u>smites</u> and offers. It is impossible to keep such things secret, particularly when men act like <u>fools</u> <u>themselves</u>, and give people proof of such things by their actions, which is always confirmation strong.¹³ I came home and felt quite unwell. I was invited to Caroline's but refused. Roundy bid us good bye at 10, starts tomorrow early with a pilot. I hurried to bed and we were all just comfortably in bed when I heard the outer door open and soon after a knock at my own door and in a second I was in the arms of Abbot. How delighted or how rejoiced I was I leave you to imagine. I was sorry to have to tell him the sick state of my dear Uncle and not to disturb him by having a noise in the house. I soon had a bed prepared on the floor for A. A. and retired myself but I could not sleep. The thought that after all my anxiety he had arrived safely and the strange feeling of seeing one of my own brothers in this country and the excitement all together quite drove sleep from my eyes. He gave me oceans of letters but I left them till morning. I recognized his voice and look at once. Indeed I think he had altered but very little. He has grown a little taller and is as brown as a <u>mulatto</u> now.

12ᵗʰ Got up this morning <u>early</u>. Ordered a Bath for Botus and Afun the <u>barber</u> which was very necessary, for his head and face was envelopped in a mass of hair of 4 months growth, and you could scarcely discern his visage. His teeth are very white compared to his brown face, otherwise I see no change.

He is astonished at Uncle's appearance but thinks with the exception of having lost my colour that I have not altered at all. I have never passed so happy a day in China with such <u>genuine</u> <u>home</u> <u>feelings</u>. If Uncle was only well! After breakfast I skimmed over my many letters and feel glad that I am still remembered. I had <u>thought</u> otherwise. I gave Abbot his but I am sure letters never got so little attention. My thoughts were completely *distrait*. I hardly knew what I was about, and in true Chinese style because I was almost surfeited with kindness and happiness, in came more letters by Dumaresq to Batavia, and Company's Ship here. So you see we have every thing at once. And this is the first time that we have any of our connections here and now here is Uncle James, Abbot, <u>Roundy</u> & Elvin Orne expected. It is always the way out here, all or nothing. It has long been a maxim here that there is no <u>medium</u> in China, and it is verified daily. We have now <u>five</u> in family, but however I will not complain but make the most of it. But my <u>economical</u> habits would led me to have spliced it out or taken a little at a time if I had had the disposing of events, but as there is a far wiser one that I am, I conclude all is right, and have made up my mind "that in whatever state I am I will <u>endeavour</u> to be content." For there is so many disappointments in life that we must enjoy the present or the future will never yield us that we wish.

I can say nothing of Salem affairs for they are too numerous and too <u>shocking</u>, and disgrace our sex too much.

I have at least found out that you were married just 4 days before Caroline. Rather singular that we should both be engaged in the same <u>occupations</u> (preparing, I mean) in different parts of the world.

Uncle seems to gain no strength and looks miserably. I may go home yet this year but if we do it will be under such circumstances that I shall hardly hail it with pleasure. Alas how soon may all our anticipations and hopes may be blasted.

I have talked to Abbot all day and now feel acquainted with you all. You will not be such strangers to me when I come home.

13th Tolerably pleasant day. After breakfast sent for the Tailor and spoke for some jackets for Abbot. I am glad he didn't have many made at home for they do not know how to make them. They <u>construct</u> them too heavily for this climate, and they should have no stuffing in them. Have not got my wedding cake yet. It's in the "<u>moon</u>" [Cap sing moon] and I cannot say when it will come down. Took Abbot and introduced him to Mrs. Colledge. After dinner we went to walk. I think A. A. has much improved in his manners. They are very pleasant and he will be liked in Canton I am sure.

14th Uncle still very feeble.[14] I have read over some of my letters and find something new in all. I did not take the sense of them at all. I have been living quite a new life this few days past. I have hardly read a line, and certainly that to no purpose for pleasure of Abbot's company and Uncle's sickness has quite discomposed my ideas. The least variation in our regular routine puts us out. We three went to walk after dinner.

15 Uncle was <u>leeched</u> last night and seems a little relieved. Abbot & I went to Church this morning. Did not much like Mr. Wimberley. Went home and read Dr. Channing's sermon till Caroline came in, but my mind was not in a state to fully understand it and I shall reserve it for a more convenient <u>season</u>. Colledge says Uncle requires great care and that it will not do for him to go to Canton this 6 weeks.

After dinner we went to the Casa Garden, but I find the <u>Palheiro</u> at Madeira puts Macao very much in the shade. But I cannot say much for the garden now. It is in a very bad state. There were some young ladies at Madeira too who seem to have made a deep impression, but I cannot discover that either in particular. So Botus I think is safe for the next 5 years. We spent this evening with Caroline. Came home early and found poor Uncle suffering with his blister, but hope it will relieve his cough.

16 Uncle had a bad night but seems better this morning. Have been trying to read today but I have got quite out of that way. My mind is in such a confused state that I have to read over three or four times.

After dinner I went to see Mrs. Macondray and then proceeded to the Peña where I had agreed to meet Abbot and Uncle James. Called in at Caroline's and found her alone and stopped and took tea but came home before 9 to see Abbot.

17 Uncle about the same. Mends so slowly that the change is hardly perceptible. Have read a little today and wrote a letter to go by *Dorothea* via Mexico. After dinner we three went to walk and Abbot & I went round the Guia, a very rough walk. The late rains have made it almost impassable. Uncle James went over the top, which was not the walk of an Invalid.

We spent the evening on the terrace talking. I am astonished to hear Abbot say he does not like reading. I thought he was fond of it, but I find <u>business</u> is his rulling passion and he begins to get impatient already to get to Canton where he can commence operations. There is not much danger but that he will be perfectly contented there.

18 Uncle seems much better today with the exception of night sweats (which weaken him very much). He is pretty well.

Caroline in this morning, not very well, looks miserably. Received your wedding cake this morning my dear. It is super excellent. I never

Facade of the Great Temple at Macao, *Thomas Allom, ca. 1840*

tasted better. Was busy all the morning looking over Abbot's things & etc. Think care would sit heavily on me now, I have been so long unused to it. Sent a piece of cake to some of my friends. It's a great treat here I assure you. The gingerbread is also very nice.

This evening I went to a party at Mrs. Davis's—had a very pleasant time. We had some good singing and danced a little which considering the heat did not give me much pleasure. Mr. Howard was there, the famous singer, and the new arrivals, and the party went off in a most satisfactory manner both to our hostess and the visitors.

19 Uncle still better. I am unsettled and hardly know what to do, my thoughts are confused and wandering. This being the case I took a little work and sallied forth to Mrs. Colledge's. Stayed there till 2 then went to Mrs. Macondray's. Came home at 3 and after dinner read Landers's *expedition to the Source of the Niger*[15] till it was time to dress to go to Mr. Plowden's to dinner. I called for Caroline and we went at 7. Our party consisted of Mrs. Daniell & Jackson and ourselves, the ladies and their husbands & Inglis, Clarke, Howard, Astell, Chinnery, & Whitehead. We had a very social party and I enjoyed it very well. It rained violently when it was time to go home, so that we did not leave till 1/2 past 12. A company's packet came in the evening and our friend Mrs. Allport came in the same Ship. Got an invitation for a party at Mrs. Daniell's on Monday evening.

20 Fox come in this morning. After dinner Abbot and I went to walk. We went to the Joss House. Could not start Uncle James, he will not condescend to admire any thing in Macao. He immediately compares with Europe, and "comparisons are odious" [John Fortescue, *De Laudibus Legum Angliae*, Chapter 19] you know. He is a very different person from what I thought him. We got caught in the rain returning and got a ducking.

21st Mrs. Allport came on shore this morning. I went to see her at 12. She appears just the same, looks in better health. Went from here to Mrs. Macondray and then to Caroline's. Came home at dinner. Colledge has told Uncle this morning that he should not consent to his going to Canton this six weeks and then he must not write again, that he ought never to pursue this employment again. He thinks it would be wise for him to go home. And will not be for want of persuasion on our part if he does not.

What is money without health though it is not that that would trouble him, but not fulfilling his duty to others that he thinks of. But if he can do nothing what is the use of his staying. Rainy afternoon and no walk.

22^d Stayed at home from Church and read aloud to Abbot two excellent sermons of Dr. Channing's, after dinner read one to Uncle James. All of which I admire, it is so reasonable, so rational the religion that he preaches that I delight in it. Abbot and I went to Caroline's this evening as he is going off tomorrow. Dr. Cox was there.

23^d Abbot and Uncle James left us at 10 o'clock this morning. I was busy all the morning helping him take an account of his clothes and books, and now he is gone and I am all alone. Oh dear. He was quite impatient to be employed and I could not keep him any longer. Beside I thought if he could be of any assistance to Mr. Heard he ought to go. But it is hard to have him go again. Perhaps I may not see him again for 5 or 6 years. Well!

Caroline came in this morning and Cox. Uncle went out in a chair this afternoon for the first time. Is much better.

I went to a party at Mrs. Daniell's this evening. All the Macao world there and a great many strangers. 4 Company's Ships in today. Was introduced to Mr. Leslie, a new production. I am beset by all these Englishmen with their criticisms and witticism upon Mrs. Trollope's, Mr. Vigne's [August 20, 1832, vol. 5], and Mr. Stuart's book.[16] I am sick of the sound of them all. Danced and had some good music. The Spanish Colonel from Manilla and Mrs. Pereira sung beautifully and Howard also.

24th A glorious day as ever shone upon this mundane sphere. I studied a little this morning, wrote a letter to A. A. [Low] Saw Sir Andrew [Ljungstedt] and Capt. Neish and worked some. Caroline came in about 2.

After dinner read and we talked of going home, a pleasing subject, and Caroline called for me to go out with her. We had a delightful walk to Casilha's Bay. The moon was shining beautifully in place of the sun which was still ting[e]ing the clouds with its beams. 4 Ships were in sight and the water looking so calm and beautiful that I looked upon it and thought with pleasure upon spending some time upon it. But alas it is so treacherous, it is dangerous to think deeply or long upon the subject, to think of much pleasure while subject to its <u>ca-prices</u>. However the dangers of the sea will hardly be thought of when I feel that I am steering toward "the land of my love."

Caroline and I sat upon the rocks a long time, then we started to go home. We were soon after joined by Fox & Inglis. C had Fox and I had the delightful Inglis. Blight walked between. I enjoyed the walk exceedingly and to make it longer walked as far as Caroline's and spent the evening with her—with Fox and Blight. 4 or 5 Ships have arrived today and as many yesterday. Several Americans among them.

25 Studied my French this morning. Wrote a letter to Rebecca Abbot and about 1/2 past 1 went to see Mrs. Macondray, took my work and stayed till near 3.

After dinner I got very much interested in Lander's *Voyage down the Niger* which they made to discover its termination and succeeded, but their sufferings must have been great. I read till dark. Then Mr. & Mrs. Allport came in & Caroline. Mrs. A. is looking much better for her voyage to England. She is quite enthusiastic in her praises of it. She says every one appeared so busy, and all engaged in some pursuit that she was amazed at first—the contrast was so great compared with the Society she had been in for the last 18 years.

26th This morning cool and delightful. Seems to restore one's energy. I felt better and brighter than I have for many a day and went to my books with fresh zeal and studied steadily till 2 o'clock to some purpose. Then I was called out to see Mr. Gover, "known all the world over" that is the <u>Eastern</u> world. He is immensely rich, but as [Philip] Ammidon used to say of old <u>Crapo</u> [Gover], "he is too ugly to eat." The great danger one has to avoid in meeting him is to shun every topic that relates to <u>Opium</u>. He brings all his forces to bear upon that one topic and if by any chance you allude to it, you cannot or but rarely have the good fortune to escape an hour's dissertation upon its rise and falls, and the prophecies which he has made regarding it. His great pleasure appears to be in <u>amassing</u> wealth but he does a great many benevolent deeds. On the whole he is a <u>bore</u>. He got into a great arm chair this morning and I certainly thought I should have to call the coolies to draw him forth again. After he was gone <u>Fox</u> came in, one of my pets. He is a good creature.

After dinner I finished Lander's Travels in Africa and sent them home and got some more. Have now got Venetian History and a tour through Holland. About six made a call on Caroline. Came home and had some tea and spent the evening in talking of going <u>home</u>. Oh only think, to leave this in January. I have hardly dare believe the hints to that effect that I have heard before, but now I think it is Uncle's intention, if possible. We were talking of our arrangements tonight. Oh how delighted I shall be and I feel almost sure the long sea voyage will restore Uncle.

The Capt. of the *Merchant* [Captain Lombard] arrived here after dinner. The *Omega* from Boston has also arrived.

27th The Capt. of the *Merchant* was here most of the morning and dined with us. Uncle feels his weakness when he is obliged to talk, and was quite exhausted before night. Mr. Davis in this morning. They are all off soon for their winter season in Canton, perhaps their last.

After dinner Caroline and I went to walk together. We went behind some huge rocks and seated ourselves out of the way of the multitude. Read <u>poetry</u> & an epistle to her from a certain friend of <u>mine</u> [W. W. Wood] in Canton. A strange being he is to be sure. We set there till quite dusk. Then I went home and took tea with her and spent the evening. Blight came in. When I went home who should I find in the drawing room but William Low.[17] I did not know him at all. He has grown very much, is a fine looking boy. The Lows swarm at this season. I never knew any thing like it. It seems his father thought he was sick and ordered him down here. I recd your letter my dear and <u>note</u> the contents. You all seem to be <u>frisking</u> about there at a great rate. Do not like Mr. Dow's proceedings in the absence of his wife.

28th Uncle seems very feeble and we said <u>not</u> at <u>home</u>. Mrs. Davis left her card. Wrote to Abbot.

Caroline came in this morning and we <u>sewed</u> together awhile, but her husband came and took her somewhere else. After dinner I made a call upon Mrs. Macondray. Spent the evening at home. Uncle applied leeches again.

29th Recd two letters from Abbot this morning. Don't tell me how he likes Canton—but says he had had the "blues" which does not say much for first impressions. However when he comes to be employed he will be contented I dare say.

Went to Church this morning, heard Mr. Wimberley preach. Came home and took Dr. Channing's [sermons], but was interrupted by Blight who thought proper to stay till 3 o'clock. Caroline came in just before dinner.

After dinner or just as we were finishing Uncle James arrived, a little more William would have been gone. Strange what a story they have got about that W. is sick. Went out in my chair to Casilha's Bay. Met Mr. & Mrs. Davis; talked with them. Hear [Henry Robert] Alexander is married in Calcutta—has espoused a niece of Mrs. D's. Not a cent in his pocket, out of employ with the Company's expiration, a <u>mere</u> <u>boy</u>, and a fickle, changeable one too, a wife to support—and several other <u>appendages</u> in Macao. Poor girl I pity her. They are expected every day. Fox joined me coming home and we had a delightful walk. Some how or other we got upon Unitarianism and religious subjects and I promised to lend him Channing's *Sermons*.

30th Four years today since we landed in Macao.

I sent the sermons today. Wrote several letters. Aunt L. went out and I read to Uncle till interrupted by Blight. He went to Canton at 3 so I had to write and prepare packages. I gave him a piece of your wedding cake. He hoped both <u>parties</u> were as <u>good</u> as that and that you would be happy. It is really excellent.

After dinner all our household sallied forth. Caroline came in for me to go with her, but I got engaged in a story from the *Diary of a Physician* and would not go. We spent the evening <u>*en famille*</u>.

Octr 1st Done nothing this morning but fly from one place to the other, looking over my clothes and sundry little jobs. Rec^d a letter from Dumaresq, he has been dismasted in a Typhoon. Capt. Macondray came in, brought me some letters, one from Susan, one from M. E. Foster. And by the way of keeping <u>alive</u> the <u>benevolent</u> feeling, I made a gum shade for Capt. Lombard while Caroline set with us this morning and sent it to him. Wrote a letter to Dumaresq in reply to his. I hear he got engaged in the <u>30</u> days in which he was at home [to Margenetta Deblois]. I give him some sly <u>cuts</u>.

Was very busy till dinner time. After dinner I rec'd a most extraordinary letter from Canton from it seems one of my admirers who I was not aware cared a straw about me, in which he makes a *declaration d'amour*—like a great fool for he <u>knows</u> I don't like him. He also sent me a pretty little pin case, which I immediately rolled in the same paper and returned, together with the letter and a few <u>civil</u> <u>formal</u>

lines to beg never to be favoured with a repetition of the act. When will there be an end of such nonsense —I am <u>sick</u> of it! It is so provoking to be bothered with people you do not care a straw about. After I had sealed this and my other letters I called for Mrs. C. to walk. Fox went with me and Rieves with C. We went to Casilha's, had a delightful walk. Came home, wrote a letter to Abbot & took tea with Caroline. Fox was there. Came home, found a letter from Abbot and Grandmother. Read them and went to bed.

I wish I dared tell you all the troubles and anxieties I have my dear Sis, but as I could not explain fully I cannot. I have more than Uncle's health which makes me wish to leave—there is a <u>demon</u> here in the shape of a man who for <u>revenge</u> has undertaken to abuse my dear Aunt.[18] Fortunately his character is so well known, all he can say makes no impression upon any one.

2^d Had a very humble note of apology this morning, as the gentleman who wrote the letter yesterday came down. He begged pardon and etc., so I <u>forgave</u> him in as few words as possible.

Uncle James left us this morning for Canton or Whampoa. Uncle W. had a blister on his throat this morning and we said not at home. After dinner read a little. Caroline & her brother came in and I spent the evening with Mrs. Macondray. Came home and walked the terrace an hour. A glorious night.

3^d Uncle seems miserable today. The northerly winds that are blowing affect him very much. I tried to study this morning, but my mind is in such an unsettled state & I feel so anxious about Uncle that I cannot do any thing. I went and set an hour with Caroline and came home to dinner and did not go out again. Commenced the *Life of Patrick Henry*.[19] Abbot brought it with him.

4th Uncle is very so so. This morning we had a few visitors. They came to falter out Adieu before leaving for Canton for the season. Clarke, Astell, Daniell & Fox, oh and Plowden "<u>shot</u> pasteboard" [left their cards]. I made an <u>appointment</u> with Fox, to go and walk with me, for I need the exercise. So he came about 1/2 past 5 and we really had a delightful walk. It was so cool and pleasant that we took a good long walk and coming home met Caroline & John [Shillaber]. I went home and took tea with her but came home just after 9. Plowden, Huddleston & Whitehead came in to tea then and we had quite a nice party.

5 This morning while the Coolies had possession of my room I lined and trimmed my straw bonnet for I begin to think I shall soon need something upon my head. Then I wrote a very long letter to Abbot and with seeing visitors my time was occupied till dinner time, when Caroline came to spend the day with us as her husband was going to dine at Gover's with all the Company. After dinner we read *Fitzgeorge*.[20] It is intended for George the 4th and I should think a correct picture of his Life & character, shewing him in his true light.

Colledge told Uncle today he thought he could not leave this place too soon, that the northerly winds that are coming are too bracing and he thinks the voyage home may restore him and it is the only thing, that he thinks his complaints are not chronic now. I wish he could leave at once but then there would be a disadvantage in leaving now because we should arrive on the Coast in a bad month. But we feel very anxious as the north winds that have commenced blowing have an uncomfortable effect upon him.

6th The Company all started for Canton this morning, with a northerly wind and rain. Sent a long letter to Botus and a box of gingerbread. Dumaresq brought us out a 1/2 barrel.

Wrote 5 letters this morning for America. Then read Memoir of Dr. Abbot[21] and some of his sermons. The evening we spent at home and talked over our plans for going home. I cannot think of any thing else my dear and you will have a dry detail enough in future.

7th Very cold, gloomy day, the northerly wind blowing and we are obliged to shut the house all up. I went to Caroline's and spent an hour or two, and read to her. Came home at 3 and did not go out again though I think a good walk would be of great service to me, but I have no one to go with me, and I can't think of going alone.

I worked steadily all the evening and really seemed quite homeish. Oh how I long to be among you. It seems as though I could hardly wait, and then if we should be disappointed and not go, oh dear! Uncle gets tired out before bedtime, does not seem to gain much strength.

Had a letter from Abbot this afternoon and wrote him another in return. We keep up the fire pretty constantly. I admire his stability of character and prudence. He is just suited for Canton and will I think get on very well. I think he bids fair to make a sterling man. I wish I could have had him here a little longer.

8th This morning I just studied my French a little and then went to work upon some flannel waistcoats for Uncle. Sewed all the forenoon. Mr. [Thomas] Beale and Mrs. Macondray were in.

A most glorious day. I feel as if I could fly. And after dinner Uncle & Aunt went out in their chairs, and knowing there were no gents in the place to bother me, I walked by the side of them (Aunty's corns are so troublesome she can't walk) and enjoyed it much. For the air was so bracing and so pure that it did me good and I left them on the plain and perched upon the top of the hill. Felt all the better for the stretch. Coming home saw the Morrisons, thought I would be very amiable, so went and joined them. They were setting there with their little family of 5 around them. I chatted with them awhile and then walked home with Rebecca. Took the chair and went to see how Caroline was—has some fever, not very well. Stayed awhile, got an armfull of books and came home.

9th Colledge told Aunt Low this morning that she could not get her husband away too soon, that he never will be any better here, and that it is necessary he should go at once. So we may be sent off in a month. I was working very hard most of the morning on Uncle's flannel waistcoat. Got tired after dinner and read Garrick's *Memoirs*.22 Had no walk, but was busy at work and thought all the evening, while the mosquitoes were regaling themselves with my person and fretting me dreadfully. Josepha came to me before bedtime and said she would cure a little sort of ring worm I had on my neck if I would let her. I enquired what she intended to perform. In bad English she explained and I concluded I should not be quite killed and I consented. So she brought up an onion and had made it quite black, how I know not, that she rubbed upon my neck till she scraped the skin off. I was almost sorry that I submitted to such quackery but if it cures he as she tells of, I don't much care. The Portuguese and Chinese have the most singular remedies, they torture themselves with their remedies. If they have a sore throat, you see their throats all in red streaks where they have burned it with hot cash. I should be very sorry to be submitted to their tender mercies.

10th Nothing to say for today, but that I have found the use of my fingers and have been exceedingly busy cutting out work. About 2 I went to Caroline's and stayed till 3. After dinner commenced Holt's Life of George the third.23 Was amused.

The evening we spent at home in talking.

11th Busy all the morning cutting work again, but the thought of the end in view softens all my labours and I would willingly wear the skin off my fingers were it necessary for the sake of leaving this place. We are thinking now of the middle of November.

About 2 I got tired and spent an hour with Mrs. Macondray. Hot day again, quite oppressive. Did not go out in the afternoon. Mrs. Allport took tea and spent the evening with us. She seems to have renewed her life by her trip to England. She was very entertaining and I know not when I have spent a pleasanter evening. She has far too much feeling for this place and is not appreciated, and she would be an ornament and delight to her friends at home. She seems to have enjoyed so much in a quiet <u>domestic</u> way while there in the society of her sisters and their children.

12th After breakfast finished little Lucy Macondray's dress. The only remarkable thing about it (Uncle says) is the <u>despatch</u> with which it has been done. Then after I had done this I worked <u>hard</u> till near 3 o'clock on divers and sundry things. Had just got dressed when Hugh Hamilton Lindsay came to pay parting compliments. He is off tonight, he is going to Bombay and from thence over land to England.²⁴ Intends taking up his abode in the <u>Pyramids</u> for a certain length of time. I never saw the spirit of <u>roving</u> and adventure more strongly developed than in him.

I wrote a letter after dinner to go home via Java. It was very short as it had no time to enter into particulars. Then I read a little till dark and in the evening I cut out a little more work. Uncle expresses great astonishment at my <u>industry</u> and hopes it will <u>continue</u>. I only want a motive to exertion and no one is more active.

13 This morning went to hear Dr. Morrison preach. Came home and commensed the <u>Koran</u>. Mrs. M. came in a little while. I had a letter from Abbot and wrote one in return, also one to S[ally] Orne. After dinner went out in a chair with Uncle. Colledge orders him out every day but he does not walk much. It was cold and windy this afternoon and we came home early, or rather he did. I went to Caroline's and stayed an hour, she has been sick for two or three days—but nothing <u>dangerous</u> I fancy. The most I think of now is my preparations and the thought of leaving here and my imagination

often pictures the joy I shall have in getting home once more, but that time is now so far distant it is hardly worth while to think of it. Even if it was only the voyage, it would be too soon to begin.

14th Went to work immediately after breakfast cutting out work for the Tailor, then worked on Uncle's flannel, and was really quite astonished at myself.

I begin to think I am myself again. I have no beau now and I cannot walk. So I stayed at home and read a little, for a book is delightful now, that is when I do not have to mull over it from morning till night, for I am fully convinced an "occasional banquet is better than a continual feast." Aunt & Uncle went out. I read till dark, then walked the terrace round and round to stretch my limbs and then went to work again.

Am sadly afraid I shall not be able to finish this book before I go, for I am short of ideas, being all concentrated at the present time on linen & a sea voyage. So my dear you must not expect much.

15 At my work again, and it was 12 o'clock before I knew it, and the bell rung and visitors announced before any one was dressed. Mr. & Mrs. Clifton and Shillaber came in—bothered us an hour. Then I took my work and went to Caroline's and stayed till dinner time. Having no beau I get no walk now a days, so I stay at home and I do not care about going out in a chair these fine days. It's stupid.

Spent the evening in working.

16th This morning the first thing, I answered a letter I received last evening from my old friend Mrs. Cartwright. She was then at St. Helena and on her way to England on account of her husband's health. She expressed strong wishes to see me in England and how delighted I should be to meet her. She was a woman after my own heart. I replied to it this morning to go by the *Scaleby Castle*. As she will be in the north of England it is a great chance if we meet. Then I wrote a long letter to Abbot by Shillaber and one to Uncle James. Worked some. Mrs. Neish & Capt. Morgan [of British ship *Pascoa* from Bombay] called, but the servants would not let them in. Then I went and spent two hours very pleasantly with Mrs. Allport.

Mrs. A. spent the evening with [us]. Her voyage has made her quite another person, has given her new life.

17th This morning I was at my work again. Mr. Inglis called and bid us good bye.

About 1 I went to Mrs. Macondray's and stayed till 3. We find the *Waterloo* is one of the first Ships and have sent up to enquire the prices of her cabins.

After dinner we received a letter from Mr. Heard proposing Uncle's taking a trip to Bombay.[25] Oh dear I fear there may be something yet to prevent our departure. And as Uncle has been better the last two or three days I fear he will wish if possible to stay. But I dread his getting a little better, just enough to feel that he must go to Canton, for a little more exertion would upset him again completely. I shall tremble till we get outside of land. If he was to go to Bombay I think I should be tempted to go on board the *Cabot* [James Low, captain] and go home alone much as I should dislike it. I do not like the idea of being the only lady on board a Ship.

Time will determine our plans. Any thing but staying in Macao another year. I went out with Uncle after dinner but it was so cold that we soon came back and I went to Mrs. Colledge's and spent the evening. We set and sewed together and had a very pleasant time.

18 This morning commenced working early and kept it up till 10 o'clock at night when I finished the flannel jackets and glad am I for I am quite tired of the sight of them. We could not give them to the Tailor. They smoke [up] every thing they take and unless the article is to be washed it is not pleasant. Mr. Colledge came in and does not approve of the Bombay speculation. He says it is a long voyage and [it is] a year or two spent without care or anxiety of any kind that Uncle needs. And I am very glad he has decided that point. Uncle's pulse has been much better for a day or two past.

19 Did some work this morning, preparing for a sea voyage and then about 1 I went to the Library but could not find what I wanted. I am very anxious to read an Embassy to Pekin but they have carried all the best to Canton. From there I went and spent nearly an hour at Mrs. Davis's and came home and dressed for dinner, and at 1/2 past 3 went to a party at Caroline's. She had Capt. & Mrs. Harris,[26] just arrived and several gentlemen. Mrs. H. is a pleasant woman, and I spent a very pleasant day with her. It seems she left England with the intent to take up her abode at St. Helena as Governess in the family of the Governor there, but fortunately the Capt. fell in love with her

and married her on his arrival there. He is a very likely man and they seem very well matched. She struck us rather singularly, she had her hair dressed in the new Style, as plain as possible. Her hair was parted on the forehead and put up plain or braided upon top in a round <u>lump</u>, and two little "spit locks" as Mrs. Trollope tells of at the side. She has a small face and after the eye became a little accustomed to it, it did not look so badly, but it would be very trying to most faces.

As she had made some stay at St. Helena I enquired about the places, feeling some interest. She told us some amusing anecdotes of the people, and I find that is very like all small places, lots of gossip and scandal and most expensive living there. Meat is very scarce and <u>fowls</u> a most exorbitant price. They live principally upon fish. The climate is fine and the society small but some very fine families there.

Mrs. H. played the piano this evening and is a great performer. She sat down and played the music of all the most celebrated composers from memory and with great execution. She sung a little. We spent a very pleasant and rational day and I came home quite gratified.

20ᵗʰ Poor Uncle seems weak and exhausted this morning. I do long to get him upon the water, for there is no change for the better here.

Did not go to Dr. M[orrison]'s this morning. I have got the "<u>Koran</u>" and got so much interested I could not leave it.

After dinner I went out with Uncle, but it was very cool and came back early.

21ˢᵗ Heard this morning of the *Morrison's* arrival and others from different places. Macondray came down and <u>whisked</u> his family off at short notice. Did not see her for I was left to take care of Uncle, Aunty had to go out—as we heard some reports about the Ship we are thinking of. But they do not amount to much. What Yankee ladies can soon get over, and what only trouble a fastidious English woman.

Uncle & Aunt went out and I stayed at home and read which I really enjoy now as I have something else to do than read from morning till night. I am as chipper as possible and growing so fat I shall be obliged to find something to <u>fret</u> about. Caroline spent an hour with us about dark. She is getting very <u>stout</u>.

22ᵈ This morning wrote a long letter to Mother, hemmed <u>pocket handkerchiefs</u> till near dinner time. Had a letter from Abbot. He has cut his hand badly. Mr. & Mrs. Colledge came in and stayed an hour. After dinner Uncle had leeches on and I went out to the "Campo" with Caroline and we had a pleasant walk. Mrs. Allport spent the evening with us.

23^d Uncle seems very feeble today, but it is owing to the bleeding. I was made happy this morning by the receipt of a letter from my dear father, by which I presume you are all well as he says nothing to the contrary. He says he shall not write me any more as you suppose I shall come in the *Cabot*. I suppose just about this time my letters per *Beta* which will alter your opinion [have arrived]. You will be disappointed I suppose. I wish you could know our plans and views, *mais c'est impossible*. I hope nothing will prevent our leaving this [place] for more than one reason. I hope I shall be able to show a <u>sufficient</u> degree of <u>sadness</u> at my departure, but I shall scarce feel a regret. Mrs. Colledge and Mrs. Allport are all the <u>friends</u> I have, my brother in Canton. The rest I say God bless them. I wish them no harm. I think if I ever arrive in Europe I shall be very soon tired of sight seeing and ready to take passage on board the Packet and once more be with you all. I am tired of living such a cold, heartless life— a life you can have no idea of. After dinner looked out, saw the Cutter come in with Mr. Alexander, his <u>wife</u>, and other passengers on board. Every one to their fancy but I cannot fancy that a sensible girl should be willing to unite herself to such a snipper snapper of a <u>boy</u>. He never has one mind more than a minute. Beside he has no money and no <u>prospects</u>. The Charter is about expiring and he is not fit for business. His father has lately lost by failures in Calcutta <u>300,000£</u> and is reduced to 100,000£ which would not be called <u>very</u> poor in America, but which does not go so far in England.

Mr. Davis was asked, how Alexander came to get married so young. He said he supposed to perpetuate <u>pauperism</u>, he could think of nothing else.

I went and called on Mrs. Allport and we went to the Peña together. It was a most glorious evening. Went home and dressed and spent the eve'g with Caroline. Mrs. Neish, Gover, Capt. Morgan were there. Hear Amelia Pereira²⁷ is to be married on Tuesday next, a sudden thing at last. Mamma has been trying for this <u>consummation</u> a long time, but Papa was not <u>agreeable</u>. But he has at last consented.

24th Uncle got up bright this morning, but before night had a very violent fever turn, and night was very miserable. He sent up this afternoon to have our passages taken in the *Waterloo* to go the middle of Novr and is obliged to give up the hope of going to Canton again. It is a great disappointment to him, but every thing must yield to health.

25 Had 3 letters from Canton this morning, all of which I replied to after breakfast. This is the way I treat my correspondence, not as you do my dear. I hear complaints of your negligence in this respect from all quarters, but I do not complain. Taking all things into consideration you have been very kind to me.

My heart leaps with joy at the idea of leaving Macao, with the prospect of meeting you once more when I shall see you a wife, perhaps a <u>mother</u>. As my time will be fully occupied I shall not have much time to write. But as I shall send you two books it will be quite as much as you will want with all your cares, and you married people are so busy generally. I can hardly expect you will get through this. But never mind, it is not worth your reading for it is stale, flat & unprofitable enough. George [her sister's husband] has not written me the last two years I believe. My mind is in such a state of confusion now that I can scarcely write.

This afternoon I went out in my chair and set down awhile and mused. Met Dr. & Mrs. Morrison and no other person I knew. All was still and quiet. Mrs. Morrison and her family leave this next month, <u>he</u> remains here. How unpleasant it must be for a poor man to have a wife and 5 children leave him at once. Mrs. Grant does the same. Hers is a still worse case for she goes to a strange land [she was French] and to strange people, among his friends whom she has never seen, and she does not know whether they will like her or not.

Mrs. Allport spent the evening with us. She is a darling woman, worth all the rest in Macao.

I shall regret leaving her more than any one in Macao. We are the only ones she visits intimately, and she will miss us very much.

26th Very busy all the morning. Uncle had a dreadful night and seems very ill today. No energy nor spirits for any thing. Caroline came and spent the morning with us. I was at work all the afternoon & evening. Mrs. Whiteman came in just about dark and Mrs. A. took tea with us. Just having made a voyage, she can tell us all we want and how to arrange every thing and she comes to look <u>after us</u>. She is a kind creature.

Abbot sent me his journal today which I shall read if I can. If not I shall beg to send it with mine to you.

27th Sunday. But I did not go to Dr. Morrison's, for my mind would have been wandering I fear. I read some but wrote letters most of the day. My time is precious now and I feel anxious to make up my accounts square before I leave this. Had a long letter from Sam Low this morning, which amused me exceedingly. He is a droll fish and inherits his <u>mother's</u> disposition.

This afternoon I went out with Uncle a little way—every body out. The weather is perfect now for walking but I have no one to go with me now and I don't know when I have had a walk. But I hope to before I go away. I am growing so <u>fat</u> that I want to walk it down.

This evening I spent with Caroline. Mrs. Harris was there, a lady "I buckle to" (as Chinnery says) amazingly. I had a small touch of the <u>Blues</u> tonight, but dispersed them in a good shower of tears.

We heard tonight of a melancholy occurrence. A Prussian Ship [*Princess Louisa*] comes here once a year & consigned to Russell and Co. And Uncle was requested to make preparations for the Lady of the Capt. [Wendt] who was with her husband in a voyage round the world, it seems she was married just before they left. And has been to Valparaiso and the Islands I believe and the Ship arrived at Manilla about a week since, but the poor Lady died in child bed about 10 days before, and the poor little infant was living. Think what a state the Father must be in. We have heard no particulars relative to her death. It is probable she did not have good attention or bad weather. I wonder Ladies have the courage to tempt the sea under such circumstances, but it is the most common thing for ladies to go on board Ship expecting to be confined there. But most likely this poor woman expected to have arrived at Manilla or Macao first, as they have been expected a month.

28th This morning went to work about packing directly after breakfast, and was on my feet till 3. Am happy to inform you I have found the use of both feet and hands, and display much [less] reluctance in packing now than when I last thought of spending 4 months on the water. We have enough to do I assure you to pack things to send home, things for the voyage, things to make ready for Auction and for England, beside Uncle to attend to and to write for him. I wrote two letters for him after dinner, and have been sewing till 10. Mrs. Allport spent an hour with us. And now it is 5 minutes after 11 and

I shall read a little of Abbot's journal if not devoured by mosquitoes and then go to bed. So good night my dear.

29th Had a letter from Abbot this morning. Uncle had one from Capt. Wendt. Poor man he seems to be quite in despair. I cannot fancy a more melancholy situation. His wife lived 10 days after her confinement, and the poor little infant still lives.

After Breakfast went to work, looking over every thing, packed up the little <u>traps</u> I find about which I shall get some friend to take home. I should like to have a green tin box that I shall send kept as it is till my return, if I should be preserved. If not, take what you please yourself my dear and distribute them as you like among those I ought to remember. It is quite wonderful the quantity of <u>trash</u> of different kinds that we have collected. We are getting on famously now, and shall be in very good order ere long.

After dinner I did a little work. Then Uncle did not go out and I took the chair and went to the Campo where I sit and mused a long time till Mrs. Harris came along and I got out walked to the Bay and home again. Called into Caroline's a moment. She was going to spend the evening with <u>Mrs. Paiva</u>, Miss Pereira that was this morning. They must have had a happy day at their house, for beside the wedding two of Mrs. Pereira's sons arrived from England where they have been many years, so that she had her whole family with her today—a fortunate and happy occurrence.

I went home from C's, found Mrs. Allport with us, and spent a delightful evening with her.

30th A lovely day. The weather is perfect now. Was busy about all the morning but sewing most of the day. Had a number of China servants offering today to go with us. I should like to shew you some of the long tailed <u>species</u> [Ayok, son of Dr. Colledge's servant Afun, was hired].

This evening I spent with Caroline. We sewed and talked very busily <u>till 10 o'clock</u>, then I came home. Brought some translations of Chinese Letters which I intend to copy. Commenced one tonight but the mosquitoes were so busy that I was obliged to quit. Had a piece of wedding Cake this morning—not such a "<u>get up</u>" as yours however.

31st Last day of October. This time last year I was at Lintin. How every thing has changed since that time.

This morning was busy till 3 o'clock, doing a little of every thing and a great deal that did not amount to much. At 1/2 past 3 I went to dine with Caroline. She had Dr. [George] Bennet[28] there, a famous Phrenologist. He is travelling about the world, has just come from New South Wales and is on his way to England. He was exceedingly agreeable, had a great deal to say for himself and seems to be a very scientific man.

After dinner Lady Robinson called at Caroline's, expressed great regret at losing us. (She don't care a straw.) Then C. & I walked out, went to the Franciscan Church yard. A lovely spot it is too, and of such an evening. We sat ourselves down under the protection of a great cross erected upon a tomb, and the evening bells were just ringing, which are always pleasing. The sun had just gone but left every thing tinged with its parting smiles, looking bright and beautiful. The water was still and smooth as glass, or moved only in a ripple. Not a discordant sound was heard, we were away from the busy world, and it was lovely. We sat there an hour and then went home lest the padres should seize us. For begging their pardon, I would not trust myself to their tender mercies more than to any layman.

We got home safe, and Dr. Bennet returned from his ride and the others, Mrs. Harris came, Chinnery, Gover, Capt. Bushet[29] spent the evening with us. Mrs. H. performed splendidly upon the Piano accompanied with her voice. She is a great performer and seems to be perfect mistress of the instrument. She plays without notes from all the celebrated composers.

Dr. Bennet and I had considerable conversation together upon different subjects. He was speaking of Miss Langdon [Letitia Elizabeth Landon] whom you know as a poetess under the signature of L.E.L.[30] She is a most extraordinary person. I told him I had heard that she was the most heartless person in the world. Her "flights of Fancy" as he terms it, (but which would be called by the world in general madness) are very strange. I have often admired her poetry, but having heard so often that she was such a flighty, heartless thing I did not read it with so much pleasure as before. But he assures me it is not the case. He says he is well acquainted with her, and to meet her and hear her talk at times people might say any thing of her. After much urging she submitted her head to his inspection. She told him there was one subject that she had kept so secret that if he would discover, she should have some faith. He told her very correctly her character—told her the organ on the <u>love</u> of <u>children</u> was strongly developed. This was the subject she had always disclaimed, and has gained her the character she has in the world, of being heartless and without feeling. She always calls them "horrid little wretches" and pretends to hate them, but Dr. Bennet says it is all <u>pretence</u>.

She still told him he was wrong, but afterwards confessed to a female friend that he was quite right. It is one of her peculiarities. She became a <u>convert</u> to the <u>science</u>. He says she is a most agreeable person if she pleases, but is sometimes quite the reverse. She has great talents, and is dreadfully <u>satirical</u>. She is exceedingly fond of flattery, and is your dear friend while you feed her with it. So you see my dear the most talented have their weaknesses. I suppose if one <u>bump</u> is more fully developed than another, it is strength borrowed from another which of course leaves a weakness. Don't know what a phrenologist would say to my hypotheses. Colledge says he will give me a "<u>Skull</u>" of a Chinaman and the Dr. says he will <u>mark</u> it out for me, but I think I shall not accept their offers. I should like a <u>cast</u> and like the study but should not like a real <u>Skull</u>. I think this would be a very useful study if one could have sufficient <u>faith</u> to educate children upon the strength of it—that is if it was <u>proved</u>. This gentleman says many do it in England now, but they would feel rather unhappy afterwards if they find their genius tended to the <u>opposite</u> <u>point</u>. I am rather inclined to the Theory myself, and the more I know of it the more I like it. Dr. B. came from Canton with Mr. Wimberley, and without having had any previous knowledge of his character, to Mr. W's great astonishment told him very correctly his character and propensities, and it seems has converted Mr. W. who was before very <u>sceptical</u>. I have heard him converse upon the Subject.

This gentleman is acquainted with all the literary people of note in England, and gave me a little sketch of the character of many whose works I am acquainted with—Mrs. [Felicia] Hemans, Mrs. [Caroline] Norton,[31] Miss [Maria] Jewsbury (lately married), Mr. [Edward] Bulwer[-Lytton], etc.

I came home about 11 very much pleased with my evening's entertainment. I have no more time to tell you the numerous anecdotes I heard brought forward in favour of the "Science of Phrenology." He spoke of Dr. Spurzheim[32] who died in America, and of his great talents, says he was a great <u>reasoner</u> upon the science and most eloquent in his lectures but not so great a <u>practical</u> phrenologist as many others.

Nov. 1ˢᵗ Cut out some work this morning, then dressed about 12 to pay some visits. Called first on Mrs. Harris, had a delightful visit there. Then went to Mrs. Alexander's. She is any thing but the woman (in appearance) that I should have thought Mr. A. would have chosen. She is not pretty at all, very inanimate. I called at Caroline's a few minutes. She says the Dr. told her all her <u>bumps</u> after I left, and I should say very correctly.

Called on Mrs. Neish, met Mrs. Fearon and Capt. Morgan there. Then I went to call on the <u>Bride</u>, Mrs. Paiva, but unfortunately it was three o'clock and she was just dressing for dinner, so I bestowed all my congratulations and good wishes upon the <u>bridegroom</u> and Mamma.

Came home, got some dinner. Had a sort of "azure spirit" creep over me about night. A lovely evening. Sewed all the evening and fought mosquitoes.

2ᵈ A dreadfully hot oppressive day—calm and the Thermometer standing at about 84. Had three or four letters from Canton this morning. Was busy at work all day mending my clothes. After dinner had just commenced writing for Uncle and who should come in but Mr. Heard. We were all glad to see him, for we all respect him. Mrs. Allport and Caroline came in just about night a little while.

Abbot sent me a pair of Chinawomen's shoes, which I shall bring or send for your first girl. They will fit it when she is about a <u>week</u> old. It seems incredible that they can wear such things, but I have seen them as small upon the Campo. The foot is above it, or as you may say out of the shoe. So dreadfully distorted that it is quite painful to look at it, when they become a little advanced, the limb is completely withered and nothing but the skin and bone remains. What astonishes me more than any thing is, that they live to arrive at old age.

Mr. Heard spent the evening with us. Uncle got so much excited, although he went to bed at 8 o'clock, that he had a restless night. We were obliged to send to Colledge—he sent him a composing draught.

3ᵈ Mr. Heard breakfasted with us. And said he should leave as soon as he had finished his business, so I went to work and wrote letters, made up a package to go home per *Dickason* [Capt. J. W. Wainwright], wrote to Canton and got my letters all ready by 12 when he started.

I did not write to you my dear because I thought I would not trust any more of my epistles to that Ship but reserve them for the next. Beside I had not time. After having done that I read 2 or 3 sermons.

After dinner wrote letters for Uncle, then went to my own room and commenced the work of <u>destruction</u> and tore up 2 large baskets full. It made me sad for I have a great veneration for these little testimonies of affection, but it is impossible to keep them for I should not like to have them exposed. Have not yet torn one third and not one of my <u>real</u> valuable ones.

4th This morning was busy writing and <u>tearing</u> letters, which seems to break my heart strings. It seems like annihilating the past and destroying all that pleased or pained.

After I had destroyed another basket full I went to see Mrs. Allport a little while. There I met Mr. & Mrs. Grant, Mr. & Mrs. Harris, Major Crossley and Monsieur Durand. Heard the merits of Capt. [W. R.] Blakely of the *Waterloo* very warmly discussed though both agreed that he was an excellent man & a man of talents. They disputed whether he was a "Lady's Man." He is a Bachelor, that is certain, and he is not a "Lady's man" in that sense. And I am sure I hope he is not a "Lady's man" in the general acceptation of the term, for I hate them—but there is no fear of that. I have heard so many speak of him, that I have made up my mind what he is and have no doubt that I shall like him well enough. I do not intend to know much of him or any one else on board if I can help it, which I think I can by keeping in my Cabin.

After dinner I went out in my chair awhile and enjoyed the evening breeze, then came home and went to work.

5th Capt. Clifton called this morning, and Mrs. Harris. Was busy as usual packing and repacking, and sewing by times. After dinner commenced a letter to you, for after all I shall send it by the *Dickason* I think.

Uncle seems quite bright tonight, which is the effect of fever. How melancholy it is to know when he seems the busy [sic] it is all owing to the excitement of fever. Flattering disorder! I do long to get him on board the Ship and see what the sea air will do for him.

I sewed all the evening, and before I went to bed drank a glass of <u>Cider</u>. Don't tell any body. Uncle James sent me a bottle.

6th Thought myself very busy this morning, but I was only "tooing" round as Aunt Orne used to say. Caroline came in about 1 and stayed till 3. We did a great deal of <u>talking</u> and some sewing. After dinner I went out in the chair. Met Colledge, said his wife had gone to "<u>the rocks</u>." I went and joined her, and we set there discussing the affairs of the nation till it was quite dark. Tom had gone to ride and we were to wait for him. We had a very interesting conversation and I walked home with them and took tea. C. and I read Paley's *Natural Theology.* Colledge came in and joined us in the midst of it, and brought in some of his books of plates and <u>expounded</u> to us. We were looking at his description of the <u>back</u> bone and Colledge brought the bones of a man who had his <u>back</u> <u>bone</u> fractured at sea on board a Ship when he was surgeon, so that we had a nice chance to see the <u>machinery</u>—truly, "We are fearfully and wonderfully made." I think I should like the study of anatomy very much. If I was a man I would be a <u>Dr.</u>, an M.D. most certainly. I asked "Colledge" to shew me some plates of the lungs, and he did and proved that a "little learning is a dangerous thing," [Alexander Pope, *Essay on Criticism*, Part II, l.15] for I saw enough to see just where Uncle is affected. I know the whys of Colledge's questions and know where his complaints are and <u>tremble</u>. It made me feel uncomfortable and my dreams were <u>anatomical</u>. I should like to have asked a great many more questions, but I felt delicate about it. I came home at 11. I had got so much engaged that I had quite forgotten how time was going and think I might have gone on an hour or two if Colledge had not have asked me if I knew what time it was.

7th Nothing occurred today worthy <u>of</u> <u>note</u> (you may be ready to say there never does), however spare me my dear. I have got almost through this monotonous life and shall soon change the <u>scene</u>. 4 months on board Ship will not be more wearisome than this. Was busy most of the day.

8th Soon after breakfast this morning Abbot arrived and Uncle James. Looks pale and thinner than when he went up but he is very well and it is only the effect of living in dark Hongs where they never see the sun. They quite put us ladies to the blush, they look so much more delicate.

    Dumaresq, Cutting, and several others came down with them. Dumaresq spent two hours with us—he looks just the same as ever.

After dinner I started to walk with Abbot and had not gone far before we were joined by Dumaresq, and soon followed in his train Mr. Cutting, Capt. [William] Russell[33] and Uncle James, so that I had quite an escort. That is always the way here, 1/2 a dozen or none at all. I did not like Mr. Cutting's face much.

I began to think what I should do with them when I got back and thinks I to myself these [are] all fresh <u>hands</u> at walking, I'll soon tire them, that they may want to go home and go to bed. So I took them through the village, a long rough walk and across the Beach home. When I got over the worst of it, I told them I <u>hoped</u> they <u>were</u> <u>tired</u>, for it would be good for <u>them</u>. Not one could give a negative except Dumaresq. I got into my chair at the gardens and left them all.

Mrs. Allport spent the evening with us.

Novr 9th Busy this morning preparing a bonnet for sea. Mrs. Neish called and I doubt if we ever see her again. She is going to Manilla in a few days. Mr. Cutting and Capt. Russell of the *Omega* called this morning. I talked till my throat was sore, these Yankees do make such unconscionable morning visits that it quite wears one's patience. I had exhausted all my small stock and was indebted to the Boy's setting the table, or I should have been "<u>hard</u> <u>up</u>" as the Sailors say. It is fortunate there is a dinner hour to bring them up. I don't like Mr. Cutting's eyes. Think Abbot must have a good disposition not to have quarrelled with him on their long passage, but he has a vast deal of prudence with considerable self control. He beats me, for I have not the <u>bump</u> of caution developed, although I have been sailing among quicksands and shoals so long. Aunt Low asked them all to come this evening. I told her I had nothing more to say to them, and I should have to resort to cards. They came, we played cards and got on very well. Abbot and I took a pleasant walk to the Penha and escaped the <u>critturs</u> on the Campo. They said they were watching for us.

10th Sealed up some more letters for the *Dickason* and my Salem letters to go by some other conveyance. Rec^d a note from <u>Fox</u> and read one or two of Channing's excellent sermons. Caroline came in awhile. Dr. Bradford arrived from Canton. Came down to see <u>us</u> <u>off</u>.

This evening walked to the "Barrier", had an escort of <u>5</u>, all of whom were very tired and myself not excepted. Mr. Cutting got a little sulky. Came home, got some tea, and Abbot and I went to Caroline's and stayed till 10. Mr. Gover and Capt. [Alphi?] were there.

11th Packed three trunks this morning and did a variety of odd jobs. All those people in again this morning. Got a letter from "George" [Archer] this morning per *Clematis*, just as I had despatched or sealed yours, but I had not time to answer it, but hope to before I leave. Had a very kind letter from Mrs. Macondray, to which I replied by Mr. Cutting who left in <u>disgust</u> to night. Suspect he was afraid he should be in for another walk.

Dumaresq and Russell came in this evening. We played whist.

12th This morning we sallied forth to see the world and falter out <u>Adieu</u>. Saying <u>Adieu</u> in this place is not like saying it in most others, it is true people do not care much about each other and do not pretend to and in saying good bye there is more of a feeling of envy than any thing else and they all congratulate you on your escape and hope their turn will come next. We called on all the Ladies almost. Say what you will of it though, it is not <u>pleasant</u> to leave the most <u>indifferent</u> with the thought it is the <u>last</u> time we may ever meet. Got home quite exhausted in <u>spirits</u>, found Caroline here, Bradford had been.

Went to walk with Abbot after dinner, had a delightful walk with him. He is a fine fellow and I like his character more and more. Came home. Dumaresq and Russell joined us. Met Shillaber and Mrs. Colledge, he is off to Manilla in a few days. Russell took tea with us and is off tomorrow morning. Promises to take the Tin Box for me and deliver it safely. He commands the *Omega*. Take care of it my dear.

Bradford put some more leeches on to Uncle tonight. His pulse is running too high again. Now here I am settling up my day's work and fighting the mosquitoes. They are horridly troublesome and I shall be delighted when I get out of their way. Bradford tells us we are to have Mr. Senn van Basel, Dutch Consul, [a] fellow passenger on board the *Waterloo* all the way to England. Oh! Hope the Capt. will lay in a good stock of <u>provisions</u>. Bradford spent the evening with us.

13th Busy as usual, no ideas beyond packing, etc. Sir Andrew Ljungstedt called to give us his blessing. Says he hopes he shall live to see me married, or rather hear of the event. He loaded us with thanks and good wishes and said Adieu.

Mr. Shillaber also came to do the same. He is off to Manilla in a few days. Mrs. Colledge spent an hour with us—went to walk. Mr. Dumaresq joined us, we had a delightful promenade and D. spent the evening with us.

14th Hear the *Waterloo* will be in the roads on Tuesday morning. I cannot realize in the least that I am to be one of the departing ones and it seems impossible that I am about leaving this place for <u>ever</u>, and so soon to be steering westward "to the land of our love!" Happy thought!

Went this morning with Abbot to Mr. Chinnery's to see his paintings. Met Dr. Bradford who was just going to ask us to go to Mr. Beale's, as we were near we went in. Abbot was quite delighted. The birds were all drest in full dress and my favourite the "Bird of Paradise" looked as splendid as ever. He had just received two Bulfinches which have been taught to sing by the organ. It sings one of the tunes of our organ. I certainly never heard notes so sweet. I thought at first it was some instrument and could hardly believe it was not, but I soon found it was far sweeter and softer than instrumental music.

Went to walk this afternoon. Met Caroline and Bradford, joined them and went to the Campo. Mrs. Allport spent the evening with us. Called at Mrs. Davis's this evening. Said <u>Adieu</u>.

15th Got up early this morning to copy one of Mr. Chinnery's sketches of Camoen's Cave, which I shall send and <u>expound</u> when I come. My dear little Bird was sent to Canton yesterday. Hope he will be taken good care of.

Bradford and Dumaresq spent a good part of the morning with me. I was at work. Was busy after dinner. Caroline and husband, Bradford and Dumaresq took tea with us, probably for the last time. Where shall we all be a year from tonight? Who knows? Had a very pleasant evening. The Organ was playing beautifully. Mr. Colledge is to have it.

16th I am ready, all packed up and I think tomorrow my book must be. I hope my next will be more full of incidents therefore more interesting. Had a letter from Mr. Russell this morning. Suspect I shall have not time to write any more letters till I get on board our "Castle." Think my dear of a Ship of 1300 tons, <u>you</u> never saw such a one. The accommodations are fine and I think of it with pleasure.

Some weeks since there was a horrid row at Cap sing moon, the English are in fault.[34] Mr. Davis says "nothing can surpass it in atrocity." The affair commenced with stealing on the part of the Chinese. It went from one thing to another, till the English armed their boats and fired into the <u>village</u>, burnt up their houses, and it is said wounded several and killed one China man. The Chinese have applied to the

Chief [Mr. Plowden] who says it is not in his department. It is referred to the *Magician* frigate just arrived, and I understand the Chinese wish one man to be given up for the China man that was killed.
They do not care <u>who</u> so that they have blood for blood. There is no
knowing how it will be settled, but it is very bad business.

Dr. Rutherford a fellow passenger called on us this morning, a
fine old gentleman. Bradford and Dumaresq were in. D. sent me a
wedding cake, Mrs. Cushing's.[35] So we are well off for the article.

Capt. Roundy arrived after dinner. It is very odd, he has been
with us at all our embarkations and has now come to see us safe off.
He is one of our best <u>friends</u> I think. So few deserve the name that
they are worth the keeping who are so.

Mr. Chinnery called this evening to bid us good bye. Went to
Caroline's and spent the evening with Bradford and Dumaresq. Felt
very *triste* and I am sure they thought me very stupid—but there are
many things make me feel unhappy now, which I shall perhaps tell
you of when we meet.

17ᵗʰ As Dr. Morrison had service this morning I went with Abbot
to hear him. I slept so little last night that I feel exceedingly stupid
today. Dr. Bradford has been in this morning and I believe is coming
this evening. I have just received several *gages d'amitié* from Mrs.
Colledge which I shall keep choice. Tomorrow we shall probably be
packing up and the next morning we shall most likely go on board,
there to remain till we reach St. Helena which will find us much
nearer home than we are now. The one <u>prime</u> and first object is to
restore Uncle's health. For that as well as every thing else we must
rely solely on the one Being who orders all things and though often
dark and mysterious to us may work out for us good in the end. My
daily prayer is that we may all live to meet once more in our own
land, where we can dwell with those "whom we call <u>our</u> <u>own</u> and
who we <u>know</u> will never change," I am tired of living among strangers as I have often told you before and long and sigh to be again at
<u>home</u>. As I shall have not more time to write in this I shall close it
now and prepare it to be sent with my others the first opportunity.

Thus finishes my <u>life</u> in China. It is useless to make reflections.
Suffice it to say that it has been like every thing else <u>variable</u>. Clouds
will rise wherever we are and the sun will shine and I can say has
often, very often shone upon me in China. Therefore with gratitude

for all the peace and quiet I have enjoyed and hoping the troubles
will serve for my good I close my book, and trust myself still further

"To him who has spread out the skies
And measured the depths of the sea,
....
We know that his presence is near,
While our bark tosses far from the land,
And we ride o'er the deep without fear
For, the waters are held in his <u>hand</u>.

Eternity comes in the Sound
Of the billows that never can sleep!
There's Deity circling us round—
Omnipotence walks o'er the deep.

Oh Father, our eye is to thee,
As on for the haven we roll;
And faith in our Pilot shall be
An Anchor to steady the Soul!"

Could I embody and unbosom now
That which is most within me, - could I wreak
My thoughts upon expression, and thus throw,
Soul, heart, mind, passions, feelings strong or weak
All that I would have sought, and all I seek,
Bear, know, feel, and yet breathe—into <u>one</u> word
And that <u>one</u> word were lightning, I would speak;
But as it is, I live and die unheard
With a most voiceless thought, sheathing it as a sword.

Hope you will approve my finale. Where shall I find an affectionate farewell to China. Would I could make it. No I can only
quote and say "Farewell."

What more can I express in a thousand words. I might say <u>fare</u>
<u>better</u> in future, but I pray that thou may'st never <u>fare</u> worse than at
<u>present</u>.

                          A Well Wisher

Volume VIII
November 19, 1833–August 1, 1834

"Once more upon the Waters, yet once more"

Hon^l E. I. Compy'^s Ship *Waterloo* November 19th 1833

Left Macao this morning at 9 o'clock, embarked at Mr. Pereira's Wharf. Went on board a "<u>Lorcha</u>"[1] accompanied by Uncle James Low and my brother Abbot, Dr. Bradford, Capts. Roundy, Macondray, Dumaresq, and our Capt. Blakely and after a little <u>squeeze</u> by the Mandarins and satisfying the Boat girls, bidding adieu to Mr. Colledge, we made sail, and left Macao I trust <u>forever</u>. Four years residence there, cools one's love for it and I for one, give up all its comforts and every thing pleasant it <u>does</u> possess, without a sigh, that is, all its <u>fixtures</u>, such as pleasant walks, pleasant views, etc. There are some <u>few</u>, aye very few, that I regret leaving, but most probably our parting will be likewise forever. For when different countries claim us and those so far separated as Europe and America there is little chance of meeting. But now, I have left the place, I will <u>in shades</u> let it rest; I shall often think of it, and with much pleasure. Time like the grave, will bury many of the thousand annoyances, I then had and I shall wonder, perhaps, at some future time, why I was not perfectly happy there; well let it pass. I trust it has not been time spent in vain. I have learned many useful lessons and if they have not as yet made me happier, they will no doubt stand as shields in my future life; I shall at least be guarded from the <u>like</u>.

But to proceed with our voyage. We made sail, with a fair wind, cool and delightful and were alongside our Castle which sat like a <u>rock</u> in the water, at 11 o'clock. Our party was all cheerful and none of us were at all sick, we were <u>whipped</u> on board, our friends saw us safe in our Cabins, in the midst of tons of baggage and had only time to say a few words as the Boatman hurried them and our Ship was under weigh. So we were soon obliged to say <u>good bye</u> again, to my dear brother and all, who it seems but a few days since, I had the pleasure of welcoming. Well we have to make the best of all these things, and with a few tears and a wave of my handkerchief as they passed our Stern, lost sight of them all in a few minutes. God bless them!

It is useless, perhaps foolish, to talk of feelings, but there is a strange one comes over you when you find the last <u>link</u> as it were broken, which connects you with land and you find yourself floating in the deep sea. The Boat and all gone we were soon obliged to give orders about our Cabin arrangements. Every thing must be "<u>Cleeted</u>" and "Lashed" to keep them from "fetching away" and the <u>most</u> must be made of room. Fortunately we remained pretty well till about dark. The Ship was steady and the Sea very smooth, at dark, the wind increased and we both began to give up what we thought belonged to us. But there was no doubting the <u>appeal</u> and we <u>surrendered</u> and were very glad, as soon as possible to resign <u>ourselves</u> to our Couches. Poor Uncle, sick as he was, was the only one not quite helpless and instead of our nursing him, he was obliged to turn nurse himself. Thus ended our first day on board the *Waterloo*. There are two other passengers from China, Mr. Van Basel, Dutch Consul, and Dr. Rutherford.

China Sea
November 20th 1833

20th I awoke this morning, but not with a desire to move, speak or look at any thing. I was sure I was alive, but I cared very little whether I remained so, or whether any one else did. More wretched I never felt, and no one can describe the <u>total</u> depression of spirits this *maladie des mers* occasions. I defy any one even the most brilliant colourer to paint the horrors of sea sickness. There I laid, seeing my poor Uncle exert himself but I could not <u>rouse</u> myself to exertion. I could only say pray leave every thing till we get well. I made out to get off my <u>night cap</u> about 11 o'clock but my night gown remained all day. And Capt., Dr., Carpenters and boys all had the benefit, but I <u>cared not</u>. They were all in, several times but I feigned sleep when I was not actually asleep and escaped all queries and conversation. I think I never was so sick before, fancy I was very bilious. Kept not a particle of any thing down, every thing was returned, without even the ceremony of I thank you. Oh *tempora*, Oh *Mores*! I shall never forget this day. A splendid breeze notwithstanding.

21st 16° North Lat[itude] China Sea This morning I awoke with a full sense of the propriety of washing and dressing myself, and the impropriety of gentlemen in night gown, a sure proof of convalescence. Also had a hope that something more than Epsom Salts Brandy and Water was to be my diet for the Day. Felt very weak however and somewhat <u>doubtful</u> but brightened up a little before dinner, but could not eat much. The Capt. and Dr. both very kind and attentive to our wants. We have fine weather a fair wind, and today are in 16 North Lat. having run 246 miles the last 24 hours.

After dinner the Capt. persuaded us to arouse from our <u>laziness</u> and go on deck, which we did and felt considerably better. Felt very <u>rum</u> and very much as though I had parted with all my <u>ideas</u> and senses as well as my food. Went to bed early and slept well.

22d 12° North Lat. Had a fine run so far, 205 miles the last 24 hours. The wind has been a little lighter. Today finding ourselves much better we dressed up and went to the "Cuddy" table to dinner. By the Bye, methinks I hear you Query? What or where is the "Cuddy," for I remember it was strange to me once. Well, I can only tell you in land phraseology it is the <u>dining</u> <u>room</u>, a room that goes the whole width of the Ship (with the exception of a small cabin off at one end) in front of our Cabins. We met at this said table in this said "Cuddy" (the origin of the word I have not yet found out) Capt. Blakely, Mr. Parkman first Officer, Mr. Caley 2d, Dr. Elliot, Mr. Miller Purser, Dr. Rutherford and Mr. Van Basel passengers, and little Johnny, a little sick boy passenger. We were introduced to those we were not acquainted with and relished our dinner very well. Felt marvellously refreshed and comforted. Feel now that we are pretty well seasoned. Poor Uncle is not well enough to go out and is obliged to dine alone. We see no change for the better as yet. After dinner we went upon the "Poop" and had tea, a clear sky above us and the clear blue waters all around us, with about 8000 yds. of Canvass to waft us along assisted by a good breeze was no mean sight. I enjoyed it awhile, and also the perfect order of the Ship. Everything goes on so regularly and with so little noise that it is really surprising when you consider that there is 150 men on board. The Boatswain's Whistle was heard while we sat there and the deck was instantly covered with men, each one bearing off on his shoulder his own hammock, which are neatly rolled up and numbered and piled upon the railing of the Ship. It was a pretty sight and looked a busy scene for the moment and all was still again.

I went below soon after and took my seat at my Cabin window where I sat musing till bed time. Have read some today for the first time, and begin to feel like myself.

23[d] 9° N. Lat. Passed "Pulo Lapato" [Pulo Sapato] in the night and are a long way past it today. We are getting on famously although the winds begin to grow light as we approach the Line. Commenced writing letters to leave at Anger today. It is rather unpleasant at first. Uncle went on deck a little while and we followed. Then came down and finished or read *Henry Masterton*[2] and finished it before I went to bed. Don't like it much. Too much murder and sudden death for my taste, not equal to others by the same author. However read it, because I was not very brilliant and could not give it much attention. Dined in the "Cuddy" and took tea on the "Poop." A lovely evening and we stayed chatting 5 or 6 of us till after 7, then Aunty and I went below to take care of Uncle. Begin to find that eating takes up a great part of the time and forms a pretty good item in the day's work, as usual at sea. What spare time I have between meals I spend in eating "oranges" (to keep them from spoiling), which hang in abundance in baskets at my cabin windows.

Sunday Nov[r] **24**[th] 7° N. Lat. This morning the wind is rather light and a beautiful day. The Capt. read prayers on deck to I should think over 250 people. It was a beautiful sight I assure you, each one dressed clean in his Sunday suit. The responses were full and distinct and it seemed as though each must feel what he uttered. It seemed more like Sunday and the Sabbath than any thing I have known for a long time. I read several of Dr. Channing's sermons which always seem to make me better at least to wish to be.

Mr. Van Basel made us a visit this morning. After dinner set upon deck till we were driven down by a Shower. The rain killed the wind and we were nearly becalmed tonight, and it was so very hot I found it impossible to sleep. We shall now have light winds till we get into the Indian Ocean.

25th 5°18' N. Lat. Winds light and hot. Begin to feel very well and go on regularly eating, drinking and sleeping, for say what you will about studying on board Ship, it is not a good place. There is a sort of listless feeling which always overpowers you and renders you unfit for exertion. However as soon as I get at my books I intend to try. I took up a novel today by Paulding, *Westward Ho*[3] and liked it very much, showing the folly and madness of dwelling too much upon Presentiments. I finished it before I went to bed. Went on deck after dinner and walked awhile with the Dr., then fell into [a] musing fit; had a slight touch of the Blues as I often do when all looks so bright and lovely above and around me as tonight. And yet perhaps it ought not to be termed the Blues. A distinction should be made between the <u>azure</u> <u>spirits</u>, and a <u>reflecting</u> humour, a sort of pleasing melancholy, which one rather indulges than seeks to dispel. However I was thinking tonight I had much rather be bound to America than England, for I want to get <u>home</u>, I am almost tired of <u>wandering</u>. Very little wind tonight, the Ship moving lazily through the water. Two "hawks" about the Ship and lighted on the Gaff. Messengers from land no doubt.

26th 4° N. Lat. This morning commenced as the "<u>Log</u>" would say with "Pleasant breeze and a little rain." Continued through the day. Spent the day in my Cabin arranging my books upon a Shelf I have had put up. Read a little French and then took up *John Bull in America*[4] which I never have read before, and was quite amused. Wrote a letter to Mrs. Colledge, dined and went on the Poop after dinner. Saw the Island of "Anambas" and several others, bearing S.E. about 30 miles from us. Several "Butterflies" flying about deck and our friends the "Hawks" found rest for their feet upon our "guards" and "<u>sheets</u>". A beautiful evening with a fine breeze. Had our little party at tea as usual on the "Poop." Stayed chatting awhile and then went below, perched in my "Cabin Window." Devoured 4 or 5 oranges, then went to my books, took Silliman's *Travels*[5] which I have several times commenced but never finished. Intend to go through with them now. Went to bed about 11 and slept well. Never slept so quietly on board Ship before it appears to me. My first voyage every little noise waked and alarmed me.

27th 2°11' N. Lat. Commenced with squalls and light airs, and plenty of rain. Saw land from the "Port" on the Lee Bow, which proved to be "Pulo Aor" and we passed that and "Pulo Domor

[Domar]." Found ourselves in Latitude 2°11' N. at 12 o'clock which is doing very well considering the very light winds we have had. The breeze strengthened before night and we glided along through smooth water most splendidly. The night was perfect, the <u>full</u> moon was shining in all its glory and set off our Ship to great advantage. What a glorious sight to see <u>such</u> a Ship under such circumstances. Uncle went on deck a little after dinner and seemed to enjoy it. We stayed up till nearly 8 bells, and then came to my window in my cabin where I have ample room for <u>reflection</u>, which tonight proved as boundless as that of the <u>moon</u> upon the <u>waters</u>.

I finished the first vol. of Silliman tonight. He gives a very interesting description of the "Mines in England." At dinner today the conversation turned upon "Rammohan Roy." One of the gents observed that he was a Christian or rather asked the Question. No replied half a dozen voices he was a "<u>Unitarian</u>," he was not a <u>Christian</u>, he was a <u>Deist</u>. They pursued the subject still further and some asked what the Unitarians <u>did</u> believe, and others answered evidently knowing as little about it as the Interrogator. I longed to put in a word but I had not confidence to meet so many adversaries at once, so I said nothing, deferring it till a better opportunity. It is rather galling to me to hear that you are not ranked among Christians, though I suppose none of these would deny but that we might be Christians in Character if not in name. But they allow no one the <u>title</u> unless he believes that Christ is <u>equal</u> with God. I long to put Mr. Channing's *Sermons* into all their hands and open their understandings that they may understand.

28th 5° S. Lat. We crossed the line this morning—rather calm before 12 o'clock but a good breeze sprung up then and it became more uncomfortable. Islands in sight all day and a Ship seen ahead which is going the same way that we suppose to be the *Farquharson* [Captain Cruickshank] which left China 12 hours before us. We shall not come up with her probably as the wind is light. Spent the day in writing and reading. Studied a little French this morning. Read the Adventures of Gil Blas in French part of the day and finished with "Silliman" who gives some interesting descriptions. On deck after dinner enjoying the breeze and the delightful evening till half past 7 when we retired to our Cabins, rather reluctantly, for after being in them all day long it is a relief to get out. But it would not be decorous to stay on deck without Aunty and she is obliged to go. So I make the best of it.

29th The last night was squally and calm by turns. We passed the *Farquharson* at anchor, while we run on and this morning she is not in sight. It is now hot and very little wind so that we can hardly expect to get into the Straits of Banca tonight, or before night. Just before night saw a Dutch Barque probably bound to Syngapore. About dark the wind died away and we were left at the mercy of the current which was fortunately in our favour. We drifted along most of the night. About dark the Hendric Rocks were bearing S.E. and the Capt. thought he should be obliged to anchor. As this rock is under water it makes navigation here rather dangerous. The moment you come within sight of land dangers begin to thicken, shoals, rocks and lee shores are not very pleasant companions. I never knew any thing so still as it was tonight about 9. The vessel was apparently motionless and every thing around and about us. Went to bed about 9 and awoke I don't know at what hour, at sound of the fiddle and a fine breeze. It was a strange contrast and a strange sound at that hour, but I soon found that we had been lying [at] anchor and they were then weighing and making sail which causes no little noise. Found myself quite cold but soon turned over and went to sleep again. We had been at anchor but half an hour I find and then a very threatening squall came up, but it proved to be nothing but a good breeze which carried us well within the "St[rait]s. of Banca."

30th The cool breeze lasted till about 10 this morning when it died away and it is as hot as possible, it is difficult to breathe the air is so close. When I got out of my couch, looked out to see what I could see, when I discovered the long low coast of "Sumatra" on one side, stretching a long distance without the slightest inequality of surface, as far as I can see. The Island of Banca is on the other side, presenting hills and vallies, which is far more agreeable to the eye I assure you. There was also a "Brig" in sight which we soon left astern, and a "China Junk" which looked quite natural—but the breeze which then favoured us soon carried us from both. We have also a Ship coming towards us, by which we hope to send letters to China—have accordingly sealed our despatches.

The day was calm with occasional squalls and wind ahead, which kept the men hard a work tacking—the most oppressive day I think

I ever passed. In consequence I went without my dinner, for it was too
much trouble to eat it. We are almost discouraged about Uncle. His
nights are so dreadful, and he loses strength and flesh so fast, and his
spirits are so low. The weather is so hot there is no hope of his getting
better till we get out of these dreadful Straits. They are tedious.

We were obliged to Anchor again about 6 as the wind was quite
gone and we were drifting on the Sumatra shore. I see with the glass
that the coast of this Island is completely covered with wood—not
a habitation is to be seen. Indeed it is impossible for it to be inhabited for the soil is a complete marsh. The trees come into the water
actually. It is an amusing sight to see them take in sail and come to
an anchor and I like it much when I can be on deck. 150 men all
busily employed. A hot night, went below and thought I should
certainly not sleep any. It was so still and airless. But I threw myself
down and slept soundly till 7 o'clock and they fiddled, weighed
anchor and made sail and I knew nothing of it. Had a fine breeze
from the land.

Banca Straits

Decr 1st Had a fine breeze from the land this morning which lasted
till 9 o'clock and here we are now in a dead calm and so hot that I
cannot write any more, so I'll read one of Dr. Channing's Sermons
and see if I can think.

It remained calm till 12 I think when we had the wind ahead
and a pretty breeze which carried us on tolerably well and at any
rate made us more comfortable. I am quite sick of the "Straits of
Banca"—there is nothing to please one in any way. Aunt Low told
the Capt. of my sleeping through all the fiddling, and they all got it
and I shall not hear the end of it for a while. The Capt. says they
cannot know all my qualifications in America. He laughs a great deal
about my being able to sleep 16 hours on one tack.

At dinner we had some of Mr. Cushing's wedding cake given me
by Mr. Dumaresq. We therefore drank to the happiness of the Couple.
After dinner went on deck, looked at the Chart, find we are approaching the "Lucepaia [Lucepara] Shoals," and in consequence of
its being difficult navigation here it will be impossible to run. The
same flat coast of Sumatra still near us. The wind died gradually away
as the sun set, and there being every appearance of a squall, we went
below. Hot and calm! Oh what miseries, and to be cubbed in a Cabin!

It soon commenced raining accompanied with wind and very vivid lightning with heavy thunder. We were cooled for a while and then it died away again, and as hot as ever. The Capt. saw a light ahead and supposing it to be a Ship sent off a <u>blue</u> light which had a fine effect. Read Young's *Night Thoughts* a while and "turned in" but it was too hot to sleep and the thunder very heavy.

Java Sea

2^d Weighed anchor this morning at daylight. Fortunately I heard the <u>fiddle</u>. Wind and tide both against us and they were obliged to drop the anchor again in an hour, so you may judge the <u>pleasure</u> of <u>Banca</u> <u>Straits</u>.

10 o'clock. Have just heard the order given to "haul up that Anchor" so I suppose we are to try again. But there is the smallest breath of wind as yet. But in this changeable place there is no knowing but we may have a gale before 12 o'clock. It is very pretty <u>fun</u> to look on and see them weigh anchor at the sound of the fiddle—and they have now done and we are moving a snail's pace but I should fancy not on our course. But I don't like to ask too many questions. There are now three vessels in sight—going the same way I believe. We had hoped to be at "Anger" tomorrow but there is very little prospect of it now.

We succeeded by squalls and favourable tide to get out of the Sts. by 2 o'clock, passed the Shoals safely but had several narrow escapes. Had a heavy squall about 2 in which we passed a "Barque" bound <u>probably</u> to Syngapore, but being in a squall we could not speak her, thus lost a good opportunity of sending [letters] to China. At the same time we had to "lay too" for one of our boats which had been out all the morning sounding and which we came very near losing. We overtook and passed an American and Dutch Ship (the latter was a Brig by the bye); the American we think must be the *Dickason* which sailed from China on the 15th. I should like much to know if it is her and to be able to put a letter on board, but think we shall not get a chance. We had a nice little breeze at dark which lasted but a short time and we were becalmed all night.

Decr 3 Was very glad to get up this morning about 6. Had a most uncomfortable night for in addition to heat we had a quantity of "mosquitoes" which we took in at "Banca" as <u>souvenirs</u> I suppose of the delightful place. They were buzzing about all night. Uncle was suffering dreadfully with perspirations and feels weak enough this morning. We are now just getting a breath of wind, and the American Ship still in sight. Now I am going to write a letter to leave at "Anger."

Wrote my letter. Finished the *Trial of Wakefield*[6] with which I have been delighted. I read it once before in the <u>hay</u> in <u>Grandmother Eaton's</u> <u>Barn</u>. What <u>changes</u> since then. Then I read Johnson's Preface to "Shakespeare's Works"[7] which I intend to go through with. It is very beautiful as almost every thing that comes from his pen is.

Dined in the "Cuddy" at 3, went on deck at 5, stayed till 3 Bells, 1/2 seven. Had a diet of discourse upon the "Poop." The Capt. was giving me a dissertation upon "Political Economy" upon which I should have <u>sans</u> <u>doute</u> been marvellously enlightened had he not in the midst of it dropped his snuff Box and broke the bottom out, thereby losing the contents, at the same moment all his ideas upon the subject vanished and we discussed the merits of "Bohea" and "Congo."[8] We ended with an argument upon servants and the comparative merits of English, American and Chinese servants, and the misery of being dependent upon them. All satisfied in our minds we then went below. Hot enough it was I assure you. I stripped myself all but my <u>chemise</u> and perched like a cat in my cabin window where I was sure no earthly being could see me, and as the angels do not wear "<u>Corsets</u>" I thought it was no matter if they did see me, and as for the spirits of the "vasty deep" I did not much care. But more than that, every thing appeared to be asleep in the Heavens above and the waters below. The waters were <u>spangled</u> as well as the Heavens, with only this difference in appearance, those below seemed to be dancing <u>quadrilles</u>. Here I sat musing till about 10, then turned in, and slept all night at the rate of 10 knot.

The American Ship was in sight all day, but we were not near enough to have any communication.

Decr 4th This morning about 2 had a strong breeze and squally, and when I got out of bed it was blowing a little gale with a great deal of rain and very heavy thunder and lightning. However we are now steering our course and getting on, and any thing is better than a calm. We lay over so much that it is difficult to write. Our fine breeze lasted till about 12 and before 2 we had a dead calm. We had the "Yankee" still in company, but she thought proper to come to an

Anchor about dark. Our Capt. thought best to make the most of a current which drifted us at about 2 knot an hour, which is better than nothing in these hard times when every inch of the way is gained with so much difficulty.

After dinner we heard the Ship's bell <u>tolling</u> as I thought. I opened our door to see what it was and they were all assembled at the gangway about to consign one of our men to a watery grave. We were not aware that one had died, but it seems he has been sick every since he left England and died this morning about 6. The Capt. read the burial service over the body. It was then consigned to the deep and all went on as before. Such an event to a reflecting mind calls forth solemn reflections, but it has a very different effect here, to what it would have in one of our small ships. For having so many, one is not missed. There is something very awful in the sound, of the last <u>splash</u>.

We were becalmed tonight till about 12. Forgot to mention that a few days since we saw a small water spout at a little distance from the Ship, the first I have witnessed and what I have always wished to see. This was rather a singular one, inasmuch as the water appeared not to be conducted to the sea in the spout but apparently broke in the air which I believe in general is <u>not</u> the case. It formed a bubbling in the water below, of course, and was a very pleasing sight. [Harriett inserts a sketch of the waterspout in the margin.]

Dec^r **5**^th The wind blowing very fresh this morning, which would soon carry us to Anger if it was but fair, but unfortunately it is directly against us, and every inch we make must be by beating. It is hard work for all on board. We had different Islands in sight yesterday. The North Watcher was bearing S.E. by E. I believe last night; we passed that and "Jason <u>Rock</u>" in the night, and this morning have Nicholas Pt. in sight. We were both very <u>doubtful</u> this morning for we have been as still as in a house for the last week. Read all the forenoon however, and ate a good dinner.

This morning went on deck to look at a Ship which was approaching us. It proved to be an American, but we were braced sharp in the wind and could not go near her, and as <u>our</u> Capt. fights shy of these Ships there was no prospect of speaking her as it was for her to make the advances. I could not help thinking she might have letters for me on board. Wish you would make my compliments to

<u>General</u> Jackson and request him to <u>order</u> our American Ships to learn to <u>talk</u>. We yesterday endeavoured to make the other Ship converse, but she had no <u>bunting</u> and was <u>dumb</u>. The English Ships all have "Mariots [Marryat's] Signals" which enable them to converse on any subject (even "<u>Metaphysics</u>"), but our Ships have not yet arrived at that pitch of perfection. This was a large Ship and she was going on her course rapidly with a strong breeze in her favour.

Went below and read till dinner time. Closed my letters after dinner then went on deck. Had Sumatra's flat coast in sight but it was varied in this view by the high land of "Raja Bassa" on the other coast towering above it. We also saw "Java." The wind and current being against us, the Capt. did not dare run, so we anchored about 8 and slept well in consequence.

Straits of Sunda, Anger

Dec[r] 6th Got under weigh this morning, with a strong <u>head</u> wind again. A fine morning and we had a pleasant run to Anger where we anchored at 12 o'clock. We passed very near to the Island of "Thont the Way" which is a very delightful little Island. We passed "Strom's Rock" too which alarmed us so much once. We should have anchored much sooner but had to make several <u>tacks</u> on account of a Ship which seemed determined to thwart us. It proved to be the *Flora* under Hamburgh colours which has often been at Macao. The Capt. and all hands get drunk together. The kindness of our Capt. would not permit him to go near him, but he deserved to suffer a little for his impudence. I was on deck to see all I could see. The scenery about here is quite beautiful. The land back is very high and covered with verdure. The coast is covered with "Cocoa nuts" and plantains and is such a perfect contrast to all that we have seen for the last 4 or 5 years in China that it is quite enchanting to one's eyes. It looks rather dryer than usual now and they appear to want rain. The Purser went on shore as soon as we arrived, carried our letters and procured all the good things he could find. The "Postman" came off but brought us no news. Plenty of "Praos" along side bringing fruits of different kinds, monkeys, birds, shells, etc. We went down into the officers' cabins and made some purchases, and spent an hour or two looking at books and sketches, paintings, etc. by Mr. C . . . [Cayley] who has great talent in this way. The Malays disfigure themselves (to our eyes) by using <u>Eere</u> [areca] and Betel nut, which they chew. It makes their teeth quite black. Indeed they consider themselves not <u>presentable</u> untill their teeth are filed off and become quite black. What different ideas different nations have of beauty as well as every thing else. It is very pretty to see them managing their little <u>Canoes</u>, but this will be but a repetition of what I have told you before. Every thing looked as when we were here before although we had different feelings. Then all was novel. They were the first foreigners or rather Indians we had seen; now they appeared to be <u>old</u> <u>friends</u>. Mr. Miller came off about 3 but brought no news at all. We have got a fresh supply of water, fowls and fruit.

The Java plantains are very delicious. There is nothing in China to equal them. We were disappointed in not getting some "Mangusteens," but it is not the season for those or Pumelos. I am very sorry, it will probably be our last chance.

The Capt. and most of the others went on shore after dinner, they wished me to go. But as Aunt Low could not leave Uncle I did not like to go without her. Beside they were going to sail which I dislike very much. As there appeared to be considerable swell I thought it best to remain on board. The Capt. is disappointed in not getting any more passengers as he anticipated, but they were not forthcoming. A beautiful evening. Our party came back about dark and we soon after came to our cabins. The town looks very prettily from the Ship. And after dark the fishermen make fires all along the shore to attract the fish, which has a very pretty effect.

Decr 7th Got under weigh this morning at daylight, and set sail from Anger. We have now a fine breeze though not fair but will enable us to lay over to the other coast and get into the homeward track. The N.E. Monsoon has not yet set in and they have had no rain for six months here and every thing is parched in consequence. The Thermom. stood at 90° yesterday on shore. We expected to have had a rough time here but it has been very pleasant. We expected a strong N. Easter but we are very fortunate. We had a fine run out of the Straits today. Passed very near the Isle of Cockatoo [Krakatoa], which is the prettiest spot I have seen for sometime. It was completely covered with wood and quite green. One high peak and the lower hills around it was beautiful, but the pencil is necessary to give you my idea of it, and I wished for the talent to use it I assure you. We passed several other Islands in the course of the day, but none so pretty as "Cockatoo." Before night we had a strong breeze and were very sure that we were once more at <u>sea</u>, for we have been sailing so smoothly the last fortnight that it has not appeared like being at sea at all and we shall most probably have to undergo another <u>siege</u> of sea sickness. Found it very difficult to walk on deck. We were braced sharp upon the wind with a head sea, which made the Ship pitch dreadfully and causes a very unpleasant sensation. We were very glad to turn in at 8 o'clock tonight, to spare our poor <u>bones</u>.

8th This morning awoke to the miseries of sea sickness. Oh the horrors that immediately fills one's mind, the disgust one feels to a Ship and the ocean and every thing connected with it. How one sighs for a quiet room even in a hovel on Terra firma, how one counts weeks and months and how interminable they appear in prospect, and how many times have I wished with the sailor today "That if Britannia ruled the waves she'd rule them straighter." This dancing up and down and depriving one of one's rights is not to be endured with complacency. Could eat no breakfast. Had prayers on deck but I could not go. Tried to read but am afraid all I profited by it was very trifling. Took a little "Porter" for my dinner which with a piece of biscuit was all I ventured. Had a most tremendous headache during the day and turned in at 7. Slept all night till 7 the next morning, which I consider <u>praiseworthy</u>. Never mind, sleep or awake, we are getting on famously and so I'll bear it patiently. Passed a Barque yesterday going our way. The Capt. thinks we have already taken the S.E. Trades which is a most fortunate circumstances and what we had no reason to expect at this season. The weather is now cooler and I hope Uncle will benefit by it.

Decr 9th Long. E.102° Lat. 8°40' Still a strong breeze and kicking up a sea. However I begin to get used to it and feel much better. Eat a pretty good breakfast and made up at dinner for the loss of yesterday's. Read all the morning a book called *Nat[ural] Magic*,[9] an interesting work by Dr. Brewster and finished the day with one of "Shakespeare's," The *Merchant of Venice* which I admire as much as any of his. Had a walk on deck and turned in at 9. A strong breeze all night and the noise under the stern was tremendous.

10th E. Long. 99° 5' Passed this day till 3 o'clock between sleeping and waking. It is true I read some, but a great deal of the time I was endeavouring to discover whether I was sick or not, which after having eaten a good dinner I decided, & that I was <u>very</u> <u>well</u>. Oh Idleness, thou art the bane to happiness or content even. Still going on well though by <u>squalls</u>. It blows <u>ten</u> <u>furies</u> now & then, and then dies away. Uncle does not seem so much better as I thought he would in this cool weather. His symptoms are no better at all. I feel quite discouraged at times. Indeed he appears to me to be worse for he can eat nothing, not enough to support life. I heard the ship's bell tolling this morning. Another body was consigned to the deep. We have now 16 on the sick list.

Went on deck a little while after dinner but were driven down by the rain. Read one of Shakespeare's Plays this evening and then "turned in," but did not sleep well.

Indian Ocean

Decr 11th 11°39' S. Lat. 96°48' E. Long. A fine fair wind blowing this morning, studding sails and of course we have had a "pull upon the main braces" or all the braces, and though she lays over considerable she goes more smoothly today. I am almost tired of walking at an angle of <u>45°</u> and fetching up in a corner, but however I do not complain for we are highly favoured in regard to weather. If this delightful sea air would only help Uncle I should feel quite happy, but he appears to be worse instead of better. Of course we take but little pleasure in any thing.

In my cabin all day till about 5, I began Goldsmith's *Citizen of the World*[10] this morning with which I was quite delighted. He is a most pleasing as well as edifying writer. After dinner challenged the Capt. to a game of Back Gammon at which I rather beat him. Stayed on deck till near 3 bells, then went to my <u>Dormitory</u>. Read *Much Ado About Nothing* and turned in but not to dream of "Benedick the married man."

Decr 12th Long. E. 93°14' Read this morning some of Goldsmith's *Citizen of the World* and a little of Sir W. Scott's *Demonology*. Then by way of variety sewed a little which passed the day off very quickly. The weather is still very fine. The Trade winds are blowing fair and steadily and we are approaching the Cape very well. When I have passed, I shall feel quite near you. If Uncle was only mending how happy I should be with the thought.

Went out after dinner and the Capt. carried us below on to the gun deck. We went forward and surveyed all the accommodations and into all the Cabins. The officers' Cabins are all neat and well fitted up, so different from our Ships. Of course the size makes a vast difference, but I doubt whether the American officers would take the trouble and go to the expense of making themselves so comfortable even if they had the room. But an Englishman must have his comforts.

Went on deck, played "Back gammon" with the Captain and beat him twice to his once. Had a long walk with him and came down at 3 Bells. Read Shakespeare's Comedy of *Love's Labour's Lost* which is the poorest I have yet read. My candle went out and I had to turn in *bon gré, mal gré*. Slept soundly all night; the noise of the water under the stern puts me to sleep when not too loud and the same noise keeps me asleep I believe, for I did not awake till 1/2 past 7. Then had to bathe and was only just ready in time for breakfast. We always breakfast in my Cabin.

Decr 13th Long. 90° Lat. S. 44° One day is a facsimile of another my dear sister and the ocean has become so familiar to me that I fear this journal will be far less interesting than the first. For how often we find that it is only the gilded charm of novelty that excites our admiration. Not that I can say that it has yet lost all its beauty to me, nor do I think it ever would. It causes deep reflection always, and in its varied humours excites our wonder and admiration, but once expressed it remains for us to admire to ourselves. And as yet we have had no variety—the weather since we left the Straits has been fine. We have been sailing over a smooth sea most of the time, with a fair wind and studding sails set. I have spent most of the day in reading. I am proceeding with the books I have mentioned before, with which I am much interested; took my sewing work while Mr. Van Basel and the Capt. made us a visit. After dinner went on to the "Poop" where the Capt. Back gammoned me. At which I was quite horrified. Had a short walk with Mr. Cayley who requested to come some morning and read *Childe Harold* to me.

Have felt quite in spirits today for Uncle has seemed a little better. His pulse has been better than any day before. But the Dr. thinks if he gets a great deal better he ought not to go further than St. Helena, that is, he ought not to go to England at that Season.

Read this evening *Taming of the Shrew*. Think Madame de Genlis has rather improved this plan of Taming a Shrew in her Tale of the *Mari Instituteur*; she acknowledges she took (which is very evident) her ideas from Shakespeare. I think it a capital plan and should think any woman might be tamed or killed with such proceedings in a husband and lover, particularly a newly married man.

Decr 14th E. Long. 86°55' Lat. 15°20' A fine breeze still and we have made a fine week's work of it. We were very fortunate in taking the trades so soon after leaving Anger, which we did not expect particularly at this season. We have run over 1300 miles this week and have got 3000 some hundred yet to run to reach the Cape, which we can do (if we average 200 miles per day) in 3 weeks. We shall most likely have the winds stronger now.

Uncle proposed to the Capt. today to leave us there (at the Cape) as it will be much better than at St. Helena as regards climate and accommodations. The Capt. has been wishing for an excuse to stop there and thinks it will do, but has not said decidedly. The Dr. thinks it the best place.

Went on deck after dinner, and chatted awhile and the Capt. and [I] played backgammon. I forgot to mention when we passed the "Cocos" (two small Islands a few days sail from Java) that an English Lady with her husband have gone to take up their abode there. I do not know whether they retired in <u>disgust</u> from the gay world, whether <u>necessity</u> or a love of solitude prompted this move, but certain it is whether they wished it or not they will have enough of their own company and very little of other people's in their present abode. It is to be hoped they love each other and are able to live on "smiles and water." The Capt. proposed making a donation of part of our wardrobe, should we come near enough to send a boat on shore as she is most likely in the state of Eve. I suppose she can find a <u>plantain leaf</u> if she cannot a fig. Ships very seldom touch here from any port and should think there were very few if any inhabitants there.

Finished Walter Scott's *Demonology* today. It gives us some good anecdotes of "witchery, ghosts," etc. I find he was a little tinctured with the Superstition of his country. Finished the evening with *All's Well that Ends Well*. Don't much like it.

Decr 15th E. Long. 83°43' Sunday morning. A fair wind and pleasant weather and we attended prayers on deck. It is a pretty sight to see the "Jacks" all dressed clean and assembled upon the Quarter deck. I enjoyed it much, it was a fuller <u>meeting</u> than I have seen since I left America. Oh I wonder when the time will come, when I can go to worship with <u>you</u> and all my dear friends again. I shall be too happy if it ever comes. Have thought much of it today and got quite *triste* upon the subject. And we all three came to the conclusion to day that we would give a great deal to be in Brooklyn. How deeply my heart responded to the wish <u>perhaps</u> you may imagine. I spent the day in reading Mr. Buckminster's *Sermons* and Young's *Night Thoughts* which I admire very much. Went on deck after dinner. Had a walk with Mr. Van Basel and a "consu" with Dr. Rutherford and the Capt. and then went below.

Decr 16th E. Long. 80° S. Lat. 17°14' Uncle's pulse has been better today than at all, being at <u>102</u>. We catch hold of the slightest clue to strengthen our hopes, but as yet I consider it doubtful whether he recovers. His feet swell and he has new complaints; his blood is so very low that he is liable to almost any thing. He proposed this morning my leaving them at the Cape and going on either to St. Helena to wait for Uncle James or going on to England. But I should be unwilling to leave him in the state he now is, although I would jump at the proposal if he were better or I could see him in a fair way of recovering. But then again I should not like to go without a female servant unless there was some other lady in the Ship. I could not bear the thought of going with all these Bachelors, for there is not a married man among them, not but that I should feel perfect confidence in the Capt. and not doubt the <u>politeness</u> of any, still it would not be pleasant. However I shall say no more of it at present. It would seem like leaving my parents again and that I dread.

Light winds today. I thought the Capt. would not count more than 150 miles today, but he says it is 192 so we shall I hope make our 1400 this week. But we who depend altogether upon the winds and waves cannot make any close calculations. Had a visit from Mr. Caley this morning, but he did not <u>read</u> *Childe Harold*. A little rain tonight. Played backgammon in the Library and read *Twelfth Night or what you will*.

Decr 17th   A rainy day and quite calm or perhaps as near it as can be. Going two knot part of the time. A state of weather very disagreeable in itself, but in these Latitudes made doubly so by its being often the precursor of a gale. So you see my dear we run from one danger to another. We have left the rocks and shoals behind us for the present and are now in these tempestuous seas. We are now nearly in the Latitudes of the "Isles of France" and Bourbon where they have tremendous hurricanes which always bring to my mind the affecting story of *Paul and Virginia* [St. Pierre] which has interested us both deeply in our <u>childish</u> days. They are very violent generally, and dismast and wreck many ships. Being rainy we did not get our Longitude today and more than that I was a prisoner for the day not being able to get my usual walk on deck.

I have become quite accustomed to <u>close</u> confinement now and never think of going out of our Cabins till after dinner, or rather till dinner time. It is rather hard at first but is astonishing how soon you get accustomed to all these things, our Cabins begin to look quite spacious as our eyes become accustomed to their limited dimensions, which certainly appeared contracted enough in comparison with our large rooms at Macao. Read part of the day and commenced <u>a little dress</u> by way of amusement.

Finished the day with Shakespeare's *Winter Tale.* Like it pretty well.

Decr 18th   76°8' E. Long. 18°8' Lat. Happy to say we have no gale to succeed the calm, but a fine breeze and clear sky. But <u>here</u> we must not "trust to the transient gleam of bright and cloudless skies" for I am told the "Hurricanes" come so suddenly that while you are admiring the clearness your masts may be gone, *par example*, the *Duneira*, an English ship, a year or two since had her three masts snapped off in <u>5 minutes</u>. They are very tremendous and sometimes last an hour, and not a cloud to be seen. However we are not in the season for them, though they are not always regular, but January and the two next months are the worst. I hope we may be spared. We have thus far been blessed with fine weather and I hope it may continue.

The Capt. tells us today he has made up his mind to go into the Cape to leave us. So we shall have this chance (if we live to arrive) of trying this climate for Uncle. He is very feeble today. Went on deck after dinner. It was a lovely evening and we are sailing along beautifully, quite the perfection of sailing tonight, and do you know my dear the <u>ingredients</u>? (Would you not fancy I was going to give you a receipt for a Cake?) Well I can tell you—a 10 knot breeze, (in a large Ship) wind on the quarter, a smooth sea, a clear sky, a beautiful sun set, the moon all ready to take her place at his departure, the bright star by her side, a <u>pleasant party of congenial spirits</u> in the "Poop," and with the exception of the last part, such was the situation tonight. Very pleasant they were, but not <u>congenial</u>. <u>Savez</u>?

Well pleasant as it all was I was obliged to leave it as my friend the moon commenced her reign, and descended to my cabin "to chew the cud of sweet and bitter fancy." [Shakespeare, *As You Like It*, Act IV, Sc. 3] However I threw the <u>cud</u> to the winds and took *Macbeth* and admired the genius of Shakespeare.

Decr 19th 72°50' [E. Long.] 19°18' [Lat.] A fine wind still, and pleasant weather, though hardly enough to satisfy our insatiable Captain. I observe they are preparing for a gale, that is rigging the storm stay sails <u>in case</u> there should be one. As it is necessary to be upon the watch, the Barometers generally indicate their approach and are generally correct. Spent the morning as usual. This fine weather ought to recruit Uncle if it is to be of service, but alas I feel almost discouraged. If he is better one day, it is only to feel worse the next. His pulse was lower this morning but was soon up again. We shall soon be at the Cape and see what that will do. I do not mention him daily, for I do not know that it can be of any use to note the changes, which are perhaps too gradual to be noticed, but you may judge how many of our thoughts are given to his situation.

I am happy to inform you my dear that I got a new idea today at dinner which I am happy to impart to you, a fact too which I think surpasses all that a spinster ever conceived of, and that is that "<u>Sugar</u> is extracted from <u>old clothes</u>." Query? How many old coats or shirts to sweeten a cup of coffee? After this I shall not be surprised at any thing. I must confess I could not restrain an incredulous laugh, but the assertor of this marvellous <u>fact</u> says it is <u>veritable</u>.

I finished the life of *Alexander the Great*[11] today. A man who with Napoleon must be acknowledged <u>great</u> by every one but I must confess <u>such</u> kind of greatness never has my admiration, for I cannot admire glory when obtained by causing the misery and death of so many fellow creatures, and all for conquest and to gain themselves a <u>name</u>. I commenced the *Memoirs of Prince Eugene*[12] of the Duke of Marlborough's time, and went on deck and saw a most splendid sunset; it was gorgeous—the first I have seen at all uncommon this voyage. A lovely evening and breeze freshened to a <u>splendid</u> <u>breeze</u>.

Decr 20th E. Long. 69°43' Lat. 20°18' I can only say for this day that it is delightful, a pleasant breeze but not enough to satisfy those who wish for speed. Passed the day as usual, find I am far more independent in being able to pass my time pleasantly than some of my shipmates. One of our passengers draws largely upon chess and cards, and of course calls for a <u>partner</u>—my books and sewing carry the mornings away rapidly. After dinner go on deck and today played backgammon awhile and had no luck. Another delightful evening. Went to my cabin at 3 Bells and read *King John*. Nothing has occurred worth note that I remember.

21st E. Long. 67°15' Wind very light all night, calm part of the time, and occasional squalls and rain through the morning. Cleared off pleasantly after noon but want more wind. Suspect we have not made our 1400 this week. Well never mind, we have much to be thankful for, and I for one will not complain while we have such weather. Saw no person till dinner time, went on deck after dinner, saw a <u>Whale</u>. He was apparently asleep on top of the water. We saw him breathing for a long time, at last he awoke, <u>turned</u> <u>over</u> and went <u>below</u>, and we saw him no more. We probably disturbed his repose. I beat the Capt. at Backgammon famously tonight. Came below and am just making up my day's accounts but my candle is nearly gone so I must say good night for it will serve me no longer. Uncle has been much better today. Sweethearts and wives tonight.

Decr 22^d 65° E. Long. "Another six days work is done" and another Sabbath has begun, with pleasant weather, every thing calm, still and quiet. Everybody dressed clean which reminds me of Sunday at home in Salem, where you know people only had a clean shirt once a week. The wind and weather being favourable, we all assembled at 5 bells on the Quarter deck to hear prayers read.

Our wind is fair but very light, and as Uncle seems to gain a very little I do not feel sorry as the sea air I hope is doing him good. Spent the day as usual in reading books suited to the day. At dinner the conversation turned upon St. Helena and <u>of</u> <u>course</u> (I may almost say) to Buonaparte. The gentlemen at table had a long argument and I find many of them agree with me regarding him. Went on deck just before six and passed an hour.

Dec^r **23**^d 62°40' Long. 22°16' [Lat.] As fine a day as you can imagine, seems as though it ought to cure Uncle if good air has any virtue. We have a little stronger breeze than yesterday. Commenced Johnson's *Journey to the Western Isles*[13] and through Scotland this morning, a book I have long been wishing to read. Find he carries his Scotch predjudices with him; he could not endure them I believe.

Uncle has had a blister on today so that he could not go on deck. Went up by myself, our party seem to be a little under the weather today. All below asleep I believe. I walked by myself awhile, talked a little with the officers, all very gentlemanly people, and watched the rising of a black squall coming up ahead. A little after 6 they began taking in sail to prepare for it; it looked wild and threatening. I sat down quite aft upon the poop, saw our Ship gradually disrobed of studding sails and royals, top gallant sails, and a reef in the top sails, which to me is an interesting performance. I sat hoping to see a pretty little squall, but the wind was not high, and it soon passed off and a calm succeeded. Some of our passengers are wishing for a gale but a squall would have quite enough of the sublime for me when exposed to the effects of the sublime. Read a little while and then went to bed to let the wind blow where it listed.

Dec^r **24**^th 60°15' E. Long. Awoke this morning and found the wind blowing fresh, and a beautiful morning. I instantly run to the side port to discover if it was fair and discovered the studding sails which quite delighted me. We have got the wind on our quarter (side of the Ship might be more correct, Miss Low) for the first time and what is rather singular in these Latitudes and at this season we have a N.W. wind, so that we are braced sharp up and although we have a 10 knot breeze we are going on steadily as possible. Spent the morning as usual in reading and working. Commenced Boswell's *Tour* with Johnson to the Hebrides.[14] What a fortunate thing for a man to have such a biographer. How many men might appear great under such advantages, not that I would say that Johnson owed his greatness to Boswell.

After dinner went into the Library and played Patience by myself, then walked awhile on the quarter deck. And as I challenged Dr.

Rutherford to a game of Backgammon and went into the Library where the Dr. <u>beat</u> me most <u>unmercifully</u>, I was obliged to retire in disgrace.

Decr 25th E. Long. 58°40' Our wind died away about 12 and we have had it very light ever since, with an opposing sea which makes our Ship pitch in a most disagreeable and <u>unbecoming</u> manner. We passed a Barque in the night bound probably to Bombay, but being the night we did not speak her. What an excitement it would have been for the day; but we are unlucky in this respect. Christmas day. Last year we were dining quietly in Macao. Oh the next I hope will be passed with my own dear friends in America. Is it too much to hope? May heaven preserve us all. Our dear Uncle has had a most comfortable day and were it not that he has the most flattering disorder my hopes would be strong. But "it is a silent cheater of the eye" most certainly, and its work is most insidious.

This nasty, pitching sea has disturbed the economy of my <u>corporation</u> and I have felt quite <u>disgusted</u> but I have just had dinner and feel better. Now I intend eating an orange and therefore say Adieu.

26th The wind continued light through the night and this morning is still so with the most disagreeable sea that we ever felt, we shall probably have it now till we get to the Cape. It is not only very unpleasant in itself but retards our progress very much.

I asked Uncle this morning if he thought he was any better. He said he felt more comfortable but he thinks his complaints are not any better. He thinks I suspect that they are seated and he hardly expects he shall recover; he is not deceived in them as people generally are. He wishes much to reach his native land once more but alas, I fear he will never be gratified. He says it is all right, and we must submit to the will of God. I hope he will live to reach the Cape. Oh my dear Sister I cannot express my feelings but you can imagine how miserable I feel.

I read a little to Uncle this morning as he wished it, and then sewed till dinner time. Went on deck at 3 bells and had a long talk with Mr. Cayley upon America, etc. Were driven down by the rain. The moon was eclipsed tonight, but as it was eclipsed by clouds from our view we could not see that any thing else intruded.

Decr 27th 53° E. Long. Fine morning, good breeze but pitching in a most <u>inhuman</u> manner, and I now find it difficult to write. Find it makes me very sleepy. Think I slept an hour this forenoon. Have been reading Boswell's *Tour,* find it very amusing, but cannot fancy how a man of Boswell's abilities could be such a shadow or tool for Johnson. It appears to have been a complete infatuation on his part. I think (begging his pardon) that the Dr. must have been a disagreeable companion, that is to be constantly with him and subject to his severe rebukes.

I find that Johnson complained a little of his exile in those Islands of a month or so and begs B. to go back that "he may commence existence again," it is a waste of life he says.[15] Do you know I began to think I was justified in complaining of my residence in Macao. Wonder what the old Dr. would have done to have been shut up there 4 or 5 years. He says a Ship is as bad as a jail, and added the fear of being drowned.[16] It is bad enough Heaven knows.

Decr 28th 50° [E. Long.] Again a fine day and a glorious breeze which strengthened after 12 o'clock. Had a bad head ache this morning and felt "no how." However read till 12, then dressed and worked till near 3. Yesterday afternoon went on deck, beat the Capt. at Backgammon, had a chat with Mr. Cayley and several others upon Americanisms. I asked if they had detected any in us or if they should know us to be Americans. The Capt. says we are all Suffolk people in America and have a tone like them, and by the tone more than any expressions he should know us to be Americans. Mr. C. says I puzzled him one day by asking him if he owned such a book. They never say Do you own a book? They say Have you got it?

The wind continued to strengthen till night and blew a most splendid breeze. Had a little rain which did its part in forming a most splendid bow in the heavens just before sunset, and contrasted with the "dark forming ocean" all around was particularly beautiful. And we see it to such advantage at sea having no houses or any thing to obstruct it, adds to its always splendid appearance. Waited on deck till 3 bells. Saw them take in royals, main and fore top mast studding sails, a reef in the main top sail and in the driver. This was done to ease the Ship and make it easier steering. Had a short walk tonight on the quarter deck with the Dr. He says he considers Uncle's a very dangerous case though not a hopeless one.

Came below and was very glad to turn in a little after 9. We were going along tremendously and the water was a complete sheet of foam for a long distance round us. How happy it would make me if we were steering directly <u>home</u> and going on so rapidly but we are steering to a strange land under melancholy circumstances. We shall soon be there and I trust it will be for the benefit of my Uncle.

29th 45°42' E. Long. 27°14' Lat. A splendid run of 254 miles since 12 yesterday, at which the Capt. professes himself <u>satisfied</u>. A remarkable circumstance, the wind still remains strong with fine weather. Sunday morning, but as we laid over so much we did not go out to prayers. Read an excellent Sermon. Capt. and Mr. Van Basel give us a benefit this morning. Went on deck about 1/2 an hour after dinner and walked awhile with Mr. Van Basel, but she laid over so much I soon got tired and as the Capt. was not on deck I came in. Was followed by Mr. Van B. and soon after Mr. Cayley. He stayed an hour and no doubt thought himself very entertaining, but people have different opinions you know. Spent the evening in my cabin reading my dear father and mother's letters. Thought much of my dear home and went to bed in rather a *triste* humour.

Decr **30**th 40°20' E. Long. 22°18' S. Lat. Wind quite light today comparatively. Going about 7 knots. Had a pretty good run through the last 24 hours of 200 miles. A beautiful morning. Uncle seems about the same, he is certainly no worse, and may we not hope he is better! Read French this morning, *Bélisaire*.[17] Took my work and the Capt. spent an hour with us. Give us a little picture of England, which he endeavours to gloss over, but it is impossible to hide that there is much misery among the lower classes and it seems doubtful whether it can be improved. It is very easy to trace the causes of this state of things, but very difficult to find a <u>remedy</u>.

At dinner we have had a variety of topics, among the last Madame La Vallette. Capt. Blakely says there is no doubt the jailer was <u>bribed</u> [see July 16, 1833, vol. 6]. I do not like to allow this because it takes the merit from the act of Madame. But still, knowing the temptation of 100£ to a poor man, perhaps was it not for stripping it of all its romance we should once credit it. But I cannot bear to have bribery at the bottom of every <u>apparently</u> noble deed, but alas it is too often the case.

Went on deck after having read an hour in what appears to me a very silly book called *Contarini Fleming*[18]. I fancied it ought to be good because it was written by the author of *Vivian Gray*. Talked awhile and walked with Capt. Blakely. We were very much amused by the Sailors, they were <u>manufacturing</u> a Donkey. We saw the thing walking round the Capstan and afforded us a good laugh. It was two men one made the head and the other the tail. They were leaning over, had something thrown over the two, and swabs, shoes and a variety of other things seemed to compose the animal; it had two panniers by its sides and mounted by a <u>monkey</u>, which they had rigged in <u>farmer</u> like style. The poor thing seemed to have the least amusement of any, being tied on and having his hands tied behind him.

It is pleasing to see the sailors so happy and to see how easily they are pleased. I could not help thinking that it is not <u>refinement</u> alone that brings happiness. Indeed I am inclined to think it causes more <u>misery</u> than any thing else. Speaking of Monkeys, the Sailors have 50 or 60 on board and it is very amusing to see them frisking about and carrying their young so carefully with them. They never come aft.

Came down after 3 bells and spent the evening in my cabin reading.

1833 Decr 31st 39°15' E. Long. 30° S. Lat. A lovely night and the wind blowing at about 7 knot. The last day of the year and a lovely one it is. A nice breeze and all delightful but the health of my dear Uncle. How happy should we all feel if he was only well.

There are very few bright spots in the past year for memory to dwell upon, my brother's arrival and our leaving China the Chief. We have many blessings to be grateful for notwithstanding, among which I think most of my good health and the preservation of my beloved parents and friends.

Spent most of the morning in writing letters. Read a little, then worked. Went on deck after dinner, played Backgammon with the Capt. at which he beat me. Sat and [had] a pleasant chat till 8 o'clock with Mr. Cayley and Mr. Van Basel, in which we all agreed if alive to meet in <u>imagination</u> the next Decr at this time. We were comparing different <u>customs</u> and thinking where we should all be and where we <u>were</u> the last year. Alas how little we know where any of us <u>will</u> be.

January 1st 1834   H.C.S. *Waterloo*

E. Long. 37°14' A *la* Log Book this morning, commenced pleasant with light airs, I therefore with like pleasure and in calmness wish you all my dear friends a happy new year, and hope the next to do it *in propria persona*. My thoughts have often wandered to you today my dear and I have <u>wondered</u> whether <u>married</u> ladies sit for company today or whether it is only for <u>spinsters</u>. But there was no one to respond to my wonders.

Spent the day in working that is from 1 till 3; I wrote a letter to you this morning to send from the Cape. Poor Uncle grows weaker I fear. He seems quite discouraged about himself.

The Capt. paid us a visit and says he expects to land us in a week at the Cape. Oh dear I don't want to go among strangers again, but it must be so!

Went on deck after dinner—a glorious evening. It is not dark now till 8 o'clock and light again at 4 with us, so our nights are very short. We were amused with the sailors again, they got up a <u>quadrille</u>—an Italian boy dressed as a girl and a very pretty one he made too. Came below and read the third part of *Henry the 6th*, Shakespeare. Very interesting.

2ᵈ **Jany** E. Long. 34°8' S. Lat. 31°40' Breeze continued light through the night—the stars were particularly brilliant and the sky <u>intensely</u> blue. Who can look on such a scene and not be filled with wonder and admiration. The breeze strengthened this morning, and was blowing a 10 knot breeze before sunset, but as clear a sky as possible. The "Barometer" was falling however and the Capt. very <u>reluctantly</u> obeyed its warning, but as he goes altogether upon the Barometer, he dared not disobey. And just before I came down the men were ordered to take two reefs in the top sails. (Was taken by surprise tonight) A landmark.

3ᵈ **January** 30° E. Long. 33° S. Lat. The wind through the day has been light and verging towards a calm and we were left at sunset without a "breath the blue wave to curl" with our mainsail reefed, our top sails also, and mizen, and royals and top gallant sails <u>furled</u>. A little breeze and fair sprung up just afterwards, but the Capt. dare not make sail, as the "Barometer" was very low. But there was no appearance of any gale at 9 o'clock.

But <u>we</u> who are exposed to the treacherous main trust not too confidently to its smiles and its placid manners, more particularly in this part of the world. Run 277 miles yesterday.

4th 29° E. Long. Before morning we were fully convinced of the fidelity of our "Barometer" and see the advantage of listening to its warnings and were awoke various times by the "fetching away" of some of our traps that had hitherto escaped our attention. I was awoke by the pelting of books which came into my couch by dozens from a book shelf over my head. Thanks to my good condition I had no bones broken. I have already been so knocked and bruised with my awkwardness in running against trunks etc., that were any one to pick up one of my legs below the knee they would find some difficulty in deciding its complexion. Well I must not be too "copious" as Haskell says, but proceed to say that a violent gale commenced about 4 o'clock in the morning of this day and continued to blow with great violence till 12 and gradually grew lighter through the day. I will not pretend to say that I saw much of the sublime outside but I can vouch for the ridiculous inside. Had I not have been violently sick I might have enjoyed the sport but I defy any one to be amused with any thing in such a situation. I succeeded in dressing myself after having risked my bones in many perils, but got through without serious injury. But every thing was in a state of confusion it is in vain to describe, for you cannot imagine how dreadful it is, and the decks so slippery that one slides from one end to the other. I did manage to look out my windows, the sea was an entire sheet of foam. And our great Ship seemed trembling for its safety, it seemed neither to advance nor recede. The wind was dead ahead and we had only 3 storm sails set, all our usual sails were furled. The sky was perfectly clear and a pure, dry air with the Thermometer about 68 or 70 during the day. I managed to get to the "Cuddy" door after dinner and stood a little while but returned to feel the horrors of sickness again. Turned in the only comfortable place and slept till morning.

5th 29° still The wind subsided in the night, the Barometer rose and our sail was set again, but we had to suffer as much from the motion as yesterday, for the wind left as its legacy a dreadful swell so that we were driven and tossed by the waves in a most dreadful manner. Eat nor drank nothing with any pleasure, and feel more annoyed as I think I ought to have been a better sailor after having been two months nearly exposed to the sea—"but so it is and it can't be no tiser" and all I have to do is to grin and bear it. After dinner the wind died away and the sea was stiller so that we had an hour or two on deck. Came below at 3 bells and turned in. Feel as though I had had a fit of sickness.

6th 27°30' [E. Long.] 34° [Lat.] Quite discouraging, a foul wind again today and the Barometer falling again and every prospect of another gale. Oh Terra firma give me one little nook upon thy shores and I'll not complain. We have the land of the Caffre and the Hottentot upon our lee, but I look to that with but little pleasure except as a resting place for a while. How useless making calculations on this fickle element. We may be kept beating about her a week to come, some of our officers have been 2 weeks getting round the Cape, in the winter season though. Fortunately today there is a current in our favor and we have made 117 miles in spite of it. Feel much better today though this morning I had one turn of sickness. Was able to go to the Cuddy to dinner, but had hard work sitting at table. Have just done dinner and have been able with some trouble to bring up my book, which had got behind hand considerable. If you could see the situation of my writing establishment, you would feel I am sure. There is my Ivory stamp and paper cutter covered with ink which will remain a monument of my misery but a truce to sighs and lamentations upon such trifles. I care not. It was upset in a lurch, so no matter.

After dinner finished the *Life of Sir Joshua Reynolds*,[19] an eminent painter whom you have no doubt heard of though not so much as I have, for Mr. Chinnery was fond of quoting him. As there was considerable sea and strong breeze and (other private reasons) we did not go on deck till after tea. Then walked awhile and amused myself with seeing them reef sails as they were obliged to do just at dark as there was evidently something ahead. The Barometer fell a little, but the squall passed over before 9 o'clock and we were becalmed. The Capt. fully expected a gale. I went down and turned in to be prepared for it. Read two Acts of *Richard the 3d* and went to sleep because my wick, waxed long and my snuffers fetched away in the gale—interesting particulars which it unquestionably behoves you to know and me to relate. They have not yet been redeemed from their sorry quarters.

Jany 7th The Capt. has gone through the form of consulting his officers regarding landing us at the Cape and all agree that he is right in so doing. 7 weeks today since we embarked, we thought to have been at the Cape today, but there is a chance if this weather holds that we may be here a week longer. A dead calm today. Had a Shark alongside today which they hooked, but he managed to extricate himself and we lost sight of the "sanguinary and voracious <u>caitiff</u>" which we used to talk so much about coming out. We have also a Ship in sight today which the Capt. thinks is the *Farquharson* which we passed at the entrance of the St[rait]s. At noon she was about 12 miles from us. We are both becalmed so that there is little chance of our speaking.

Have been packing up books today and thinking of landing again. And as I have challenged the Capt. to a game at Backgammon, I will bid you good bye for the present.

Went on deck at 6—no wind, the sea looking like a sheet of glass, a beautiful sky however—and if we only had a wind we should soon bid adieu to the Ship. But our luck seems to have <u>blown</u> away in the <u>gale</u>. The "Black Cats" are <u>petted</u> but all to no effect. Our Capt. pretends to have great faith in these creatures, but he is far too sensible a man to credit such <u>superstitions</u>. However they are always treated with <u>great respect</u>, while the poor <u>tortoise shell cat</u> is sadly abused if she goes further aft than the main mast. Played with the Capt. till nearly dark, then walked awhile and went below.

Saw a most brilliant meteor this evening from my window which appeared to cross the constellation of the Southern Cross which was just visible from the Stern windows. The atmosphere was exceedingly clear and the stars <u>splendid</u>. <u>Something new</u>.

January 8th The Longitude I <u>do not know</u>, a <u>point</u> you perhaps never heard of, but it lies somewhere off the Cape. Awoke this morning and found a fresh breeze blowing and our Ship contending with a heavy swell, which if the wind is <u>fair</u> must retard our passage. However I soon discovered it was dead ahead. We have only made 66 miles in the last 24 hours. But there it cannot be helped and as Mr. Miller says, there is a time for everything; therefore we hope there is a time for us to arrive at the Cape. But it seems a pity that we should be going back again in spite of my philosophy—but there, we <u>can't help it</u>. Hark, I hear a <u>small pull</u> on the yards, perhaps it is coming. Uncle seems a little better. The Digitalis seems to have had a good effect. Oh that it may continue.

The small pull was only to brace more sharply, and before night we had a very strong breeze which would have carried us straight to the South Pole if we had been disposed to go. Top Sails reefed and I went below to secure myself in my couch before it blew any harder. It was a most uncomfortable night and I slept little, for I was pitched about in a dreadful manner.

[Marginal note] found out at night that Long. 25°37' Lat. 35°17'

9th 24°35' [Long.] The wind decreased before morning but the sea was tremendous and most disagreeable—we were obliged to keep in our couches till dinner time as much as possible as there was no such thing as sitting or standing. The Capt. Says he hardly ever saw such a sea, so irregular and confused. Poor Uncle has hung in his Cot all day, for his poor bones would suffer from the bruises mine get. Was reading the *Lives of British Sculptors and Painters*[20] all the morning. We begin to wish for a little quiet on land. After dinner found ourselves <u>becalmed</u>. O the <u>pleasing</u> <u>varieties</u> <u>of</u> <u>a</u> <u>sea</u> <u>life</u>. We may be here a week yet. Went on deck after tea, had a Ship in sight, and amused ourselves with imagining what it <u>might</u> be. Perhaps our friend *Tommy Dickinson*—but we cannot see her hull on deck.

10th A very pleasant morning with a smooth sea for our comfort. Looked out the first thing to see where the sails were or if there were studding sails, but they were not to be seen—indeed we were then <u>becalmed</u>. However looked again after 12 finding a little breeze had sprung up and to my delight saw the sure signal of a fair wind. I immediately went to the Cuddy door and had the good news confirmed, for it is delightful after having a week of storms, headwinds and calms. It was really cheering and I could have sung "Merrily every bosom boundeth" if I had not turned and looked upon my dear Uncle. He is so weak that he can scarcely move and—but it's no use. Took my work and worked till 3, marvelling in my own mind what we shall see at the Cape, how long we shall stay, and how we shall get <u>from</u> there. The wind continued fair till midnight when it grew calm. I was awake most of the night and a little of every thing passed through my brain. Read till 10 o'clock Mrs. Piozzi's *Anecdotes* of Dr. Johnson.[21]

11th 21°30' [Long.] The wind <u>began</u> again about 5, not quite fair till after 2, but I heard the officer on deck say at dinner "Land on the Lee bow," so I suppose we are in sight of "Agulhas Pt." which is the first we shall see. A small Ship in sight, and the Capt. thinks <u>if the</u>

wind holds we shall see the Cape of Good Hope tomorrow morning. I cannot realize as yet that we are going on land again. While we have nothing in sight but the sky and water it seems impossible. Have read part of the day and worked the rest, just done dinner. Went on deck and found "Agulhas" nearly abreast of us. Low land and bears this name from its resemblance to an eagle. Had a long walk on deck, then the Capt. and I played Backgammon. He beat me and then I beat Dr. Rutherford. Had a walk with Mr. Cayley and came below at 8 o'clock. Then it was quite light. There is a very long twilight here.

Table Bay

12th A fine day with a fresh fair breeze. Looked out after breakfast and found we had the Cape of Good Hope nearly abeam. Attended prayers on deck at 10 o'clock being Sunday. Then went on to the "Poop," looked at the Chart and found out our situation, had a walk and came down. We have been sailing past it rapidly and I have been watching its changes from our port.

Table Mountain was covered as Capt. says with a cloth which looked light and airy, but which Capt. Blakely says is a sure sign of a S.E. gale. This Mt. is 3582 ft. high. I wonder if I shall ever attempt its summit. Our abode will be at the foot of it. The land all along here is black and barren, not a trace of a shrub or any thing green have we seen as yet. Not much to be wondered at perhaps, when we think of the scorching suns and the bleak breezes that are continually playing upon it. The Purser will go on shore tonight and get some accommodations for us, and we shall go tomorrow morning. I almost dread it for Uncle, he is so weak, but we must trust to Providence. We do what we think for the best, and I hope he will find benefit. We are all packed up now.

We anchored off Cape Town about 4 o'clock, and after I wrote the above and we came nearer the shore, there was enough to delight the eye. We went on deck and the Health Boat came off. Told us of the Annihilation of the [East India] Company's Charter as a Trading Body, of the abolition of slavery in the West Indies, and a variety of other matters, but nothing from America. Query? Where is the English government to get 20,000,000£ Sterling for the emancipation of her slaves. Well never mind that. The Purser, the two Drs., and Van Basel went on shore tonight and are to find us accommodations.

Now it will be proper before I proceed to say what I think of Cape Town in the distance. First it has a most singular appearance. The land is so curiously formed. Table Mt. is directly back of it and so flat on top and so well deserving its name that it actually looks as though it had been planed off. Its sides are rugged and barren apparently—there is also a very curious Peak near it, called the "Cloof" [Kloof] I believe. The Town itself looks prettily and more like civilization than any thing I have seen for a long time.

We are at some distance from the shore, therefore could only see with a glass. Table Bay is not deep and a shelter for ships only in the S. East Monsoon or Trades. They have now a Light House established on Green Pt. which is the first I have seen since Bakers's Island [off Salem harbor]. A most lovely evening. Walked my last walk on board the *Waterloo* with Mr. Cayley and the Capt. Never shall I forget her though. Every one has been so kind and attentive, and we have been so comfortable that I shall hold them all in grateful remembrance.

Cape Town Cape of Good Hope

13th This morning feels sharp and cool and reminds me of our delightful summer mornings or May mornings in America; it brought the colour into my cheeks at once and it actually seemed as though I was breathing my own native air. We breakfasted at 1/2 past 7 and had our selves and baggage put into the Boats for landing. Uncle had a couch fixed so that he got on shore very comfortably. We were landed at the jetty about 9 and a <u>Coachman</u> walked up and said the <u>Carriage</u> <u>was</u> <u>ready</u>—a novel sound to our ears, who have not seen a Carriage for nearly 5 years. Nevertheless we jumped into it and we went to our boarding House. Every thing looks strange of course though many look homish, and though I do not feel at <u>Home</u> yet I feel as though I was nearer it.

I shall never be able to tell you of all the strange things I have seen, but Here I am, on Afric's shore and by degrees you will know how and where we live. To describe my <u>feelings</u> would be impossible—they were so varied! but that you will gladly dispense with and imagine them if you can.

We drove to our boarding House then, and were introduced to a young lady, very pretty and genteel, whose name I have not yet attempted to pronounce, being Dutch, but I have since then learned it and may venture to write it. It is "Cruywagen."[22] There is a widow lady and two daughters. The latter speak English and have the care of the establishment. They had a breakfast ready for us which we could not resist. Oh the delicious bread and Butter, the tempting Apricot, the fig and the grapes, think you I could resist. We are just in time for fruits of all kinds.

We soon after breakfast had the pleasure of seeing a Highland regiment and hearing the most delightful Band. It seemed as though all our senses were to be regaled at once, I was in a maze I assure you. I set at the window all day gazing. Every one seemed so busy and so many running about and what astonished us most was, to see ladies so plenty walking about so briskly in the middle of the day. Our officers were in and out all the morning but at 2 went on board after having bid us Adieu.

Had a delightful dinner and such a appetite. After dinner as we had the carriage at our disposal for the day, and Uncle feeling too tired to go out, the two ladies and myself jumped in and we had a delightful ride. Went to Green Pt. and saw the *Waterloo* some way out with a fine breeze and all sails set. God bless them all. Saw many odd things which I may describe hereafter. Stopped at Mr. Vallet's [Charles Mathurin Villet][23] on our way home and got some splendid flowers, the mignonette, the Heliotrope, and a thousand others that I have no name for. The weather is delightful. The people call it warm but we do not.

Mr. Vallet had some strange animals natives of this country. I saw the "Gnoo" [gnu] a very ugly but powerful creature, the Spring Bok, a very pretty creature resembling a little the Deer, which he had there, a most lovely creature, the Laughing Hyena too, he has several and a number of others. Came home and brought our load of flowers, I have not seen such a collection before for years. Every thing grows in profusion I noticed while riding a hill covered with geranium growing wild. We passed some lovely little cottages, the grape vines growing over them and forming such a pretty contrast with the white houses. The houses have all flat roofs, and at first had a very odd appearance, but I begin to like it.

14th A most lovely morning, but I was up rather late having been very tired last night. Soon after breakfast the Highland Regt. passed with the most delightful band I ever heard. They played most delightfully. Their dress is very picturesque, but I am sorry to say they wear the Trowsers and not the Short dress (kilt) I believe it is called.

Dr. Murray [Dr. John Murray][24] called this morning to see Uncle. Says he must go directly into the country where he will have finer air and that he does not intend to give him any medicine but to eat every thing good—in fact to live on the fat of the land, which is rich enough I assure you. Every thing is so abundant particularly compared to Macao that we are quite ravenous. You would think I had been starved to see me eat, but coming from sea every thing tastes so fresh. The Dr. says also, that Uncle wants building up, that he does not need medicine. Oh I do hope he will cure him with God's blessing. I really have hopes again. He is a most skillful Physician and every thing else is in his favour.

I have spent most of my morning in gazing about and wandering from place to place. After dinner I went to walk with Miss <u>Franchy</u>. Went to the Company's Gardens, a most delightful shady walk. Very extensive and two rows of Oaks on each side, it is laid out in large squares and turfed. It seemed to be the resort of ladies and gentlemen and children.

15th Am still amused at looking out the windows, to see the variety of faces, the African, the Hottentot, and the Caffres, all ugly enough in their way. The ladies all look alike, that is their dresses. We find ourselves quite *outré*, but I do not care much. After dinner Uncle, Aunt and I had a very pleasant drive. Uncle enjoys it very much. This is certainly a very pretty place. The flowers are beautiful, particularly the Oleander which grows very high and in great perfection. The evenings here are very cool and we do not dare expose ourselves to the night air as in Macao. It seems more like our summers in America. Heard of the arrival of Sir Benjamin D'Urban[25] this evening, the future Governor of this place.

16th Miss Cruywagen and myself dressed and went <u>shopping</u> this morning—what I have not done for 5 years. I made poor work at it, for I did not understand the money at all. Rix dollars and Schelins [schellings] are new to me. After we had shopped we walked in the gardens, a delightful cool and shady walk, but I was astonished to find myself very comfortable in walking in the sun about the streets in the middle of summer. We went to Mr. Vallet's Museum and saw a great collection of stuffed animals, birds, snakes, and a great variety of insects and Butterflies from Rio. The animals and birds were mostly natives of this country. I saw an Ostrich for the first time, and find the splendid head dresses we have from that bird owe much of their beauty to the <u>dressing</u>. It is a very ugly bird—an immense straight neck and very long legs. The feathers are taken from the wings and tail. I cannot describe all I saw but I recognized many that I have looked at in days of my childhood in the <u>Primer</u>. There was a Flamingo a very handsome bird. I saw a hideous snake about 50 ft. long from Syngapore. It is not venomous, but coils himself round you and presses you to death. Snakes are very common in this country. There were a great variety of small and very beautiful birds, also a fine collection of shells. But in all the collections of birds I have ever seen, I have never yet seen any thing to equal Mr. Beale's "Bird of Paradise."

The Governor his lady and suite landed this morning and there has been such a running to and from by the slaves to get a peep at him. They all fancy they are to be liberated at once. Poor creatures, they will never be so comfortable and well off as they are now in my opinion. In this family they are treated like children more than servants—I never saw any thing exceed the kindness.

After dinner we went to ride. Went to Green Pt. It was a lovely afternoon apparently. But there was a S.W. wind blowing which is considered very bad and all invalids are obliged to keep close, but we did not know it, and poor Uncle soon felt the ill effect of it. We find the evenings exceedingly cold.

17th The S.W. still blowing this morning, and Uncle has coughed incessantly. Has had a blister on today.

Mrs. Murray, the wife of our good Dr., called upon us this morning, a pleasing woman.

After dinner the wind increased and blew quite a gale; the clouds of sand were rolling in the air so thick that we could not see across the street. We were obliged to close every window and even then the sand came in. The S.E. they say are much worse. I have often heard of them. Every <u>place</u> as well as every <u>body</u> must have its "something."

18th A fine morning. Had a good deal of rain which has laid the dust and made it very pleasant. The Highland guard has just passed. Such a band of music as I have not heard for many a day. Read most of the day *Ivanhoe*, [Sir Walter Scott] except when I have been run-ning about from place to place. Mrs. Murray's little girls came to see us. A dull evening and we did not walk, except upon the <u>stoop</u>.

19th A rainy morning. The Church Bell rung at 8 for the Dutch service and the people came pouring in from all parts—the Church is just opposite our house. At 11 I am going as the English service then commences. Oh how delightful it will seem to go once more to Church and hear the music. I can hear the sound of the Organ at my window.[26]

Went to Church, heard a pretty good sermon and was delighted with the organ. It sounded something like <u>ours</u> at Dr. Prince's Church and aroused many pleasant associations. I heard one of the familiar tunes <u>we</u> used to sing. I cannot tell you how pleased and yet how sad I felt. For pleasant as this place is all are <u>strangers</u> and every <u>thing</u> strange, with an <u>uncertainty</u> how long we shall be here—but we hope Uncle is getting better and I ought not to complain.

Well to the Church. The English I am astonished to find have been indebted to the Dutch for the use of their Church for the last 20 years and are just now building one. It is rather small but neat and I should think easy to speak in. The Dutch service commences at 8 and lasts till 11, the English at 11 and lasts till 1/2 past one, then the Dutch again in the evening. The Sunday is very strictly observed here. The town was still as Salem of a Sunday—in Macao it was the same as any other day. It was very rainy all day and very cool. This climate is very like our summers in America.

20th A fine day, the rain has laid the dust and the air is delightfully fresh. Was busy all the morning putting away clothes. It is a deal of trouble to make long voyages. After dinner Miss Joanna and I went a shopping. Then we went to the Gardens of a German Baron [Carl Ferdinand Heinrich von Ludwig].[27] They are splendid—the most commanding situation, having the town, the "Bay," the "Blue Moun-tains" in the distance, and a full view of Table Mountain on the right. The <u>gardens</u> are extensive and a great variety of flowers of the most rare and beautiful kind. The old gentleman was rather stingy how-ever, but by looking very hard at some and praising them a great deal, managed to bring away a very beautiful bouquet, consisting of "Heliotrope," the Myrtle in full bloom, a very beautiful crimson flower, etc. Miss Joanna and I got them all—the three other ladies got none at which they were very much <u>annoyed</u>. The myrtle here grows as high as my head and is most lovely. He had the "<u>Cochineal</u>," a little <u>insect</u> that lives on the prickly pear, had a variety of the "Passion" flower—but I cannot tell you all that delighted me. The gardens were laid out very neatly and kept with great care. The old gentleman was very polite and invited me to come again.

21st I wish you could just take a peep at our breakfast table. We have 7 different kinds of fruit upon it and those the most delicious. There is Grapes Green & Purple, fresh figs, Pears, Apricots, Peaches, Green Gages & Damsons, sometimes Mulberries. This climate produces all the fruits that ours does and more too and in the greatest abundance. Then beside we have the most delicious bread and Butter & etc. So you may judge that I eat a good breakfast. I expect before long to be a "Dicker fatty" as the Dutch say. I have such sport with this language. I hear it constantly spoken here but I doubt if I ever speak it. I have tried to pronounce many words but they are so guttural I cannot. The above and one other make the chief of my Dutch vocabulary at present. I do not much like it.

This morning being very fine, Aunt Low went into the country of Castenbosch [marginal note: spelt properly Kirstenbosch] to see the house where we intend going as soon as the Dr. thinks best. I stayed at home to take care of Uncle who certainly seems much better. If he gets no cold we think he will do well. She came back at 3 and says the country is delightful—but I can better describe it when I have seen it.

After dinner the Miss Cruywagens and myself took the carriage and went to ride. It was a lovely afternoon and we went to Green Pt. Got out and run upon the rocks at the sea side till nearly sun set. The air was so pure and beautiful we enjoyed it much. Saw a French Brig coming in and a Ship in the distance. We got back just before dark and then took a walk on the <u>Parade</u>. Came home, took some tea and spent the evening upon the "Stoop." I was amusing myself with <u>Dutch</u> words.

22^d Find one cannot sit on "Stoops" and expose themselves to the night air as in Macao with impunity—got a cold in my head by it. Mr. and Mrs. Thompson [George Thompson][28] called upon us this morning, a very nice woman apparently. We called on Mrs. Murray, talked a good deal of China; they seem to know no more of it here

Merchant Shipping in Table Bay, Cape Town, Chinese Artist, *ca.* 1805 (*Martyn Gregory Gallery, London*)

than in America. They asked many questions, many of them <u>posers</u>. Had a very pleasant call, for I had much rather talk of it than be there. Came immediately home, for Uncle is quite miserable again today. I feel quite discouraged again, but poor Aunt I am afraid is too much encouraged; we have been flattered but to be deceived I fear.

Aunt Low went out after dinner to buy a few <u>comforts</u> for him and when she came back I went round the Parade with Miss Joanna, or as she is called in Dutch, Miss <u>Hainachy</u>. This said "Parade" answers to our "<u>Common</u>" and is used for the same purpose. Another delightful evening. Now there is an opp[ortunit]y to write to China so I must improve it.

23^d A cold in my head which is very uncomfortable. Uncle told the young ladies I got it opening my mouth so wide to speak Dutch. It amused them very much. I should think it might make one hoarse. Was in my room most of the morning with a bad head ache. Uncle has been better today than he has at all. Wrote to Abbot today.

This afternoon a South Easter was blowing and we could not go out. We were obliged to shut the house up quite close to keep out the dust. We are obliged to be much more careful here not to sit in the air than in China; there we were always in a draught. The Dr. came in this morning and found me sitting with the window a little open. He closed it at once and says you must not sit by on open window. And although the windows are closed, the house is perfectly cool and comfortable.

We see very little company here; it is just the reverse of what we have been accustomed. Before we have seen mostly gentlemen; now it is all ladies. We have [a] nice old lady the mother of the young ladies, one of the kindest and best of women. She speaks no English and we cannot have much communication except by interpreters, but she gives me a motherly smile now and then and allows me to call her "<u>Mamachy</u>," the Dutch for Mama. The young ladies are both very pleasant and very kind. They spare no pains to make Uncle comfortable, and to get him every delicacy.

24th Mr. Eksten [Dirk Gysbert Eksteen]²⁹ our future host at "Castenbosch" called to see us this morning, a handsome and pleasant looking person.

The S. Easter blowing again this morning and increased before night to a heavy gale, so that we were obliged to shut the house again.

I have been very busy cutting out a muslin print, we must be a little modernized. The day passed off very rapidly I was so industrious. I have nothing of consequence to relate to you—have been in my room most of the day.

25th No wind this morning and very warm. The Dr. thinks Uncle must prepare to go to the country by Tuesday. He brought another Physician to consult with him this morning.

Finished my dress before dinner. Bought it, cut it out, and made it since yesterday at 10 o'clock, so you see I am good for something yet. Five Ships arrived today, one from China, but no news. After dinner went a shopping and then walked in the gardens with Miss Joanna. A lovely evening which we spent upon the "Stoop."

26th A lovely morning. Intended to have gone to Church but Mrs. Thompson did not call for me therefore I did not go. Wrote a letter to send per *Thames*. Dr. Baylies [Dr. Samuel Bailey]³⁰ and Murray called this morning. They held a consultation and advise Uncle's going at once. He has had a very sick day today. Mr. and Mrs. Ebden [John Bardwell Ebden]³¹ called upon us this afternoon. Her little grandchildren came in to see us and her own little girl. Sweet little children, we had Mrs. Murray's children here too.

Two bands play in the Comp[any]'s gardens on Sunday Evening, but as the _canaille_ only go there on this evening _we_ did not go out. It seems very like our Sunday evenings in America in <u>Salem</u>. Now it is near 10 o'clock at night and another S. Easter is blowing. Exceedingly disagreeable, it raises such clouds of sand and dust.

Jany 27th The wind blew very hard at night but was a fine morning. The mountain was quite clear of clouds till about noon when they came rolling over in immense columns. It has a very singular appearance. The vapours from the sea condense on the top of the mountain and roll down into the valley very much to our annoyance when we contemplate a visit to the Beacon as we did this afternoon. Mr. Etson, Mr. Gordon (not Gaffer) and Mr. Taylor had engaged to go with us but we were obliged to give it up on account of the <u>S. Easter</u>. Was busy all the morning packing up and preparing for the country as we contemplate going in the afternoon of tomorrow, wind and weather permitting. Was writing for Uncle and doing a little of every thing.

After dinner in spite of S. Easter Miss Joanna and I did a little Shopping, then Aunt & I called on Mrs. Thompson. She has a house that looks so <u>Salemish</u> I felt quite at home. The room looked snug and comfortable with an English air of comfort. The Dutch houses have a more foreign air, tiled floors, etc. The rooms all look very small after our large rooms at Macao.

The young ladies and myself took a walk in the garden, which is very sheltered and pleasant, and being gravelled walks, we are not troubled with dust. I tell the young ladies I shall write you word the young ladies at the Cape all have dirty faces. For my own part, I cannot keep my face clean. This red sand keeps one dirty the whole time. I can't bear it, every thing you touch is covered with it. We spent the evening in amusing the ladies with anecdotes of the Chinese. I believe they were often inclined to doubt us, but we told nothing but the <u>truth</u>.

28th A S. Easter blowing again today so that we could not have gone into the country even had they been ready to receive us which they sent word they were not. Uncle had a very sick day. I really dislike leaving this family already, they are so kind and attentive. They are full of the milk of human kindness, unsophisticated and ignorant of the heartlessness of a great part of the world.

Went to walk in the gardens this evening with Miss Joanna. Mr. Thompson called this evening, another kind and excellent person. He was telling us of an expedition to be made by about 60 gentlemen into the interior of this country, to the "Mountain of the Moon." He wishes very much to go, but cannot. He has been once some distance and one would suppose he had suffered enough to be glad to remain behind, but this sort of excitement seems like all others to grow with the gratification and one feels the want of it after a time. For my own part my desire of travelling would lead me to <u>civilized</u> countries, though this being quite unknown will be exceedingly interesting. He says he found the people where he went very interesting. He has published a book which I intend reading.

Kirstenbosch Africa

29th Finished packing this morning and made ready to leave our kind friends again to go among strangers. However I am not long in making myself at home any where now. I shall never forget the kindness of this family; if we were their own relations they could not do more. We dined here and at 1/2 past 3 we bid them good bye. And with Dr. Murray to accompany us, we had a most delightful ride through one of the most charming countries I ever saw. Nature seems to have done her best to bring every thing to perfection and to have concentrated them all here. The tall pines and magnificent oaks that line the roads are superior in size to those of our own forests, the "Silver tree" [*Leucodendron argenteum*] grows in great abundance and looks very beautifully, a great variety of Heath too in full flower to delight the eye and "any quantity" of Blackberries would have delighted the taste could we but have got them but we could not stop. Well I am sure by describing on paper I never shall give you any idea of the beauties that nature presents therefore I may as well be mum.

We arrived at Kirstenbosch about half past 4, at a most delightful little thatched Cottage situated directly under the mountain, not at the foot of it but some way up. We see it towering directly above us, and being high we have a fine view of the Country around us. We were kindly received by our host, hostess and daughter who all speak English, and a very genteel and respectable family. The air is very different here from what it is in town, cool and bracing and we hope it may be beneficial to Uncle. He bore the ride well and was quite comfortable after it.

We are now upon the other side of the mountain, the side which is most productive. Being the[re], we [are] not exposed to the S. Easters and not so much exposed to the scorching sun. There is a vast difference in the appearance I assure you. Dr. Murray left us after having seen us safely landed and we surveyed the premises. My room would look quite English had it not Dutch tiles for the floor. It opens on to the "Stoop" in front of which the roses are blooming in great abundance.

I took a short walk with Miss Ecstein [Anna Catherina Eksteen, the oldest daughter] to one of the most romantic little spots I ever saw. It was through their gardens to the side of a fountain where there is a fine spring of water. They have with great good taste a seat placed under the shade of a weeping willow from which there is a most lovely view in the distance and no sound was heard but that of the Turtle Dove in the forest behind us. We passed through the vineyard where the grapes are growing of every kind. Came back to our cottage with a splendid collection of flowers.

Nature is certainly most bountiful to this part of Africa. If she had been less <u>partial</u> in the distribution of her favours, it would have been more satisfactory to those who live in some other parts of the continent, and more especially to travellers in the Deserts.

We passed a very pleasant evening in company with this interesting family, which consists of Mr. and Mrs. Ecstein, [Anna Catherina Cloete Eksteen] a <u>noble</u> looking couple and apparently very happy and <u>much</u> <u>attached</u>. (You will think I am premature in this last assertion, but that I have heard from others who know more than I do of them.) Then there are their three nice daughters and one son all under 16 years. The youngest [Geesje Wilhelmina Maria Eksteen] is about little Ellen's age (7 years old) and these have an English Tutor who lives in the family and completed our group this evening. The young ladies give us a little music this eve and then we retired.

30th Slept pretty well considering it was a strange place—my poor bones have not had so soft a bed for <u>many</u> a <u>day</u> or night— Uncle is pretty comfortable too. A cloudy morning but cool and comfortable. Amused myself this morning by surveying the premises. I feel once more as though I had my <u>liberty</u>, which is a happy feeling, so I ranged through the orchard and picked Blackberries, which are large and nice and admired every thing I saw and came in to my books.

Mr. Ecstein killed a "Hyena" last night near his house. He came down from the mountain to secure the remains of a dead horse and met his <u>untimely</u> <u>fate</u>. They have long shaggy hair and are the size of a large dog. Tonight we heard the cries of another which they supposed was coming to prey upon the dead carcase of his species. Mr. Jones [Rice Jones Jones][32] was out endeavouring to put him in the same <u>condition</u>, but did not succeed. To support my assertion a few pages back, that every place has its "sussin" [something] as the old woman said, I must tell you what this has, for it is not without millions of <u>fleas</u>, as large (Aunt L. says) as <u>coach</u> <u>horses</u>. Now no doubt this is exaggerated, but I assure you they have power enough, whatever may be their size, to make me exceedingly uncomfortable and disturb my repose. Uncle says he should have no amusement if it was not for them, but I must confess I am too much fretted with them to be pleased.

After dinner we all went to walk Mr. Eksteen myself and all the children. We went I cannot say <u>where</u>, but this I know, that we brought home some beautiful flowers, some pears, and some <u>lemons</u>. We came back through the grounds of Mr. Breda [Michiel van Breda][33] (I dare say it is not spelt right) very extensive—laid out in squares formed by immense oaks and pines, the center of these squares filled with fruit trees of every description. The lemon and orange trees looking beautifully. Although this is said to be not the season for flowers yet, you cannot step without finding them. The flowering heaths too are rich and an innumerable variety of them— a splendid country for a botanist. Dr. Murray tells me his wife has painted 101 different kinds of Heaths.

[marginal note] There are 700 different kinds of Heaths about here.

We came home a little tired, very dirty and myself not a little worse for brambles, having <u>slit</u> a large place in my stocking. Brought home some *pommes d'amour* [gooseberries] which are of golden colour and pleasant to the taste and about the size of a cranberry. They grow in a sort of pod, one in each.

31ˢᵗ Jany Uncle had a comfortable night and feels a little stronger. He has commenced taking "Asses Milk" which the Drs. trust very much too if he can bear it. It is excellent for his complaints.

Passed most of the morning in reading and eating <u>fruits</u>, for they are so delicious. The Blackberries are very fine.

We took a long walk again to a very delightful place. It was rather an adventurous one however for not one of the party had ever been before. It was a sort of <u>ramble</u>, but made it more interesting. Came back very tired. Dr. Bailey had been while I was absent. Thinks Uncle perhaps a little better.

This evening we played whist, passed it very pleasantly. This is a most delightful family, every thing so orderly and so pleasant. [Illegible] and every thing within <u>appears</u> to harmonize with the prospect of <u>quiet</u> from my windows. It seems so delightful to me who have been so long without seeing the delightful domestic circle, that I look with admiration, and it only makes me wish they were <u>my own</u>, but patience I must have. And another thing that recalled the home circle so much was, Mrs. Eksteen sat by us with her <u>knitting work</u>. She is I am sure in every sense of the word a "<u>Goody Vrow</u>."

Having found a pretty piece of poetry in the *Literary Gazette* published at Cape Town, I insert it here for your perusal as it is applicable and descriptive of this delightful country.

Farewell to Southern Africa

1

Farewell to the land where the wild heath and vine,
Their blossoms and tendrils uniting entwine;
Where the orange and citron abound in the dale,
And waving acacias breathe sweet on the gale.

2

How genial thy clime! Thy breezes breathe health,
That blessing more precious than all India's wealth,
Inviting the stranger to haste to thy shore,
Where fondly he hopes his lost strength to restore.

3

And glorious thy heavens where [when] mighty [nightly] do shine
In matchless effulgence, each planet and sign;
And the moon's mellow light uncloudedly beaming,
Round the mountain King's brow brightly is streaming.

4

Here Flora has fixed of her Empire the seat,
No chill blasts of winter compel her retreat,
In endless progression her treasures are spread
O'er forest and moorland, o'er mountain and mead.

5

Pomona too, scatters with bountiful hand
Her choicest productions abroad o'er the land;
The seasons acknowledge her gentle controul,
As marked by her fruits, [in] successive [succession] they roll.

6

From the deep ocean's bound the hoar mountains rise
Majestic, showing [elancing] their peaks to the skies;
While the dark gathering clouds roll awful above
Like thine, distant Scotia, the land of my love.

7

Still green be thy vallies, and fertile thy plains,
And numerous the flocks and herds of thy Swains;
Remote each disaster the true heart that grieves,
For leal is the <u>welcome</u> the <u>stranger</u> <u>receives</u>.

8

Farewell to thee, Afric'-land, sky, and ocean,
Hush'd in my soul be each swelling emotion;
To me, no <u>relation</u> e'er hallow'd the scene,
Yet still will I bless thee for that which has been.

Signed S -

Copied at Kirstenbosch, from the *Literary Gazette*
[*Cape of Good Hope Literary Gazette* 4(1833):151]

February 1ˢᵗ Abbot's birth day. Many happy returns to him. Mother's children are fast growing up, she has a family of men and women round her already.

Oh such a lovely morning. I was up at six, the birds were singing and all besides was still and quiet as possible. How much pleasanter than the town, where there is nothing heard but the rattling of carts, carriage and Dutchmen's whips. By the bye, these said whips are worthy of note. Coming from the country with loads of wine, over the mountains and the sandy plains they are obliged to have an immense team. I have seen often 10 yoke of immense oxen. A boy runs ahead, guides the head ones with a rope, and the driver sits upon the waggon <u>far</u> <u>aft</u> and wields the immense whip which reaches to the foremost of the oxen. You can judge its length. I should think it required much strength of men to hold it even, and I am told it requires a great <u>knack</u> to use it.

I spent the morning in reading the *Literary Gazette*. I want to get a little initiated into the <u>politics</u> of the Cape, find out the state of society. I suspect from this writer's observations that there is a great deal of nonsensical aristocratical feeling there, and great divisions in the society. And moreover there are too many people to make one set and too few not to have all known. As he says parties are given and half the town offended because they were not invited, upon which he proposes parties given upon the <u>Parade</u>, rather to ridicule the idea of being offended because a lady cannot accommodate every one at once. But these things must be, and we find here as well as in the world in general "That all save the spirit of man is divine," [Byron, *The Bride of Abydos*, Canto 1, Stanza 1] for nature is here most harmonious but men and women will quarrel, for they will not support the <u>Divinity</u> of <u>their</u> nature I do not question 'but' 'they were made upright but they have sought out many inventions.' [Ecclesiastes 7:29] However this also is disputed so I'll een leave the subject.

After dinner we sallied forth again and went part way up the mountain, to what they call the "bosch" or bush, and it was thick enough. I must confess I thought of snakes, Hyenas, etc., but I marched on and got back safely.

The Blackberries were growing in abundance at ever step. I have not felt so free and happy for a long time. It is what I have long been wishing for, to feel that I can move my <u>length</u> without constraint. Spent the evening in telling of the <u>wonders</u> of my travels, astonishing my friends here, for they have few ideas beyond Cape Town.

2ᵈ A beautiful Sunday morning, and as we had no temple to worship in, I thought it best to go to the woods where none but pure and lovely feelings can be excited. So Miss Eksteen and myself first went to the orchard and admired the ripening fruits. We then came back, got our bonnets and books and went to *La belle fontaine*, where we spent two hours very pleasantly. We had the Lemon, the Citron, the Loquat, and the Willow to shade us from the sun and to shed their fragrance upon the breeze. The birds were making music in their branches and every thing around was so still that one could not but adore the Author and disposer of all.

> Soft roll your incense, herbs, and fruits, and flowers,
> In mingled clouds to <u>him</u>; whose Sun exalts,
> Whose breath perfumes you, and whose pencil paints,
> Ye forests, bend, ye harvests wave to <u>him</u>.

Oh that beautiful hymn of Thompson's. One feels its power in such a place if not elsewhere. I can say with him,

> When I forget the darling theme,
> Whether the blossom blows the summer ray
> Russets the plain, inspiring Autumn gleams;
> Or winter rises in the blackening east;
> Be my tongue mute, may fancy paint no more,
> And dead to joy, <u>forget</u> <u>my</u> <u>heart</u> <u>to</u> <u>beat</u>!

Well we sit in the delightful retreat far from "the busy haunts of men" [Felicia Hemans, *Tale of the Secret Tribunal*, 1.203] till the sun was rather hot, when we returned home. I read an excellent Sermon to Uncle, then dined and after dinner we took a very pleasant walk "over the hill and far away" and came back loaded with flowers, and among them a "White Rose" which <u>smelt</u> of home, and I have not seen one since I left America before. There are many things here that call that blest place to my mind.

We made a call upon four gentlemen. The fact was we went rather farther than was prudent, but as we were hurrying back we met Mr. Eksteen on horseback going to visit a sick man, so we turned back with him and went to the house where we saw all these gents, and the lady of the house was too much engaged with her sick child to see us. They were all very pleasant and polite and spoke English very well. We got home in very good time not much tired but dreadfully dusty.

Dr. Bailey has been today and finds Uncle much better. He puts great faith in a medicine he is taking now. It is a Caffre medicine made of Herbs from the Caffre country. If he is cured I shall think it is a most providential thing that he put in here. It seems to me little short of a miracle if he is restored.

The *Marquis of Huntley* [Capt. John Hine] has arrived from China today, and several other Ships. Dr. Bailey says the heat has been intolerable in town for the last few days, while we have been delightfully cool and comfortable out here. In going from here to the Town you have two or three different temperatures.

Poor Dr. Murray has lost his dear little girl that only last Sunday we had [been] playing with, then the picture of health. The servant exposed it to the sun and it had convulsions, he has another case of the same kind from the same cause. These slaves are not to be trusted, they are miserable servants. People talk of slavery and consider that their emancipation will make them happier, but is far otherwise in my opinion. [Slaves were emancipated December 1, 1834.] If there is any advantage, it will be for their masters, for they are great torments. Now they are well fed, clothed, and taken good care of. Then, they must look out for themselves and I suspect they will not be able to say then, as now, that we have no beggars, no town paupers.

3ᵈ A very hot day. Dr. Murray was out this morning and says the heat in town is intolerable—poor man, he seemed much depressed, but says it is all right. He found Uncle not so well as Dr. Bailey represented yesterday. Indeed he has been much worse today than yesterday. Was sitting with him till dinner, at work. One day we hope and the next <u>fear</u>.

After dinner took a walk with the young ladies, and called on our next neighbour about 3/4 of a mile from here, Mr. Bedat [van Breda] has an immense place, we walked in the gardens for a long time. I hope to give you a description of them *in propria persona* one of these days—it was quite dark before we got home. Passed the evening under an oak tree in front of the house talking with Mr. Jones and some others of the family till we were disturbed by the Hyenas which appeared to be approaching from the mountains. It set the dogs to howling and barking and we thought best to go into the house where it was even cooler than out of doors.

4th The wind of this morning is burning hot. Feels as though it had blown over fire and answers to all the descriptions we have had of the Simoon of the Deserts. My face felt quite scorched passing along the stoop to breakfast. Uncle has been very ill today, much weaker. He is now to change all his medicines and to give up the asses milk for a day or two. Every thing sours upon his stomach. We were obliged to keep quite close today, shutting all the glass to keep the air out. It was too hot to walk far and we only rambled a little about the house.

5th Another hot day but a cooler air than yesterday. Dr. Murray was out after dinner, thinks Uncle is no worse, he says the heat is intense in town, the Thermom. having stood at 96° in their houses in the day and 90° at night, this beats China. This is very uncommon. Mr. Thompson made us a visit tonight so we got all the news from China, which is not much, no letters.

We had a short ramble about the orchard and to the fountain accompanied by Mr. Jones. Several Dutch gentlemen here to tea complaining sadly of the English government and ridiculing their customs. It seems they do not like to loose their <u>slaves</u> as some of them have half their property invested in them and they will not be 1/2 paid for them. Played whist in the evening.

6th Cooler this morning and Uncle feels a little better. Was sitting in my room this morning. Saw a carriage with a lady and several gentlemen drive up. Who should it be but Mr. & Mrs. Grant

[Alexander and Maria Teresa Grant], Mr. Jackson [John Jackson], and Lieut. Tindale. I was delighted to see her but got nothing new from China. Says Abbot was well when she left. I took a walk with them to my favourite seat at the fountain which they admired much. They stopped about 2 hours and bid us good bye, but I hope to see her again.

After dinner Mr. & Mrs. Eksteen, the young ladies and myself jumped into the <u>Cart</u> as the Dutch call it and had a very pleasant ride to enquire after a sick person. These waggons are commonly used here and on a good road are very comfortable. It holds 6 or 8. It was a pleasant afternoon and we went into their garden and thinking it a pity the "flowers should lose all their sweetness on the desert air" [Thomas Gray, *Elegy in a Country Churchyard*, Stanza 14] we plucked them and brought them home. There was a great variety and very beautiful. I was introduced to Mr. Fashfield [Versfeld] and two Mr. Lowins [Louws]. Got home about dark and found Dr. Bailey at the house. Dr. Macartney [Dr. H.E. Macartney][34] came with him, and was sitting in the drawing room with me while Dr. B. was with Uncle. Such a talker I scarce ever met before. He touched upon every thing. Was enthusiastic in his praises of America, and pretended he did not know I was an American till I asked him if he was aware that he was praising <u>my</u> country. I must confess I a little doubted the <u>negative</u>. Miss Eksteen and I played <u>Patience</u>, a virtue required every where, I find.

Stellenberg

7th Was reading all the morning. Dr. Murray came, finds Uncle a little better. Poor man, he says his wife was so ill last night he thought she would have died. He looks quite dejected and worn down, the heat has been so dreadful, and his afflictions and his arduous duties are almost too much. Riding about in the hot sun is too much.

After dinner we all went to ride again. Went to "Stellenberg," a very pleasant place, to a sister of Mrs. Eksteen.[35] The Dutch are so kind friendly and hospitable, I like them much. There is no formality, they are a great contrast to the English in this particular. They like good frolics. I was introduced to about 20, I should think in all. There was grandpapas and grandmamas, Uncles and Aunts, <u>lovers</u>, governess, etc., all in one house. It is a novel and a pleasant sight to me, to be once more where the bonds of family affection are so visible. We had a very pleasant walk in an extension garden and got home about dark. Capt. Hyne [John Hine] and Mr. Marshall had been at the house. The jolting cart give me a good appetite for my nice bread and butter, and after that we played whist.

Newlands

8th A fine day here but the S. Easter is blowing very strong in town. The mountain is quite covered with clouds and has a singular appearance from our windows. It is very sickly in town owing to the hot weather we have had. Read to Uncle this morning *Insect Architecture*.[36] Dr. Bailey called this morning and finds Uncle better.

After dinner Mrs. Eksteen, the young ladies and myself walked to "Newlands," formerly the residence of Lord Charles Somerset[37] when Governor of this place. It is a splendid place, laid out with great taste. Mr. Cruywagen [Johannes J. Cruywagen],[38] the present owner, told me that Lord Charles spent 70,000£ upon it for government and Mr. Cruywagen bought it for 3000£. The grounds are very extensive. After walking through immense avenues of pine trees, you ascend a hill which is flattened at the top and excavated to the depth of 20 ft. say, at the bottom of which there is a find spring of water which is constantly running summer and winter and supplies two mills. On the flattened top of this hill there is a broad gravelled walk round the fountain where there are seats and tables placed for the loungers and picnics, and on each side rows of tall trees which form an arch on top as well as over the fountain. It is a most romantic place. On our way to the house we regaled ourselves with grapes and peaches, and after having collected handsome bouquets we went back to the house. Mr. Eksteen came for us in the carriage and took us home. [A sketch of the fountain is in the margin.]

9th Was writing letters and reading to Uncle alternately this morning. Did not walk after dinner except about the house. Was talking with Mr. Jones about the missionaries. He says the Moravians are most numerous and the Wesleyan Methodists. I rather approve of the system they follow. They teach the natives the arts of life first, teach them to be industrious, provide them with tools and land, and give them instruction and gradually instruct them in the religion they profess.

10th Uncle seems very unwell today. I feel quite discouraged about him. Dreadful cold and fever [by] turns. Dr. Murray was out today, says he is very ill but he shall do all he can, but I think he almost despairs of effecting any thing. There is a great deal of sickness about here now. An interesting young man was buried in the neighborhood today. The heat has been excessive and people expose themselves too much to the burning sun.

We did not walk except about the house. I went about to see them feed the chickens, milk the cows, which is to me very pleasant, and to see the mules, the cows and every thing returned to its nightly shelter. I was also amused with the children and the Ass. They saddled him and rode him about the house, and your humble servant for the first time mounted a <u>Donkey</u>, but I very soon got off, for there was no bridle. The poor animal was a patient as possible under all his troubles and he was very well <u>tried</u>. Spent the evening in <u>social</u> <u>conversation</u> round the table. Poor Aunt is never of our party, Uncle does not like to have her leave him. Had a good feast of peaches under the tree this afternoon.

11th Most of the morning I was reading aloud to Uncle. He seems more comfortable though very weak and so thin.

After dinner Miss Eksteen, myself and Mr. Jones mounted horses and went a long way up the mountain. Had a fine view of the country and the sea in the distance which I had no idea was so near us. Heard the noise of the Baboons which are <u>plenty</u> in the mountain and sometimes come down into the orchard. After letting our horses breathe a little, we turned their heads downwards and took a good canter nearly down to "Newlands." You would have laughed to have seen our equipment and our party, and the boys would certainly have hooted after us if it had been any where out in the <u>bush</u>. We neither of us had habits. Miss E. put on a skirt of her mother's over her pink dress and I had a black silk. And little Jesse was mounted with Mr. Jones. Had a very pleasant ride though my horse was not very easy. I had a pretty decent jolting, but still meditate another excursion tomorrow.

Bergvlyt

12th Spent the morning in my room reading. We dined early and about 1/2 3 o'clock Miss Eksteen, Mr. Jones, myself and Johnny [Johannes Paulus Eksteen] mounted our steeds and commenced our ride to Bergvlyt [Bergvliet], the residence of Mr. John Eksteen. We arrived about 5 and I must say it was any thing but <u>pleasure</u> to me. In the first place, my horse was lazy and if perchance by whipping I urged him into a canter it was almost at the expense of my poor bones, for I had not yet recovered from yesterday's frolic. To add to my miseries, the breeze was strong and got the pins out of my dress, and I had great difficulty in keeping it in <u>decent</u> order. Then my bonnet kept blowing off and what with my lazy horse, my sore bones, my whip, the reins, my bonnet and my dress, I had more than I could manage. I could have cried almost with vexation. Whether Mr. Jones saw my <u>knees</u> or not I do not know, but he was kind enough to keep in front a little. Before we got to our destined end my comb had contrived to make its escape and my hair was hanging over my back, so you may judge how I looked, but I cannot tell you the agony I was suffering. Miss Eksteen had an easier horse, an easier saddle, and was enjoying herself comparatively, although her hair plagued her some. We arrived at last and after having arranged our hair and dresses a little we took a walk in the garden with the young ladies. I enjoyed this for it was a pleasant spot. After walking through beautiful shady walks we come to a flight of steps which opens upon a beautiful pond of water very clear and deep, in the center of it a little Island say 100 feet in diameter, round and enclosed by a white wall in the bottom of which are nests made for the hawks and geese that live here, and birds, etc. The Island appeared to produce flowers of different kinds, but we had no boat and could not go to it. It was as romantic a spot as I ever saw. We sat here some time, then went to the garden, got some peaches, and prepared our return, which I <u>dreaded</u>, my bones were so stiff. I gave my horse to Mr. Jones and took his, hoping it might be easier. He was not quite so lazy, but cantered much harder. There was not so much wind going home, and saving the pain I endured, it was pleasant. I certainly never felt so tired before. We made out to get home after 7 and never was I more happy to find a resting place. Nothing would induce me to suffer so much again. I got some tea and felt a little refreshed but was sorry to find the Miss Cruywagens had been here in my absence. Went to bed before "<u>Burgher</u> time" tonight.

13th Was very restless all night in consequence of my fatigue, but got up before 7 and went to the orchard hoping to get a little limbered before making my appearance at table. Felt half sick all the forenoon and was asleep most of the morning. Felt better after dinner, but could not be persuaded to ride. So we went to the vineyard and eat grapes and to the potatoes field to see them digging them and we were rambling about, enjoying my freedom I assure you till near dark. Then set upon the stoop and Joanna [Johanna Pauline Eksteen] sung to us. In the evening we played whist. Dr. Murray has been out and says Uncle is better today.

14 Still quite stiff, and the bed being the most comfortable place, I laid there and read most of the morning. Could neither walk nor ride after dinner except to the vineyard. Dr. Bailey was out today and tells us of a shocking occurrence in the town, the second of the same kind since we have been here. A celebrated physician in town quarrelled with his wife and then blew his brains out. Nothing to tell today, eat and drank as usual and went only to the vineyard this afternoon.

Cape Town

15th Was up at six o'clock this morning to make preparations for going to the Cape. Gathered a splendid bouquet for Miss Cruywagen and started at 1/2 past 8. A beautiful day, but much pleasanter in the country than in town, but I want to get some comforts for Uncle and a comb for myself otherwise I would not have gone. In my ride the other day I lost my comb. And tortoise shell is very dear here. A common sized comb cost me 16 rix dol[lar]s, 6 Spanish dollars.

We arrived in town about 10. Went to Mrs. Cruywagen's, found them very glad to see me. I tell Mrs. Eksteen she is related to every body in Africa, for between Kirstenbosch and the town and many miles round in different directions there is no one but Cloetes and Eksteens. Every birthday all the families meet at one place, and for 3 days and nights they keep up a regular frolic, dancing and feasting, and I am told it is the bounden duty of all the <u>old</u> (alias married) men to get tipsy and the young ones are thought more agreeable if a little <u>funny</u>. They are jolly people and very social in their habits. A kind hearted people the Dutch, but I think I should not like them tipsy.

Well to proceed, I spent the forenoon in shopping, called on Mrs. Ebden, dined and at 5 we started for Kirstenbosch. 2 American whalers came in this afternoon. I think there are 7 or 8 now in the Bay.

Had a delightful ride out. Enjoyed my own thoughts most of the way, for Mrs. E. was talking <u>Dutch</u> most of the time. Got home after six and then we had another dinner. Mrs. Eksteen sends us all to bed at 10 o'clock. She says it is "Burgher time" that is <u>genteel</u> time, though burgher means farmer. Yet I fancy it answers to time all honest people were abed, as we say in English.

Constantia

16th Sunday morning, a beautiful day, read two sermons aloud to Uncle. While at dinner Miss Eksteen asked her father to take us to ride as it is too dusty to walk. He consented and after dinner we went to the famous "Constantia." I had an idea it was a village, but it seems it is the residence of Mr. Jacob Cloete, Mrs. Eksteen's brother. Here is where all the celebrated Constantia wine is made. It is a most delightful place, a fine house and from the Stoop we have a fine view of the country round & of False Bay in the distance, also "Hanglip," one of the Southern Capes. Mrs. Cloete has a large family and an interesting daughter grown up. I am astonished to find what polished and elegant manners all the young ladies have here. You would suppose they had been brought up in a great deal of society. I was much pleased with Miss Maria. There was also a Miss Van Reenan [Reenen] an interesting girl. All the Mr Nashfeldts [Versfelds] were there. This place was built many years ago by one of the old Dutch governors and named for his wife (in English Constance). The wine made here and which is so famous is very rich. She tells me of the real Constantia there is only 30 leaguers (150 gals.) [153.7 U.S. gals.] made a year. They leave the grape till it is so ripe that it begins to look wilted like a raisin, so that there is very little juice to express. It is consequently very sweet and rich and I am told that if the seed of this grape is sown elsewhere, the flavour of the wine is different from "Constantia" wine. It may not be correct, but it may [be] the peculiar situation. There is no doubt an immense deal of spurious wine is exported & no doubt much of the common sweet Cape wine is drank for Constantia. They say to witness the making of the wine is quite enough to sicken you. And from all accounts I should think would be as good as a <u>temperate</u> society—the little <u>sweaty</u>, <u>dirty</u> negroes are sent into the tub to express the juice with their feet, they cannot do it by machinery lest they should break the stones.

After they have got the juice out, then the skins are pressed to give the wine a colour.

There are five different kinds of Constantia wine, the White Muscatel and the red, the Frontignan made of a light coloured grape, and the Pontac which is the most expensive, and the most rare. There are now several other places built near Mr. Cloete to which they have given the name of Constantia, but this is the <u>real</u> one. Before coming to the house we ride through long avenues of old majestic oaks while the milk white house in the distance has a very pretty appearance. And oh if you could see the beautiful myrtle hedges. They grow above my head and so luxuriantly that they look splendidly. We took a walk in the gardens, and after talking awhile we bid them good night and had a delightful moonlight ride home. These people all live very genteelly, very different from our Country people; more like the Virginia farmers, from descriptions I have had of them. They have a great many slaves who do the work of the farms.

17th A cold rainy day, what a change from yesterday. This will injure the grapes very much. The crop of grapes is quite as doubtful as the crop of rice in China.

Mr. Thompson and Mr. Van Reenen were out this morning in spite of the rain, but they bring no news except the arrival of two more American whalers. The English are getting very jealous of the Americans about here. I think there has 10 or 12 whalers been in here within the last week. Spent the day in reading, played whist in the evening.

18th No rain this morning, but cool and pleasant. Dr. Murray and Bailey were both out. Think Uncle much the same. Dr. Bailey cheered him up a little. He has been in the navy many years. Was in the battle of Trafalgar and has been in many other battles.

Afternoon started for the vineyard but were obliged to take shelter under the trees before we reached there to avoid the rain. Got but few grapes and hurried home. A very cool evening. We played whist and got dreadfully beaten.

19 Dreamed Mrs. C[olledge] had a boy.

Poor Uncle had a very sick day and I was with him most of the time. He says he is quite worn out. He suffers a great deal of pain. Went to bed myself tonight at 9 o'clock with a violent nervous head ache.

20th Uncle a little more comfortable today. Dr. Murray and Bailey both out. They give us but little hope and I suspect have little themselves. I was with Uncle all day.

21st Uncle was very sick today. We were quite alarmed and sent to town for one of the Drs. Dr. Bailey came out immediately, says he is very low indeed. The complaint now seems mostly in his bowels, his lungs are much better, and Bailey thinks breathes very freely on both sides. It is wearisome to live in such a state of hope and fear, one day we think he will certainly recover, the next that it is impossible. 'Tis true indeed that Hope deferred makes the heart sick. And to see a friend suffering so much for such a length of time. I never saw any one so completely emaciated.

22d Uncle is a little more comfortable today. Dr. Murray was out, says he finds we all look better when he is better, and indeed it makes a vast difference in our spirits. I have nothing to say, do, or think of at present but him.

23d While Uncle was asleep I went out and sit in the trees in the orchard. Reminded me of the days of my childhood when I used to climb trees and fences and every thing else. Came in soon after, found him again in great pain, sit with him till after 2, then dressed for dinner. Dr. Bailey came out after dinner. Thinks him a little better notwithstanding. Dr. Bailey tells us Dr. Macartney is going to America, the little man I think I mentioned having been introduced to. He is a clever man they say and has an astonishing memory. I believe he purposes delivering Lectures on Natural Philosophy, etc.

We had a delicious water melon today, just like ours in America. It reminded me of the days when Father used to deal out after church of a Sunday afternoon.

24th Oh if you can conceive how I am tormented at night with these abominable <u>fleas</u>. They are so thick and bite like the <u>deuce</u>. We sometimes pick 14 off before going to bed and still manage to have some remain. I have no peace night or day for them, so you see there is always something to disturb one's quiet.

This morning I found our hostess was to have company and a little after <u>9</u> this morning 4 ladies were seen approaching the house. Ye powers! said I, are they coming to spend the day? I soon found them "located" in the drawing room. I kept close to my own and

Uncle's room, for I could not think of spending a whole day with them, so I was very busy reading till dinner time. I sallied forth once to see how they were employed and found them all at work, some knitting and some sewing, looking as cozy and social as possible. Had they not all been strangers I think I should have enjoyed [it]. It revived my own kind and social home feelings to see them, and caused a sigh for home and friends. The Dutch seem to be more like the Americans in their habits and feelings than the English. There is none of the formality and stiffness that you find in John Bull wherever he is. I do like them much. I never saw more domestic happiness, more quiet and contentment than in this family through all its branches. The family is very large and they all appear to be on the best of terms. About 5 times in the year they tell me they meet at the different families houses and for three days keep it up, eating and drinking, with music & dancing, without formality, each suiting himself and gratifying his own humour. Drinking among the <u>elders</u> seems to be the fashion. They have large brimful glasses which they are obliged to fill and drink at every toast, and it seems to be no disgrace to say such and such a one was so <u>tipsy</u>. Now this part of it I do not subscribe to, but the good feeling that is occasioned by these meetings is very delightful.

But to return to my day's account, I was introduced to three ladies, the 4th (Miss Breda) I knew. I stopped but a few minutes, then returned again to my books. Met at dinner and found them very pleasant. After dinner Mr. Thompson called and Dr. Murray was out. Finds Uncle better. If he only remains so a few days, I shall feel quite encouraged. The ladies left us before dark and we played whist in the evening.

I was looking over the newspaper and discovered a late arrival from Boston, and before I went to Bed I wrote a note to the Capt. to see if he had any papers, so that I could send it to town in the morning. Went to bed and had a comfortable night's sleep having had <u>no fleas</u>. A most remarkable circumstance and worthy of record, whatever you may think to the contrary.

25th Your birth day my dear Sis, many happy returns of the day to you. Would I could give you a good pinch. Oh futurity lift the veil one moment; let me know that I shall be near enough to commit so kind an act before another anniversary and I will rest content. But my dear Uncle is again better and I must not complain at any thing. If he is spared to his dear wife I would undergo much. I really hope now the <u>cause</u> is removed and that the complaint is not so much in the lungs as the liver. Dr. Bailey was out after dinner. Miss Eksteen and [I] read together till dark. Oh Dr. brought me two Boston papers, Dec. 4th and 5th, but I could not glean much news from them, some few scraps, and the assurance that America still <u>exists</u>. A fact I had not much reason to doubt, but it is pleasant to be <u>certain</u> on any subject. The sight of familiar names even is pleasant, when in a strange land and away from all communication with our friends. But it is useless to make these remarks to one who has never been from among her own friends, but brought up in the midst of friends and kindred, for one must feel them to have a <u>true</u> sense of them.

26th Uncle again better. Mr. Eksteen killed a beautiful little buck in the "bosch" this morning. A very hot day. Was reading all the morning. And after dinner Miss Eksteen and I were reading Shakespeare's play of *King Lear*.

What do you think the farmer's signal for his bullocks is? Mr. E. had to send this morning for them to come; he spied them with a glass coming very lazily along the road. He went and got an enormous whip, measuring 5 or 6 yards and snapped three or four times, each of which reverberated through the mountains, making a great noise and the bullocks were immediately seen quickening their pace. They know the sound at once, although they were distant a mile.

I do enjoy this country life when Uncle is well enough to enjoy any thing. There is a kind of grape just now ripe, called by the Dutch "harney pote" [*hane poot*] or cock's foot, that is most delicious. It is as large as a pigeon's egg, of a bright yellow, and the most delicious flavour I ever tasted. I only wish I could share them with you. The grapes are considered very wholesome and we can eat them at all hours without injury, and in any reasonable quantity. A most lovely night I was out on the stoop till very late—so quiet and still that it seemed as though all thoughts and feelings should be as calm and tranquil. It seems to be a <u>holy</u> stillness, almost as though it was wrong for any but holy thoughts to arise, and I could cry almost when I cannot still each anxious feeling and desire and be as still, calm and celestial as every thing in nature seems to be. I long to fly beyond the earth, to <u>see</u> if the heavens so bright above will bear examining and to be assured that those bright worlds above are the habitations of happy spirits enjoying the reward of their merits. Oh how happy to <u>know</u> it! To feel <u>assured</u> that when the spirit leaves this abode, it will go on progressively till it reaches perfection, to feel that each step we make in moral and intellectual good is one step further in our course to glory and happiness. And have we not in the writings of our Saviour sufficient to warrant such hopes. I think so.

Excuse these aberrations. I went to my room, wrote two letters to town and then to bed.

27 Uncle still continues better and he has deigned to bestow an old fashioned smile upon us, which rejoices the <u>cockles</u> of our heart.

Spent the morning in reading. Uncle being so much better I accepted an invitation to "Wynberg" with our family. Had a very pleasant ride. Wynberg is a thriving little village, has a neat little church and some delightful residences. We stopped at Mr. Maguier's [H. F. W. Maynier].[39] Saw his two daughters in the bloom of youth and loveliness, with their hearts all unsunned and as cheerful as their ignorance of ills and wickedness can make them. You will I dare say think I make some queer observations, but you know my dear I am a novice to the world at large. I have been living among people of <u>one</u> age so long and among people well versed in the ways of the world, that I am quite enchanted with being among all ages and sizes, and where they laugh at <u>nothing</u> as I used in my <u>young days</u>. But one cannot help giving a sigh to days gone by and say with Byron, "There's not a charm [joy] the world can give, Like that it takes away, When the early glow of youth declines, In feelings dull decay." [Byron, *Stanzas For Music*] But a truce to romance, I thought I had done being sentimental.

You would be delighted with the splendid avenues of trees and the beautiful myrtle hedges we ride through. I never saw any thing more beautiful. We got home a little after dark, and played Whist this evening.

28th Uncle still continues better. I begin to think I shall learn something in the way of cooking here, for the Dutch ladies are obliged to oversee their slaves, and I go very often into the kitchen to see Mrs. Eksteen and if you will believe it, I have made two puddings with the aid of the receipt books. Mrs. E. comes to me to read them for her as she cannot read English. The Dutch here are fond of good living and have some famous stews, which I often think my father would like.

After dinner we took a walk to Mr. Breda's, a splendid place. Walked round the grounds, had some fine fruit, saw all the good people, heard a great deal of Dutch spoken, one word of which I do not understand, and I do not think I ever shall. Mr. Eksteen brought the cart after us and we came back to tea about 8.

March 1st It appears to me it is Josiah's birth day [b. March 15, 1821]. God bless him.

We have had a party of young ladies today, two Miss Maguier [Maynier] and two others. Walked from "Wynberg" this morning. We had a fine swing fixed upon a tree in the "bosch" after dinner which reminded me of the days of my childhood when I used to swing and touch the beam. The young ladies left about dark as they walked back with their father, and in the evening we had a party of gentlemen, the three Mr. Versfeldts. Expected some other ladies but they sent an excuse.

2d The *Duke of Sussex* [Capt. W. H. Whitehead] arrived yesterday from China. For the three last days the wind has been blowing tremendously in Cape Town, while here we could sit with a lighted candle upon the stoop, and hear the wind roaring on the other side of the mountain. Dr. Bailey says he could not get his horse to face it the day before, the dust and sand was quite smothering. Some of the Ships were driven out of the Bay, and there were 9 trying to get in without success. These S. Easters, as they are called, are confined chiefly to Cape Town, a few miles in the country they are not felt.

Wrote to Whitehead this morning to try and get some news. After dinner they proposed a walk and asked me where we should go. I said to the "Brewery." They seemed to shrink at first, but finally we started and arrived there about 1/2 past 6. Found a great many visitors there. I thought there was no end to the ladies and gentlemen. It is a handsome house and the grounds extensive. There is a large brewing establishment carried on here. It is a most delightful spot. And Mr. & Mrs. Van Reenen [Dirk van Reenen]⁴⁰ are said to be the best people that ever lived. I cannot vouch for it, not knowing them, unless the good condition of themselves and daughters go to prove any thing. I can assure you they all merit the term of "Dicker fattys." The two Mr. Versfeldts who dined with us and Mr. Jones with all the children walked with us and we found it very pleasant. Came home in the cart, the gentlemen on horseback. Took tea, came to my room, and have now finished my day's work and think it must be after 11 so will bid you good night.

3ᵈ Rose at 7 after having dreamed I paid Aunt Porter a visit and she did not know me. Was writing for Uncle most of the forenoon. Read a little. After dinner the horses were tackled and Mr. Eksteen invited me to go to Wynberg with him to <u>inspect</u> the Church which is undergoing repairs, and he is <u>deacon</u>. I am always ready for a ride and accepted, but we were stopped by lots of visitors till quite late. First came Mr. Thompson and brought us all the news. Says the last S. Easter was terrific and did an immense deal of damage. The gravel stones in some exposed situations drilled holes through the glass. Then came Dr. Bailey and soon after I saw a coach and four drive up to the door and Mr. [W.H.C.] Plowden and Capt. Locke jumped out, just from China in the *Duke of Sussex*. Nothing particularly new from China. I was very glad to see Mr. Plowden. He made us a short visit as he was obliged to go back to dinner. After they had all gone we had a very pleasant ride to Wynberg. It was a beautiful evening. Has been dreadfully hot in town, but we are very comfortable out here. Mr. Plowden was quite delighted with our situation.

Dr. Bailey thinks Uncle is going on very well and he has had no perspirations for two nights which is more encouraging than any thing, and it is the first time since he has been ill that they have stopped.

March 4ᵗʰ A very hot oppressive day, but our little thatched cottage is very comfortable, particularly the rooms with the <u>tiled</u> floors. You have no idea what a romantic little place it is, but I mean to try to make a little sketch of it that you may better be able to understand my descriptions of it. How much I wish for a painter's talent, for I always wish to transmit to you the beautiful scenes I enjoy. I was very busy all the morning (for a wonder) writing for Uncle, and it passed rapidly enough, as it always does when employed usefully.

After dinner swung a little. Dr. Murray came and finds Uncle still improving. Miss E. and I read till nearly dark, then eat our usual quantum of grapes which are now delicious. Evening we spent out of doors, it was lovely. We heard the Hyenas in the mountain apparently very near us. There are a great many about here, but they generally run from man. They prey mostly upon dead carcasses, which they smell very quickly. Further in the country I believe they often attack live animals, such as horses, sheep etc. By the bye, the Cape Sheep are very different from ours. They have hair instead of wool, and very large thick and long tails, weigh a great deal. It is used for many domestic purposes, most of the oil burnt here is sheep's tail melted. It burns very well. (Dont you admire my sheep?) The tail is all I aimed at and that looks a little like it. [Harriett inserted in the margin a tiny sketch of a sheep with a large tail.]

5th Uncle still continues better and the Drs. now think his disease proceeds from the Liver, which encourages us that he will yet recover. A very hot day which keeps him quite weak. Was busy writing for Uncle part of the morning and read a *Literary Gazette* published at the Cape. After dinner Miss Cruywagen and another young lady made us a visit. We read part of the afternoon, in *the Abbot* [Sir Walter Scott]. Miss Eksteen and self swung a little, in the evening played cards as usual, and finished the day.

6th A rainy and a cool day. Dr. Bailey was out today. Says Uncle is going well. I am now his private secretary and was busy writing for him this morning. Am happy to find myself of some consequence. Spent the rest of the day as usual. Quiet and contented at present, supported by the hope of carrying my Uncle away restored in health, it will seem almost like having him raised from the dead.

March 7th This morning read till 12, then wrote for Uncle again.[41] A fine cool day.

After dinner we all went to Wynberg and from there to Stellenberg. Had a fine drive. Got no new idea, I believe and saw only what I have seen and described before, "the church and no steeple and all the good people." Dr. Murray was out, is much pleased with Uncle's appearance. Says it is blowing terribly in the town just the other side of the mountain while here it is still as possible. We can hear it roaring like thunder on the other side. The mountain is quite covered with clouds when these S. Easters blow so.

8th Was busy writing for Uncle and squaring my books. I now find myself in the very important office of private secretary to Uncle and am delighted to be of any use. I was too lazy to walk after dinner and therefore stayed at home and read. Nothing new under the sun in our little world. We have no neighbors but the wolves and Baboons. We are further on the Mt. than any one and it is so quiet here that I admire it, for unless I can be among my own friends I do not wish to mix with the world.

9th Sunday Morning. After I had done what little I could for Uncle, Miss Eksteen & I sallied forth into the bosch where I read aloud [to] her about two hours, seated upon a rock under the shelter of the fine oaks which abound here and which make such a cool retreat from the burning sun. About 12 we went back. I read one of Channing's excellent sermons, then wrote several letters. Dr. Bailey was out and finds Uncle doing well. Capt. Whitehead of the *Sussex* also called and gave us some information from China. Aunt L. took a walk for the first time.

March 10th Commenced with strong breezes and rainy. Cleared off after breakfast, very pleasant though the wind continued high through the day, and what is rather curious the S.E. and N.W. winds were contending together. The N.W. rather beat today.

We are now just on the borders of a peninsula. The flats which connect us with the main land are directly within our view and within a mile or two of us. Then the S.E. blows over from False Bay and the Southern Ocean, while the N.W. comes from the Atlantic on the other. These flats are supposed formerly to have been covered with water, which would make the place where we now are an Island. They conclude so having found the wreck of a Ship in the sands some years since at a place called Tygerberg and some distance from the Shore.

Spent the day in reading, my journal will I fear be more destitute of events than ever. Amused myself after dinner with looking round the <u>lot</u>, seeing the cows milked, eating grapes & etc. Had some flowers sent me tonight, brought from the top of Table Mountain. They were very beautiful and unlike any I ever saw before.

This evening we played whist and got a most unmerciful drubbing and now I think it is after 11 and I must go to bed. How fortunate we are situated on a <u>peninsula</u>. Had we not been you would not have had the above <u>interesting</u> description but would have been dismissed with an account of the weather.

11th Commenced with heavy rain but cleared up before night. Commenced reading French again for I shall forget all about it. Dr. Murray finds Uncle still better. Not a remark to make today.

12th A beautiful day. Read all the morning, that is all the time I had. After dinner Mr. Eksteen took us to Wynberg, from there to Stellenberg, and home a road I have never been on before. Passed through Schoenberg where Sir John Herschell is residing, son of the great astronomer. He has got an immense Telescope here, not so large as his father's, but one by which he has discovered <u>volcanoes</u> in the <u>moon</u>. He pursues the study of the worlds above, and I suppose will one of these days tell us what the inhabitants in those unknown spheres are like—and heaven only knows what else.

We came home through Mr. Breda's and made them a call. Had a large basket of grapes to eat on the way, remains we distributed at Mrs. B's. They are very delicious now. There is one kind now ripe called the <u>Hanny pota</u> [*hane poot*] (as it sounds). Some of them measure two inches in length and an inch thick. They are of a bright yellow colour and very sweet when ripe. These make very good raisins. It was quite dark before we got home. Spent the eve'g very pleasantly in reading and conversation.

13th A beautiful cool morning. Did very much as usual, except going up [the] garret to see them stow apples which they are just gathering and laying in for <u>winter</u>. I am afraid we shall be obliged to winter at the Cape. I almost despair of ever reaching my native land again; it seems as though the fates opposed me. It will be a very long while before Uncle gains his strength. He is dreadfully weak though all his symptoms are better.

After dinner Miss Eksteen, the children and myself walked to Mrs. Versfeldt's to see Miss Van Reenen. Spent an hour walking in the garden, till Mr. Eksteen came after us in the waggon. We had a dark ride home and a bad road but arrived safely after having been tossed about as in a Ship at sea. It was so dark Mr. E. said he could hardly see the road.

14th Short and sweet today. I have nothing to say for myself, having had a face ache.

15 Uncle was very anxious to have me go to town today and notwithstanding a strong S.E. was blowing as I could hear from the

Stoop, we started after breakfast, Mr. & Mrs. Eksteen, Joanna and Jesse [Geesje], and arrived safely. The houses [were] all shut up and but few people to be seen in town, the dust rolling in clouds along the streets. I attempted to do a little shopping but could not force myself along. However did all my odd jobs in the house and as that was the principal object of my visit I left the out of door business for future time. I had a *triste* day of it enough. Saw Dr. Murray, he tells me he has no doubt now that Uncle's lungs are the seat of his disorder. That being the case we have little hope of his recovery. His perspirations have returned and he feels himself growing weaker instead of stronger. He told Aunt Low this morning he thought he never should be any better.

After dinner I had a dreadful spell of the face ache, and at 4 left Mrs. Cruywagen's, the wind blowing dreadfully and quite cold. Took off my hat and covered my head with a large shawl and with my cloak got home pretty comfortably. Was very glad of an excuse to keep my mouth shut, for in truth I felt little disposed to talk.

March 30th A dreadful chasm since I last wrote, fifteen days, in which time I have witnessed one of the most solemn scenes possible, the sick and dying bed of my dear Uncle (my father in feeling) and I pray that it may make a lasting impression upon me, that I may never forget it. And I pray also that my last end may be calm, peaceful, and happy like his.

He failed rapidly for the last week. On the 18th he told me it was impossible for him to live, that he had hoped to see me safely in my native land, but that it was the will of heaven that he should leave us in this strange land, but that God would take care of us, and he did not doubt it was all rightly ordered. He talked very kindly to me several times in the course of the day every word of which I hope will be engraven upon my memory. He got out of bed on the 18th but said it was for the last time alive, and indeed it was. Every moment appeared to deprive him of strength, of body, for his mind was strong till he was struck with death. He seemed to wish to have his whole thoughts devoted to his Maker, and regretted that he must take opiates, as it stupified and rendered him unfit to watch at the last hour. He was perfectly calm, peaceful and happy, and seemed to die at peace with all the world and happy in the thought of meeting his father in heaven, and Jesus his Intercessor; he said he had prayed to be forgiven and trusted he had received pardon. He was so happy too in having a firm and full faith. He said it was the greatest comfort to him and he often spoke of it with tears, so grateful was he that it continued firm and unshaken to the last. In his wakeful moments he would get us to read to him the Bible, Sermons or hymns, and as soon as the effect of his draught was over he would call Aunt Low to read or talk to him. It was delightful to sit by him, to hear his thoughts expressed and witness his patience through all his sufferings, [deleted: to see] the calm and sweet smile with which he would tell us he should soon die and that God would protect us. He seemed to trust so fully in his God that his own protection seemed to him nothing and he gave us up with full confidence. The 18th, the anniversary of Caroline's marriage, when he was sitting at the head of his own table, only one short year ago, in the pride of life and health! Alas how changed! Now sick, feeble and emaciated, the bones actually through the skin, yet blessing God for his mercies, and uttering scarce a groan in all his pains. I scarcely thought he would live the night through. I watched with him till 12. I shall never forget how kind and affectionate he was. He laid his hand on my head as I stooped to kiss him, called me his blessed child, his only daughter. He says "Make religion your study, my child," and then said it had always been a source of consolation to him that I had a well grounded faith. Never till his illness have I seen its value. It is such a source of consolation and comfort to him that I shall I trust think more than ever of it.

On Saturday the 22d, he appeared much weaker, and prayed that it might please his father in heaven to take him to himself. He seemed very quiet all day, no pain and very little cough, for which he seemed very thankful. Dr. Murray came to see him after dinner. He said nothing to him scarcely. After he had left, we were sitting on either side of him, and he talked with us for near an hour, and I never shall forget it. He said he was happy and I asked him if he feared to die. He said "No, I long to die and be with my father and Jesus my intercessor," and then said he hoped he did not use his father's name too frequently. I never saw greater humility, greater calmness, and every feeling appeared so purified. His worldly feelings were all subdued.

Such complete resignation and submission to the will of God, and such confidence that all was right, was very consoling to us. He spoke of his mother and many of his friends, and of his life in China, particularly regretted that he had not given more of his time to his Maker, and told us how happy we were in being spared and at having time to take warning by him. He felt his sickness was occasioned by too close <u>application</u> to business and the desk.

I was crying while he was talking with us. He says, "Harriett I hope you do not weep for me." I told him no, I weep for myself that I must lose so good, so kind an Uncle. "My child," he says, with such a sweet expression "I am your <u>father</u> I consider you as much my child as though you had been born of your aunt." It is impossible to write all he said in this last hour. Suffice it that he died at peace and in love with all mankind, forgiving all who had in any way injured him, thankful for all the blessings he had received, for his comforts in his illness and beseeching us always to remember the sick and afflicted. As far as morality goes, he was always perfect. For integrity and uprightness in thought, word and deed no one could surpass him. And at last he was adorned with the graces of the Christian, purified and prepared to join the Society of the "just made perfect."

He asked Aunt L to lie down early that she might relieve me in the morning and about 1/2 past 8 p.m. she did and went to sleep. I sat by him and wiped the cold perspiration from his forehead. He asked me once for a little tea which I gave him. He coughed once soon after and said "that is the <u>last</u> of it." Soon after I noticed a strange appearance in his eyes, and got up to give him something but I could not make him speak. I took hold of his hand and it appeared stiff. I awoke Aunt Low with the dreadful sound of "my dear Aunt I believe he is dying, I cannot make him speak." We found it but too true. He was quite speechless and hardly appeared to know us, though he once turned his eyes upon her as though he knew her voice. My poor Aunt took his hand, prayed that Jesus might receive his Spirit and at about 11 he yielded up his Spirit to the God who gave it I trust. Such an hour I never passed before, my dear Sister. His two sole relatives in this part of the world sitting by him as he requested. We called no one till all was over. It was 1/2 past 9 when I awoke Aunt and 10 minutes past 11 when he breathed his last. He died quite easy, no convulsions, not the least, the spark of life went out like an expiring lamp.

What an impressive scene! To see his poor wife sitting by him offering up prayers for him to the last, holding his hand and calm and collected till all was over, it was almost too much. It was agony but still we supported each other. I took example from her and remained quiet till the last. Oh how I longed to <u>know</u> where the Spirit had fled, I fancied it winging its way to purer, happier spheres and at last finding a resting place in heaven. Can it be otherwise, no, if there is a world of happy spirits, his <u>must</u> be among the number. Would that I could <u>know</u> how such a Spirit exists, in what body it shall live, but alas such queries can never be answered. It is to be left till we ourselves shall be summoned to experience the great change. But were it not for the blessed hope of the resurrection and of the pardoning mercy of our God where should we be, when called to part, with all that has made our happiness in this world, and without which we cannot believe even heaven will be perfect. If it was not for this, what would prevent us from ending our own lives that in such cases become burdensome, and at such moments would be too much to endure, if it was not for the hope and assurance of a blessed immortality for those who <u>endure</u> unto the end.

And now one word for my dear Aunt, who is one thus afflicted. It is truly the last link, it is <u>all</u> she had loved on earth, the idol of her heart, and the sharer of every joy and every sorrow. He is now gone, taken from her, and she is to live on solitary and as it were alone. She has for the last six months devoted her whole time and strength to him, and at the last has not only ministered to his bodily wants, but has assisted in preparing him for to meet his God. Truly she has been a ministering angel to him. I never saw her equal, for devotion, for firmness & fortitude, for tenderness, kindness and deep enduring affection she is unsurpassed. She would not let him concern himself about her, but bid him give his whole thought to his Maker, telling him his time was short, praying for him, with him, and that she herself might be strengthened till the last, receiving all his last requests, and disguising the agony of her own feelings that she might not give him pain. My dear Sister if I am not made better by such lessons as these, what am I made of? Oh God, grant that each may make a <u>deep</u> impression, let not the remembrance <u>ever</u> be obliterated, and may they serve to make me wise unto Salvation.

After we had done all in our power we called the family and they kindly performed all the last sad affairs for our dear departed one. Need I, can I tell you the dreadful feelings when all is over and we see our dear friend a cold and lifeless corpse? No, I cannot. Although strangers and in a strange land we have been thrown among the best and kindest people. They have done every thing for us and they will have their reward. The remains of my dear Uncle were consigned to the grave on the following Monday, the 24th. He was buried in the Episcopal Burying ground, Cape Town. And the first that lies there, it is a new one and lately consecrated by the Bishop on his way to Calcutta.

The body was examined (by Uncle's request) by Dr. Murray and Bailey, and we have the satisfaction of knowing, that every thing has been done for him possible. His disorder was wholly in the lungs. The right one was <u>entirely</u> gone, the left nearly so, but we shall bring the statement with us.

We remained at Kirstinbosch till Thursday, 26th [27] and then we thought it best to change the scene and go to town where we should be making preparations for leaving this, for now all our duties are performed, nothing more calls us here. The spirit of our dear friend is I trust happy in heaven and all has been done for the poor body that we are permitted to do. It now remains for us to resign ourselves to the dispensation of our Father in Heaven who works in mysterious ways, but we do not doubt these means (though hard) tend to some wise end. Though the wisdom is far beyond our ken. It remains also for us to be watchful, to profit by his last words and the spirit he showed that we may be ready when called, to meet him in heaven. Never lived a man more upright, of stricter integrity, and of more unblemished conduct through life. He had no dishonourable acts of any kind to reproach himself with, but he mourned that he had not devoted more of his life to his God, that he had neglected him in searching for worldly treasures. How I long to be with you my dear Sis that I can tell you how happy were his last moments.

24th [27] Returned to Cape Town. Mr. Thompson & Dr. Murray both called. They are both excellent men and have been very kind.

26th [Sunday March 30] Went to Church this morning, heard Mr. Hough [Reverend George Hough].[42] An excellent sermon and truly comforting, the subject was the Immortality of the Soul, a subject that deeply interests us, when we have just parted with one of our dearest friends, whose spirit has gone "to that bourne from which no traveller returns" [*Hamlet*, Act III, Sc. 1].

27th [28] We are anxiously looking out for a Ship. Shall probably go to England as there are no American Ships here.

29th My dear parents' birth day. May God bless them and preserve their lives and health.

31st The last day of March. I have nothing to say nowadays. My dear Aunt though greatly depressed, murmurs not and bears her sorrows like a true Christian. Dear creature, if afflictions are sent to purify us and prepare us for heaven, I am sure she ought to be fully prepared, for how many and how severe have been hers. It seems now as though her cup was full. Indeed I know of nothing else that would really afflict her, all other woes would be light in comparison.

April 1st We begin now to be very anxious about some Ship. We hear the *Buckinghamshire* is not coming, and we shall probably be obliged to go in some nasty India Ship, full of Cockroches, Centipedes, and Scorpions, to say nothing of hosts of passengers. And two lone females, it will be very unpleasant, but go we must, before we can reach our journey's end. Once there, appears to me I never shall be induced to leave again.

Mrs. Cruywagen has her house full now. She has 4 ladies and a gentleman and 7 children of the most noisy kind. They however go on in a few days. Two Ships going on but all full.

2d An arrival from England, Ships detained in Channel three months with head winds. Went out a little this evening shopping. A nasty place this is—the dust is so dreadful. Aunt Low & I spend most of our time together in my room. She has not yet left the chambers.

3d The *Madras* sailed today and our house is quiet again. All the people have gone again. How little you know in America of the miseries of the rest of the world, India I believe is full of it. I could fill volumes with anecdotes of unhappy marriages, of dreadful separations of parents and children, indeed domestic misery in all its most dreadful colours. The evils of ambition, envy, jealousy, and all the bad passions are fully displayed.

4th An American Brig arrived here today, but as yet I have heard no news form her, but hope to. Dr. Murray made me a long call this morning. Aunt did not see him. He is a kind creature, I like him much. He gave me something for my face, for the last 4 weeks I have been most dreadfully afflicted with a pain in it. With what the Dutch call the Sinkings, a sort of rheumatic pain. It is nasty stuff and I hope will do me some good.

5th Mrs. Murray paid us a long visit this morning, a nice little body. After dinner went a shopping a little, looking anxiously for Ships, but none in today.

6th Sunday. Did not go to Church, but read some good sermons at home. Was in my own room by myself all day thinking much of my dear departed Uncle, and fancy him enjoying a Sabbath in heaven, with angels and the Spirits of the just made perfect. What a delightful thought! How dreadful it would be to be deprived of the hope of immortality. What misery it would be to suppose our friends, both soul and body were annihilated at death, how foolish indeed it would seem to form ties today which tomorrow were to be burst asunder and leave us today on a wearysome life, without the hope of being reunited. But thanks to our Father in heaven and our Lord Jesus Christ, we have that hope to lean upon and which will support us in the hour of adversity and urges us to press onward in a moral and religious life that we also may be ready when we are called.
     In dreadful pain all day with my face.

7th Got a few papers from the Liberator, but none later than we had seen, but I see father's name in Dec. so I suppose he is alive and well. I feel so anxious to leave this that I may be coming nearer to you. The Bland and Marian both arrived today but are quite full of passengers and Cockroches and no room for us. So we must wait awhile longer. There are plenty more coming. We had an addition [of] 10 to our family tonight from the Madras. It is melancholy to notice these Indian Ships. Ever[y] day almost brings the widows and the fatherless in great numbers, bound once more to their native land. Owing to the gentlemen being more exposed to the climate than the ladies, there is many more widows than widowers. This Ship has in it 10 ladies and of the 10, 7 are widows. We have three at this house and one poor lady mourning for her husband, and three children, her all.

She goes home childless and alone. As we dine in our own room, I have no opportunity to observe how their afflictions sit upon them. I can only witness the sorrow of my dear Aunt, who bears hers with the most Christian feelings and resignation, though at times it seems as though her heart would break. But she knows where to go for consolation. I long for the power to soothe her grief, but alas what is human aid at such times. Hers is a loss that can <u>never</u> be made up to her, the master chord is broken and cannot be repaired. Oh how desolate and alone she feels, and yet she does not wish <u>him</u> back, she is not so selfish, she feels that he is happier, she only longs for the time to come when she may meet him in heaven. I long to get her away from here. She has nothing to do, nothing to take up her time or thoughts, and nothing but employment can ever divert them.

8th Am still troubled with my face. Every evening is quite lost I am in such pain. See no one here but Mr. Thompson occasionally who is very kind and calls to tell us of every arrival.

9th Mrs. Murray spent an hour or two with us. Sent us afterwards some of her paintings to look at. They are very beautiful. She has painted 100 different kinds of Heath, all beautiful. Mr. Jones called tonight.

10th Dr. Murray called this morning professionally and has taken me under his care. Says I must take an Emetic and all sorts of stuff. Thinks I am a little feverish. Dr. and Mrs. Bailey called upon us, a nice fat Dutch woman, but a kind hearted creature as ever lived. She was very good to Uncle.

At 5 commenced operations with my medicine and disgusted my poor stomach, but hope to feel better in consequence.

11th Took Calomel last night and another nasty dose this morning of Senna & Salts and feel "<u>no</u> how" today, as the <u>Kentuckians</u> say, "No account, no how." Dr. Murray came, says I am better, and I suppose he knows best. Face is better, that is the main thing.

12th Mr. & Mrs. Eksteen, Miss Eksteen & Jesse called this morning from Kirstinbosch.

Dr. M. came also and said he would give me another day without medicine; he is very kind certainly. I have had enough I am sure for one month.

No arrivals today. When shall we get away? I am sick and tired enough of this place. You will say what a restless mortal you are Harriett. Yes I shall not be easy till I arrive in Brooklyn. I <u>hope</u> I shall then.

13 A beautiful Sunday Morning. The Dutch begin to go to Church at 8 o'clock in the morning. At 11 the English go. I hear the beautiful organ now. I do love the sound.

Spent the day in reading in my own room. Ayok came to me at noon and told me he had been to Chin Chin at his Master's Grave. He asked me if it was not our custom to do so too? I told him No. He said with great feeling that he thought it a very good custom, and with them they go twice a year.[43] I was pleased with his attention and apparent good feeling, indeed I have never met a Chinaman who has manifested such good feelings as he has ever since he has been with us, at Kirstinbosch particularly. We have become quite attached to him, he has been so faithful. If he only continues so we must consider ourselves very fortunate.

14 Dr. Murray came to see me this morning, my face still troubles me. He gave me some medicine tonight which made me very ill in the night. No Ships yet for us. We begin to get very anxious as it is getting very late in the season. There is nothing here to take our attention or to interest us in any way, and not feeling quite well in body either adds to my <u>mental</u> troubles.

Mrs. Murray sent me some *Reviews* in which I have been endeavouring to drown all my sorrows. They are effectual for a certain time, but I find my eyes often wandering from the books, to the <u>steeple</u>, to discover from whence the wind is blowing.

15 A rainy, cold morning, cleared off at noon. Mrs. Murray paid us a visit. Aunt Low was not in spirits to see her and she stayed but a short time. Said she should send her husband to see me for I was looking very bilious, indeed I felt so. We both had a violent attack of the Blues.

Dr. M. came. I told him I should complain no more, he gave me such doses. He was quite astonished at the effect it had, but said I needed it.

16 A S.E. wind blowing. 3 or 4 Ships came today and raised our hopes, but none of them bound to England. Feel better today.

17 Mr. Thompson called and lent me Mr. Rush's visit to the *Court of London*,[44] a work in which, the Reviewers say Simplicity is its greatest merit. It is a pleasing style and correct and I was interested in it. They say he seemed charmed with all he saw, but it is the work of a diplomatist and no doubt intended to flatter. There is no pleasing Englishmen though, and they must sneer at America and Americans. What provokes me is the contemptuous way in which they treat every thing not emanating from themselves.

18 Finished the book this morning. Mrs. Murray paid us a long visit, in which time we had a dissertation upon "Master Richards" alias, Flannel Petticoats. Myself being found <u>minus</u> a flannel petticoat, in my present state of health, (<u>Rheumaticky</u>) was considered a strong proof of insanity or aberration of <u>prudence</u> and I was forthwith to be reported to the Dr., her husband, which report it was believed by the two ladies would produce great astonishment, and orders would be immediately issued for a flannel petticoat to supersede a cotton one. The good lady enlarged upon the dangers of the climate to say nothing of the eloquence spent upon a display of figure and "<u>feet handles</u>." She went home fully charged with all my imprudence and soon after dinner I had a visit from the Dr. which gave me great pleasure. He looked at me with great gravity when I asked him if his wife had been telling tales, but I laughed heartily and at last promised to supersede the above mentioned article for one of warmer properties. He paid us a long visit and it was worth a little to have it. Think I shall not get well quite yet.

This climate is not at all like China. There you can take great liberties with yourself but here no. Any exposure gives you colds and pains.

Spent the evening in working, for a wonder.

19 Finished the "Reviews" and sent them back today. Mrs. Murray sent me the first volume of *Men & Manners in America* by the Author of *Cyril Thornton*.[45] Like it pretty well, but displays the Englishmen throughout, that conceited feeling which is in all of them, and that disposition to sneer at every thing American. And I do not at all like his observations upon New Englanders generally, and particularly upon Unitarians.[46] Many of his remarks are no doubt very correct, particularly upon <u>manners</u>, as far as I can judge, but as regards morals I should think not. I wish the Americans would improve in their manner of eating; they are I know <u>piggish</u> in that particular, and especially so in public houses and steam boats. I should think they would profit by the observations of all travellers and foreigners. The fact is there is not enough attention to *les bien séances* of life in America. They are too much for money getting and not given to *les politesses*. And more than all they have inherited much of the conceit of their mother country, which with their ignorance of things in other parts of the world makes them appear very ridiculous to enlightened travellers. They have much to learn. I only wish they would be more modest and not boast so much of their government and institutions, and let their visitors admire or not as they please. Well to leave the Americans. I put on my flannel this morning. The Dr. came to enquire and finding my face still obstinate in spite of all his medicines, he has been examining my teeth. Thinks it may proceed from them. Told me to take a walk. Ordered some thing new, which I tried and the first time for six weeks slept all night without pain, at which I was perfectly delighted.

Took a long walk with Miss C[ruywagen] by the sea side. A most lovely evening.

20 We intended to have gone to Uncle's Grave this morning but the S.E. is blowing a gale and we could not move out. Now I have made up my week's work and I will read my sermon. This wind must bring some Ships and I hope before another Sunday we may be again on the "briny deep."

21ˢᵗ The S.E. yesterday brought in the *Alexander* and one or two other Ships. The *Lady Nugent* which we have been hoping to go in came in, but she is quite full. We are almost discouraged. It is getting very late and we are getting very impatient. Dr. Murray came to see me, tells me to go to walk again. I have been too much shut up of late he says. So I obeyed after dinner and went with Miss Kitchy. Do not much enjoy walking in this place. The sand is so unpleasant and every one I meet is unknown, so different from what I have been accustomed to that I do not like it. In China my trouble was to keep out of the way of people, for every body knew me, but now the most uninteresting face there would please me here, where all are strange.

22ᵈ The passengers from the *Alexander* came on shore this morning. 4 ladies and a gentleman, 5 children, and three servants came to our house and put the house in commotion. Mr. Thompson came in to see me to say there is perhaps one Cabin in her that we may have, but also another lady has the refusal first, and at noon Mr. T. wrote me that it was engaged and there is no chance for us there. There are others expected yet. The *Royal George* [Captain Embleton] was signalized just before night so that there will be another chance.

I have got such a sweet little pet now in the house, a little boy about three, a darling little creature. He is going from India under the care of one of the ladies. It must have almost broken his mother's heart to have parted with him, but it was necessary on account of his health and she sacrificed her own feelings to his good. Oh India, India. . . .

Mothers in India give their children birth it is true but little do they know of them afterwards. Their children are sent from them at 3, 4 or 5 years old, perhaps younger. They go to England, receive their education, know nothing of their parents but by name. At 16 or 18 they go back to India, get married and that is all the poor parents have of them. There is another fine little boy of 8 and a little girl about 5 going under the charge of the Capt. and his wife— all interesting children. And I have amused myself with them. I do love to hear their little voices. It reminds me of home so much.

23 Mr. Thompson writes me word there is one Cabin vacant in the *Royal George* that we are now thinking about. The Capt. is exorbitant in his demands.

Went out this morning shopping. Called on Mrs. Murray. There was a Race Ball last night nearly opposite here, a poor gentleman dying under neath. How horrid! What a world this is.

Mrs. Murray sent me the *Headsman*, [James Fennimore] Cooper's last. I do not much like it. In fact I have not been pleased with any of Cooper's last.

24th No other arrivals. Mr. Thompson came to see what we think of the *Royal George*. I have agreed to go off tomorrow morning and see what her accommodations are. Ah this makes one feel what is lost. So helpless is a poor female! particularly when abroad in the world.

25th This morning at 9 Mr. Thompson and Capt. Embleton and Mr. Bonnifier, one of the passengers, called as agreed for me to go off to the Ship. I tried very hard to get Miss Cruywagen to go with me, but she had a bad cold and the face ache and could not, and Aunt Low did not feel like it, so nothing was to be done but to go by myself. Not very pleasant, but I started off and said nothing. We were three quarters of an hour beating off. A fine breeze but dead ahead. Found the Capt. a pleasing person, and the Ship very neat and very small compared to the *Waterloo*, but I smelt no Cockroches and think the accommodations are as good as we can expect. There is but one small cabin for us and we shall be well squeezed. There are many passengers mostly French, so we may learn to <u>speak</u> French. Stopped about a quarter of an hour. Was introduced to the Surgeon and made sail for the Shore. Very glad to leave the Ship. My reflections were melancholy enough as you may imagine, both past and present. There is only the hope that I <u>may</u> see you all once more that cheers me, but the recollections of when we last landed here and the changes since was almost too much. I was glad Aunt L. did not go. Walked home with Mr. Thompson. He carried me into the Public Library, a large and well filled Library and into the Exchange, a fine building upon the Parade.

Came home, reported favourably to Aunt Low, and she has made up her mind to take it. I am sorry to say she will not sail till a week from tomorrow.

Got a bad headache by the trip, and now begin to think of the horrors of sea sickness once more. Well it cannot be helped.

Dr. Murray came in to see me just before night, found me playing with my little <u>pet</u>. I shall really hate to part with him, and they go tomorrow morning.

Dr. M. thinks I had better have a tooth out which he thinks may be the cause of all my pain. I think I had better before I go to sea.

Saw this afternoon the hearse pass about to attend the funeral of the gentleman who died the other night. It was dressed with plumes. The top was covered with ostrich feathers (Black) and the horses' heads also. I must confess to me it made no impression of solemnity, mere pomp and show and nothing to rouse one's feelings like the tolling of the Bell which they omit here. Then they have 8 or 10 men behind dressed in black with feathers and black bands, etc. No one but gentlemen ever follows the body to the grave. This poor man had no relatives I believe here. He was obliged to leave India in search of health, and to leave his wife very ill at the Nilgherry [Nilgiri] Hills in India. Thus families are separated in this part of the world. How dreadful it seems, one wandering in one place and another in another, seeking climates favourable to them, and at last dying strangers in strange lands without a friend to smooth their pillow or administer consolation in their dying moments.

26th Capt. Embleton called this morning. Seems to be a kind, obliging person and promises to be attentive to us on board as well as when we arrive in England.

Dr. Murray came afterwards and brought his cold iron in his pocket, so without any further demur I summoned all my resolution, raised my courage to the striking point and sat myself down to the dreadful operation. Unfortunately instead of coming out, it broke short off. It gave me great pain for an hour or two, the nerve was quite bare and he gave me an opium and Camphor pill to kill it, which I kept in my mouth all the evening and all night.

Our house was emptied again today.

27th Another Sunday gone and we are still here. Another week must roll away before we shall bid adieu to the Cape of Good Hope. Feel exceedingly stupid this morning. Suppose I swallowed the Opium. My face is very sore yet and some pain still. A strong S.E. blowing again today. Two more ships in from Calcutta and one from England.

People flocking here in great numbers, under all circumstances and bound east, west, north and south. Misery has abundance of company here, the victims of sickness of poverty and every ill you can name. Dr. M. came to see me after dinner; we had a long conversation with him.

28th Capt. Embleton called this morning and our passage is engaged in the *Royal George*. Think, my dear of the pleasure I shall feel in starting once more for home, but alas it is with the dreadful uncertainty of what may have happened among my friends. But I will not borrow trouble but trust to the goodness of God, who afflicts but for our good. We are making some preparations for our departure, of course. Shall not sail before Sunday next certainly.

29th I don't know what to say for today. I am out of tune. I am kept awake at night by the tooth ache and my days are spent in dreading its being extracted. It must come I fear, and I am a coward that is certain.

Mrs. Murray called, but I did not see her. Dr. M. also. Some more people came to the house this eve'g.

30 Persuaded Aunty to go down to breakfast. It is better she should
meet some one before she goes on board. There she must, for we
have only one small cabin. We were not either of us sorry we went
below afterwards. We were introduced to Col. and Mrs. Craigie, very
pleasant and delightful people, she particularly. Her appearance was
to me exceedingly interesting, her countenance of rather a grecian
cast, I should say, regular features, and what adds to it, she wears her
hair *à La Grecque*. Her manners are elegant and easy, affable and
pleasant. From the first I was prepossessed in her favour. The Col.
appears a gentlemanlike man and I think must be a sensible one from
having chosen such a wife. Methinks I hear you say you are very
hasty in your conclusions, so it would seem. For these observations
were all made on account of the pleasing countenance and though
I write them afterwards, they were all made in my mind after leaving the breakfast table. I said to myself, if that eye does not speak
purity of mind I will never trust again to appearances. She went on
board ship again to get her things and I saw no more of her till night.
From an observation I heard her make and some little conversation
I had with her I pronounced her a sensible and a religious woman.
All this I discovered in one day or in a few hours. She had three fine
children with her.

Mr. & Mrs. Eksteen and family called and bid us good bye today,
also Mr. Jones. We all part never to meet again in this world probably.

May 1st Mrs. Bailey called and paid parting compliments, also Mrs.
Murray, Mr. Thompson, Dr. Murray, and our Capt. Altogether we
have had a busy day. Dr. M. came just at dinner time. Says he shall
take out the remains of my tooth. It keeps me awake every night.
But as it was just dinner time I told him I must have some first.

After dinner we went to visit Dear Uncle's grave, a melancholy
act enough. It is [a] quiet spot looking upon the sea, towards Green
Pt. There is an iron railing 5 ft. high all round it, and we are going
to have the cypress & myrtle all about it.[47] How one longs to know
when standing by the grave of a near and dear friend where and how
the Spirit is existing. How glad we are to turn our thoughts from the
mortal part which lies mouldering in the dust, to the immortal which
we fondly trust is in the society of Jesus and the angels, perhaps
watching over us and interceding for us at the throne of our father
in heaven. Sublime thought!

We returned and spent the eve'ng in company with Mr. & Mrs. Craigie who has not as yet disappointed my first impressions. On the contrary, my opinion of her firm and unbending religious principles and holy, pious feelings increases with my knowledge of her character. Her mind is highly cultivated, and I have discovered she is a descendant of the Duke of Marlborough, and nearly related, but I have since heard her say she tolerated no aristocracy but that of mind. Our conversation turned upon Stewart's and other works upon America and divers other subjects. The Col. is a great admirer of Mr. Channing. His religious views seem to suit him very well, but his wife is a Trinitarian, though she had read Channing's works and speaks highly of them. They were enthusiastic in their praises of America. They had gathered their ideas from Stewart [James Stuart, *Three Years in North America*] mostly. I told them they might have altered their minds had they read the work I read last week. [Hamilton, *Men and Manners in America*] Passed a very pleasant evening.

2^d The place is crowded with strangers. The nobility have been in an uproar today on account of the arrival of the Commander in Chief having arrived from India. And we had one of the party from the Ship here, the Hon. Mrs. Churchill, relation of Mrs. Craigie, a handsome woman but not so pleasing as Mrs. C. Dr. Murray came today would not let me escape, took out the torment and I behaved very well.

Seven Ships arrived yesterday, all full of passengers.

3 Some depart and others come today. Capt. E[mbleton] and Mr. T[hompson] called this morning and say we shall not sail till Monday so that we shall have another day. Shall leave my eulogium on Mrs. C. till we meet. I hope I never shall forget her. She is I am sure worthy of being remembered. I have been reading books she lent us most of the day. At night we walked to the grave yard. Now adieu till I am once more on the blue water. Then I will endeavour to bring up my accounts.

On Saturday evening the 3^d of May went to the grave yard for the last time to that little spot where lies all the remains of the corporeal part of my dear Uncle. But ah what pleasure to turn from the melancholy thought to the contemplation of the purified spirit in heaven and to the goodness of our father in heaven who by his Son brought life and immortality to life. Ought it not to be enough to induce us to lead righteous and holy lives not only for our own sakes but as what we <u>owe</u>, and all he asks us to return. It is a sad and melancholy thought to think we went for the last time, that we leave his remains <u>here</u> without one relative to shed a tear upon his grave, and yet why should we mourn for the body. Ah my dear we try to reason with ourselves, but mourn we must, for man was made to mourn.

A plain inscription stone bearing his name, place of birth and age will mark the spot where he lies, and if any who ever <u>knew</u> him in life should chance to read it, I am sure a tear and a sigh will be their legacy at his grave, but none, none can know but us who witnessed his death, how calmly, how willingly, how cheerfully he resigned his breath in submission to the will of his heavenly father.

We spent this evening most delightfully in conversation with Mrs. Craigie, the most interesting woman and the most profitable companion I have met for many a day. I believe she is a true Christian, though perhaps a little wanting in Christian <u>charity</u>. Religion the subject on which she most delights to <u>dwell</u> was introduced, and one thing leading to another, we at last ended in a pleasant though warm argument. She is a thorough Trinitarian and I could not entirely agree with her. We each urged our favourite opinions and ended as such arguments generally do in being of the same opinion still. But I gained something for I brought out many of her high toned and noble feelings and though having neither convinced nor been convinced I was pleased with my evening. To me it appears that a creed is of little importance, that is one may be as profitable as another, provided we have weighed the subject well, read, meditated and inwardly digested the holy Scriptures and at last feel perfectly persuaded in our minds that things are as we believe them to be. Not so my friend. Well perhaps as I grow older and wiser and have read as much as she has, I may alter my mind, far be it from me to condemn her. Would that I were more like her, she is an ornament to the religion she professes, so cheerful, so kind, so affectionate, so humble, so devout, and I may add so energetic, so indefatigable in the performance of her duties, and so desirous of finding the means of doing good. But I will cease, lest you should charge me of my old propensity, of judging too hastily. It does appear hasty I grant, but I have seen sufficient in these few days of her character to warrant all I have said. And I regret deeply that she did not come before, for I feel that intercourse with such a person would do <u>me good</u>. She has rather courted our acquaintance and regrets as we do that we are not to be inmates together longer. To me it will be a "bright spot" in my remembrance of the Cape, and I shall often think of her with pleasure. By the bye, speaking of Dr. Channing's works, I asked her, how she liked them. She admired the language she said, but she added she regretted "that he was not more deeply read." This surprised me as I always had supposed Dr. C. an eminent <u>theological</u> scholar. I told her so, but she said no! Another thing which I wish to remember and which I therefore note here, was that she understood Dr. C's mind had been very much shaken or disturbed by Prof. Stuart. This was also new and which I could not contradict, because I did not know, but if I ever live to get home shall make enquiries about. Perhaps Mr. C's works would rather lead you to suppose him a man of great <u>genius</u> rather than a deeply read man. But though he has no occasions to borrow ideas I cannot believe Mr. C. has ever been content without <u>reading</u> much upon the subject his writings prove him to have <u>thought</u> so much of. She made a curious request today.

4th Aunt Low and I went to Church this morning for the last time at the Cape and heard a very good sermon from Mr. Hough on the benefit of afflictions, very appropriate to our situation. Mrs. C[raigie] came to our room after church and brought us some of her good books and is going to make us a list of some that have given her particular pleasure.

After dinner Dr. Murray called to see us, the last time we shall meet on earth, in all probability. I shall always remember him with kindness and gratitude for he has been faithful in his attentions to us. Ah my dear Sister where ever we have been whether on land or on the sea, we have found kind friends and some with whom we are sorry to part for the last time, and in every place we are led to exclaim *c'est un* <u>triste</u> <u>plaiser</u> *de voyager*. And yet how truly *triste* I would be if we found none in our voyages and travels with whom we would like to remain, or that would not embitter a farewell. After Dr. M. left us, I sat till long after dark by myself reflecting on our sojourn at the Cape, the remembrance of which must always be sad.

On the *Royal George*

5th Got up early this morning, packed up our last trunk and made preparations for our departure, which was all completed about 10 o'clock. Just before leaving we heard of Uncle James' arrival at St.

Helena which gave me pleasure. He will take to you all my letters I suppose. At 1/2 past 10 Mr. Thompson called for us and we bid adieu to our kind hostess and her family with much sorrow. We have experienced great kindness from them; had we been their sisters they could have done no more for us. We parted with real regret too with Mrs. Craigie, for though our intercourse had been short it had been exceedingly pleasant, as you will know from my previous pages. The society of such a woman must make one better. She gave me a little book when I left her, and lent us several others of a religious order which I shall read with pleasure. Col. Craigie and Mr. Thompson waited upon us to the boat and we retraced the steps which three months before we had passed under such different circumstances.

There was a busy scene enough at the landing place. Eight Ships had arrived the day before and one or two this morning all full of passengers, which were landing with their baggage as fast as possible, others were going and we among the number. I could not help thinking what different histories they might all give. We should hear truth more strange than fiction and find that things had occurred which had "never been dreamt of in our philosophy" [*Hamlet*, Act I, Sc. 5]. And then I could not help thinking that of all these probably few were acting from <u>inclination</u>. It was no doubt their own pleasure to land when they got here, but how few find themselves here to gratify either curiosity or inclination.

Well leaving the inclinations of people to themselves or any one else, we went on board the *R George* where there was as much confusion as upon the jetty. The passengers were coming in rapid succession with quantities of baggage and the like, and the deck was hardly to be seen. And thinks I to myself all this is for the comfort of these poor bodies of ours. Well we proceeded to our cabin which looked as though it w[oul]d contain little but our bodies, but we set Ayok to looking into the berth and drawers, and we found it contained many other bodies beside our own, in the form of <u>Cockroches</u>, to our great horror. Then there was the smell, and a thousand other little miseries, all of which are ready to salute one on first entering a Ship. All of which we become accustomed to after a certain time, but untill that time arrives they are hard to be endured. After a while we learn to move in a smaller space, and our cabins begin to grow larger. I must not be too prosy. Mr. Thompson stayed with us some time and then bid us <u>good bye</u> and we began to arrange our things. Had time enough as we could not sail till the following day. Managed to keep very well all day and we thought got things in pretty good order.

We had dinner about 5. I made my appearance and did justice to a very nicely cooked dinner thinking it best to improve the time as I shall get none tomorrow. We had about 20 at table, mostly French, so that I understood very little of what was going on. Shall describe them at some future time. Aunty was not well and did not come out. We went to bed as soon as possible, to forget our miseries in sleep, and "tired nature's sweet restorer" [Edward Young, *The Complaint: Night Thoughts*, I, l.1] did not refuse to come to our relief. There was a heavy sea and were pitching badly all night.

6th Raining hard this morning, but cleared up about 11, when we got under weigh and took the last look at the Cape where lies the remains of our dear, dear friend. Our ship was anchored abreast of the grave yard so that we could see the spot. Ah my dear, sad, sad were we today.

We were both in our births most of the day, with nothing to cheer us but the thought that we were once more starting for home, and should be every day coming nearer. And it was a comfort to me, and I said "Blow breezes blow" and waft us speedily. I do like to dwell on the thought of being once more with you. We had a fine wind which took us outside the Islands before night, and a fine fair wind all night.

7th We were both very sick all day, though I think not so much so as in the *Waterloo*. The Ship rolls very easily. Last night we had but little sleep, for there was a heavy sea and the wind aft, and almost every thing in our cabin gave way and we were in perpetual commotion. The man had lashed nothing properly and our wash stand upset, bowls broke and there was no sleeping for noise. However the like troubles have all been detailed before and I will not fill up my book with them.

8

9

10th Had strong and fair winds all these days and averaged 200 miles a day. We both became convalescent and took our places at table and performed no mean part at the knife and fork, and tonight (Saturday), got a walk on deck and ventured a few words in French to some of the passengers.

11 Sunday Wind still continues fine and the prospect is in favour of our having a short passage to St. Helena. Have been reading all day. We are close prisoners in our cabin till dinner time, and as usual I begin to find abundance of occupation, in reading, writing, etc. My book will be neglected till I have passed St. Helena, then I shall say something of out party.

12 Breeze getting light but fair and is now quite smooth.

13   "   "   "   "   "   "   "   "   "   "
Venture a little more french daily and am making friends with the children.

14 The sun out today and very fine with a little breeze. We have had no observation for 4 days till today, and now find ourselves a little farther from the Island than we thought for as the wind has been so light we shall have rather a long passage. There is no calculating upon the sea. Every day proves the propriety of the <u>adage</u> "as fickle as the wind."

Commenced reading French to one of the young ladies this morning, she says I read <u>very</u> <u>well</u>. N.B. [*nota bene*] Make allowances for french politeness!

Fair moonlight night. Had a long walk then had some bread and milk and played a rubber at whist.

15 The wind is still light with every prospect of our being out till Sunday. Thus you see are all our calculations on a short passage to the Island disappointed.

16 A little more wind today but before night we were braced sharp up and every prospect of a head wind. Still a long distance off, we begin to get rather impatient and faces look long. It is dreadful the thought of being penned up in this place for months & months and poor Aunty is most unpleasantly situated. There is no peace nor quiet for her, and the constant noise in the Cuddy is most discordant to her feelings. Our cabin is more noisy than the others as it joins the Cuddy, and these noisy French people keep such a chattering from morning till night that there is no such thing as reading in peace. After breakfast many of them remain at the table and commence with Piquet, back gammon, écarté, chess and all sorts of games and keep it up pretty well most of the forenoon. At 4 we all

assemble to dinner where we are wedged in so tight that it is difficult to <u>eat</u>. And such <u>eaters</u> as our friends are I never saw before.

After dinner Aunty and I generally take a constitutional walk
together, and we walk till we are quite tired rather than join the
party, where we find it difficult to make ourselves understood. At
7 we have tea, etc. and as soon as that is over you see the different games commenced again, the old and the young, the
grandmama of 70 and the child of 7, both and all deeply interested. We do not join. I sometimes look on, but most generally
return to the deck.

17 The last night was very squally with a head wind, and I got up
feeling quite doubtful. Went to the table, but thought it prudent to
leave it before the others. The wind died away and the sea became
like a river, with a clear sky, but we are very little further than we
were yesterday. We are still braced sharp up and it is becoming tedious enough. Time flies swiftly enough but I wish we were making
progress. I am at present very much interested in Cobbett's *French
grammar*.[48] It is the most simple and the idiom of the language made
more easily understood than any I have seen. Must not forget this.
Hope Sarah is studying it. I am also reading Spruzheim on <u>Phrenol-
ogy</u> and begin to look at people's heads very <u>scientifically</u>. Wrote a
letter to Abbot today to leave at St. Helena. Today completes my
24ᵗʰ year, and what account can I give of it?

Was on deck all the evening. A most lovely night and we were
cheered with the sound of a fair wind, but alas so little of it that I
fear we shall not reach St. Helena tomorrow night as we might very
easily do with a little breeze. We were only about 150 miles from it
at noon. We shall probably spend one day there in which time we
shall visit "<u>Longwood</u>" and the tomb of the <u>great</u> man Napoleon as
we shall probably never have another chance.

18 After breakfast of a Sunday morning. A calm hot morning and
here we shall be most likely a day or two. We have an anxious party
on board and all desirous of pressing onward but alas we are so de-
pendant on this fickle element that we can only submit and make
the best. All our wings are spread today, but the winds refuse to bear
us on. I have been obliged to take my writing, these people have
kept such a chattering in the cuddy it was impossible to read. Now,
the bell strikes 11 and the Capt. calls us to prayers.

The wind continued light through the day. A most lovely evening and we endeavoured in vain to see the land. The breeze freshened a little just at night, which served to cheer us at once, for it is tiresome to have a passage protracted to such a length, after having been so flattered at first. We set on the Poop all the evening.

St. Helena

19 Wind still light, but about sunset the Capt. called me to see the Island which he had just discovered, and one but the eye of a mariner would have supposed it any thing but a small cloud. We all hailed it with joy and anticipated the pleasure of being <u>near</u> it tomorrow morning.

Spent the evening in conversing with Madame Munro, a lady of <u>70</u> years. What would grandmother say to that. This is her sixth voyage. She has seen great changes in her day. She is <u>nobly</u> related in France, has lived in great style and had a first rate education. She is now elegant in her manners, full of life and very active. She was this evening giving me some account of her adventures, which interested me much and approaching the famous Isle of St. Helena our thoughts were naturally turned to the <u>fallen</u> hero, who died there. She was in the same convent [Les Carmes] with Josephine at the time she was separated from her first husband "Beauharnais," just before he was guillotined. She says she was loved by all and gives the same account of her character and manners that we get from books generally.

Went to bed hoping to find ourselves at St. Helena when we sh[oul]d awake.

20th When we awoke found we were very near the Island and dropped the anchor about 8 o'clock. Dressed ourselves accordingly to go on shore. There is no bay here but good anchorage under the lee of the Island. I know not how to give you an idea of this place from the Ship, but I will do my best. The first appearance is like a huge rock rising <u>perpendicularly</u> out of the sea. After a while you discover a few houses and some trees at the entrance of a ravine between <u>two</u> mountains, which appear to have dissolved partnership (from the <u>unknown</u>) and retired from each other in mutual disgust or by mutual consent. Since which time the <u>town</u> has grown up between them, which place, is inhabited by <u>most</u> of the people on the Island. But stop, I am now giving you the appearance from the Ship. Except in this valley, to <u>our</u> view, there is not a spot of verdure to be seen, excepting a strip or two of <u>water</u> <u>cresses</u> growing by the sides of the springs. On the summits of these mountains and on other high places are fortifications, for the defense of the Island. And on the sides of these mountains you discover the roads which give you an idea of the winding paths of the Alps, but more of this anon. [Harriett inserts in her text a tiny sketch of the town in the valley between the mountains.] Then there is the vast ocean around us, and one wonders in vain what could have produced this enormous excrescence in the midst of it. Two Ships anchored near us, the *Duke of Argyle* which had as long a passage as we had, and a French Ship from "Bourbon."

After having had our breakfast and having gone through the customary visits from health boats, etc., with our best bibs and tuckers on we were whipped into the boat, in company with Madame Grant her three children and two sisters, and several gentlemen of our party, and in a few moments were again on terra firma, which is always pleasant, be it what land it may. But how delightful it will be when we again step upon our native land, *la terre, la terre*, will then have charms it never had before. There are very good steps for landing and all convenient, but such a queer place I never saw before. Our eyes had not deceived us, we were actually walking on the quay with the rock rising a thousand or more feet perpendicular and in some places jutting over our heads, and not a trace of vegetation to be seen. Some miserable little houses were built at the foot of the rock, the sides and roofs of some being formed by it, and making one tremble lest some convulsion should bury them all. We marched on a little further and the next [thing] that struck our eyes was a <u>ladder</u> from the foot of the hill or mountain reaching to the fortification on the top. This is also nearly perpendicular, or at this slope. [A mark practically vertical is inserted to give the angle of the ladder.] The idea of going up made one dizzy. I have been told it is 3000 ft, it certainly looks 2500. I shall endeavour to find out. It was built by the E[ast] I[ndia] Company and cost 200,000$. We walked on a little further and entered a gate which locks up the <u>city</u> at night. Passed through a very clean street, the principal, saw some pretty looking houses and <u>one</u> <u>pretty</u> girl and arrived at the Hotel of Mr. Solomon, a <u>Jew</u>—a very neat and commodious house and well furnished. Made inquiries at once for American papers and letters, but the only one for us had been sent to the Cape (very gratifying). No papers of late date could be obtained. (Well one must pocket one's disappointments and see others reading theirs with <u>patience</u>.)

The Capt. immediately ordered carriages to take us to the tomb of Napoleon, as we had no time to lose. The sight of the roads we were to mount were rather awful in appearance. However we soon saw our *voitures* at the doors. I hardly know what to call them; I should say they resembled mostly double buggies with four wheels very small, which brought us very near the ground. A driver sits upon the horse and leads them part of the way. There were no tops so that we were exposed to the sun which was not very agreeable. Well we started, Miss Grant and Aunt Low on the front seat, Miss Grant and myself behind, and the other carriage contained the Miss Bestels, two children, and Miss Counter. Our course was a zigzag path up the side of the mountain, the valley below us at the distance of many hundred of feet, the mountains towering above us. There is a little wall to guard us from the precipice on one side.

Being above the valley we had a fine view of the town, which runs up some distance between the mountains till it finally tapers off <u>and</u> <u>is</u> <u>no</u> <u>more</u>. It is not a quarter of a mile wide, the streets very narrow but looked clean, the houses mostly small and built of mud and stone. We saw some pretty gardens and a variety of most beautiful green <u>trees</u>—the banana and other tropical fruits. They have one church, plenty of fortifications, mountains on three sides of them and the beautiful blue waters in the distance, or on the fourth side, visible. [Harriett makes a sketch of the town in the valley with the road winding up the mountain. The sketch is labeled <u>My</u> <u>private</u> <u>mark</u>.]

After losing sight of the town our attention was drawn to the little chateaux or cottages perched about in the little spots capable of cultivation. The scenery is grand, the ravines and the precipices are magnificent, looking as though they had been torn asunder in every direction. Some of our party confirmed my opinion that it gives one a very good idea of the Alpes, as he had been there himself. In certainly accords very well with the account I have read, except in <u>magnitude</u>.

[Marginal note] except in dangers, heights, <u>depth</u> and every thing else

The roads are made in precisely the same way. I was enchanted with the scenery and as we gained the <u>summits</u> felt <u>much</u> <u>nearer</u> <u>heaven</u>,

for some how or other it always seems to exalt the feelings to be towering so high. But I hope soon to be able to tell you in *viva voce* all I
admired. As I hope to come with this, I shall only give enough to
recal[l] the scenes and places to my memory. When we had nearly
gained the summit we were obliged to get out of our carriages and
descend a little way into the valley to visit the tomb. Our companions
were all violent Bonapartists and looked sad and sentimental as we
approached. It was indeed a time for *réflexion*. It recal[l]s so many facts
and leads to so many conclusions, that one is almost *égaré* and again
I could not but in the midst of all, rejoice that my dear Uncle was not
brought here. I am sure he would not have been half so comfortable.
The valley must be dreadfully hot and the ride up the mountain would
have been far too fatiguing for him to have bourne. Then again I
could not help thinking how much he would have enjoyed it, had he
been here with us in good health. *Allons*, a truce to reflections.

The tomb of the great man, of whose fame the world knows
enough, is situated on the side of the mountain in a most quiet and
delightful spot. There is not a letter upon the stone, to say <u>who</u> or
<u>what</u> lies there, owing to the foolish jealousy of the English govern-
ment. The tomb is enclosed by a neat iron railing, a sort of lily growing at the two head corners and the four sticks remaining which supported the "Forget me nots" planted by Madame Bertrand after his
decease, but which has since died. [Includes a sketch of the tomb
surrounded by the fence.] Within the outer enclosure there are two
large willow trees which <u>waved</u> over the grave, but they too must die
and they are nearly <u>dead</u>. A few green leaves upon the branches show
they once had life, but the trunks are quite white. The present Gov.
Dallas has planted some cypress trees which are growing well. An old
Sergeant lives near by and will give you [a] slip or two which was
there during Napoleon's residence and looks like a piece of antiquity.
His little cottage is just above surrounded with geranium, growing
wild and luxuriantly. It is a most enchanting spot. But far too quiet
for the spirit of such a man as rests here, as Byron says, "Quiet, to
'quick' spirits is a hell" [*Childe Harold*, Canto 3, l.370] and it must
have been so to him, for how could he reflect upon his career, in this
lone and desolate place with any <u>peace</u> of <u>mind</u>? What a change to
be sure! from the courts and palaces of kings in the midst of courtiers
and dependants, to this isle in the ocean and the cottage, <u>in com-
parison</u>, on St. Helena heights!! Whew!! A prisoner! and alone!

Finding a book at the entrance for the travellers's name to be inserted I took it up and how quick it recalled the favourite saying of Napoleon himself, "There is but one step from the sublime to the ridiculous," [To the Abbé du Pradt, on the return from Russia (1812), referring to the retreat from Moscow] for one glance at this said receptacle for names and remarks, was quite sufficient to excite one's risibles. Here were huddled together eulogy and invectives, sentiment, of all kinds, of friend and foe, poetry and prose, good and bad, of the literate and the illiterate, of all nations, tongue and kindred. One bit I was particularly struck with but unfortunately I remember only part of it, but enough to give you some idea of its merits. "Here lies Bony part . . . He rests in peas," written in a very bad hand, and much more of the same kind. Such a book of trash I never saw before but no doubt is like many others adapted to such occasions or places.

I merely wrote the names of our party and we bid adieu to the tomb and returned to our carriages and proceeded to Longwood where Napoleon lived and died. But there is hardly a trace of what it then was. It is in a most shocking state of filth and delapidation and converted into stables, etc. It is a pity I think that they did not let it fall honourably to decay, but his bed room is now turned into a stable, his sitting room where he died, is a room for machinery in a wretched state, his flower garden into a pig stye. Pity, pity, I think. They shewed us the grounds etc., but there was no trace of anything that belonged to him. The house stands on one of the highest points and has a most commanding view of the sea etc. They shewed us the rooms of Las Cases and Montholon, and we also passed the house of General Bertrand.[49] I was amused to see our friends carrying away large pieces of the wall and the floor where he died and saying how happy they should make their friends in France and at the Mauritius by dividing the Spoil.

The Dr. and Capt. Fewson joined us here. They had been to plantation house, the residence of Sir Hudson Lowe [1769–1844, English governor of St. Helena] but we had not time to visit it. So we left Longwood, saw the new house built by Napoleon containing 52 rooms, but as the Gov. is residing there at present we could not go to it.

We went down the same way we came up and were almost suffocated with dust, and the sun was very hot. Thus finished our excursion. Our next demand was for a bath (I told you keep in mind, Mr. S. was a Jew) which we had and felt exceedingly refreshed and comforted by it, for we were quite fatigued. This done and dressed again, we sallied forth into the streets, bought a spool or two of cotton, and enquired the prices of some things, all and every thing here are the most <u>awful</u> prices.

As we went along, we were stopped by a gentleman who made himself known as the <u>American</u> <u>Consul</u>, Mr. Carrol [William Carroll].[50] He was very liberal in his offers of assistance; would be "<u>too</u> <u>proud</u>" to do this, that, and the other. He <u>humbugged</u> a long time and expressed a great desire to serve us in some way, said he should be "<u>too</u> <u>proud</u>" to introduce his daughter. We said we should be most happy to see her. Soon after we went home he came in [and] introduced Mrs. Brookhouse, the wife of J. Brookhouse of Salem, a pretty and interesting little woman, and his other daughter. She told us some melancholy news from Salem (she has come from there recently) of Mr. Dodge's [Pickering Dodge] death and Mrs. Jenks' [Mary Jenks], of Mr. Deland's marriage, etc. It made me feel quite unhappy, but she told me Fisk [John Fisk Allen] had arrived home, which gave me pleasure.[51]

We dined at 5 o'clock, had a good dinner, which cost <u>15</u> <u>shillings</u> sterling <u>a</u> <u>piece</u>. It was a very nice dinner to be sure, and relished well, consisting of Turkey, Goose, partridges, Fowls, pies, pastry, etc., fish & soup of course, and fruits, Figs, delicious plantains, Pears, Guavas, fruits of the Islands and dried imported fruits. But we should have said nothing of this but when we were demanded <u>7</u> <u>shillings</u> <u>sterling</u> for each Bath we exclaimed in perfect astonishment and I said N.B. never say any more of <u>Chinese</u> <u>imposition</u>, they are excelled by Europeans'. But there was no disputing this charge and we found every thing else was charged accordingly, and we were not all sorry to bid adieu to St. Helena, or to think our stay was limited to one day. But I hope you will remember Mr. S. is a Jew, though he is not alone in these charges. There may be reasons for all this, that is living may be very dear, but I cannot forget the hot water. It is true they are very nice rooms well fitted up, and then I suppose they do not get customers very often. But hope I shall remember to warn my friends when they may go to St. Helena to ask the price of a bath before they call for it.

At 8 o'clock our party mustered. A most beautiful moonlight night and we walked to the Quay and went once more on board our ship and were quite tired enough with our day's exertion to go to bed.

May 21ˢᵗ 14° S. Lat. We got under weigh about 1 o'clock last night and were out of sight of land at breakfast time this morning. I for one was not at all sorry, for now every day will be bringing us nearer home. We have fine wind now and the next land we shall probably see will be the Island of Ascension in about 8° S. L.

Beautiful weather. The nights are quite perfect, so that we are able to sit upon the poop all the evening.

22ᵈ After breakfast we remain in the Cuddy awhile and mutually assist each other in French and English, and in pleasant weather our time passes rapidly. Cannot help feeling grateful for this charming wind and weather and pray that it may continue. I cannot complain of minor evils, such as heat, cockroches and want of room, when I feel that every day is leading me on my way. How happy in the thought that I <u>may</u> be at <u>home</u>!! Nevertheless I am sometimes impatient.

23ᵈ 12°15' As yesterday, fine wind and weather. Fully employed all day and am busy now reading Spurzheim on *Phrenology*. Think it a pleasing theory at any rate and very plausible. Whether it is ever of any great use remains to be proved.

24ᵗʰ S. Lat. 11°45' Five years today since we bid adieu to home and friends and took the last lingering look of our dear native land. Have recalled it all to my mind. The weather is getting very hot as we come to the <u>top</u> of the world, but we are chasing the sun yet, and shall have it still hotter when we get further North. We find Cockroches begin to feel the effects of it and come out abundantly.

25ᵗʰ Lat. S. 9°18' A dreadful hot morning, but good wind and weather. Attended prayers on deck this morning, then returned to our Cabins and I read aloud one of Dr. Wardlaw's sermons on the "Divinity of Jesus Christ."[52] In reading these different views of the same subject I get puzzled my dear Sister. The texts brought forward and shewn in different lights, confute without convincing me, and I am left, though in the same faith essentially, yet puzzled regarding the meaning of many parts of the bible. I get perfectly lost at times, for the more I think the more I am puzzled, and the more I reflect on the holy life we are called upon to lead and the weakness of our powers to overcome all the obstacles that are thrown in our way, the more I feel the impossibility of ever arriving at any thing approaching perfection. I sometimes think I will never read any book upon religious creeds, but the bible, then again I should feel that I was sinning against my own conscience, because I feel that it is right to read all sides of the question before we make up our minds, at the same time I feel that it only sets my mind in a turmoil without leading to any good result. For while you find many texts to support both sides and you are puzzled in both, what can you do. I sometimes ask if it depends upon ourselves whether we understand aright or not. It depends upon the powers we have given us. If the power is not given us, where are we to get it? By prayer and supplication? Yes. We are told "if we seek, we shall find" [Matthew 7:7]. I pray most sincerely that my understanding may be enlightened that it may understand the scriptures. But alas there are many things hard to be understood and to me particularly the 8th and 9th Chapter of Romans.

I find it very difficult to write as it is all to be done in my lap.

26th I find a sea life has become so familiar to me that my journal is neglected for many days together and I sometimes think it best to spare my paper all together and reserve it for something more interesting on my approach to land. There my poor brain will be overrun and I shall be glad to relieve it of its burden.

27th [Deleted: It is now the first day of June,] untill the 28th we had a good breeze, and on Tuesday morning the 27th passed the Island of Ascension, but as it was foggy and in the night could not see it. And we did not pass as near it as we expected to, as there is a strong current setting us to the west. But in this I for one was not much disappointed. The weather is getting dreadfully hot and as we approach the line we shall have lighter winds and consequently hotter.

28th Still fine weather and all our party appear grateful for mercies received. We are all well and with the exception of minor evils get on amicably and cheerfully. We begin to have some communication with our fellow passengers, as we find they are ready to excuse without laughing at our blunders, and with pleasure assist us in our endeavours at acquiring their language, and we readily return the favor. The Cuddy is regular school room after breakfast and might well be called a Bedlam. There are <u>couplets</u> of <u>readers</u>, and <u>couplets</u> engaged at piquet or écarté. There [are] couplets of talkers and now and then a solitary reader and it [is] with perfect astonishment that I see him engaged without a <u>murmur</u> or a sign of being disturbed by the noise around him. Perfectly abstracted, he knows of nothing that is passing around him. This is the public resort as it is cooler than any other place. About 11 we all disperse and then there is a little peace. The evenings are generally spent by us on deck and our quiet is very much distracted by the nocturnal rambles of the cockroaches which sometimes take the liberty of promenading our necks and heads. Poor Aunty has no peace. We are generally all in bed before 10 o'clock.

29th Dreadfully hot wind, getting light. Today finished Spurzheim on *Phrenology*. Studied Cobbett's *Grammar* which I admire more and more. Hope Sarah Elizabeth is studying it.

30th 1°16' [S. Lat.] We are now within a degree of the Equator, with a three knot breeze. Soon, tonight I trust we shall pass the line, I hope for the last time. We shall then be heading towards America for some time, then must tack and bear away. Alas, I shall give a sigh for we shall be within a week or two's sail of New York I suppose. Well, patience! Once more at the north of the Equator every mile will count.

This evening about 6 o'clock a delightful 7 knot breeze sprung up which <u>wafted</u> us most splendidly across the <u>line</u>, and we are now once more in the N. Atlantic. We feel truly thankful that we are thus favoured.

31st 2°28' N. Lat. Awoke this morning with the Sun and saw him rise from his watery bed in great splendour. I* fancied the sky looked more <u>homish</u> than usual.

[Marginal note] *How much fancy will do

The breeze continued this morning but grew rather light through the day. Suppose the winds will be very light and variable for the present. The weather is very hot and the cockroaches swarm. Those in the lower cabins say, they have them by the 500,000. They are a great nuisance, in fact I cannot relish any thing for them. If there is the smallest crevice in any thing, they will enter, they are in our drawers, they eat our apples, and in fact there is no peace for them. Breeze freshened tonight—Oh blow, breezes blow!

June 1st 3°26' Attended prayers on deck, then read one of Wardlaw's Sermons, then Burns' *Principles of Christian Philosophy*,[53] a very good work. How I long to get home to talk with my father on these books and these subjects.

After dinner went on the Poop a little while but we were driven down by a squall and kept in the Cuddy all of the evening by the rain. Very little wind today except in squalls, but that cooled the air and made us a little more comfortable. But it is sad work. We went to bed about eight. It is astonishing how calms lengthen people's visages, and a fair breeze sets them all to smiling and raises their hopes of a short passage which the next day may sink lower than before. Such is a sailor's life, and a tedious one it is!

2ᵈ A veritable calm, the most distressing of evils. The sea like a piece of Ice, the sails beating the masts, and not a breath to cool one, is enough to inspire one with the blue devils!

Saw a small shark today for the first time. He kept round the ship most of the day. A little breeze just at night, and we set upon the poop enjoying it till 1/2 past 8, watching the squalls that threatened, and at last burst upon us. Had a squally night with considerable thunder.

3ᵈ Wind light through the day and the most indeed all that we made was in the squalls that came up at night. Rained tremendously and blew very hard for a while this morning.

4ᵗʰ "   "   "   "   "   "   "   "   "   "   [ditto]

5ᵗʰ Had a little more breeze today and were in hopes we had got hold of the Trades again, but they changed again at night, and we groan in the Spirit at times. But nevertheless are <u>calculating</u> to arrive in about 23 or 4 days.

6ᵗʰ The wind from the N.E. today and we have relaxed our muscles a little. Have made but little more than 20 miles a day for the 4 or 5 last days. Distressing. However, once out of it, we hope for good winds. So much for <u>hope</u>.

7ᵗʰ 7°34' Just before I was dressed heard the sound of the trumpet, Ship Ahoy. And where are you bound? Looked out of the <u>Scuttle</u> and saw an English Brig abreast of us. We sent a boat, got 3 newspapers and some nice Potatoes. She was 24 days from Syllie [Scilly Isles] & 32 from Liverpool. I assure you it was no small pleasure. However did not get much news and not one word from America.

Saw another Ship just after breakfast, but going the same way. The Brig was bound to "Rio Janeiro." We had the mortification of seeing the Ship out sail us. In the afternoon, saw another Brig bound to the Southward, but did not speak her. I am sorry to find our Ship is rather a slow sailer. She is not in good trim, has a "list to Port," which retards her progress. However they mean to "fix" her tomorrow—as the Yankees would say. A smacking Breeze today and we are pitching about merrily. Go as rapidly as she will, it seems slow to me, for my wishes go and come back again. Every thing is accomplished in my imagination very often.

Sunday 8ᵗʰ June N. Lat. 9°2′ Intended when I rose this morning to spend the day in a most Christian like manner and arranged in my mind my books and employments, but so little can we control events and so much are we the creatures of circumstances that not for one little day can we pretend to say what we will or will not do. Untill 11 o'clock I read as I intended and then went out to prayers, which were shortened as there was a Ship on our lee bow, outward bound, and the Captain knew we were anxious and in hopes of meeting an American. We immediately went on to the Poop, and what was our joy when we discovered she was an American. We bore down upon her and found the Capt. was rather unwilling to take in his studding sails to speak to us, but finding we were resolute, he slackened sail and in a few minutes we were alongside the *Italy*, Capt. [A.A.] Ritchie. Found he was from New York and bound to China. Sent a boat to see if he had any news or letters. I assure you I was made quite happy by hearing you were well or rather as far as he knew and he had a note from father a few days before he left which was about the 9ᵗʰ of May. A most happy encounter. He sent us a lot of papers, some few stores as a mark of attention to his countrywomen and was exceedingly kind. So our day was spent in reading News papers. Find Uncle James had arrived, and not much else in the papers except politics which I regret to find are in such a state. Our old general [President Andrew Jackson] seems to be wishing to play "Napoleon" or dictator. Seems to be sounding the people and should fancy from the papers we have, that he finds it won't go! Oh dear I hope we shall not find civil war when we get home. He is carrying it with a high hand certainly. Many failures too on account of his measures, and this subject is now worrying me. I have looked in vain for my

dear father's name in the advertisements in the *Journal of Commerce*
where he always appears, but alas it is not there. What is the reason?
I hope nothing has happened to him, but I cannot help [word illegible] and thinking of it, for I have always seen it before.

We were busy all day reading the news, and thus all my plans of
the morning were deranged. I could not help excusing myself for this
innovation on my usual practices as I had heard nothing of consequence for many months from my home. We bid adieu to the *Italy*
and her kind commander after having finished our business and we
both proceeded on our respective courses. Every thing was in prime
order on board the Ship and nothing to blush for but every thing to
be <u>proud</u> of. We drank some <u>Philadelphia</u> Cider at dinner, which was
very nice. Spent the evening on the Poop and saw the beautiful appearance in the water I so often spoke of going out, the animalculae.

9th 10°12' Fine weather and braced sharp up with the N.E. Trades.

15th June 22°5' Since my last date my dear Sister nothing has occurred worthy of note. We have been jogging along in the 22d degree of Lat. and if our Ship was good for any thing in my opinion
with the fine breezes we have had we ought to have been much
further, but perhaps it is my impatience. We have seen nothing on
the face of the waters since last Sunday and have been employed in
the regular routine of eating and drinking, sleeping, etc. You may
think with so many passengers I might find something interesting to
relate, but to tell you the truth I can say but little in their favour.

Could I have the privilege of conversing with them, I should hear
some sage remarks and perhaps be regaled with a "feast of reason
and a flow of soul" [Alexander Pope, *Satires, Epistles, and Odes of
Horace*, Satire I, Book II, l.127] but unfortunately it is otherwise.
For their rapidity of utterance debars me from any intercourse in the
general conversation and in my private chats I never venture to
express my sentiments. This being the state of the case we keep out
of the way, and either sit upon the poop or read in the eve'g and in
the day are in our own cabins. The manners of the party are not
very elegant and judging from the very frequent utterance of *Mon
dieu* I should not say much for their reverence of one whose name is
so irreverently spoken but on this subject I dare not judge. To our
ears it is very unpleasant. We had the misfortune to lose one of the
invalids this week who has been ill a long time which is the princi-

pal occurrence of the week. The three last days we have had a "powerful" strong breeze and we have been pitched about unmercifully.
However thank God I am very well and happy in the thought that
every day is carrying me to the end of my voyage and my dear Sister
(a thought that will come) nearer to the end of my life. Yes every
day I am wishing away is taking me from the little space of time that
should be employed in preparing for an entrance upon another!

I have just been reading two of Mr. Wardlaw's sermons, which
if I live you will hear me speak of. He is clear and powerful in his
reasoning.

We have passed the "Cape de Verds" and next shall come to the
"Azores." I have been obliged to make these observations with a pencil
for the ship is in such commotion I can have no safe place for ink.
Good bye my dear (if nothing particular occurs till next Sunday).

Monday 16th 24°39' A fine strong breeze all day and at noon found
us in 24°39' North, a very good run. Our ship seems to have caught
the spirit of her inmates and seems to be pressing on with all possible dispatch, though she seems more inclined to head towards
America than England. If we were only bound there we should set
our studding sails and soon be among you, but alas, alas we want to
go very near where the wind is coming from. We begin to count
the days now before we arrive, and the heads are thick round the
chart. It is curious to watch the different feelings which are busy
among the different parties. Our Captain to begin with is anxious
about his ship, his passengers, and all his trouble is to be repaid by
the happy meeting between his wife and child. We have another
Shipwrecked Capt. on board, and he is anxious to meet his family
and settle his troubles. We have another family consisting of the
grandmother, son, & daughter and grandchild. They return to their
friends and *la belle France* after three years's absence. Another family consisting of a widow lady, her three children, two sisters and
nephews. They have left their native country to take up their abode
in France for the good of the children. The young ladies (the sisters) are anticipating the pleasures and gayeties of Paris with some
<u>faint</u> regrets for friends left behind. The eldest of the three chil-
dren, a young lady of about 16, seems to think more of friends left
than the joys to come and manifests no impatience to arrive. I can
sympathize with her, for I remember my first <u>essay</u>. I was not at all

anxious to arrive, but I must leave the rest till I see you, for my book is filling up. A beautiful evening.

17th 26°56' Thus far pretty well, but now the wind is getting light, only 5 knots, and weather quite perfect. Really if we had started on a party of pleasure we could not have wished pleasanter than we have had most of the time. We have had very cold winds of late and shall not be surprised to hear of late summers, blighted fruits, etc. A fine moon now and daylight not gone till nearly 8. Sit on deck this evening, looking towards you and fancying the clouds the shores of America. Hum. Brilliant fancy, *n'est ce pas?* Went below at 8 and took a lesson in Chess of Mr. Fewson & Mr. Drusine.

18th 28°12' Better than I anticipated today, but now there is no wind at all. Suppose we have lost the N.E. Trades and in a little while hope to get something better. Most lovely weather and being so still I have thought proper to bring up my book. Having done so I shall take my work till time to dress for dinner. I have had another lesson in Chess. Suspect it will hardly do for my crazy head. If I thought it would be the means of giving it any stability I would willingly give the time but I rather grudge the time it requires, though it is very interesting.

19 29° We have made precious little since yesterday and shall make still less today. Now find ourselves in what is called the "Saragosso or Grassy Sea" on account of a grass or sea weed that is seen in great quantities in these latitudes. Are now surrounded with it.

The weather is very hot now, there is so little wind, and faces begin to lengthen and prospects of a long voyage to be feared. Thus we go! Saw three Dolphins pass today. They look splendidly in the water. <u>Never</u> saw, no I will not say never, because I have, but there was a most <u>glorious</u> sunset. This last you will pass as very trite and common place and perhaps think it too common a sight to be no-ticed. But not so my dear. We do not see a glorious sunset every night nor even a pretty one—but I assure you it leaves any thing but a common impression on my mind when I do see it. And I only regret that there are not words more adequate to express it than the most superlative in our language, for they give you no idea at all of it.

20 29°49' Winds still light and weather warm. All our calculations upset as to arriving the last of June. We sigh in the spirit I assure you and complain that the weather is too fine. Though in my heart feel that it is all right yet I cannot help wishing the right were <u>otherwise</u>. "Patience is having her perfect work with me" [James 1:4].

21ˢᵗ 30°46' Now we are just getting into the Lat. of the U. States and our time begins to accord so well with yours that I can actually fancy what you are about. In China I was always obliged to suppose you <u>snoring</u> while I was employed and vice versa.

Hot and light wind, or I may say no wind at all, for a great part of the time there was not. The sea resembles a piece of glass, and we invoke the clouds in vain for <u>wind</u>. They come and go but heed not our wishes. Had a Ship in sight two or three days but cannot get near her. Fairly got the blues tonight, a dead calm, and was glad to go to bed and forget myself in sleep. It was a most lovely night too.

22 31°35' Made more than I thought we should, but fortunately a little breeze sprung up after breakfast and carried us on a little, but the weather is still too fine and we are creeping along at the rate of a knot or two. —Slow work—

Attended prayers, then read one of Wardlaw's Sermons, an excellent [one] "on the practical influences of the Atonement." It gives one great subject for meditation. But a Ship is a bad place for either reading or meditating with attention, especially with a lot of <u>magpies</u> on board. We quite lose patience sometimes, they keep up such a <u>chattering</u>.

Another week has rolled over our heads since I wrote and that week has placed us in the Lat. of New York.

23ᵈ Winds still light and we are moving at only about 2 or 3 knots an hour. We were sitting in our Cabin wrapping our thoughts in our books this morning when the sound of a Ship in sight roused us from that to a very different course of proceeding. Thinking it might be an "American" as she was steering W. I sat down and wrote a letter if we should chance to speak her. She bore down to us and we soon discovered her to be a Spanish Man of War. She passed directly under our bows, but manifested not the least anxiety to know any thing about us, although she had made advances to speak us. Capt. E. hailed her and asked the usual questions. From the replies, we found she was from "Madeira" and on a mission, where or what we know not. She went her way and we ours. I could hardly fancy they descended from <u>Eve</u> like ourselves.

24 Weather still very fine and the only complaint is the weather is too fine, indeed if we were on land nothing could be more perfect—but we are all too anxious here to enjoy it. But all the passengers bear it exceedingly well. None growls so much as the Grandmama.
Capt. Fewson is giving me lessons in Chess and I get on very well. I admire it very much.

25 A fine morning. Had a shark along side, but he "was not to be caught with pork."

This evening we were all cheered and delighted with the appearance of clouds and squalls which burst upon us about dark, plenty of rain, wind and lightning. The Second brought a grateful Smile upon the countenances of all. We are now nearly in the Lat. of the "Western Islands" where we must expect squalls and gales perhaps.

26 35°45' The wind continued to blow through the night and we have now a good strong and steady breeze which will carry us in a short time beyond the Western Isles. Begin to find a great change in the temperature and it is so cold in the evenings that we have the Cuddy full, some reading and some playing. All look serene and contented—because *nous allons bien*.

27 38°15' A fine breeze from the S.E. All well. Have been reading today a history of the *Mutiny of the Bounty*,[54] very interesting, which took place many years ago. Still growing cold and being all summer birds on board, there is great shivering among us.

28 40°50' Still a fine breeze which rejoices the "cockles of our hearts." All we want is plenty of exercise to make us feel delightfully, for I really recognize my native air in these breezes, though I do not know you will account for it when I declare they are from the S.E. Never mind, they are just like them at any rate. Today we are in the Lat. of New York. Even that is pleasant to me. I only wish I could turn our Ships head and bring her up in New York Bay or harbour.

About 12 had a sail in sight. As we gained upon her (as we actually did) we found it to be a Brig bound the same way as ourselves. About 8 o'clock we came up with her and spoke her. She was from the W. Indies bound to Cork. Had considerable conversation and then wished her good night, and a pleasant passage and in a few moments she was far behind us. We shall now probably meet vessels every day. It is very pleasant I assure you. The *Hielands of Scotland* was the name of our friend.

29ᵗʰ 42°45' The Long. I have forgotten, but this I know, we shall not arrive this week yet unless this vessel moves a little faster. However we have still a S.E. wind and are obliged to be braced sharp up, and *par consequence* she does not sail so fast. A fine bracing wind that actually brings back the fading roses. Sunday again. Have attended prayers and read another of Dr. Wardlaw's Sermons on "The Divinity and personality of the Holy Spirit." I cannot say I feel any wiser than before. It is a doctrine that confuses and disturbs the mind and is not at all suited to settle and confirm us [deleted: for how can we have true faith in we know not what]. I get up from reading those sermons without feeling any wiser or any more settled—and often confuted without being convinced. I endeavour to determine whether it is from habit and education that I believe as I do, or whether it is from my understanding and my heart. My only desire is to know the truth.

Cloudy with rain at night. Reading in the Cuddy.

30ᵗʰ The last day of June. Fine strong breeze, only not quite fair for us. However we are getting on very well. Find it very cold. A full assembly in the Cuddy in the evening. The weather here seems more like Nov. than June.

1ˢᵗ **July** Fine wind still, overtook another Brig today. The *Penelope* of Glasgow from Trinidad, spoke her and soon left her behind. So we do sail faster than some things.

A most lovely evening and every prospect of being in in a few days, say 5 or 6, and all our passengers seem happy in the idea of setting foot on shore again.

2ᵈ **July** W. Long. 23°4' Lat. 47°4' As beautiful a day as ever shone, *parce que* the sun is shining, the wind strong and carrying us swiftly in. My heart is warm with gratitude to the giver of all these blessings, and my best wish is that all may be as bright at home. I have been reading this morning Edwards on Redemption,[55] an interesting work.

A large Whale has just passed our port.

July 3ᵈ 4 Ships in sight before breakfast, but soon shot by us. About 11 we spoke an English Ship bound to Quebec and soon after another Dutch vessel passed within hail, perhaps bound to New York, but she was not inclined to speak. We have had a dozen ships about us today, and have been quite amused by beating several them. It is very cheerful after a monotonous voyage of six weeks.

Played Chess with Mr. F[ewson] after dinner. Am very much interested in the game but do not like being <u>beaten</u>, as I most generally am.

July 4 And the 59th (I believe) of our Independence. We had lots of Ships in sight today and I believe one of our countrymen, but we were not near enough to speak. Fine weather yet, though the breeze is falling off a little. The "peace and prosperity of our country" with a pretty little speech from Captain Embleton, was proposed as a toast and drank in good fellowship by all after dinner. I cannot better express my feelings on the occasion than in a little piece of poetry I came across yesterday, a part of the piece addressed to the American Eagle by Mr. Thompson—

> My native land! My native land!
> To whom my thoughts will fondly turn;
> For her the warmest hopes expand,
> For her the heart with <u>fears</u> will yearn.
> Oh! May she keep her eye, like thee,
> Proud eagle of the rocky wild,
> Fix'd on the sun of liberty,
> By rank, by fortune unbeguiled;
> Remembering still the rugged road
> Our venerable fathers trod,
> When they through toil and danger pressed
> To gain their glorious bequest,
> And from each lip the caution fell,
> To those who followed, "Guard it well."

I think them particularly pretty and very applicable to the present time. I hope the spirit of our "Washington" is still alive, as well as all the noble spirits that lived in his time, for there are many that deserved to be immortalized.

July 5 Wind light today but we are getting on shall probably make the land tomorrow.

6th A fine breeze the latter part of the day but thick weather in the evening. Plenty of vessels about us. This evening a Ship passed us, bound to the Westward, which we fancy by the "cut of her jib" is the 1ˢᵗ of July packet. If it had been in the day time we might have determined.

7ᵗʰ A thick foggy morning. Notwithstanding a pilot boat came along side from Sylla and told us we were 27 miles from there. About 4 it cleared up, and Sylla Islands [Scilly Isles] were bearing N.W. half West. At the cry of "land ahead" we left the dinner table as soon as possible and soon discovered the coast of England, "Land's End." Much to our joy, the fog had entirely disappeared and we had a fine breeze which cheered us up at once. We had the *Duke of Argyle* ahead that left St. Helena the day we had. By the means of Mar[r]yats signals people can hold long conversations at the distance of 5 miles or more. They are quite delightful, but not generally in use with our countrymen. Suppose the bunting costs too much for "Jonathan,"⁵⁶ but it is very stupid to meet a <u>deaf</u> and <u>dumb</u> ship now a days.

When I went on deck heard a great noise, looked half way up the "<u>rattlins,</u>" and there was two jacks busy in tying the legs of one of the passengers, to these said rattlins. I found it was the first time he had been <u>aloft</u> and they immediately took advantage of his novel situation by practising the <u>permitted</u> joke upon him, <u>sanctioned</u> by old custom, to the great amusement of the party on the poop who all witnessed his struggles for liberty without assisting him. Made the "Lizards" before dark.

8ᵗʰ Wind quite fair today and running along finely. Had the coast of Devonshire on our lee, and about 10 o'clock three of our impatient gent passengers left the ship in pilot boat and made the shore thinking to land at Plymouth.

It looks good to see land again, though at a distance, and I would gladly land too. The land on this coast appears well cultivated, and I observe all the divisions of land are made by beautiful hedges, which have a far better appearance than our dreary <u>stone</u> <u>walls</u>. On enquiring I find it is the case <u>generally</u> throughout the Island. This coast it is said is rather barren, though a few miles inland it is the richest county in England and celebrated for pretty girls, the "<u>Devonshire</u> <u>lasses</u>." After leaving those passengers, we were obliged to change our course and with a fine fair wind and the most beautiful weather possible we steered for "Havre" where we land our passengers. Had the Island of Alderney in sight about 7. Shall reach tomorrow morning if the wind continues. It is now daylight at 10 o'clock, that is day light is still in the sky.

9th Was awoke this morning at 3 o'clock by the Capt. rousing his french passengers. I got up at 4 to see them off. We then had the coast of France in sight, and the Pilot boats all in readiness. The immense quantity of baggage delayed them a long time as there were 20 people in all to leave. They did not get away till half past 6. When we bid them all adieu, which is always painful, I felt it particularly in parting with the three sweet children. They made themselves beloved by all on board. We were saluted in French style by a kiss on each cheek. I was amused yesterday to see the young ladies and all offer their cheeks, with the most perfect nonchalance to a french gentleman who left. It is true he was a married man and an elderly one. I do not know whether it would have been the same with a young one or not, but however custom sanctions every thing. At eight o'clock we lost sight of the boat and our friends probably forever. I should like much to hear from some of them. We parted good friends with all, and could we have had a little more communion with them, think I should have become much attached to the young ladies. Fortunately, perhaps! We have now our head again turned towards England and shall tonight make the land again. Most lovely weather, we are particularly favoured. I am thankful I am sure. Had a beautiful run and made Beechy Head light at 9 o'clock, a revolving and very brilliant light.

10th Capt. E. called us early this morning as [we] were nearly abreast of Dover. Dressed and went on deck, realized the sight of "Dover's chalky cliffs" I have so often heard of, we were then abreast, distant 1 mile & 1/2. Took our pilot last night off "Dungeness"—beautiful breeze this morning and we run through the "Downs" finely, chasing the American Packet, *Montreal* of New York. A fine looking ship [in which they sailed a month later to New York].

I like the looks of Dover very well, an ancient castle crowns the summit of the cliffs at the right of the town (entering). It is said it was built by the Romans. It looks very grey but I should think must have been rebuilt since that time. There is a cave about midway, in the solid rock which is also mounted and must be quite inaccessible from the outside I should judge, the houses are all built of free stone and has rather a somber appearance. That part which fronts the sea is wholly occupied by boarding houses, large & lofty. On the beach were many bathing <u>carriages</u> which are run into the sea. Saw a good many places that pleased me much at Dover, we soon after passed "Deal" with which I was also pleased. Indeed my dear sister I fear I shall not have receptacles in my brain for all the fine things I shall be called upon to admire. I shall be obliged to entrust them to my memory instead of my book for it will take too much time and paper to note them all, and my memory is not a faithful friend. I give many things to its charge and when I demand them, they are either lost or so snugly stowed away that they are not to be found in proper time and place. My head I think resembles <u>chaos</u>. I would <u>somebody</u> would put it in order. Passed many splendid palaces along the coast of "Kent" and I have made the most of it. Passed "Margate" & "Ramsgate." All appear to be built of free stone, castles, fortresses, and lighthouses in their respective places, and bring all sorts of things to one's mind, of the bloody battles & etc., but in a word the scenery here is beautiful. Would you could look at it with me. For in enjoying a thing, I always want those I love with me to participate. Plenty of boats alongside and to make the water around us cheerful, the Ships and brigs and all sorts of vessels are flying about, (no doubt, for our express amusement.) As we got abreast of "Dover" this morning the "Steam boat" had just started for Calais. It is really beautiful to see them, they truly go "like a thing of life." Ayok was highly delighted and says, they say, "Suppose have got foul wind can walky." I replied yes, "suppose no got wind at all can walky" which seemed to heighten the pleasure & surprise. Have now turned the <u>corner</u> being noon and are steering west for the Channel. Our wind is no longer fair, and we are beating up. Have been making preparations for landing today. Think I had formed a very good idea of the appearance of England, I am not disappointed, nor had I exaggerated.

We were boarded this morning by a boatman with yesterday's paper. Says, "Sir, the <u>Vig</u> ministry is dissolved," the queen has gone to Germany. These people I find, (the boatman I mean,) all call for "Rum." Temperate societies do not flourish here I fancy. Heard nothing very interesting. We cannot catch "brother Jonathan" [a reference to the American packet *Montreal*]. The pilot says we sail well to keep up with her, as they are built for <u>sailing</u>.

11th Having a head wind and tide yesterday we and all our <u>companions</u> were obliged to anchor being among the shoals and quicksands. A lovely evening and a boat came off to us and brought <u>cherries</u> & all the tempting things from shore. Six years since I have eaten any. Assure you we did not grudge 4d. the pound.

We were obliged to remain quiet till 10 this morning, still a head wind and very little of it, but we have had plenty to do this morning in arranging our luggage, and preparing to land tomorrow. We have Essex on one side and Kent on the other, a most beautiful country. All <u>looks</u> peaceful and happy, but we cannot always judge from <u>appearances</u>. Though I certainly have seen no appearance of starvation in any of the boats, every one looks well and worthy of the title of John Bull. The <u>packet</u> is still by us, and a beautiful ship she is. A splendid steamer passed just now, full of passengers, and the band playing merrily on board—running easily over tide and <u>wind</u>, while we are tacking and toiling and shall shortly be obliged to anchor again. It calls forth a eulogy upon steam I assure you.

Anchored at 4 o'clock. With lovely weather, a beautiful moon and time enough for silent meditation, for every thing was quiet except now and then a schooner or smaller boat would pass us, one playing the flute, another beguiling the time by exercising his own vocal powers. I was walking by myself on the poop till near 10 or quite, when I went to bed. Oh that I was a poetess for rather than express my feelings in bad prose you will lose all my <u>musings</u> my dear which would no doubt be highly <u>edifying</u> and amusing at the same time, but alas, alas, nature as I have said before, was certainly going upon an economical plan when I was created both <u>physically</u> and <u>mentally</u>.

12th When we got up this morning found our friend the Packet had had the aid of a Steamer and was out of sight. We made sail about 10 and got under weigh, with hundreds of vessels of all descriptions and sizes, of all nations and from all nations. Such a busy scene I never saw before. We were in the narrow part of the river, land very near us so that we had a delightful view of the most charming country that ever was seen, most highly cultivated and is what I always imagined it, <u>beautiful</u> without being grand, hilly in some parts, but nothing approaching a mountain or a good sized hill, but the beautiful lawns the thick set hedges occasionally a venerable looking church "with its spire pointing to heaven." Indeed my dear Sister go to Washington Irving's *Sketch Book*[57] and find beautifully expressed what I would fain give you some idea of—suffice it that I was much pleased and it recalled all my fancies and they were embodied before me.

We were in a perfect Babel till about two o'clock nothing but tacking Ship, & etc. till we arrived at Gravesend where confusion was made still worse by the landing of live stock, the pigs were rebellious and the geese do [ditto]. Then all our steerage passengers went, and soon after a steamer took us in tow and we went on smoothly defying the wind. At about 5 we were at Blackwall and our trunks were looked into on board, but passed without trouble, and we congratulated ourselves, but when going on shore at Blackwall in full view of all the houses on shore our boat was stopped and another "Philistine" boarded us, demanded our keys and overhauled them; my blood boiled but we were obliged to submit, and bear it patiently, but I never felt so much annoyed. We got off very easily however, and landed in a few moments—called for a coach to proceed to Capt. Embleton's house, and were put into an "Omnibus" after some fighting between the coachys to know who should have us. Capt. E. was obliged to collar one man who was running off with my dressing box. I thought upon the whole we were in a sad place. In a few moments we were kindly recd. by Mrs. Embleton. They live away from the city at No. 5 Canton Place, East India Road. We received every attention from them, but she is in miserable health.

It was pleasant and yet painful to see the happy meeting between friends when there were none to welcome us, but our turn will come, and we have become accustomed to strangers now. We had a fine treat of strawberries, gooseberries, cherries, etc. tonight. Went to bed quite tired by our day's excitement.

Sunday 13th And very like a Sunday at home. No mails today no penny post, so that we could have no communication with Mr. Bates [Joshua Bates].[58] Did not go to church. Was writing to you in the morning. At noon Mrs. E's mother and sisters called from the country. I was delighted with them. One reminded me of S[ally] Orne. They invited us to go to their country house on Sunday which I hope we shall be able to do. They appear to be just the kind of people I like.

After dinner Mr. Ibar [Joaquin Ybar] our old China friend, and Mr. Iglesia called to see us. I was most happy to see the first I assure you. He told us much news, of marrying and giving in marriage. My

<u>friend</u> Vachell is married and gone to China. We spent the evening very pleasantly with our friends.

14th July This morning took a "<u>Fly</u>" and started for the city—the busy bustling city, the noise of which almost stunned me and the many fine things nearly dazzled me. We passed the great St. Paul's and heaven knows what else—carriages innumerable, and such quantities of those detestable "Omnibuses." I can't abide them. We drove first to the "Adelphi" and engaged lodgings at Wright's Hotel, No. 2 Adams St. where our dear Uncle wished us to go, and where he put up before. It is a nice house and a respectable landlady.

After we had engaged to come tomorrow morning we drove to the <u>Pantheon</u> a new Bazaar just opened;[59] to attempt to give you an idea of it would be great presumption. There was a little of every thing under heaven in the building.

But to begin at the beginning. In the entrance hall there is some splendid specimens of marble, highly polished and made into stands for busts, etc., statues and groups of figures, which are no doubt very fine, but though I <u>know</u> they pleased my eye, yet do not pretend to be a judge. We ascended the stairs and were surrounded with fine paintings—some of which were beautiful, there were many ancient paintings very valuable and from the best artists. I was particularly pleased with some by 'Taylor,'[60] his dead game are perfect, but I should give you little pleasure in enumerating them. The light is from above, the centre roof of the Bazaar is all of glass. From the painting room you enter the gallery where are all the stalls, fitted in the most tasteful manner, with every tempting thing. Really one might spend a fortune in a few minutes. A dangerous place for ladies who cannot resist temptation, but I flatter myself I can. I longed to seize many of the pretty things for my little friends in America, but I then thought of the trouble of transportation, etc. and deferred it at any rate. Went from the gallery to the "<u>eating</u> <u>stall</u>" below, eat <u>nine</u> <u>pence</u> worth which refreshed me much, walked around the lower hall and went into the "Conservatory" and aviary. In the centre there is a handsome *jet d'eau* the birds singing the gold fish playing below, the flowers blooming, and completed the beauty of the whole. This is all under a glass arched way. Nicely paved, we walked through this to a sort of pavilion nicely <u>couched</u>, <u>carpeted</u>, and <u>mirrored</u> for the use of ladies waiting for their carriages. Called ours and being quite fatigued we returned home, at 4 o'clock. Passed the celebrated "<u>Newgate</u>," [prison] a dismal looking place enough, one would think it would be a warning to all evil disposed persons.

At dinner had a note from Mr. Bates, and had the <u>pleasure</u> of hearing all our letters had been sent to the <u>Cape</u>. So it goes you see— I could have <u>cried</u>, but I thought it best to laugh!!

15th After breakfast put on our bonnets and walked to the W[est] I[ndies] Dock with Capt. E. (very near our house), and went to the baggage warehouse where we had our trunks examined. Went home had Tiffin and started for our lodgings. Was very sorry to leave Mrs. Embleton, she wished us to stay but her health is very miserable. They have been exceedingly kind and attentive to us. Indeed we should have been unpleasantly situated had we not have found such friends, for one is lost in such a place as London at first. I hope we shall see them in America one of these days and be able to repay their kindness. Arrived at our lodgings about 2. Arranged our affairs, and did not know what to do with ourselves, not a book had I, the tables chairs etc. would afford me no amusement, I was tired of seeking a familiar face among the myriads that were momentarily passing, in short we felt as desolate as possible. We at last determined to sally forth, and we sauntered through the Strand, passed Charing Cross, and found our way to St. James Park, I had studied the map before leaving the house. We should have enjoyed this much, but we took Ayok with us which made us so conspicuous that we were glad to return. The Park is a most delightful place, a beautiful Pond in the centre of it, the fine old trees and the pretty shrubbery surrounding it, the Palace of St. James on one side, and the venerable churches in the distance— altogether making a most lovely place, and perfectly picturesque. Again I sigh for the painter's or the poet's art to bring to you some of the fine things. Where the beauties of art and nature are so beautifully combined as here I am <u>charmed</u>. Here we are away from the noise of the world, yea, even in the <u>heart</u> of London. The birds were singing around us and it seemed quite like the country.

The weather is perfect. I had no idea we should have it here. It is not dark till after 9. We returned home and dined and after a little while sallied forth to a booksellers for we had nothing at all to read. Walked as far as Waterloo Bridge then having bought some books returned to those dear companions which cheer us in every situation. They are indeed the only antidote to the <u>blues</u>.

Soon after I got engaged with my books, a gentleman from Boston was announced, and who should it be but <u>Mr. Odin</u>, the gentleman who fell in love with Jane Steele in the coach and followed her to Salem. I did not remember him, but he told me where he had seen me before. How singular that we should meet here again. He advises our going to Liverpool to embark.

16 This morning sent our letter of introduction to Mr. Borradaile [Abraham Borradaile].[61] He and his wife called at noon, but we were out. Went shopping after breakfast, that finished we walked to "Somerset House" where we saw a vast collection of paintings and were very much delighted.[62] The house is immense. There was one room filled with statuary, looked very old and extremely dirty. I could not prevent a blush when I entered the room. For it seemed indelicate and hardly fit for a lady, however I thought it would never do to be so <u>unfashionably</u> delicate and I walked through with apparently great nonchalance, but I was very glad to make my exit. I am a novice at these things as yet, indeed I would not be quite dead to these feelings, but I saw some ladies sitting down and enjoying it. I must confess I <u>directed</u> my attention to the models of <u>buildings</u>, with a <u>sly</u> look at figures, but this was nothing to some of the public exhibitions.[63]

We stayed here till near 4 and could have spent days, it was highly gratifying. We dined and then walked to St. James' Park. A most delightful evening. The grounds were full of people though not the most fashionable, multitudes of children, amusing themselves in different ways. We took a chair at the side of the pond, for which a youngster demanded a <u>penny</u>. It is a lovely place, the towers of Westminster were in full view in front, raising their heads above the trees. That place we have all heard so much of and think of with a feeling of veneration. The associations we have with all these places give plenty of subjects for reflection. We have a great desire to visit it, but we have no one to call upon and we should hardly like to go alone. We sit there till near 8 and though the sun had not then set, we thought best to retrace our steps. We were both dreadfully tired. It seems to be all day here now, for daylight is not gone till long after 9, then there is a beautiful moon and the streets so well lighted that it is almost the same as the day.

17 A very hot day. But our friends Capt. & Mrs. E. called and wished us to go to the Zoological gardens, we got a carriage and went, but it was so hot there we could not enjoy it. It is a delightful place, a sort of menagerie, the gardens were scented and beautiful with flowers of all kinds, and laid out with great taste. From thence we went to the Colisseum.[64] In the first place we descended and passed through a gallery lighted with lamps and felt so delightfully cool that at the moment I felt that I could pass my life there. We entered a <u>statue</u> gallery next with a mellow light thrown in from we <u>knew</u> not where, but through tapestry which covered this semi-circular apartment in the most fanciful and elegant manner. All around this place in arches there were little marble tables placed, and delightful crimson spring seats, where we immediately seated ourselves and partook of ices and cakes and felt much refreshed, for we had been nearly <u>parched</u> in the gardens. Then we examined the busts and groups, some of them beautiful and very few that the <u>most</u> <u>modest</u> would blush at. We admired as long as our time would allow, we then went into a little octagon room of about 10 ft. in diameter and were wound up to the top of the building where we saw a Panorama of London. It is quite perfect. I began to doubt every thing around me, it looked so like nature, that I thought I might be deceived with regard to my standing ground. Ayok was quite <u>stabbergasted</u>, to use a most vulgar but expressive word. We descended again and went to the Conservatory filled with plants from all countries. You could fancy yourself any where. Then there were beautiful grottoes, *jet d'eaux* and indeed it was [so] enchanting, that we said what cannot art and man's device accomplish? I cannot describe half I saw for it appeared so magical that I could not comprehend it, the principles of the thing I could not understand, and had no one to explain to me. We entered a dark cave and you would have sworn you saw a Ship on the beach, another very near being wrecked, there was the noise of the surf and every thing imitated nature completely. This was a peep from some cave in Africa, I believe. There was the Stalactites perfectly formed, giving us a perfect idea of what we had often read. They had also here a fine collection of birds which added to the <u>harmony</u> of the place, I do not mean in the cave, outside. Then we went to the Swiss Cottage a sweet little place—then the African Glen, where we saw some beautiful scenery and a great variety of animals and birds stuffed. Drove home quite tired enough. All the gaiety and fashion of the place were out as we drove through Regent St. a most magnificent place. Had an old letter from Mrs. Colledge when I got home.

18th A rainy day. Was busy all day writing letters to China and the Cape. Considerable thunder in the afternoon. Mr. Borradaile called on us again.

July 19th Still rainy. Now I must leave my book for the present, I am going to gad and to see about going to Liverpool.

About 2 we started in a one horse "<u>fly</u>" for Bedford Square to Mr. Daniell's [William Daniell],[65] the Artist, where we saw the pictures of Mrs. and Mr. College and were very much pleased. It seemed like bringing them before us. Ayok burst into quite a hysterical laugh when he saw his father's face in the picture.[66] Mr. Daniell was out, but we saw his wife. We saw Mrs. Davis' picture too. They were all too late for the exhibition, unfortunately. Chinnery's paintings are liked much here, but they say his greatest fault is <u>deadness</u> of colouring. I noticed this myself the other day at "Somerset House."

We next drove to Mrs. Borradaile's to Fenchurch St., where we were introduced to her ladyship, a very pretty woman, very genteel and <u>prim</u> like Cousin S. Orne. House splendidly furnished, and like all English houses, exceedingly <u>comfortable</u>. I do admire their domestic arrangements very much.

Poor Ayok excites so much attention that I believe he will be very willing to doff his China Costume. Being rainy today he had on his great umbrella hat, and cut a curious figure to be sure to those who are not in the habit of seeing them.

We started for Mrs. Embleton's but found it very difficult to get on, being a rainy day there were millions of carriages. We arrived at last and as usual were kindly received by our friends. Dined with them and about 6 took a carriage and went to "Woodhouse" Eastham, Essex, the house of Mrs. E's mother, where we were invited to stay as long as we could. We arrived about 7 at one of the sweetest little places, a fine large house, handsomely furnished, quite <u>enveloped</u> in trees & shrubbery the gravelled walks and the smooth lawns, all so delightful, but it rained so hard we could not enjoy that much. However there were attractions inside which prevented our sighing for those without. In the first place Mrs. Moates, the Mamma, a very fine looking & extremely kind personage, who welcomed us as though we were old friends, making us quite at home at once, then come two unmarried daughters, very pleasing both, who seconded all their mother's endeavour to entertain us, then there are four Sons all at home to spend Sunday with their mamma, with Mr. & Mrs. Embleton & ourselves made quite a table full. Then comes the respectable look-ing footman with his <u>breeches</u> so <u>tight</u> and so <u>white</u>, and which seems to be a necessary appendage to such a place. There appeared to be every comfort and many luxuries in the house. We took tea, then adjourned to the drawing room (which is always up stairs in an English house, that being the <u>parlour</u> on the first floor) and heard the young ladies upon the Piano, played and sung most of the evening. Shewed us their paintings, etc., and what was more beau-tiful than all, Miss Sylvia the eldest, has made a Chess board, inlaid the black squares and painted flowers from nature upon them, and the white ones have each a little picture upon them <u>transferred</u>, the whole then varnished. Perhaps this is common in America, but I never have seen it before. There is a splendid wreath of flowers round the edge. It would have done any one credit. At 10 we had a little supper then prayers and retired for the night.

20th **Sunday** Still rainy, however we had a carriage that held six and the gents walked and we went to the little village church. Built in the year 1100, it has been lately repaired and looked in good order, though very ancient, as you know by the date. There were several ancient monuments of noble families who lie buried there, one particularly conspicuous behind the communion table, and some <u>rude</u> statuary, the whole family kneeling and praying before the tomb of their friend. We heard a very good sermon by the Vicar of the Parish, came home quite pleased. Cleared up at noon. Took a walk round the grounds, had a pull in a little boat in the fish pond, got some fine fruit in the gardens and seated ourselves in the garden house or summer house and had an interesting chat with the young ladies. Had some sacred music after dinner, and passed the evening very pleasantly.

21 Raining again, however I do not mind it in pleasant company. Played Chess with Miss Sylvia this morning, we play about alike.

Cleared up at noon, and we gathered some beautiful flowers and at five reluctantly bade them adieu, for they are just such people as I like and should like to live with. I shall not forget them. These dear little spots on Memory's waste and the remembrance of kindnesses received in strange lands <u>shall</u> 'brighten and brighten as time steals away.' For I will fondly cherish them that when in my power I may impart the same to others. There is nothing like <u>feeling</u> to know the value of these things. We spent this evening and night at Mrs. Embleton's.

22 This morning had all our baggage examined, and at 12 we took a carriage and first drove to St. Katherine's Dock to look at the *Montreal* and were very much pleased with her accommodations, and finding it will be an immense deal of trouble and expense to transport ourselves and luggage to Liverpool we at last determined to take a Cabin in this Ship the first of August. Once decided we all felt relieved of a heavy load, for it had caused us great anxiety before. The Ship is splendid in her accommodations, and having no "<u>Cockroches</u>" we shall feel quite happy.

From the Docks we rode to St. Paul's—that noble building that we have so often had exhibited to our 'mind's eye.' It is noble, grand, magnificent, stretch your imagination to its extent my dear and apply those words in all their power, and then you will fall short of the reality. We spent a long time there looking at the monuments and went as far into the dome as the whispering gallery, but Aunt L. was too much fatigued to go further, we were then about a third of the distance to the top. The whispering gallery is curious. We sat on the opposite side of the gallery to the man who whispered. Around it were hung the trophies of many victories— every thing looked smutty, dirty, and ancient. We descended again and waited till divine Service commenced at 3 o'clock, the sound of the organ reverberating through the arches was grand, and rolled forth such volumes of sound, that seemed as if it would bear you aloft upon it.

They are just now erecting a monument to the memory of Bishop Heber.[67]

We went from this place to the Soho Bazaar to make some purchases.[68] Then returned to our lodgings, found a number of cards left for us in our absence, Mr. Bates and Mr. [Rev. David] Abeel among the number, Mr. Odin, Capt. Champlain, etc. Being then after 5 we ordered dinner and were alone the rest of the evening.

23 A very pleasant morning and we sallied forth to the Strand to see what we could see, walked through the Louther Arcade,[69] made a few purchases, and returned. Soon after Mrs. Bates and Mr. Odin called, Capt. Embleton and after dinner Mr. Bates. Heard tonight that Mrs. Colledge has a son [born February 1, 1834], but not very well. Poor thing, I was afraid she might not get over her confinement well.

24 Finding it a beautiful day and being alone, we thought it proper to take a drive, accordingly jumped into a fly and drove to Westminster Abbey. A porter opened the door and said if we should like to go to the House of Lords we could, as it was then open. We gladly availed ourselves of it,—we entered through Westminster Hall (in Gothic style). There is nothing grand in the appearance of the House, and struck me as being very small. The King's throne is opposite the entrance door and fills the centre, & nearly one side of the hall. Directly in front is the Lord Chancellor's <u>Woolsack</u>, covered with crimson moreen I think as are all the other seats in the House. Each of the four corners were tied with <u>common rope</u>. Why or wherefore, I cannot say. At the side of this, or rather back of it, there were two others of the same dimensions and I should think might be yclept woolsacks as well as the other, they are the seats of the 12 judges. Had I have named them I should have called them all Ottomans, but the Lord Chancellor's has had his named for ages.

Then on each side the house there were the benches of the Lord Bishop & Archbishops. We passed from this to the King's robing room, covered with tapestry representing the battle at Bosworth field in the days of Queen <u>Bess</u>. After having had the honor of <u>speaking</u> in the House of Lords, we took our departure and went to the Abbey of Westminster. We entered at Poets' Corner where were monuments erected to the memory of those whose name, characters and writings are familiar to us. There lies Milton, Gray, Gay, Shakespeare and many, many others. We passed to the Chapel of Henry 7th, to the tombs of the Dukes of Buckingham, of Kings, Queens, which have lived, reigned, and departed, <u>where</u> who can say? But let me refer you to Washington Irving's *Sketch Book*, to his reflections in this place.[70] Be assured my dear, it is impossible to enter such without moralizing on the mutability of all things. It would take volumes to tell you the heaps of reflections that rush upon one in such an ancient and venerable building. We went to the Chapel of 'Edward the Confessor' who built this place. See *Sketchbook*. By his side is Henry the 3d in whose reign it was rebuilt. Here is also the immense tomb of Edward surnamed Longshanks, he was 6 ft. 4, I think. There is also the tombs of Elizabeth and her sister lying together and in the opposite Chapel Mary Queen of Scots, all with effigies lying in state upon their tombs. In another chapel there are wax figures of Elizabeth, William & Mary, Queen Anne, & many others, all in their own robes, in the fashion of the day the ornaments were imitations. They were all quite dusty and defaced by time. Queen Elizabeth struck my eyes the moment I got up the narrow staircase, an ugly looking, <u>rattish</u> sort of face, but very like the pictures we have seen of her, and seemed to display her character completely. Some one has seen fit to clean her face round the features, and has left the dust upon her forehead, making a circle of dirt round her features, which certainly does not add to her <u>beauty</u>. Next to her stands Nelson to the life I should think judging from pictures. Over it the words he used when he went to battle, "Victory or Westminster Abbey." He has had both; he fought bravely no doubt and was a gallant hero, but I cannot think of him with any pleasure for his private character is always before me. He has a monument erected in St. Paul's also. But two more and I think I am done, though I might fill sheets, but we have a book which will tell you all.

You will see in the *Sketch book* one mentioned, of a Mrs. Nightingale, which I think with W[ashington] I[rving] particularly horrid but is considered a masterpiece of sculpture. However we will allow that to be there, for after thinking of the horrors of the tomb which this brings so awfully to your mind, you have but to turn your back to that and behold one of the most beautiful, with one of the most pleasing ideas imaginable; the contrast is striking. There is a glimpse of heaven, an angel descending and taking a lady and bearing her to her departed husband to place her in the vacant seat at his side. Another angel above waiting with a crown of laurel, to put upon her head, it is I think the most pleasing of the whole, and pictures so beautifully the reunion of friends, the hopes which support us through this life and takes away the sting of death and the horrors of the tomb. We wandered about a long time and could have spent much more. Oh we went to the Chapel where the Kings and Queens are crowned and had the pleasure or <u>honor</u> of sitting in the Coronation Chairs,—old fashioned things and under the seat of the King's chair is an immense rock of granite brought from <u>Scone</u> where the Kings of Scotland used to be crowned. Our guide amused me very much, reciting what he had to say. I suppose he has said it so many times that he has it all at his finger's end, he went through it so rapidly that it was difficult to follow him. We left at 3 and drove to Hyde Park. The first thing that meets your eye on entering is an immense statue of [the] Duke of Wellington in Bronze. Quite <u>naked</u>, erected by the <u>ladies</u>. If it had been an equestrian statue I think it would have been more to the purpose, and done greater credit to the delicacy and good taste of the said females. Here we see the gaiety and fashion a most lovely place. Ladies & gents walking, <u>riding</u>, driving, sauntering, <u>flirting</u>, reading, musing, etc. We passed the Kensington Gardens where there were many carriages in waiting, the ladies had left them, and we could see the different groups among the trees. The Serpentine river runs through both and adds to the beauty of the whole. Here were children sailing their boats, and all seemed innocent & happy.

Had an invite to dine with Mrs. Borradaile again but declined. We came home from our drive very much pleased with what we had seen.

25th Mrs. and Miss Morrison [Eliza Morrison and her step-daughter Mary Rebecca][71] called to see us yesterday and told us much news with regard to our China friends. We were at home all day. Had a heavy thunderstorm tonight.

26th Felt "no how" this morning. Long to get away from this place. At 2 we started to go to Mrs. Bates but something prevented and we merely drove round Hyde Park and to the Pantheon to make some purchases and see the pictures. Some of them are beautiful. Came home, spent the evening in gazing at the multitude.

27th This morning at 9 went down to Mrs. Embleton's to go to Church with her. They have a fine organ and I find it is the Custom for the Charity children of the Parish to sing and make the responses, but they make too much noise and untill you become accustomed to it, it disturbs one very much. It was a very pretty sight to see them all dressed alike and ranged round the galleries, —the little girls wore black or dark blue dresses with white bonnets and mits, looked as neat as possible, the boys had brown linen frocks, looked neat, and behaved well. There were about 600 of them. When we went in, there were about 6 couples at the Altar being married. I thought from that and the number of publishments that there is not much regard paid to either Malthus or Chalmer's *Political Economy.*[72]

We heard a very good Sermon from the vicar of the Parish, a venerable old gentleman of <u>80</u>, the curate performed the first part of the service, reading prayers etc. in the most hurried & I thought irreverent manner. I did not like his appearance at all. In the Evening attended the Limehouse Church, and heard a most solemn and eloquent sermon from Rev^d. Mr. Williams—singing by the children, the same as this morning, their dress a little different, neat white Caps instead of bonnets. Behind the Altars of each of these Churches there are handsome painted windows with a figure of our Savior pointing to Heaven, very well done but savouring of Popery very much. This Church is very ancient. They have a perfect organ here and the Evening Hymn closed the Service, which was altogether very solemn and gratifying. Spent the night at Mrs. Embleton's.

28th We intended to have visited the Tower this morning but Capt. was too busy. Therefore we spent the day with his wife and at 7 jumped into an "Omnibus" to go home. These things are no doubt exceedingly convenient, and one is privileged to be sulky in them, which is agreeable. We arrived home safely after having taken up and dropped our passengers all along the roads.

29th At home all day 'tooing' about and making preparations for our departure. One more voyage and we are done for the present I hope, for it requires all one's energy to be moving about in this way. <u>N.B.</u> Never travel for pleasure without a gentleman at your <u>command</u>, for there is no pleasure [in] it. In our case it is misfortune, and sad it is. However I do not complain, we have too much to be thankful for. Our Capt. came to see us this evening. Says his Ship is quite full of freight & passengers.

30th Mrs. Embleton & Mrs. Moates called to see us this morning. After dinner we sallied forth to find Westminster Abbey, but we were so long getting there that it was near six the hour for it to be closed and we contented ourselves with admiring the outside, and then retraced our steps by St. James Park, a most lovely place, and went to the Adelphi terrace where there is a most delightful view of the river, the magnificent bridges, churches, St. Paul's, and a million other objects with the beautiful county of Kent *à la distance*. Returned home quite tired. Read this morning Sheridan Knowles' Play of *The Wife*.[73] Liked it much.

31st This morning took a carriage to pay our parting calls. Went first to the Jerusalem Coffee House and delivered some letters to the far-famed <u>Mr.</u> <u>Hardy's</u> care, went to the Watch maker's. Were much surprised to find our Coachman could not read even a <u>sign</u>. Who would have thought we should have found such an instance in London. I was quite astonished! It came on to rain violently, but we drove on and paid our visit to Mrs. E[mbleton] first, came back, drove to 30 Portland Place to Mrs. Bates, found her ladyship at home, spent an hour with her, then drove to the 'Panthenicon' a magnificent establishment.[74] The first is an arcade and shops on each side, the second floor a Bazaar, another room occupied wholly by China and India goods, a China man presides. The third floor contains furniture of all kinds and descriptions, another building on the opposite side containing pictures, paintings, Pianos and carriages of all descriptions. I suspect we saw the Lord Mayor's carriage here, a gaudy thing enough.

We left this and paid another visit to Westminster Abbey, where we remained till 6 and saw much more than before, as one part was closed being under repair. We left the guide and walked round by ourselves and stayed as long as we pleased at each. Went into the Cloisters dark gloomy places. Saw the Library door but we could not get admittance—being private property. Quite fatigued with our day's exertions we drove home and dined. Found Mr. Gregusson, of <u>Salt's</u> memory had been to see us [see entries for June 14 and 20, 1833, vol. 6].

August 1st Got up early and packed up our <u>duds</u> to send on board with Ayok, at 10 they started. And we go tomorrow to Portsmouth and that is all for the present my dear. Think I shall not edify you with any more of my long stories, my next will be *viva voce* I hope. Adieu.[75]

Volume IX

August 2–September 21, 1834

Homeward Bound

Left London August 2ᵈ for Portsmouth in a very nice Coach which holds four persons inside and loaded outside with all sorts of etceteras. We had two very pleasant ladies who were on their way to the Isle of Wight to rusticate for a time during the warm weather. The Steam boats are constantly plying between that and Portsmouth and are generally full. The Isle is called the garden of England and I should think from description and pictures, deserving of the title. The famous castle of Corysbrook where Charles the first was <u>checkmated</u> is an interesting ruin, and many delightful seats of English noblemen add to the beauties and combine all that is lovely in art and nature. We travelled through the most delightful country imaginable, and passed through the town of <u>Guildford</u> the only <u>large</u> town on our way. The scenery after passing that from the hill is very beautiful. You have every thing to make a perfect landscape; there was a romantic old ruin, a castle in the distance, a highly cultivated country, and in short was delighted and want to bring it all to America. I am charmed with England, but do not be jealous, I am ready to leave it, for the heart the heart is [word effaced—possibly American] still. Well, we drove on and so we [sentence unfinished].

We left our lodgings at 9 in the morning and arrived at the Fountain Hotel, Portsmouth about 6 in the evening, not having left the <u>Coach</u>. We changed horses 7 or 8 times with the greatest despatch and were never detained many minutes. For the noble horses were all harnessed and waiting for us, splendid animals; think we do not have such in America.

It was very hot and dusty and our wheels were troublesome on account of the friction. We were obliged to <u>quench</u> it. The roads are very fine and I do not wonder Englishmen complain in America when they make comparisons.

When we got to the Hotel and found ourselves all <u>alone</u> we began to be very miserable, feeling tired and solitary and wondered then what we came for. However we had some tea, went to bed and rose refreshed the next morning.

July [August] **3rd** Spent our day quietly and satisfactorily rather, being Sunday, the first quiet Sabbath for many months.

But an Inn is a disagreeable place at any time.

Monday 4th We were at home all the morning reading. I was finishing the Life of Legh Richmond,[1] a good and valuable man, pity there were not more such. After dinner we sallied forth and surveyed the place, it is strongly fortified <u>I</u> should say. It is surrounded by embankments or bastions or both (for I am quite out in these descriptions) and a moat below, running all round the city. A gravelled walk shaded by trees on the embankments makes it very pleasant, and on the sea side a cool and delightful evening walk. We have the beautiful Isle of Wight in full view and pleasure yachts and other vessels in abundance. There is nothing particularly novel or <u>lion like</u> in this place except the Docks and a <u>block</u> manufactory which is very famous, but as we had no one to wait upon us, of course we did not see them. Were quite satisfied with Portsmouth when we got back and sorry not to see our Ship in sight, but head winds prevail.

Tuesday 5th Got up very leisurely this morning but heard the summons before long that our Capt. was below. Said we must be ready at 10 to go on board. Ate our breakfast and met him at the boat. Were put on board a Cutter where were many of our passengers. Went on board the ship and had all the confusion attendant on such occasions. However we are so accustomed to this that we take it very cooly and astonish the rest of those who are inexperienced. Got our things all to rights and fully expected to be saluted with the usual feelings, but wonderful to relate I was quite well, went on deck, read papers, walked and felt as though I was on land. We have 15 ladies on board and confusion worse confounded no doubt. Everything seems nice and comfortable, <u>and</u> <u>no</u> <u>Cockroches</u>. Did not sleep much tonight.

6th Head wind this morning and a rough sea, but I am very well, while all around me, are ill. Indeed I never was in such a scene before, but I shall not be very particular in describing though it would be most amusing. Some are very, very ill and suffer much, others doubtful and all envious of me and two other young ladies who went on board at London.

Wind continued ahead and a most uncomfortable sea was pitching in from the westward which made it exceedingly disagreeable— no prospect of our getting out of the Channel. Our cabin and indeed the whole Ship is a perfect hospital.

The first thing we heard this morning was that a man in the steerage had cut his throat and thrown himself overboard in the night, judge of the feelings of all if you can, particularly those in the steerage. The weather is dark, rainy and dismal and all together we have an odd mixture of the comic & tragic. Some of the ladies are much alarmed tonight with the sea. We do not get on at all.

Tonight about 6 Miss M. one of our passengers, a young lady, was taken very ill, fainted, and remained so for a number of hours. Felt seriously the need of a physician and think it very wrong for these ships to be without one. It was difficult with the most powerful remedies to keep life in her. Was up with her all night, her head was in a dreadful state. I feared the dropsy.

7th Weather still bad. Miss M. remains very, <u>very</u> ill. Fortunately Aunt & I are both well enough to attend upon her for she has no friend on board. We were obliged to blister her, and at last bleed her, or rather Mr. Sutton [Amos Sutton][2] kindly did that, which at last relieved her but she was insensible all the morning and I thought she must have the dropsy or inflammation of the brain. We felt miserable enough I assure you for it is an awful responsibility. We feared doing any thing, and yet powerful medicines were necessary. The blister relieved her at night. We had a change of weather and wind for a while and our faces and hearts were brightened. I never was in such a scene before, hope in mercy we shall have a short passage.

9th Tolerably pleasant day and the invalids begin to turn out. An odd mixture we have enough it may with propriety be called a menagerie. To see the people perched about in their respective berths reminds me of the Zoological gardens.

A dead calm this day, not out of the Channel yet.

10th Revd Mr. Sutton gave us an excellent sermon on deck this morning. A very pleasant person, a missionary in India. This evening Mr. S. made an excellent prayer in our Cabin and proposed having it every evening, which would be very agreeable to part of us, but does not meet with the approbation of all, therefore we must give it up, being a public place.

Calm all day today. A general turn out of Invalids. I have certainly not laughed so much for the last year as I have the last week on board. I shall tell you many anecdotes if we ever meet, at present I see no prospect.

11th A little breeze this morning which I believe took us a few miles beyond Scilly. By night it strengthened to a small gale, so that we carried but very little sail, a monstrous and frightful sea was pitching us about tremendously. And all though it was very awful yet we could not help laughing, and I defy any one to help it in the scenes we had tonight. Many of our party wisely kept their births.

12th Wind increased. I am a day before my story. Wind commenced the night of the 11th and after breakfast this morning was sick for the first time. However was determined not to give up to it, therefore went on deck and even walked with Mr. Mein . . . the German. However was glad to return and planted myself with Miss M. in the gentlemen's cabin because the couches in our Cabin were all engaged. I took a book, but read very little having a raging headache. However ate my dinner at 4 and felt better. At tea time commenced the sport. It was almost impossible to keep our seats, the lurches of the ship were dreadful; one came and overthrew the crockery, over went plates, pitchers, cups, and saucers, and it was with great difficulty we saved ourselves. Mr. S[utton], who was sitting on the lee side, was deluged in milk. He looked so perfectly ridiculous, with the milk dripping from eyes, nose, and mouth, and his coat and all completely covered with it, that though we trembled at our danger yet we could not resist laughing. Another lurch, and over went another pitcher of milk and a lady had the contents who was lying on the floor faint, however it restored her so it was no matter. Altogether it was such a mixed scene that we knew not what to do, laugh or cry. In one place was heard vomiting, another fainting, another sighing, and another laughing. But the night was dreadful the sea tremendous. Some of us dared not undress. Miss M. and myself [word illegible] each other upon one corner of the Cabin and there were various groups in different places, but very little sleep. The sea came over us and we jumped about like a <u>bear</u>, but more anon.

13th Wind ceased this morning and left us in a few hours nearly becalmed, the motion not much better than before, for it takes a long time to smooth the water again. Our Invalid getting on pretty well, appetite returned, pretty generally restored before the 14th.

14th Was reading this morning Mrs. Trollope in Belgium, Germany etc.³ Was reading aloud to Miss M. & Miss [?]. Very entertaining. After dinner walked on deck, calm again. We have been all this time doing 4 days work. We are now only 14 1/2 degrees W[est]. Horrible.

Was amused tonight by one of our passengers telling me neither he nor his wife had ever seen the sea before. Could not imagine there were not fields and trees on our way. They are missionaries. Calm all night. Had a long argument in the Gents cabin tonight regarding slavery etc. Never get to bed before 12 at night and often later. We have several very pleasant passengers on board and many the reverse.

22^d Since my last date we have had very little besides head winds and calms, but much of the whole calms, till since last night we have had a good fair breeze.

28th Have now been out 24 days and we had only 30 hours of fair wind in the whole <u>time</u>. We are quite discouraged for we have all the disagreeables combined. Then the anxiety of getting home and not getting there quite unfits me for any thing. I certainly never read so little on board before. I cannot compose my mind to anything. The weather is very pleasant but we are not yet half way and although we have been going at 8 & 10 knots the best 3 days we have not made more than 1 degree.

Were yesterday running here in sight of the U. S. Packet, the 8th of August from Liverpool. At dark we had her astern very much to the delight of the Captain. Kept the U.S. in sight a day or two and in tacking lost her.

Saturday 30ᵗʰ Head wind again. Dreadful smell of Bilge water, disagreeable company on board who will raise breezes inside and never fair, (*à la mode*). Miss M. was found faint in her cabin tonight. We were afraid we were going to have a second edition, but she soon recovered.

Sunday 31 Rainy day. Had a very excellent sermon from Mr. Brooks in the cabin. We have been cheered with a fine 10 knot fair breeze since 12 o'clock, which has cheered us all, and we begin to make our calculations for going on shore. But I am too used to this fickle element to be very sanguine. We were all very much alarmed tonight at tea time by the alarm of Fire, one of the worst dangers on board ship, but it was a trifle and soon over.

Sept. 1ˢᵗ Our fair wind lasted till this morning when we had a most <u>magnificent</u> squall and, received as its legacy a head wind. We were all in the round house admiring the scene. The glass fell very much in the course of the day and after dinner we had another squall which ended in a severe gale. I never experienced any thing like it before. Every bit of sail was taken in but the foresail, and the noise of the whistling winds was tremendous. But I hope to <u>tell</u> you of the strange scenes, which will need no other tablet but my memory for they are deeply engraved. We were all alarmed in the night, we shipped such seas. Many of us did not venture into our births. The gale broke about 12, but the sea was worse afterwards.

2ᵈ We are all <u>worser</u> this morning, feeling as though we had been beaten. The sea is grand this morning. Kept up till 12 and then had a nice <u>snooze</u> till near 4 when I felt better, dined, had a walk on deck. Spent the evening in chatting with Mr. S[utton], Mr. O., Mrs. S. etc—the breakfast table was the place. The adventures of the night before were <u>marvellous</u> and <u>amusing</u>. I for one felt grateful that we had been preserved. Going on our course today.

3ᵈ A fine squall this morning. A ship in sight, glass falling, and a prospect of another gale. The weather changed and we had a calm instead.

Saturday 7ᵗʰ [6] Another week gone and we have not made much more in it than we did Sunday last. It is dreadfully tedious. We get on only by 1/2 a degree a day. Now we are in the banks of Newfoundland

and last night had a specimen of the fogs which are so celebrated together with a calm which does not conduce at all to our mirth. It seems as though I never should reach the desired spot, hope deferred truly makes the heart sick. We have such a strange medley of passengers on board that we shall not have many regrets at parting, though with Miss M. a sweet girl I shall hope to meet again.

I never heard the King's English so maltreated before. It affords me some fun. It is worth while for Englishmen to laugh at Americans. The H is totally dismissed where it is generally required and called into office where not necessary. They talk of "'orrible 'ot", leading ladies to the "Haltar", of "hanchoring". One says when he gets to New York he'll have a "Pat of Parter" [pint of porter]. That is Hampshire dialect. Indian Carn, farks [illegible words]

6th Sept. Morning calm, fair wind about 10, which increased before 12 to a violent gale. We went on deck at 10 or 1/2 to look at our Ship flying through the water. We were then sailing at the rate of 14 knots through a smooth sea. The sight was grand, but a cloud in the N West out of which proceeded vivid lightning added much to the brilliancy of the scene, yet predicted a head wind and we soon after left the deck and had one of the most awful nights I ever experienced. We were up till near 5, the wind blowing tremendously and a frightful sea. We felt our dependence on an Almighty power in such a time and have great reason to be thankful that we were preserved. The Captain says we were in great danger. I came very near a hurricane.

7th This morning (Sunday) is still very uncomfortable and had we not had the wind so much higher we should think this very dreadful. Still pitching in an awful manner—and what is worse, the wind is ahead again. We do have the luck, but we ought not to complain. We have made only one good day's work in the last week—every inch of water is fought for. We had a little push across the banks yesterday, but are now going back again, I believe. We were all tired enough today and had no sermon on account of that and the motion. Had prayers in the gentlemen's cabin this evening and all turned in early.

[8] **Monday** Head wind again. Had a specimen of foreign manners this morning. Got on very well, however. Surprised at nothing. Play Chess with Mr. O [Oppenheim] almost every evening.

Tuesday, 9ᵗʰ Had a little fair wind this morning, but only lasted a few hours. We only made one day's work last week—how tedious. My patience is almost exhausted, and wardrobe too, as is the case <u>generally</u> I am afraid. Squally night.

11 Sept. [10] **Wednesday** <u>Head</u> <u>wind</u>. Are now in 57 longitude, only 3 days run with a good wind, but alas, alas, the fates are against us. O dear. Finished a little piece of work yesterday therefore indulged myself today in lying in my birth and reading. Felt uncomfortable, so much wind and all ahead, pitching and wretched. Had a specimen of German imagination this morning. Oh, what a place a Ship is, but I shall leave my stories for propria person. On deck after dinner, but very unpleasant.

Calms and head winds till the morning of the 18ᵗʰ, when we were rejoiced by a fair breeze, but we rejoiced with trembling, for they are always fleeting. We feel anxious enough to get in, for every one or at least many of our passengers are at swords' points. I do not think there was ever such a *mélange* of people before.

18ᵗʰ Being charmed with a fair wind this morning we were <u>all</u> on deck, and by way of variety went with Mr. Oppenheim to visit the steerage. Enquired for their health and condition. Poor creatures we complain, but we might not when we consider how comfortable we are in comparison. There are 120 people huddled together, getting short of provisions, and quite comfortless.

19ᵗʰ Fair wind continued all day and night, but we hardly dare mention it. However we all have our <u>private</u> <u>opinions</u>, as well as public, and I for one was anticipating the pleasure of crossing Brooklyn ferry tomorrow night at 6 o'clock, which we might easily have done had the wind have lasted, but alas, we appear to be doomed to be tried to the extreme and the wind gradually died away. And we are becalmed now this morning of the 20ᵗʰ.

[20] Oh dear, I am almost sick with anxiety and hope deferred. The time since we heard from you seems so dreadfully long that the dread of what I may hear takes from the pleasure of arriving, and though I am wishing it were over yet I tremble too when I hear we are going on well. It is a strange feeling, and one not easily described. Went on deck after dinner and found ourselves becalmed in a thick fog— pleasant prospect. All our speculations as to arriving tomorrow at

an end, so you see hope protracted one moment and raised the next and vice versa varying with the wind. And to prove it before we left the deck, the wind increased and we fully expected to have land ahead and in sight by day light. We went to tea, the haze had vanished, the moon was just rising clear and beautiful from her watery bed, and all were again cheered. And my poor little heart was going pit a pat at the thought of once more meeting my dear mother father and all hands.

About 10 was playing chess, the reports from deck were wind dying away and just 90 miles from Sandy Hook—a few hours drive. The next sounds on retiring to our cabins was haul in the studding sails and brace the yards. There is the end of the ups and downs of this day. Say you my dear there is no variety in the life of a sailor? I sat up till after 12 and no change came for the better. The night was perfect save and except we were two points off our course.

21st Think you will begin to look anxiously for us now for we are a week or two over our time. The first question this morning was, any land in sight, and how's the wind. The responses were any thing but agreeable. No land, wind ahead and but just moving. Can't possibly get there today.

Got up and eat my breakfast as usual. Not so usual either for I breakfasted in the ladies' Cabin. Stoned some raisins with several other ladies, for plum pudding. Next time hope it will be for Thanksgiving at home. It reminded me of old times.

Went on deck, walked awhile, a Ship and Brig in sight. A most lovely morning it would have been to have gone in to the Bay. So bright and clear. Went on to the round house, wind light and ahead. Have no work to do, cannot read and the day has seemed as long as six when employed. I sit and muse and cannot fancy at all how I shall find you, but I endeavour to keep myself quiet trusting to that being who has been so merciful to us in all the perils by which we have been surrounded and not doubting that whatever he sees fit to do will be for our good, and feeling too that sufficient unto the day is the evil thereof. I cannot explain how I feel. It is a sort of all overness and yet it appears to me that I am going to a strange place as I have been to so many before —

Notes to Volume V

1. Philip Dumaresq (1804–61), who was educated at Gardiner, Maine, commanded a ship at the age of twenty-one, and for thirty years thereafter. On June 9, 1836, he married Margarita Deblois, and with his wife arrived at Macao in the *Levant* on the following October 20. He was captain of the ship *Luconia*, in which James P. Sturgis died at Anjer on his homeward voyage in August 1851. R. B. Forbes calls him "that prince of Cap[tain]s (*Reminiscences*, 152)." See Harriett's description of him, September 7, 1832.

2. Thomas Henry Lister, *Granby; a Novel* (London: H. Colburn, 1826).

3. Josiah Orne Low (1821–95), younger brother of Harriett. Upon Abbot Low's return from China in 1840, Josiah became his partner in the new firm of A.A. Low & Brothers, which built ships for the China trade. In 1845, he married Martha E. Mills.

4. A Catholic procession, usually held on August 15, commemorating the assumption of the Virgin Mary into heaven.

5. James Fenimore Cooper sets *The Bravo* (1831) in the sixteenth-century Venetian republic. The "hero," a hired assassin for the Doge, finally turns on his employer and goes to his death rather than murder a nobleman whom he had come to admire.

6. No rice is used in making this paper; it is the pith of a plant, *Tetrapanax papyriferum*. The "rice paper pictures," so common at this time, were called by the Chinese *t'ung-chih hua* (pictures made of the *t'ung* plant).

7. Abiel Holmes, *The Annals of America, from the Discovery by Columbus in the Year 1492, to the Year 1826*, 2d ed. (Cambridge: Hilliard and Brown, 1826).

8. Sir Walter Scott, *Count Robert of Paris* (Boston: Bazin and Ellsworth, 1831). Scott followed closely the story of the first Crusade in 1096, in which Alexius, emperor of the Byzantine empire, called on European knights, led by Godfrey of Bouillon, to free the Holy Land from the Arabs, who were also threatening Byzantium. The story of the kidnaping of the Count of Paris, one of the leaders of the Crusade, is characterized by turgid prose which does not improve until the Count of Paris appears 123 pages later. There is much emphasis on the code of chivalry but little action to leaven the stilted language.

9. Frances Trollope, *Domestic Manners of the Americans* (London: Whittaker, Treacher and Co., 1832).

10. Probably the review of *Domestic Manners* which appeared in the *Quarterly Review* 47 (March, 1832):39–80. The reviewer writes at length

about the geographical, social, and political differences between England and the United States in order to point out cleverly the superiority of the old country. He uses examples of Mrs. Trollope's most satiric comments to prove that while she "carried with her to the New World the most exaggerated notions of liberalism," she "seems to have returned, if possible, a stouter enemy of all such notions. . . ."

11. Godfrey Thomas Vigne, *Six Months in America* (London: Whittaker, Treacher and Co., 1832).

12. While Harriett was musing over the "inconsistences of men," John Murray Forbes was busy writing Augustine Heard, William H. Low's partner, about Harriett Low and Caroline Shillaber. His initial impression of Caroline Shillaber as "exceedingly pretty and agreeable" changed when he next saw her in daylight. "By day light she looks <u>haggard</u> and old - her Hair and eyes are very beautifull and her figure is good - but she has not been enough in Ladies society to be exactly 'the thing' - she is too independent - perhaps from having been a great deal about the world - she is clever & can be very agreeable -" For a "rib" [wife] Forbes would much prefer Miss Low though he was not tempted. He confirms that James P. Sturgis [Uncle Jem] was smitten with Harriett and would probably propose if he thought she would accept. "She pretends to certain romantic notions about "Love" etc - which would I fear prevent her acording -" He cautions Heard not to mention his "fault finding" to Low since it might "come to the Ladies' ears" (John Murray Forbes to Augustine Heard, August 18, 21, 24, 30; September 10, 1832, BM-8-1, Heard Family Business Records, Baker Library, Harvard Business School, Boston, Mass.).

13. An anchorage, known to the Chinese as *Chin-hsing men* (in Cantonese, Kumsing moon). The characters mean Gold Star Gate. The place is twelve miles north of Macao.

14. *The Canton Register* (3 September 1832) quotes Capt. R. Wallace's log, stating that the *Sylph* left Calcutta August 13 at 6 am and reached Macao Roads August 31 at 11:30 pm—or seventeen days and seventeen hours. She sailed from Calcutta to Singapore in nine days and twenty hours; and from Singapore to Macao, in seven days and twenty-one hours.

15. Frances Wright (1795–1852), a Scottish reformer who tried out her ideas in utopian settlements in Tennessee and Indiana, was one of the first advocates of woman's suffrage. She was considered a scandalous figure on the basis of her public lectures, her open friendship with the Marquis de Lafayette and French liberals, and her advocacy of marriage based solely upon affection rather than religious or state ceremony.

16. Harriett had met the German missionary Rev. Charles Gutzlaff, whose wife and two children had recently died in Bangkok, on an excursion to the Lappa on December 16, 1831. Two days later she heard him preach in Macao and, in a letter to her brother Abbot written later that day, praised his zeal for bringing the word of God to the heathen Chinese, his ability to speak twelve languages, and his agreeable company. While on Lappa they talked at length and Gutzlaff proposed that Harriett write "a

little history of myself and compare it with the degraded state of the thousands of poor degraded beings in this vast Empire." He would then translate it into Chinese and distribute it as one of his tracts. Telling Abbot not to laugh at the idea for Gutzlaff was really serious, Harriett related that he excited so much pity by his tales of "cruelty and uncivilization among my fellow beings" that for a moment she almost agreed. "But alas, I told him that I was too feeble a creature, and incapable even of writing anything." Their conversation ended on Gutzlaff's: "But try," as the handsome Lt. George F. Dashwood joined them (Loines, *The China Post-bag*, 48). Harriett's "*recherché* admirer" may have had more in mind than religion since he married three English wives in rapid succession.

17. "Parson Dana" was Rev. Samuel Dana (1778–1864), who graduated from Harvard in 1796, was ordained in 1801, and was pastor of Old North First Congregational Church, Marblehead, for more than thirty-five years. It seems likely that the son mentioned here was Samuel Turner, who was born in 1810 and was later a "merchant in Boston." The other sons were Joseph William (baptized 1804) and Richard Perkins (a twin brother of Samuel).

18. Sarah Procter Shillaber (1758–1832), widow of Capt. Benjamin Shillaber (d.August 16, 1823) and mother of Caroline Shillaber, died on April 22, 1832 (Danvers *Vital Records* 1:288; 2:456).

19. Charles Sidney Bradford (1804–93) was a younger brother of Dr. James H. Bradford. He graduated from the University of Pennsylvania in 1822, studied law, and practiced in Pittsburgh. He resided for some years in Paris where he married in 1850 Helen Mary Fisher (1818–63).

20. William Paley, *Natural Theology, or Evidences of the Existence and Attributes of the Deity, Collected from the Appearances of Nature* (London: Richardson, 1821).

21. James Warner Sever (1797–1871), also spelled Seaver, entered Dummer Academy in 1811 and graduated from Harvard in 1817. He studied law in Worcester, but in 1820 entered the employ of Thomas Perkins of Boston. He made trips to China until 1835—his ship *Alert* being later immortalized in R. H. Dana's *Two Years Before the Mast* (1840). In 1836 he married Elizabeth Parsons of Boston. In 1866 he was elected president of the General Society of the Cincinnati (*The Seaver Family, A Genealogy of Robert Seaver of Roxbury*, 23–25).

22. James Kirke Paulding, *The Dutchman's Fireside. A Tale* (London: H. Colburn and R. Bentley, 1831).

23. Rev. Charles Wimberley arrived with his wife in the American ship *Israel*, on September 5, to serve as the Company's chaplain for two years (salary £800), during the absence of Rev. Vachell, who left for England October 25 in HCS *Canning*. The *East India Register and Directory* lists Wimberley as chaplain at Dinapore in 1836.

24. A. J. Donnelly and Mrs. Donnelly arrived in HCS *Asia* September 3; and a Mr. and Mrs. Donnelly sailed in the *Jamesina* (bound for Calcutta) March 16, 1833. See entry for October 25.

25. Ana Rita de Paiva (b. 1804) married Bernardino da Costa Martins on this day in the Church of St. Lawrence (*Galeria de Macaenses Illustres do Seculo XIX*, 131). His ship, the *Camoens*, arrived at Macao from Bombay on July 27.

26. George H. Williams was clerk to Capt. Lyman Hunt of the *Neponset*. He was sent out—on this his first trip—to transact business at Canton for the firm of Richardson and Whitney of Boston. A George H. Williams is listed in *Salem Vital Records* (4: 474) as having declared his intention of marrying, on July 4, 1835, Julia A. Deland.

27. Catherine Maria Sedgwick, *Clarence; or, A Tale of Our Own Times* (Philadelphia: Carey and Lea, 1830); Thomas De Quincey, *Confessions of an English Opium-eater* (London: Taylor and Hessey, 1822).

28. James Beattie, *An Essay on the Nature and Immutability of Truth, in Opposition to Sophistry and Scepticism* (Edinburgh: A. Kincaid and J. Bell, 1770).

29. W. Massie, *Alice Paulet: A Sequel to Sydenham, or Memoirs of a Man of the World* (London: H. Colburn and R. Bentley, 1831).

30. Benoni Lockwood (1805–51) of Pawtuxent, R.I., was master of the ship *Panther* which arrived on September 16. In 1830 he married Amelia Cooley at Providence. He sailed first for the Carringtons of Providence and later for William Platt and Sons of Philadelphia (*Lockwood Genealogy* [1889], 524).

31. Captain and Mrs. Underwood arrived September 16 in HCS *London*. Mrs. Underwood was a talented musician whom George Chinnery painted while she played her harp. For a description of this portrait see entry for December 1, 1832.

32. Washington Irving, *The Alhambra: A Series of Tales and Sketches of the Moors and Spaniards* (Philadelphia: Carey and Lea, 1832).

33. George Barrell Cheever, *The American Common-place Book of Poetry, with Occasional Notes* (Boston: Carter, Hendee and Babcock, 1831).

34. George Gordon Byron, *The Byron Gallery: A Series of Historical Embellishments to Illustrate the Poetical Works of Lord Byron* (London: Smith, Elder, 1832). This book was advertised for sale at Markwick & Lane's for $1.75 (*Canton Register*, 20 December 1832).

35. While imprisoned in Les Carmes during the Reign of Terror in 1794 because she was the wife of Vicomte Alexandre de Beauharnais (now judged an enemy of the Revolution), Josephine recounted to her fellow prisoners the prediction of an old black soothsayer on her native island of Martinique that her husband would die a violent death and she would be "even greater than a queen." Her husband was sent to the guillotine on July 22, 1794, five days before the end of the Reign of Terror, and Josephine lived to be crowned Empress of France by her second husband Napoleon Bonaparte on December 2, 1804 (Evangeline Bruce, *Napoleon and Josephine: The Improbable Marriage* [New York: Scribner, 1995], 61–62; *The Court and Camp of Bonaparte* [New York: Harper and Brothers, 1831], 112).

36. Harriett's secret engagement to William W. Wood had been revealed to her uncle and aunt. From this time forward, William H. Low and his wife

Abigail exerted pressure on Harriett to break the engagement. Harriett's daughter Katharine Hillard summed up the family opinion of Wood: "The Mr. Wood so often referred to as so clever and so charming must be the person whose addresses were not received favorably by the wise uncle, who knew him to be a man of irascible temper, little steadiness of character, and with neither fortune nor prospects, with nothing, in fact, but his brilliant talents to recommend him. Miss Low fully acquiesced in the wisdom of her uncle's decision later on, though it was hard to bear at the time. We can realize, however, that the blow was not altogether a crushing one, when we find her on the evening after this most melancholy morning amusing herself with the incipient mustache of one of their visitors" (My Mother's Journal, 162).

37. Mrs. G. Luke and Edward Luke Esq. arrived in HCS Marquis Camden on October 18, and sailed from Macao in the same ship January 24, 1833 (Canton Register, 3 November 1832; 16 February, 1833).

38. This island in the mouth of the Pearl River, eighteen miles from Macao, is called by the Chinese Ling-ting "lone nail" because of its pointed summit. It was the anchorage for opium store ships, or for other vessels whose destination was Whampoa farther up the river. It was a place from which ships engaged in the illicit opium trade could go to sea at short notice.

39. A ship of 564 tons register, launched at Philadelphia early in 1832, and named by the owner, D. W. C. Olyphant, after Dr. Robert Morrison.

40. The Lintin (390 tons), built for Robert B. Forbes in 1830, arrived at Canton on November 17 of that year to be a "receiving ship" in the opium trade at the island of Lintin. Forbes had command of her until the spring of 1832, after which she was owned in part by Russell and Company and commanded by F. W. Macondray.

41. William McKay was in charge of William Jardine's opium ship, John Biggar, stationed at Lintin. He signed as McKay to resolutions that appeared in the Canton Register in January,1831, and February, 1832, though the spelling Mackay had current use. He is probably the Captain McKay of the brig Fairy who, together with many of the crew, was murdered by pirates in the summer of 1836. On August 2, 1837, a year after the tragedy, fifteen members of the crew reached Canton.

42. Probably Capt. Williams Howland, a native of Bedford, Mass., who was born in 1804. He began seafaring early in life. According to Franklin Howland's genealogy of the family, he married, first Mary R. Wood (1832), and in 1849 Sarah Philips Nitchie. After 1854 he was a merchant in New York City, living in Brooklyn. His remains were interred at New Bedford.

43. Frederick Marryat, Newton Foster; or, The Merchant Service (London: J. Cochrane, 1832).

44. George Sturgis (1817–57) was the ninth child of Nathaniel Russell Sturgis and Susan Parkman Sturgis. The American ship Lyon (Captain Rich) in which he came from Boston reached Macao on November 5. He was connected with his brother's firm in Manila—Russell & Sturgis—a firm established July 1, 1828. On April 22, 1849, he married in Manila Josefina Borras (1828–1912), and had three sons and two daughters. After his decease, his

wife married Don Agustin Ruis de Santayana, and in 1864 gave birth to the well-known Harvard teacher and philosopher, George Santayana.

45. Letitia Elizabeth Landon, *Romance and Reality* (London: H. Colburn, 1831).

46. David Geisinger (1790–1860), a native of Maryland, entered the Navy in 1809, was commissioned master commandant in 1829, and captain in 1838. The USS *Peacock*, carrying twenty-four guns, was a new ship built in New York in 1828 to replace its aging namesake, a survivor of the War of 1812.

47. Edmund Roberts (1784–1836), a merchant from Portsmouth, N.H. who had lobbied intensely the U. S. government to expand American trade in the East, was appointed on January 26, 1832, special agent of the United States to negotiate treaties with Cochin China, Siam and Oman. In his book *Embassy to the Eastern Courts of Cochin-China, Siam, and Muscat During the Years 1832-3-4* [(New York: Harper and Brothers, 1837), 67] Roberts described his walk on shore a bit differently: "The next afternoon we landed on Linting, with a small party, at a miserable filthy village. . . . When we entered the village, (containing about twenty or thirty huts,) every man, woman, and child, turned out to see the barbarian ladies and gentlemen. A more ragged, filthy assemblage was, perhaps, never before seen. We hurried through, obliging them not to press too closely upon us, fearful some of their old acquaintance, apparently the rightful inheritors of their persons, might, contrary to our wishes, transfer themselves to us."

48. Robert B. Cunningham, a native of Ireland, became a citizen of Maryland, entered the U.S. Navy in 1814, and was commissioned lieutenant in 1825.

49. Lt. Cunningham was repeating the accepted medical view of the day that the principal cause of cholera lay in the atmosphere—the miasmatic theory of disease—which he had heard from Dr. Benajah Ticknor, the naval surgeon on the *Peacock* (Hodges, *The Voyage of the Peacock*, 138–46).

50. Another account of the visit of the officers of the USS *Peacock* to the *Lintin* that evening can be found in the journal of Dr. Benajah Ticknor, a serious and sober surgeon. While he did not dance and probably disapproved, he enjoyed Miss Low's company and gained from her a first-hand description of her secret trip to Canton in 1830 (Hodges, *The Voyage of the Peacock*, 153–55).

51. Benajah Ticknor (1788–1858), a native of Jericho, Vt., entered in the Navy in 1815 as surgeon's mate, but was not called to serve until 1818, rising to surgeon in 1824 and fleet surgeon in 1837. He received an honorary M.D. degree from Yale in 1836, and graduated from Berkshire Medical Institute in 1838. His career in the Navy continued until his retirement to his farm in Ann Arbor, Michigan in 1854. Among his many naval voyages meticulously recorded in a series of journals was the first U.S. diplomatic mission to Southeast Asia and the Arabian peninsula on the USS *Peacock*, 1832–34. For another account of the picnic on Lintin peak in Ticknor's journal, see Hodges, *The Voyage of the Peacock*, 158–59.

52. *The Court and Camp of Buonaparte*, vols. 1 and 2 in *The Family Library* (London: John Murray, 1831).

53. *Court and Camp of Bonaparte*, 321–49.

54. Charles Edward Grey (1785–1865) was educated at University College, Oxford, and was a fellow of Oriel College. He was knighted in 1820; made judge of the Supreme Court Madras, 1820; chief justice of Bengal, 1825–32; commissioner to Canada 1835–36; M. P. for Tynemouth, 1838–41; governor of Barbados, 1841–46; governor of Jamaica, 1847–53 (*DNB* 8:623).

55. Capt. Thomas Larkins of HCS *Marquis Camden* from Bombay. He was master of this ship as early as 1822 (see Robert Morrison's *Life* by his wife, Appendix, 25). W. C. Hunter describes him as "a well-known and general favorite in the community" (*Fan Kwae*, 75).

56. William Russell, *The History of Modern Europe* (London: G. G. J. and J. Robinson, 1789).

57. Miss Jones, *The False Step . . . and The Sisters* (London: Edward Bull, 1832).

58. Oliver Goldsmith, *An History of the Earth, and Animated Nature* (London: J. Nourse, 1774).

59. Joseph Tuckerman Jr. (1811–98), son of the Unitarian clergyman, Joseph Tuckerman (1778–1840) of Boston. He made several voyages to China over a period of five years—this time in the *Cowper* (Captain Bartlett) of Russell and Company. In 1845 he and his brother Lucius began an iron business in which both prospered. About 1865 he retired from business and lived sometime in Paris (Bayard Tuckerman, *Notes on the Tuckerman Family of Massachusetts and Some Allied Families* [Boston, 1914]).

60. Abel Sampson, called Dominie Sampson, was a comic character of a failed clergyman who served as tutor to young Harry Bertram and confidant to his father, the laird Godfrey Bertram. When Harry was kidnaped at age five while in Dominie Sampson's charge (fulfilling a prophesy of harm on his fifth birthday made at his birth by the astrologer Guy Mannering), the distraught Dominie transferred his affection and allegiance to Harry's infant sister Lucy. He refused to leave her side for the next seventeen years until she was reunited with her brother, known as Vanbeest Brown, after many adventures leading to the solution of his kidnaping.

61. John Shillaber, U.S. consul in Batavia since 1825, while on leave in New York in 1829 wrote to Secretary of State Martin Van Buren to request that he be allowed to continue as consul. He also suggested that an American naval vessel be sent out to Southeast Asia to visit Cochin China and Siam with the intention of negotiating a commercial treaty. Just before leaving the U.S. in late 1830, Shillaber wrote to Van Buren once again proposing commercial treaties and himself as the negotiator since in his nine years in Java he had acquired "some knowledge of the languages, many peculiarities & commerce of these people." Van Buren instructed him to send a formal communication to the Department of State describing the advantages of commercial treaties. Shillaber complied with this request and wrote at length on the government of Siam, stressing the necessity of un-

derstanding their customs and providing appropriate gifts. His list of suggested gifts of rifles, looking glasses, cut glass, and watches was followed almost to the letter by the State Department, but the agent chosen to negotiate the treaties was Edmund Roberts (John Shillaber to Martin Van Buren, 21 October 1829; 10 December 1830; 30 May 1831, Department of State, Despatches from U.S. Consuls in Batavia, Netherlands East Indies 1818–1906, MC 449, Roll 1, National Archives, Washington, D.C.).

62. "The unceasing prosing" of Jonathan Oldbuck, the Antiquary of Monkbarns, was the complaint of family and friends in Sir Walter Scott's witty examination of a north-country squire who shunned the practice of law and forswore marriage for a life of research and arguing obscure points of ancient history. Around this humorous character, Scott wove a tale of solving the mystery behind the supposed illegitimacy of the hero, Mr. Lovel, so that he would be a worthy suitor of the beautiful Isabella Wardour (*The Antiquary* [1816; reprint, Edinburgh: B & W Publishing, 1995], 168–70).

63. Diana Vernon, the heroine of *Rob Roy*, was characterized by Sir Walter Scott as "a mixture of untaught simplicity, as well as native shrewdness and haughty boldness in her manner" (Signet Classic ed. [1995], 50). Harriett compared this free-spirited young woman of eighteen (initially described as an orphan), who rode like the wind and relished a romp more than the polished graces of society, to Caroline Shillaber, who unlike Harriett, could still choose her destiny.

64. The day was the anniversary of the hanging in 1830 of Joseph J. Knapp, Jr., Abigail Low's brother, for the murder of Joseph White of Salem.

65. M. Burroughs, who arrived December 10 in the American brig *Caroline*. He seems to have been a naturalist and taxidermist.

66. Maria Edgeworth, *The Modern Griselda. A Tale* (George Town: Joseph Milligan, 1810); *Leonora* (London-New York: I. Riley and Co., 1806).

67. John Fisk Allen (1807–76), a native of Salem, entered the employ, as a supercargo, of Pickering Dodge (1778–1833), who owned many East-India-going vessels, including the *Mandarin*. In 1833 Allen married Lucy Dodge (1810–40), the daughter of Pickering. After her decease he married Mary Hodges Cleveland (1817–73). He wrote on horticultural subjects. A miniature portrait of him is in the Peabody Museum, Salem.

68. Joseph Coolidge Jr. (1798–1879), a native of Boston, received his A.B. degree at Harvard in 1817, and his M.A. in 1820. He traveled in Italy and there made the acquaintance of Lord Byron. On May 27, 1825, he married at Monticello, Eleanora Wayles Randolph (1796–1876), a granddaughter of Thomas Jefferson, who was then still living. They had six children. He entered Russell and Company, first as a clerk, but was admitted as a partner in 1834. Many who knew him remarked on his cultivation and on his "remarkable conversational powers." He seems to have left China in 1844.

69. The brother was Charles Blight (d. 1864 in his 70th year), who married Julia Fulton (1810–48), daughter of Robert Fulton, the inventor. Charles Blight was associated in Canton with Thomas Dent and Company,

but his interest with that firm ceased on June 30, 1827. He left China permanently, and with ample means, the following February 3.

70. Maria Edgeworth, *Patronage* (London: Printed for J. Jonson and Co., 1814).

71. Thomas Henry Lister, *Arlington* (London: H. Colburn and R. Bentley, 1832).

72. Battledore and Shuttlecock was a children's game played with a bat of wood strung with catgut (battledore) and a shuttlecock made of feathers stuck into a ball of cork. The object of the game was to hit the shuttlecock and keep it up in the air for as long as possible. The game was traditionally played on Shrove Tuesday.

73. Writing in the *Chinese Courier* (24 November 1831) under the pen name Hesperus, William W. Wood explained in "A Defense of Bachelors" why bachelors never marry: "There are men who pretend to despise women *in toto*, and for themselves; they hate the sex as Frederick the Great did black beetles; they profess no specific dislike, but hate all indiscriminately. These prejudices are doubtless induced by the operation of *jilting*, one which is no doubt very agreeable to the fair renegade, but has the same effect upon a lover's temper as thunder upon small beer. Could we but accompany these misogynists in their dreams, follow them in the retrospections of their memories, we should find a cause,—this cause,—none other." A prophesy for his future perhaps.

74. [Herman, L. H., Puckler-Muskau] *Tour in England, Ireland, and France in the Years 1828 and 1829 . . . By a German Prince* (London, 1831).

75. Probably Eliza Bartlett Sprague (baptized 1810) of Salem, who married Maltby Strong of Rochester, New York, on September 9, 1835 (*Salem Vital Records*).

76. Samuel Johnson viewed with contempt the idea that the weather influenced man's mental state: "Surely, nothing is more reproachful to a being endowed with reason, than to resign its powers to the influence of the air, and live in dependence on the weather and the wind for the only blessings which nature has put into our power, tranquillity and benevolence" (*The Idler*, no. 11 [London, 1761], 62-24).

77. The reference is to Captain Garstin of the Bengal Engineers. He sailed back to India on April 10 in the *Falcon* (Captain Ovenstone).

78. On February 3, 1833, John R. Latimer wrote to Hormuzjee Dorabjee in Bombay: "I am just going to Macao to pass the China new year holidays where I have not been for nearly three years" (Letter Book, vol. 3, Latimer Papers, LC).

79. William Godwin, *St. Leon: a Tale of the Sixteenth Century* (London: G.G. and J. Robinson, 1799).

80. Napoleon Francis Joseph Charles, Duke of Reichstadt (1811–32) was the son of Emperor Napoleon and his second wife Marie Louise of Austria. His early death from tuberculosis removed the possibility of any Bonapartists in France being able to support a Napoleonic revival after the revolutionary upheaval of 1830 (*Encyclopaedia Britannica* 19:77).

81. *Cha* denotes tea in both the Cantonese and the Peking pronunciations. Our English word tea derives from the Amoy and Swatow pronunciation *tay*. *Bebe cha* means to drink tea.

82. A variation on the quotation: "From envy, hatred, and malice, and all uncharitableness, Good Lord, deliver us." *Book of Common Prayer. The Litany.*

83. J. Labouchère arrived on the French ship *Cathinka* on January 26 and left on the same boat February 23.

84. Eyre Evans Crowe, The *History of France* (London: Longman, Rees, Orme, Brown and Green, 1830), part of Lardner's *Cabinet Cyclopaedia,* vol.10–12.

85. John R. Latimer's account books show that between the years 1827 to 1833 he paid variously $25, $30, and $36 for one-way passage between Canton and Macao. Once he paid $30 for the round trip.

86. Dr. Benjamin Cox (1806–71) who came to be known as "the good physician" of Salem. He was born in Norman Street, Salem, and graduated from Harvard in 1826. He married (1) in 1841 a widow, Sarah Aborn (Silver) Daland; (2) in 1860 Susan Daland (*Essex Institute Historical Collections* (October, 1948), 345). See Harriett's entry on April 13, 1833, vol 6.

Notes to Volume VI

1. George James Welbore Agar-Ellis, Lord Dover, *Life of Frederic the Second, King of Prussia* (London: Longman, Rees, Orme, Brown and Green, 1832).

2. Charles Mills, *The History of the Crusades for the Recovery and Possession of the Holy Land* (London: Longman, Hurst, Rees, Orme and Brown, 1820).

3. For an excellent reproduction of this painting, see Conner, *George Chinnery*, 232. Harriett viewed it again in London when it was on exhibit at Somerset House. The Chinese servant Ayok, who accompanied the Lows on their homeward journey, was startled to see his father Afun's likeness in the picture (July 19, 1834, vol. 8).

4. *The Liberal Preacher; A Monthly Publication of Sermons by Living Ministers*, Thomas R. Sullivan, ed. (Keene, N. H.: J. Prentiss, 1827) began in July (vol. 1, no. 1.) and continued in 1828 from Boston, edited by David Reed.

5. Marie (de Rabutin Chanta), marquise de Sévigné, *Lettres de Madame de Sévigné à sa fille et à ses amis* (Paris: Garnery, 1811).

6. An old-fashioned expression implying George Chinnery's attachment to or fondness for Harriett Low.

7. After the Great Awakening (an evangelical movement that swept England and America in the mid-18th century), doctrinal disputes broke out among clergymen who became divided into New Lights and Old Lights. New Lights adhered to a faith based on pre-destination, emotional revivalism, and missionary zeal; Old Lights defended a more rational faith based on individual choice and responsibility for one's actions. Unitarianism, Harriett's denomination, grew out of the doctrines of Old Lights, hence her suspicion of a New Light minister.

8. John Gillies, *The History of Ancient Greece, its Colonies, and Conquest* (London: A. Strahan and T. Cadell, 1786).

9. Amelia Opie, *The Father and Daughter: a Tale* (London: Longman and Rees, 1801). It is the story of Agnes Fitzhenry, who eloped with Captain Clifford who had no intention of marrying her. When she finally decided to return home, she found her father had gone mad from grief. Resolving that the restoration of his sanity and his forgiveness would be the sole object of her life, Agnes supported herself and child by needlework and slowly nursed her father back to health. Shortly before his death he pardoned her, but the strain was too much and she died a few hours afterward. Clifford then acknowledged his son and made him his heir. Mrs. Opie's moral is that a woman who has strayed beyond society's bounds can redeem herself by hard work and patient suffering even unto death. Ferdinando Paer turned this story into *Agnese*, an opera in two acts, first performed in Parma in 1809.

10. Ram Mohan Roy (d. 1833) was a reformer of outmoded Indian social customs; a pioneer in modern education; and founder, about the year 1820, of the religious society known as Brahma Samaj.

11. Frances Anne Kemble, *Francis the First. An Historical Drama* (London: J. Murray, 1832). Fanny Kemble (1809–93) wrote this play in her seventeenth year but it was not produced until 1832.

12. *The Unitarian Miscellany and Christian Monitor*, Jared Sparks, ed., vol. 1–3; F. W. P. Greenwood, ed., vol. 4–6 (Baltimore: The Baltimore Unitarian Book Society, 1821–24).

13. Amelia Opie, *Tales of Real Life* (London: Longman, Hurst, Rees, Orme and Brown, 1813) or Amelia Opie, *Tales of the Heart* (London: Longman, Hurst, Rees, Orme and Brown, 1820). It is not clear which collection Harriett read.

14. Amelia Opie, *Temper, or Domestic Scenes: A Tale in Three Volumes* (London: Longman, Hurst, Rees, Orme and Brown, 1812).

15. James Sheridan Knowles, *The Hunchback* (London: E. Moxon, 1832).

16. Stéphanie Félicité de Genlis, *La Duchess de la Vallière* (Paris: Maradan, 1804); *Madame de Maintenon, pour servir de suite à l'histoire de la duchesse de la Vallière* (Paris, 1806).

17. *The Evangelist*, a religious newspaper about the size of the *Chinese Courier*, had just been published by Robert Morrison (William H. Low to Samuel Russell, April 29, 1833, Reel 3, Russell and Company Papers).

18. This monthly was inaugurated in May 1832 by Elijah Coleman Bridgman. He was assisted in later years by a fellow-missionary, S. Wells Williams, who arrived in China in October 1833. The periodical ceased publication in 1851. Its twenty—now very rare—volumes constitute a rich and authentic source for the history of the period.

19. Charles Gutzlaff's account of the voyage of the *Sylph* appears both in the *Canton Register* and in the *Chinese Repository* for May 1833; and in his *Journal of Three Voyages along the Coast of China in 1831, 1832, & 1833* (London: Thomas Ward and Co., 1834), of which the third edition has an engraving showing the author dressed as a Fukien sailor.

20. William Jardine (1784–1843), born in Broadholm, Lochmaben, Scotland, had served as assistant surgeon and later surgeon on East India Company ships from 1802–18. Since surgeons were entitled to ship a certain amount of tonnage for their personal trade, Jardine by 1817 had become more interested in trade than medicine. Jardine left the Company, bought a share in a trading vessel, and settled in Canton from 1820 as a commission agent. By 1824 he was associated with Magniac and Company, one of the leading opium firms of Canton. On June 30, 1832, the interest of Hollingworth Magniac in the firm ceased and the remaining partners, William Jardine and James Matheson, carried on under the firm of Jardine, Matheson and Company, which became the chief rival of Russell and Company for trade at Canton. For portraits of Jardine, see Conner, *George Chinnery*, 214–15.

21. Jacques Henri Bernardin de Saint-Pierre, *Studies of Nature* (Worcester: J. Nancrede, 1797).

22. "The *unalterable* laws of the celestial empire were held forth to justify the treatment we had experienced. 'If the laws are indeed unalterable,' we replied, 'then we ought to come hither freely, for the ancient edict issued under Kang-he permitted foreigners to enter all Chinese ports. The unchangeable laws, which, as you assert, allow not the least deviation from ancient custom, are in our favour, and we plead them in our behalf'" (Gutzlaff, *Journal*, 155).

23. This *Sylph* is one of the three Canton and Macao passage boats of which the others were the *Union* and the *St. George*. The *Sylph* and the *Union* could accommodate six passengers, the *St. George* four. The fare for one passenger to Lintin or Macao was $30.00 (Advertisement, *Canton Register*, 3 October 1832).

24. A small passenger boat in the Macao area which took its name from local aborigines whose families lived in them. The derivation "egg-boat" in reference to the shape is a misnomer.

25. In opposition to President Andrew Jackson's support of the protectionist Tariff of 1828, South Carolina had passed an Ordinance of Nullification (November 24, 1832) which forbade the collection of tariffs within the state and threatened secession if force was used by the Federal Government. By early 1833, a compromise tariff was passed and South Carolina rescinded the Nullification act thus ending the dispute peaceably.

26. *Fazio, a Tragedy* (Oxford: S. Collingwood, 1816), a drama by a dean of St. Paul's, Henry Hart Milman (1791–1868).

27. *L'italiana in Algeri*, a *buffo* opera by Gioachino Rossini, first produced in Venice in 1813.

28. John Shillaber had failed in business in Batavia before he arrived in Macao with his sister. In January, 1832 he applied to Jardine, Matheson and Company to back him as a rice merchant in Anjer but the company declined. Jardine even counseled his partner Matheson not to consign any opium to Shillaber for fear that it would be seized to satisfy Shillaber's debts. Evidently Jardine changed his mind since by early 1833, Shillaber was shipping rice to Manila under the cover of Jardine, Matheson and Company. That was not

enough for W.H. Low who distrusted Shillaber. In thinly veiled contempt, Low wrote his partner that Shillaber "is ingratiating himself into Society here, transacts business through Jardines assistance & has made some money" (Low to Russell, February 17, 1833, Russell and Company Papers; John Shillaber to J. Matheson, January 3, 1832, B7, Macao 677; W. Jardine to J. Matheson, January 26, 1832, B7, Canton 327, Jardine Matheson Archives).

29. Sir Walter Scott, *Woodstock; or, The Cavalier* (Edinburgh: A. Constable and Co., 1826).

30. Horatio Smith, *Brambletye House; or, Cavaliers and Roundheads* (London: H. Colburn, 1826). A novel written in imitation of Sir Walter Scott.

31. Scott, *The Antiquary*, Chapter 18.

32. Henry Lawrence, a native of New York, was the son of Jonathan Lawrence of the New York firm of Lawrence and Whitney. He was a merchant in Manila until his retirement in 1858 to New York. He reached Macao in the Spanish brig *Brilliante* on May 17, 1833, and sailed in the same ship June 8.

33. A play by Giovanni Schmidt turned into the opera, *Eduardo e Cristina* (1819), by Gioachino Rossini.

34. The war between Holland and Belgium had resumed over the question of the dissolution of the Kingdom of the Netherlands (1830), which had called for the separation of the two countries. In August 1832, Holland refused to accept the settlement and invaded Belgium, defeating its army. France rushed in and forced the Dutch to leave Belgium but King William of Holland refused to evacuate Antwerp. It took a combined British/French fleet and a French army during November and December, 1832 to expel the Dutch from Antwerp and force an armistice.

35. On December 10, 1832, President Andrew Jackson issued his "Proclamation to the People of South Carolina" to refute the South Carolina Ordinance of Nullification of the tariff acts of 1828 and 1832. Jackson asserted the supremacy of the Federal government and declared that no state could refuse to obey Federal law or attempt to leave the union. Any attempt to dissolve the union by force would be treason. The Proclamation was written by Edward Livingston, Secretary of State. Jackson's firm stand and a compromise tariff bill enabled the South Carolinians to suspend the Ordinance of Nullification and end the crisis.

36. Sermons 4 and 5, *Sermons by the Late Samuel C. Thacher* (Boston: Wells and Lilly, 1824). The text was Psalm 139:23–24, "Search me, O God, and know my heart; try me, and know my thought; and see if there be any wicked way in me, and lead me in the way everlasting."

37. George Melville was master of the British ship *Charlotte*, which left Bombay April 14 with a cargo of opium from Jamsetjee Jejeebhhoy and Company, reaching Lintin June 9.

38. John R. Morrison had been interpreter and secretary to Edmund Roberts, the American diplomat who had negotiated a successful commercial treaty with Siam in Bangkok in March 1833. For Morrison's role see Hodges, *Voyage of the Peacock*, 9, 228–20, 242, 259–60.

39. Harriett may be referring to *Vie de Rossini par M. de Stendhal* (Paris: Chez August Boulland et Co., 1824), which was an extremely popular biography of Rossini.

40. G. Gregerson, master of the American ship *Ninus*, reached Macao on May 4 and sailed for Cowes on June 25.

41. *Numa Pompilio, segundo rey de Roma: poema del caballero de Florian* (Madrid: B. Cano, 1818).

42. John Marshall, *The Life of George Washington* (Philadelphia: C.P. Wayne, 1804).

43. Lantau, the largest island in the estuary of the Pearl River leading up to Canton, is fifteen miles long and about five miles wide, with a peak about 3,000 feet high. It had several villages on its shores, and formed the northern boundary of what was called the Lema passage up the river.

44. Montanha is an island south, and slightly west, of Macao. The Cantonese designation is *Tai-wang-kam-to* (Peking *T'ai-heng-ch'in tao*)—literally Large Horizontal Lute Island, as contrasted with another nearby, called Lesser (*siu* or *hsiao*) Horizontal Lute Island.

45. This was the Beach Hotel, kept at this time by Richard Marwick (1791–1836), an Englishman. It was situated on the Praya Grande, facing the outer harbor.

46. Temple Hillyard Layton was assistant tea inspector in the Company's service at Canton—having arrived in HCS *Broxbornebury* on November 5, 1832. A student of Corpus Christi College, Cambridge, he married in December 1837, Sarah, daughter of Edward Rea of Ludlow, Salop, England. The ceremony was performed in the British Chapel at Macao by Rev. G. H. Vachell. In 1845 he was British vice-consul at Ningpo, and the following year consul at Amoy.

47. William Wood, unable to find an opera critic for his newspaper, had to go to Macao to see for himself. His review of *Edoardo e Cristina* was restrained. He pointed out that it contained "some passages of great beauty; but is not perhaps, upon the whole one of the most effective that could have been chosen; and with so small a company, the success with which it was accomplished is certainty entitled to much admiration." For someone condemned to live in "villainous Canton" the sight of the audience was "rival to the stage. We shall live for a month upon the remembrance of bright eyes and soft voices" (*Chinese Courier*, 2 July 1833).

48. This observation is confirmed by John R. Latimer in a letter he wrote his sister in Wilmington, Delaware, on March 28, 1831: ". . . the old fashioned manners have been preserved at Canton, & on arrival here most men are admitted to better society than they have been accustomed to at home - the extreme forms of politeness among the Chinese keeps our own alive - " (Box 1, Latimer Papers, LC).

49. The oil which was used by the common people, both for cooking and for lighting, is a vegetable oil called *Yu-ts'ai* (*Brassica campestris, L.*), one of several species of mustard. The oil is extracted from the seeds. Writing in 1841, E. C. Bridgman described the lamp then used as "a small glass

cup, partly filled with water, and the oil is poured upon its surface; the wick, made of rush pith, is suspended in the vessel by means of wire, and burns till the oil is consumed" (*Chinese Chrestomathy*, 140).

50. Jean François Paul de Gondi de Retz, *Mémoires contenant ce qui s'est passé de remarquable en France pendant les premières années du regne de Louis XIV*, 7 vol. (Geneva, 1751).

51. Frances Trollope, *The Refugee in America: A Novel*, 3 vol. (London: Whittaker, Treacher and Co., 1832).

52. Harriett's intolerance of the "heap of married ladies" was not unlike that of Miss Caroline Gordon, in *Refugee in America*, who found little in common with the housewives of Rochester, N.Y. who talked of nothing but "'*helps*' and the 'last sermon'"(Trollope, *Refugee* 2:108).

53. William Dallas arrived in the British ship, *Charles Forbes*.

54. Joseph Priestly, *Memoirs of Dr. Joseph Priestly, to the Year 1705, Written by Himself* (London: J. Johnson, 1805–7).

55. Fanny Trollope notes the use of "fix" as an example of ancient English when a farmer's wife who had no butter hoped that her guests "'would fix a little relish with our crackers,'" and "eat salt meat and dry biscuits." *Domestic Manners of the Americans*. Reprint (Dover, N. H.: Alan Sutton Publishing, 1993), 175.

56. Etienne de Jouy, *L'Hermite en province: ou, observations sur les moeurs et les usages français au commencement du XIXe siècle* (Paris: Pillet, 1818–27).

57. Harriett's coolness toward Wood on the Campo on June 23, 1833 showed enough spirit to satisfy her uncle who heartily disliked William Wood.

58. Jared Sparks, *The Life of Gouverneur Morris with Selections from his Correspondence, and Miscellaneous Papers* (Boston: Gray and Bowen, 1832).

59. *Jawaub* is said to be (see *Hobson Jobson*) a Hindi word meaning dismissal, "also used in Anglo-Indian for a lady's refusal of a marriage offer, whence the passive verb 'to be jawaub'd'."

60. Antoine-Marie Charnans La Valette, *Mémoires et souvenirs du comte de La Vallette* (Paris, 1831).

61. Johann Georg Zimmermann, *Über die Einsamkeit* (Leipzig, 1785). Harriett probably read a French or English translation.

62. The *Nabob* (Capt. George W. Putnam) left Boston on March 15 and reached Macao July 15.

63. Aunt Eaton was Hannah Low (b. 1786), a sister of Harriett's father, Seth Low. She married Washington Eaton (1788–1841) and lived at Weare, N. H.

64. Antoine-Marie Chamans La Vallette, a close supporter of Napoleon throughout his campaigns, had married Emilie-Louise de Beaucharnais, niece of Empress Josephine. He became Directeur General under Napoleon until ousted by the Bourbons in 1814. Remaining faithful to Napoleon, La Vallette aided Napoleon in his return from Elba. After Napoleon's defeat at Waterloo and the return of Louis XVIII to Paris, La Vallette was tried for treason and sentenced to death. The evening before he was to die, his wife visited him in prison heavily veiled. She changed clothes with him and

with the help of a bribed guard, the "sobbing wife" was able to leave the prison and escape. Madame La Vallette was imprisoned for some time and when released became mentally ill. He was able to publish his memoirs based on papers that his wife had collected before she became ill (Pierre Larousse, *Grand dictionnaire universel du XIXe siècle* 10:263–64).

65. See n. 35 above.

66. Throughout the first half of 1833, Augustine Heard was increasingly plagued with ill health. Low finally prevailed upon him to visit Macao. He was accompanied by Joseph Coolidge, who was being sent to Bombay to buy opium for Russell and Company. Coolidge had been disappointed in his reception in Canton since he had not received the partnership that he had been promised. He admired Heard and Low as business men, and found Heard kind and friendly, but felt that Russell and Company labored "under one serious disadvantage; which cannot but be, in time, an injury to their business: this is the unpopularity of Mr. Low" (Joseph Coolidge to Samuel Russell, April 6, 1833; June 29, 1833, Reel 3, Russell and Company Papers).

67. Edwin Stevens (1802–37), a native of New Canaan, Conn., graduated from Yale in 1828 with high honors. Appointed by the Seaman's Friend Society as chaplain for the port of Canton, he left Philadelphia in D. W. C. Olyphant's new ship *Morrison* June 29, 1832, and reached Canton October 26 of that year. In March 1836, he became a missionary of the American Board of Commissioners for Foreign Missions, but died at Singapore in 1837. He contributed a number of articles of worth to the *Chinese Repository*. His obituary appears in that journal for March 1837.

68. *The Works of James Barry* . . . *Historical Painter* (London: T. Cadell and W. Davis, 1809).

69. Charles Pearson, master of the American ship *Gaspar*, which arrived on June 5 and sailed July 22.

70. Sodium bicarbonate, commonly called baking soda, used for indigestion.

71. It was the Empress—not the Emperor's mother, as stated below—who died on June 10, 1833. She is known in Chinese history as *Ta-hsing Huang Hou*. The prohibitions and ceremonies connected with this event are set forth in detail in the *Chinese Repository* for July 1833.

72. The Irish painter James Barry had an irritable temper and was often contemptuous of the opinions of contemporary artists. He lived in poverty, dressed like a beggar, and shocked people who admired his painting by his coarse language filled with oaths. He was relentless in his pursuit of artistic truth. His mind was so commanding on any subject he pursued that his manners and dress were overlooked by his admirers (*The Works of James Barry* 1:329–37).

73. Two operas of this name were current in the Italian repertoire: *I baccanali di Roma* (1801) by Giuseppe Nicolini (1762–1842) and *I baccanali di Roma* (1816) by Pietro Generali (1773–1832).

74. Vicomte d'Alincourt, *Le Solitaire*, 10th ed. (Paris: Bechet aîné, 1823).

75. Stéphanie Félicité de Genlis, *Le philosophe pris au mot, ou Le Mari*

corrupteur, vol. 5 of *Nouveaux contes moraux, et nouvelles historiques* (Paris: Maradan, 1819).

76. J. Goddard arrived at Macao in the *Water Witch* on July 5, 1833, and sailed in the *Falcon* the following November 8.

77. The quarrel was about the alleged refusal of the authorities of the East India Company to permit the body of a boy of the ship *Guardian*, who had drowned in Macao harbor, to be interred in the Company's burying-ground. The letters on the subject exchanged between Bartolomeo Barretto and Plowden, who was then Chief, appear in the *Canton Register* for July 30. Barretto, a member of an old Macao family, acted as W. C. Hunter's "security" while he was living at Canton (*Bits of Old China*, 156).

78. William Wood described Chinese street theater in even more critical terms: "Throughout the day the audience is perpetually changing in the various idlers who throng the public thoroughfares of a Chinese city, and the hideous music which accompanies the play, joined to the uproar and confusion which constantly occurs among the crowd who obstruct the passage, renders the Chinese 'Sing Song,' as it is called, intolerable to an European, after the first impulse of curiosity is satisfied. At intervals there is a sort of screaming recitative, howled forth in a shrill and drawling voice, which is highly esteemed, the pauses being filled up with a frightful burst of gongs, trumpets, cymbals, etc." (*Chinese Courier*, 14 April 1832).

79. The young English heroine, Caroline Gordon, was puzzled when she overheard the sharp comments of American women when she walked across the room on the arm of her father: "I cannot realize how any girl can get upon such a lay, and yet keep her standing." "If I live from July to eternity, I shall never obliviate that go." "How she swiggles her way through the gentlemen! Did you ever?" (Trollope, *Refugee* 2:73)

80. The reviewer in the *Quarterly Review* describes *Refugee in America* as a story of "absurd nonsense from beginning to end . . . To say that this tale is singularly unskilful, would be almost flattery;—we have seldom met with more of childish improbability, combined with less of surprise and interest. It was intended, we suppose, as a peg whereon to hang the drapery of the satire; but it is a peg wretchedly ill-fashioned and ill-covered" (48 [October, 1832]:509–11).

81. Laure Saint-Martin Permon Junot, *Mémoires de madame la duchesse d'Abrantès, ou Souvenirs historiques sur Napoléon, la révolution, le directoire, le consulat, l'empire et la restauration* (Paris: Garnier frères, 1831).

82. A catty (*chin* in Chinese) is 1 1/3 pounds avoirdupois. A tael (*liang* in Chinese) is 1/16 of a catty, though the word tael is more properly used to represent an ounce of silver.

83. The slaves were probably owned by José Bernardo Goularte, a prominent merchant. In 1830 it was estimated that there were 350 male slaves and 779 female slaves at Macao (Ljungstedt, *Historical Sketch*, 28).

84. de Genlis, *Nouveaux contes moraux*, vol. 1.

85. Laure Junot, *duchesse d'Abrantès*, had known Napoleon since childhood when he was courting her widowed mother. As wife of one of

Napoleon's most trusted friends and generals, and lady in waiting to Napoleon's mother, Madame Junot had intimate knowledge of court life and the relations between Napoleon and Josephine. When Napoleon returned from his Italian campaign and heard reports that he owed a debt of gratitude for his success to Josephine's intrigues, he was deeply wounded by every contemptuous look, when he heard the expression:"'It is his wife's influence that upholds him.'" Junot pointed out that this expression was "false and ridiculous" and Napoleon reacted by forbidding Josephine to talk politics unless he gave her permission (*Memoirs of Emperor Napoleon from Ajaccio to Waterloo as Soldier, Emperor, Husband* [New York: M. Walter Dunn, 1901] 1:168–69).

86. An example of Junot's attention to detail for benefit of her French readers was her description of seventeen-year-old Hortense de Beauharnais, Empress Josephine's daughter: ". . . she was fresh as a rose, and though her fair complexion was not relieved by much color, she had enough to produce that freshness and bloom which was her chief beauty; a profusion of light hair played in silky locks round her soft and penetrating blue eyes. The delicate roundness of her figure, slender as a palm tree, was set off by the elegant carriage of her head; her feet were small and pretty; her hands very white, with pink, well-rounded nails" (Junot, *Memoirs* 1:339).

87. The specimen play-bill here mentioned, giving the cast and the "Argument" for Rossini's opera *La gazza ladra*, is preserved in vol. 6 of the original journal in the Library of Congress. On the reverse is written the name, "William Low, Esq." The fun consists of the hilarious translation of the story of the opera from Italian to Portuguese to English.

88. The preferred spelling is *Tso-tang*, the designation of the Chinese sub-magistrate who was appointed by the magistrate of the neighboring district of Hsiang-shan to be the judge of the Chinese inhabitants of Macao, and to transmit communications to higher Chinese officials.

Notes to Volume VII

1. George Stanley Faber, *A Dissertation on the Prophecies That Have Been Fulfilled, Are Now Fulfilling, or Will Hereafter Be Fulfilled, Relative to the Great Period of 1260 Years, the Papal and Mohammedan Apostasies, the Tyrannical Reign of Antichrist, or the Infidel Power, and the Restoration of the Jews* (London: R. C. and J. Rivington, 1806).

2. Andrew Bigelow, *Travels in Malta and Sicily, with Sketches of Gibraltar in 1827* (New York: E. Bliss, 1831).

3. N. G. Dufief, *Nouvelle Grammaire française-anglaise, ou Cours d'études de la langue française*, 4e (Paris: Picard-Dubois, 1817).

4. Jean Pierre Claris de Florian, *Guillermo Tell, ou la Suiza libre*, trad. de français al castellano por J-Ant. J.(Paris: Masson y Hijo, 1822).

5. Possibly a later edition of the encyclopedia of Robert Goadby, *The Family Library: or, Instructor in Useful Knowledge* (London: R. Goadby, 1755).

6. Henry Nelson Coleridge, *Six Months in the West Indies* (London: J. Murray, 1826).

7. James Low, brother of Seth Low, was master of the American ship *Cabot* which reached China September 2 in the service of J. W. Perit. Harriett contemplated for a time returning home with her uncle in the *Cabot*.

8. Robert Chambers, *The Life of King James the First* (Edinburgh: Constable and Co., 1830). Instead of Robert Bruce of Scotland, Harriett probably referred to Francis Bond Head, *The Life of Bruce, the African Traveller* (London: J. Murray, 1830), a more "promiscuous" choice.

9. Sermon on Immortality in *Discourses by William Channing* (Boston: C. Bowen, 1832).

10. Henry Hart Milman, *The History of the Jews* (London: J. Murray, 1829).

11. Discourses 10 and 11 employ the same biblical text: Ephesians 6:24.

12. William H. Low arrived in Macao with an active case of tuberculosis that forced him to give up work and eventually leave China. His symptoms and treatment can be followed in almost clinical detail in daily letters to Samuel Russell (September 18, 1833ff, Reel 3, Russell and Company Papers, LC) and to Augustine Heard (September 9–October 24, 1833, 1 BM-10-4, Heard Family Business Records).

13. The "smites and offers" that Captain Roundy had heard about in Batavia refers to Harriett's rejection of William Wood's offer of marriage. Harriett blamed Wood for the gossip because of his refusal to call on the Lows or even to speak to Harriett in public in Macao after the engagement was broken.

14. On September 14, Low wrote to his partner in Canton: "I am sorry to say, that I am no better. My cough is more troublesome than when at Canton & I perspire profusely nights, which cause me to feel great exhaustion in the morning. Colledge seems to think that the cause of my cough is deeper than the throat & intends applying leeches to my chest this evening" (1 BM-10-4, Heard Family Business Records). After leeching, Dr. Colledge applied a blistering plaster between Low's shoulders and administered digitalis to bring down his pulse.

15. Richard Lander, *Journal of an Expedition to Explore the Course and Termination of the Niger* (London: J. Murray, 1832).

16. Frances Trollope, *Domestic Manners of the Americans* (1832); Godfrey T. Vigne, *Six Months in America* (1832); James Stuart, *Three Years in North America* (Edinburgh: R. Cadell, 1833).

17. William Low, son of Capt. James Low, had been aboard the *Cabot* in Whampoa.

18. The "demon" was James P. Sturgis, who since 1832 had been in an open feud with W.H. Low over losing a share of the opium storage ship *Lintin* that he had been promised by Robert B. Forbes. As Russell and Company became the dominant American merchant house in Canton, Sturgis had become more embittered. Around this time a broadside entitled "Air" that alluded to Abigail Knapp Low was pasted on the door of East

India Company factory in Macao and 500 copies were left on the doorstep. Rumor had it that Sturgis was the author. The scurrilous ditty referred to the murder of Joseph White by Abigail Low's brothers:

> Now Joe and Frank they both are hung
> And Phip is like to swing.
> What horrid grief and trouble too
> My thieving brothers bring.
>
> For tho' they killed old Uncle White
> They got but little plunder,
> Therefore if I'm 'a drop too <u>low</u>'
> I'm sure its no great wonder.
>
> For after sticking the old Wretch
> And knocking on the knob him,
> How it subdues my weaker part
> To think they did not rob him—

John R. Latimer felt that Sturgis was responsible because he had left publications about the murder referring to the Knapp family on his table where everyone could see them and was the only one who had ever expressed a personal dislike of Mrs. Low. Sturgis denied composing the song and excused his ill will toward Mrs. Low by saying that she had cast a stain on his character in Macao by "asserting that my father's 'reputation' was such that <u>She</u> could not <u>know</u> his family at home.— The only proofs that I can adduce of the 'respectability' of Mrs. Low's family are in the printed records of a court of Justice which shall not be withheld when called for" (Sturgis to J.R. Latimer, October 16, 1833; Latimer to Sturgis, October 19, 1833; Sturgis to Latimer, October 22, 1833, Box 6, Folder 1833, Latimer Papers, LC).

19. William Wirt, *Life of Patrick Henry*, rev. ed. (New York: M'Elrath and Bangs, 1833).

20. *Fitzgeorge; a Novel* (London: E. Wilson, 1832).

21. *Sermons by the Late Abiel Abbot of Beverly, Mass., with a Memoir of his Life, by S. Everett* (Boston: Wait, Greene and Co., 1831).

22. *The Private Correspondence of David Garrick, With the Most Celebrated Persons of his Time; and a New Biographical Memoir of Garrick* (London: H. Colburn and R. Bentley, 1831–32).

23. Probably a reference to John Holt, *Characters of Kings and Queens of England, Selected from Different Histories* (London: G.G.J. and J. Robinson, 1786–88).

24. Lindsay's account of this trip appears in the *Chinese Repository* 3(1834): 252–55.

25. "Your Bombay scheme does not meet with Mr. Colledge's approbation, in fact, I do not much fancy it myself, for my wife is determined I shall go <u>no where</u> without her, & as I could not leave Harriett here alone, I should have to take her, & the trouble & expense, would be about the

same, as going to Europe or America -" (W. H. Low to A. Heard, October 18, 1833, 1 BM-10-4, Heard Family Business Records).

26. H. Harris, captain of HCS *Lowther Castle*, had also been in Macao during the 1831–32 trading season.

27. Amelia Pereira (baptized 1816) was the daughter of Antonio Pereira, a heavy dealer in opium, a consignee of British and Portuguese "country ships" form Calcutta and Bombay, and a judge in the local court. On October 29 she married Francisco José de Paiva (1801–49) who was a judge in Macao in 1833. In P. Manuel Teixeira, *Galeria de Macaenses Ilustres*, 574, the bride's name is given as Aurelia.

28. George Bennett (1804–93), naturalist, was born at Plymouth, England. A fellow of the Royal College of Surgeons, he wrote *Wanderings in New South Wales, Batavia, Pedir Coast, Singapore and China; Being the Journal of a Naturalist in Those Countries During 1832, 1833, and 1834* (London: R. Bentley, 1834), which gives a good account of the opium trade and has an excellent painting by Chinnery of the British Factory at Canton. He settled in New South Wales in 1836, was the first curator of the Australian Museum, Sydney, and the first person to discover the pearly nautilus in a living state (Fred Johns, *Australian Biographical Dictionary*, 1934).

29. Possibly a reference to the master of the French ship *Pactole*, which arrived October 13. The *Canton Register* spells his name Bousses.

30. Letitia Elizabeth Landon (1802–38) earned her living from the age of fifteen by writing romantic poetry for *Literary Gazette* and later editing an annual, *Drawing-room Scrap-Book*. With no family protection or support, she led the independent life of a writer (highly unusual for a woman in the 1820s) and her name was linked with several married men who fostered her career. In June 1839, she died of poison four months after she married George McLean, governor of the Gold Coast. It was never determined whether it was suicide or murder by her husband's disgruntled mistress (Alison Adburgham, *Woman in Print*, 244–48).

31. Caroline Sheridan Norton (1808–77), whose poetry *The Sorrows of Rosalie* (1829) and *The Undying One, and other Poems*(1830) had probably been read by Harriett, was later more widely known for her support of married women's rights that led to passage in England of the Infant Custody Act of 1839 and the Divorce Act of 1857.

32. Johann Gaspar Spurzheim (1776–1832), author of *Phrenology; or, The Doctrine of the Mind, and of the Relations between its Manifestations and the Body* (London: C. Knight, 1825).

33. Capt. William Russell (1785–1857) of the ship *Omega* was a son of John Russell (1737–1813) of Providence, R. I. He went to sea early and remained in the India and China trade for twenty-four years. He married Rebecca Snow Gair of Medfield, Mass., and they had ten children. His portrait and biographical sketch appear in John R. Bartlett, *Genealogy . . . of the Descendants of John Russell of Woburn* (Providence, 1879).

34. About October 12–14, a violent quarrel took place between the crew of the opium ship, *Samarang*, which previously had been beached in

a storm, and the inhabitants of the nearby village of Keeow. In the affray, each side lost a life. The Company's Select Committee put much of the blame on Capt. Alexander Grant of the *Hercules*, an opium ship under Grant's command.

35. John P. Cushing, the old China hand of Boston, had not long before married Mary Louise, daughter of John Sylvester J. Gardiner, rector of Trinity Church, Boston.

Notes to Volume VIII
November 19, 1833–August 1, 1834

1. Lorchas were cargo boats of from fifty to one hundred tons, of combined European and Chinese design with Chinese rigging. Often they were armed and had a mixed crew of Chinese and Portuguese. There is a detailed account of them with an excellent drawing, by a Chinese artist, in C. A. Montaldo de Jesus, *Historic Macao* (Hong Kong: Kelly and Walsh, 1902), 319.

2. George Payne Rainsford James, *Henry Masterton; or the Adventures of the Young Cavalier* (London: H. Colburn and R. Bentley, 1832).

3. James Kirke Paulding, *Westward Ho!* (New York: J. and J. Harper, 1832).

4. James Kirke Paulding, *John Bull in America; or, the New Munchausen* (London: John Miller, 1825).

5. Benjamin Silliman, *A Journal of Travels in England, Holland, and Scotland, and of Two Passages over the Atlantic—in the Years 1805 and 1806*, 3d ed.(New Haven: S. Converse, 1820).

6. Probably a reference to Oliver Goldsmith, *The Vicar of Wakefield: a tale. Supposed to be written by himself* (Dublin: W. and W. Smith, 1766).

7. Samuel Johnson, *Mr. Johnson's Preface to his Edition of Shakespeare's Plays* (London, J. and R. Tonson, 1765).

8. Bohea tea derives its name from a range of hills in the province of Fukien from which it comes. Congo or Congou is an imitation of the Amoy pronunciation of a black tea known in the Peking and Canton dialects as *Kung-fu*. Since the characters mean work or labor, westerners rather pointlessly called it "working" tea.

9. David Brewster, *Letters on Natural Magic, Addressed to Sir Walter Scott* (London: J. Murray, 1832).

10. Oliver Goldsmith, *The Citizen of the World: or, Letters from a Chinese Philosopher Residing in London to his Friends in the East* (London: T. Vernor, 1792).

11. John Williams, *The Life and Actions of Alexander the Great*, 2d ed. (London: J. Murray, 1829).

12. Eugene of Savoy, *Memoirs of Prince Eugene of Savoy* (London: Henry Colburn, 1811).

13. Samuel Johnson, *A Journey to the Western Islands of Scotland* (London: W. Strahan and T. Cadell, 1775).

14. James Boswell, *The Journal of a Tour to the Hebrides, with Samuel Johnson, LLD* (London: T. Cadell and W. Davies, 1807).

15. Boswell, *Tour*, Sunday, September 12 and Friday, October 8, 1773 (Penguin Classics edition [1984], 264, 339).

16. Boswell, *Tour*, Thursday, September 23 (Penguin Classics edition, 308).

17. Stéphanie Félicité de Genlis, *Bélisaire* (Paris: Maradan, 1808).

18. Benjamin Disraeli, *Contarini Fleming: A Psychological Auto-biography* (London: J. Murray, 1832).

19. James Northcote, *The Life of Sir Joshua Reynolds, . . . Comprising Anecdotes of Many Distinguished Persons, His Contemporaries; and a Brief Analysis of His Discourses* (London: H. Colburn, 1818).

20. Allan Cunningham, *The Lives of the Most Eminent British Painters, Sculptors, and Architects* (London: John Murray, 1829).

21. Heather Lynch Piozzi, *Anecdotes of Samuel Johnson, LL.D. During the Last Twenty Years of His Life* (London: T. Cadell, 1786).

22. The boarding house at 27 Heerengracht (now Adderley Street) was owned by the widow of Adriaan J. Cruywagen. Her daughters were Johanna and Francina *(South African Directory and Almanack, 1834).*

23. Charles Mathurin Villet is described in the *Directory* of 1834 as "naturalist and seedsman, 100 Long-street—menagerie and botanical garden, Somerset Road."

24. Dr. John Murray, inspector general to the forces and principal medical officer, lived at 2 Strand-street. In 1837 he was listed as president of the Medical Committee of the Colony.

25. Sir Benjamin D'Urban (1779–1849), after whom the city of Durban was named, was appointed governor of Cape of Good Hope in 1833. He took occupation of Natal for the crown.

26. The organ, costing about £1,500, was presented to the Dutch Reformed Church by "Jan Hoets, esq." in 1830. St. George's Church (Episcopal) was nearly completed when the Lows were there. The *South African Directory* for 1834 reports that the church would "provide for 1,000 sittings" of which "300 seats will be set apart for the poor."

27. Carl Ferdinand Heinrich von Ludwig, an apothecary and proprietor of the garden called Ludwig's-burg, was a much respected botanist in Cape Town. The garden was located in what is now called Tamboers Kloof, above central Cape Town on the lower slopes of Lion's Head.

28. George Thompson, author of *Travels and Adventures in South Africa* (London: H. Colburn,1827), was a trustee of St. George's Church and a partner in the firm of Borradaile, Thompson, and Pillans, 2 Heerengracht, which did business with Russell and Company in Canton (*South African Directory*, 1834).

29. Dirk Gysbertus Eksteen was listed in the *Directory* (1837) as residing at Kirstenbosch. He was a member of the Agricultural Society of Cape Town and elder of the Dutch Reformed Church at Wynberg.

30. Dr. Samuel Silverthorne Bailey, a former surgeon in the Royal Navy

who lived at 57 Long Street, founded the Somerset Hospital at Cape Town in 1817, and in 1834 was resident surgeon there. He also acted as medical officer in charge of the Town Prison and the House of Correction (Peter Philip, *British Residents at the Cape 1795–1819* [Cape Town: David Philip, 1981], 12).

31. John Bardwell Ebden, who in 1834 was a merchant at 28 Heerengracht, and his wife Antoinetta Adriana Kirchmann Ebden. In 1837 he is listed as trustee of St. George's Church (Philip, *British Residents*, 112–13).

32. Possibly a reference to Rice Jones Jones, who is listed in the *Cape Town Directory* for 1837 as living in the Kirstenbosch neighborhood. He is mentioned several times later on.

33. It was in the Boshof orchards of Michiel van Breda, owner of the estate, Oranjezigt, in Table Valley, that Harriett had her first taste of a Cape gooseberry.

34. Dr. H.E. Macartney, MRCS, advertised in the *Cape of Good Hope Literary Gazette* (13 December 1833) that he would give "10 or 12 weekly lectures" on "natural history" at the price of fourteen Rix-dollars for two.

35. Harriett visited Sebastiaan Valentijn Cloete, Mrs. Eksteen's brother, and her sister-in-law, the former Maria Johanna van Reenen, at Stellenberg.

36. James Rennie, *Insect Architecture* (London: C. Knight, 1830).

37. Charles Henry Somerset was installed governor of Cape of Good Hope on April 6, 1814, and left on leave in 1826.

38. Johannes J. Cruywagen lived at Newlands in 1837 and probably in 1834. Like D. G. Eksteen, he was deacon of the Dutch Church at Wynberg. There is an engraving of Newlands in Thompson, *Travels and Adventures in South Africa*, 393.

39. H.F.W. Maynier, son of H.C.D.Maynier, owned the old homestead of Protea, a farm established in the 1650s by the Dutch founder of the Cape settlement, Jan van Riebeeck. It was later acquired by the Episcopal church and renamed Bishopscourt.

40. Dirk van Reenen is listed, in the *Cape Town Directory* of 1837, as living at the Brewery. An engraving of D. Van Reenen's mansion appears in Thompson, *Travels and Adventures in South Africa*, 312. This country seat is said to have been "situated about six miles from Cape Town, on the Newlands road."

41. In a letter (dictated to Harriett) on March 7 to his partner Samuel Russell, William H. Low says that his physicians are now of the opinion "that the chief cause of my disease proceeds from the Liver, for the month past, have been treating me accordingly . . . I am now reduced to the last stage of weakness and obliged to keep my bed, but they have commenced giving me Tonics and assure me that I shall be stronger and better soon." In a postscript dated March 11 to a copy of this letter, Low describes his turn for the worst: "Since the date of my last I have gained no strength, in fact see no improvement in my health, and am unable at this time on account of my cough to dictate. I must therefore refer you to Miss Harriett's letter for particulars regarding my health. . . ." Harriett's "very important office of

private secretary" came at a terrible price (Low to Russell, March 6, 7, 1834, Reel 4, Russell and Company Papers).

42. The Reverend George Hough (1787–1867), M.A., formerly fellow of Pembroke College, Oxford, was senior colonial chaplain and minister of St. George's Church, then being built.

43. This was the month when, in China, it is customary to pay respects at the tombs of the departed. In South China this is normally done twice a year: about the day called Ch'ing Ming (Clear and Bright) which falls on April 5, and again about the Mid-Autumn Festival (15th of the 8th moon) which occurs in late September or October. In North China the autumn ceremony is not much observed.

44. Richard Rush, Memoranda of a Residence at the Court of London (Philadelphia: Carey, Lee and Blanchard, 1833). An English review that Harriett probably read considered the book "rather trivial" and its author "somewhat credulous—and rather too easily amused with objects because they were new" (Quarterly Review 49 [July, 1833]: 322–49).

45. Thomas Hamilton, Men and Manners in America (Edinburgh: W. Blackwood, 1833); The Youth and Manhood of Cyril Thornton (New York: J. and J. Harper, 1827).

46. Thomas Hamilton found scarcely anything to admire in New England character: ". . . while the great body of the New Englanders are distinguished above every other people I have ever known by bigotry and narrowness of mind, and an utter disregard of those delicacies of deportment which indicate benevolence of feeling, [in Boston] the higher and more enlightened portion of the Community should be peculiarly remarkable for the display of qualities precisely the reverse" (Men and Manners 1:231). He particularly admired their love of literature, philosophy, and their tolerance of stranger's opinions. But he reserved his scorn for Unitarianism, "the democracy of religion," where reason and dogmatism suited to the cold, calculating New England temperament had overcome the tenets of Christian faith (1:159–65).

47. The Somerset Road cemetery at Green Point was condemned as unsanitary by the city authorities of Cape Town in 1870. Remains and stones were not removed until 1900 when they were taken to Maitland in the northern suburbs. The original site of the graveyard was leveled and no trace of Low's gravestone has survived (information provided by Langham Carter, Cape Town, 1994).

48. William Cobbett, French Grammar, or Plain Instructions for the Learning of French in a Series of Letters (Paris: Bosange Père, 1824).

49. Napoleon was accompanied to St. Helena by his aides Comte Henri Bertrand, General Comte Jean-François-Charles-Tristan Montholon, and Comte Emmanuel Las Cases.

50. According to William Carroll's notices in the Canton Register during 1832–33, he was appointed "Consular Commercial Agent" for the Island of St. Helena on February 4, 1831. He kept a variety store with "supplies of every description."

51. The Mr. Dodge is Pickering Dodge (1778–1833), owner of many ships in the China trade. In 1801 he married Rebecca Jenks (1781–1851). The Mrs. Jenks whose death is here recorded is Mary Jenks, the wife of Daniel Jenks. She died June 11, 1833, age eighty. Fisk is John Fisk Allen (1807–76), Harriett's cousin.

52. Ralph Wardlaw (1779–1853) was a Scottish Congregational minister. The sermon mentioned here appears in his *Discourses on the Principal Points of the Socinian Controversy* (Glasgow: Andrew and James Duncan, 1815).

53. John Burns, *Principles of Christian Philosophy*, 3d ed. (London: Longman, Rees, Orme, Brown and Green, 1829).

54. Sir John Barrow, *A Description of Pitcairn's island and its Inhabitants. With an Authentic Account of the Mutiny of the Ship Bounty, and of the Subsequent Fortunes of the Mutineers* (New York: J. and J. Harper, 1832).

55. Jonathan Edwards, *History of Redemption: on a Plan Entirely Original* . . . (New York: T. and J. Sword, 1793).

56. Jonathan is a name used by the British to refer to Americans.

57. Probably referring to the chapter "Rural Life in England." See Washington Irving, *The Sketch Book of Geoffrey Crayon, Gent.*, Library of America ed. (New York, 1983), 795–801.

58. Joshua Bates, an American from Weymouth, Mass., had been sent to London after the War of 1812, as an agent for William Gray of Boston. By 1826 when he formed a house with John Baring, he had inherited all the other business of the major Boston merchants known as the Boston Concern. He joined Baring Brothers and Company in 1828 and became the partner who handled all the American business, including Russell and Company of Canton (Jacques M. Downs, "American Merchants and the China Opium Trade, 1800–1840," *Business History Review* 42 [Winter, 1968:430]).

59. The Pantheon, a stylish three-story building with an elaborate columned portico located near the east end of Oxford Street, had been designed by James Wyatt for balls but by 1834 had been turned into a bazaar, following the pattern of the more famous Soho Bazaar. Individual stalls sold accessories such as lace, millinery, jewelry, gloves, and refreshments (Alison Adburgham, *Shopping in Style* [London: Thames and Hudson, 1979], 60, 66).

60. The painter of dead game was Stephen Taylor, who exhibited at the Royal Academy 1817–49.

61. Abraham Borradaile (1789–1857), a leading London merchant who handled Russell and Company business in London. A branch of his firm in Cape Town—Borradaile, Thompson, and Pillans—had been solicitous of W. H. Low and his family during their stay there.

62. Somerset House, beginning in 1781, was the site of the annual art exhibition of the Royal Academy.

63. Harriett's shyness at seeing nude antique sculptures was in direct contrast to Fanny Trollope's reaction in Philadelphia in the Academy of Fine Arts in being urged by an attendant to hasten her view of the sculptures while no men were in the gallery. "I never felt my delicacy shocked at

the Louvre, but I was strangely tempted to resent as an affront the hint I received, that I might steal a glance at what was deemed indecent" (Trollope, *Domestic Manners*, 197).

64. The Colosseum was built in Regent's Park in 1824 by a group of speculators as a pleasure palace to provide paying members in London a club-house with the amenities of a rural villa. The separate idea of creating an enormous diorama of London as seen from the top of St. Paul's was being pushed in 1823 by Thomas Hornor, an artist and surveyor, who had made 2000 sketches of the view from scaffolding around the dome. The two ideas were incorporated in the architecture of the Colosseum which contained a dome thirty feet wider than St. Paul's rising 112 feet above the ground. From 1825 to 1832, Hornor and other artists labored to transfer his 2000 sketches onto 46,000 square feet of canvas stretched around the bottom of the dome. Spectators climbed to the viewing platform or rode up in the first elevator in London to look down on a view of the city stretching for twenty miles in every direction. The view was so realistic that spectators drew back from the edge of the platform with alarm at the thought that they might fall from a parapet on St. Paul's. A sculpture gallery, gardens and grottoes, and a Swiss cottage completed the other attractions on the site (Richard D. Altick, *The Shows of London* [Cambridge: Harvard University Press, 1978], 141–51).

65. William Daniell (1769–1837), a landscape painter who visited India and China. He had published with his uncle Thomas Daniell, A *Picturesque Voyage to India; by the Way of China by Thomas Daniell and William Daniell* (London: Longman, Hurst, Rees, and Orne, 1810). The pictures of Dr. and Mrs. Colledge, and Mrs. Davis, were painted by George Chinnery.

66. For Harriett's description of Chinnery's painting of Dr. Thomas R. Colledge and his servant Afun, Ayok's father, see March 30, 1833, vol. 6.

67. A monument to Reginald Heber, bishop of Calcutta, who died in 1826, is in the crypt of St. Paul's.

68. A shopping bazaar was opened in a building in Soho Square in 1816 with rents for stalls to benefit the widows and orphans of soldiers killed in the Napoleonic Wars. All types of merchandise for women and children were sold there (Adburgham, *Shopping in Style*, 60).

69. Lowther Arcade located in the Strand was renowned in Victorian London for its toy stores (Adburgham, *Shopping in Style*, 104–5).

70. Irving, *Sketch Book*, 894–908.

71. Mrs. Eliza Morrison left China in the ship *Inglis* (Captain Dudman) December 14, 1833. According to Harriett's entry on October 25 of that year, Mrs. Morrison was leaving China with five children. Her step-daughter, Mary Rebecca, accompanied her, but was not counted among the five. Dr. Morrison's obituary, published by his close friend E. C. Bridgman in the *Chinese Repository* in August 1834 (3:181), states, "In December last, Mrs. M. and six children embarked for England, leaving his eldest son [John Robert] with him in China."

72. Thomas Chalmers, *Political Economy in Connection with the Moral State and Moral Prospects of Society* (New York, 1832); Thomas Malthus, *An*

Essay on the Principle of Population, as It Affects the Future Improvement of Society (London: J. Johnson, 1798). Both writers warned of the perils of overpopulation.

73. James Sheridan Knowles, *The Wife: A Tale of Mantua* (London: E. Moxon, 1833).

74. A two-storied bazaar named the Pantechnicon opened on Motcombe Street in Belgravia in 1830. It was described as an exhibition place for artistic work to avoid Belgravia's prohibition against retail trade, but sold carriages, furniture, toys and other household necessities (Adburgham, *Shopping in Style*, 109).

75. Sometime later Harriett copied at the end of volume 8 an unidentified passage from Henry Wadsworth Longfellow's *Outre Mer* (1833). She felt that it matched her own feelings about foreign travel. Amid all the excitement of new places, there was always a "longing after the land of my birth, lurking in the secret corners of my heart. When I stood by the seashore, and listened to the melancholy & familiar roar of its waves, it seemed but a step from the threshold of a foreign land to the fireside of home; and when I watched the outbound sail, fading over the water's edge and losing itself in the blue mists of the sea, my heart went with it, and I turned away fancy sick with the blessings of home & the endearments of domestic love. At times I would sit at midnight in the solitude of my chamber and give way to the recollections of distant friends. How delightful it is to strengthen within us the golden threads that unite us with the past! to fill up as it were the blanks of existence with the images of those we love! How sweet are these dreams of home in a foreign land!"

Notes to Volume IX

1. Gregory T. Bedell, *A Life of Legh Richmond* (Philadelphia, 1829). Richmond was an English evangelical clergyman.

2. Amos Sutton (1798–1854), a native of Sevenoaks, Kent, England, went to India in 1824 as a missionary of the General Baptist Missionary Society, stationed at Cuttack, Orissa. He translated the entire Bible into Oriya—a language related to Bengali. He also compiled a dictionary and grammar, and translated many European works into the Oriya language. See *Encyclopaedia of Missions*, 714.

3. Frances Trollope, *Belgium and Western Germany in 1833, Including Visits to Baden-Baden, Wiesbaden, Cassel, Hanover, the Harz Mountains, etc.* (London: J. Murray, 1834).

Index

Some page numbers refer to information in the notes

Norton, Caroline Sheridan, 648
nuns, 56, 237, 242, 583

O

opera, 11, 72, 120, 310, 450, 474,
533–534, 541, 545, 547–548, 554,
556, 558–562, 564–565, 569, 571,
580, 586, 591, 597–598, 604,
606–608, 615, 617, 623–624
opium, 2–3, 9, 12, 57, 63–65, 68,
71, 76–77, 81, 98, 116, 119,
143, 145, 148, 153–154, 161,
172–174, 188, 191, 226, 243,
250, 258, 365, 436, 441, 453,
454, 459–461, 544, 555, 564,
573, 587, 597, 607, 633, 636,
643, 647, 654, 736, 767
Orne, Edward, 57–58, 60, 69, 75,
91, 93, 447
Orne, Sarah (Sally), 91, 113, 441
Orne, Susan, 92, 117, 451, 476, 532
Osgood, Capt. W., 56–57, 60
Otaduy, Eugenio de, 104, 114,
117–118, 121, 127, 131, 135–143,
146, 152, 154, 177, 181, 433
Ovenstone, Captain and Mrs., 119,
501

P

padres, 108, 130, 136, 174, 212,
242, 297, 421, 491, 508, 600, 647
Paiva, Amelia Pereira de, 643, 646,
649
Paiva, Miss Ana Rita de, 440
Paiva, Mr., 313, 334, 442, 450
Peacock, USS, 161, 343, 458–459,
461, 463, 482, 564
Pearson, Dr. Alexander, 68, 75, 97,
101, 127–128, 166, 178, 210,
480, 487
Pearson, Capt. Charles, 62, 139,
185, 197, 587
Peña Church, 265, 421, 446, 596
Pereira, Francisco, 263

Pereira, Antonio, 63–64, 68, 71,
101, 111, 136, 153, 171, 214,
227, 236, 241, 352, 358, 362,
477, 480, 657
Pereira, Mrs. Aurélia and family,
78, 86, 90, 107, 146, 168, 171,
180, 203, 219, 223, 229, 232,
234–236, 254, 263, 282, 313,
322–323, 330, 334, 337, 340,
343, 347, 365, 429, 432, 440,
442, 452, 474, 498, 517, 519,
522, 540, 544, 554, 601, 632, 646
Perit, James Dunlop, 351–353,
355, 361, 363, 365, 429, 431,
433–434, 438–439, 442–445
Perit, John Webster, 622
Petrie, Miss, 269, 271, 280
Phillimore, Captain, 71
Phillips, Capt. John, 148, 164
phrenology, 647–648, 744, 751, 753
Pierson, Dr., see Pearson, Dr.
Alexander
Pinkham, Lt. R. R., 336
Playfair, Major William Davidson,
276, 279
Plowden, Mrs. Annette Campbell,
237, 433, 436, 440–441, 469,
473, 480
Plowden, William Henry Chichely,
65, 68, 72, 76, 86, 100–102, 237,
427–428, 431, 517, 521–522, 543,
545, 547, 551–552, 559, 563,
572, 577, 596, 631, 636, 655, 719
Porter, Elijah, 65, 441, 491
The Portuguese, 3, 12, 64, 66,
68–69, 71, 73, 78–79, 90, 100,
104, 108, 120, 136–137, 155,
192, 199, 211, 230, 242,
248–249, 252–254, 266, 271,
275–276, 313–314, 337, 349, 426,
450, 483, 507, 516, 559, 609,
638, 643
Potomac, USS, 331–332, 336–337,
339
Prince, Dr. John, 28, 91

U

Ullman, Misses Ana Margurida and
Joana Ana, 80–81, 90, 92, 121,
133, 152, 157, 166, 233, 259,
298, 450, 507, 554, 617
Ullman, Jacob Gabriel, 76, 78, 80,
99, 144, 150, 318
Underwood, Captain and Mrs.,
442–443, 470, 473
Unitarians, 3, 7, 14, 24, 28, 35, 117,
215, 222, 283, 288, 498, 518,
532, 537, 574, 635, 662, 732
Upham, Rev. Charles Wentworth,
28, 35, 64, 107, 216, 477,
562–563, 567

V

Vachell, Rev. George Harvey, 6–8,
10, 63, 73, 76, 80, 83–84, 88,
90, 92–93, 96–103, 109, 131,
141–144, 147–152, 154–161, 164,
167–173, 175–177, 179–180, 182,
185–186, 197–198, 200–214,
216–217, 219, 221–249, 251–252,
255, 257–264, 266–268, 273,
281–283, 291–292, 294–297,
304–308, 313, 316–317, 328, 330,
352, 354, 357, 362, 364–365,
422, 425–427, 430, 438, 440–444,
482, 499, 548, 568, 768
Van Basel, Magdalenus Jacobus
Senn, 64, 110, 204, 214,
219–220, 223, 227, 252, 254,
277, 325, 358, 423, 485, 543,
601, 653, 658–660, 672, 674,
681–682, 688
Van Breda, Michiel, 701, 706
Van Caneghem, S., 64–65, 104
Van Reenen, Dirk and family, 707,
713, 718, 722
Villet, Charles Mathurin, 690
Vincennes, USS, 95, 332, 343
Von Ludwig, Carl Ferdinand
Heinrich, 693

W

Ward, Eliza Wetmore, 65, 104, 122,
138, 156, 209, 236, 325, 498, 626
Ward, Horatio Gates, 352–353, 427,
430, 431
Warriner, Francis, 332, 336
Waterloo, 12, 81, 129, 589, 623,
641, 644, 650, 653–654, 657–690,
735, 742
Webb, Captain, 97
Wemyss, Mrs. Robert, 159, 189,
342, 564
Westray, Juliana, 7, 197
White, Mrs. George, 75, 154–156,
264, 266
White, Joseph, 7, 12, 177, 181, 201,
219, 301, 485, 636
Whitehead, Capt. W. H. 64, 67–69,
71, 73, 75–79, 86, 97, 261, 265,
267, 275–276, 281, 631, 636,
718, 721
Whiteman, John C. and Mrs.,
103–104, 107, 148, 150, 183,
189, 198, 209, 225, 228, 233,
235, 241, 248, 252, 255–256,
260, 262, 264, 266, 271,
273–274, 276–279, 283–285, 288,
309, 317, 320, 330–331, 422,
425, 431, 440, 448, 465, 469,
477, 487, 492, 497, 505–506,
534, 539, 544, 562, 568, 580,
623, 644
Whitney, Captain, 311
Wilcocks, Benjamin Chew, 77, 98,
148, 194, 266
Williams, George H., 441, 461
Wilkinson, Robert, 121, 125,
128, 130–131, 135, 137–139,
142–144, 146, 149, 254, 257,
259, 261–262, 267, 334, 336,
338, 434, 441, 495–496, 505, 521
Wimberley, Rev. Charles and Mrs.,
63, 438, 441, 447–449, 451–452,
468–469, 499, 501, 505, 507,
518, 522, 527, 533, 544, 547,

About the editors

Dr. Arthur W. Hummel (1884–1975), editor of *Eminent Chinese of the Ch'ing Period* (1943), began his distinguished teaching career in Japan in 1912, moving to China in 1915, where he continued to study and lecture in Chinese history until his return to the United States in 1927. From 1927 until 1954, he was chief of the Division of Orientalia, Library of Congress as well as conducting seminars and classes in Chinese history at major American universities. Dr. Hummel held a Guggenheim Fellowship (1954–56) and lectured in Chinese studies at American University and George Washington University until 1963. His knowledge and love of the Chinese language and people did much to promote the study of Chinese history and culture in the United States.

Nan P. Hodges, M.A., a former editor of The University of Washington Press, has been cited for her work in historic preservation in Michigan. Hodges first encountered Harriett Low when editing *The Voyage of the Peacock: A Journal by Benajah Ticknor, Naval Surgeon* (1991). Any young American woman who would climb a 1800 ft. peak in China in 1832 to have a picnic with Dr. Ticknor and a group of naval officers was certainly unusual enough to warrant a book of her own—thus *Lights and Shadows of a Macao Life: The Journal of Harriett Low, Travelling Spinster*. When not editing 19th-century diaries, Hodges actively promotes the Methow Music Festival, a chamber music festival held every summer in Mazama, Washington.